THE ENTREPRENEUR & SMALL BUSINESS PROBLEM SOLVER

THIRD EDITION

WILLIAM A. COHEN, PhD

WILEY

John Wiley & Sons, Inc.

Published by John Wiley & Sons, Inc., Hoboken, New Jersey.
Published simultaneously in Canada.

For general information on our other products and services or for technical support, please contact our Customer Care Department within the United States at (800) 762-2974, outside the United States at (317) 572-3993 or fax (317) 572-4002.

Wiley also publishes its books in a variety of electronic formats. Some content that appears in print may not be available in electronic books. For more information about Wiley products, visit our web site at www.wiley.com.

Library of Congress Cataloging-in-Publication Data:

Cohen, William A., 1937–
   The entrepreneur and small business problem solver / William A. Cohen.—
3rd ed.
      p.   cm.
   ISBN-13: 978-0-471-69283-6 (pbk.)
   ISBN-10: 0-471-69283-2 (pbk.)
   1. Small business—Handbooks, manuals, etc.   2.
Entrepreneurship—Handbooks, manuals, etc.   I. Title.
   HD62.7.C63 2006
   658.02′2—dc22
                                                      2005012593

Printed in the United States of America.
10   9   8   7   6   5   4   3   2   1

CONTENTS

CONTENTS

SECTION III
MANANAGEMENT PROBLEM SOLVING

LIST OF DOWNLOADABLE WORKSHEETS

CHAPTER 1

So You Want to Go into Business for Yourself

If you weren't thinking about going into business for yourself either by starting your own business and becoming an entrepreneur or by taking over an ongoing business, you wouldn't be reading this book. Just thinking about this possibility marks you as someone out of the ordinary and makes you stand out from the rest. Moreover, because of your interest, I already know a few things about you.

I know that you seek more out of life than just a paycheck. You may want to be your own boss so that you control more of your life. Or your boss at work may have rejected your ideas in the past: Later, you saw others either inside or outside your company implement the same ideas with great success. You don't want this to happen again. You want to be in charge because you know you can do better.

You may have had difficulty in getting a job that you really didn't want but had to accept to support your family or yourself. And in getting this dissatisfying position, you may have been rejected many times. You were told you were too young or too old, lacked an education or had too much education, had the wrong kind of education, didn't have the experience or had too much experience. All the time, you knew that you could not only do the job but also do it better than most others. Or maybe you have a passion for a certain kind of work, but the requirements of your current position are such that you just don't have the opportunity to concentrate on the work that you really love.

Maybe you retired after years on one job and now want to take this opportunity to do what you've wanted to do for a long time. Or perhaps you realized from the start that the corporate life is definitely not for you. You completed high school or college or dropped out from either and decided that you wanted to go a different way. Many have done this successfully, too. Douglas Becker founded Sylvan Learning Systems and owns universities all over the world, some of which offer doctorate degrees. However, Becker himself never went to college. He finished high school and founded a company teaching learning challenged kids how to learn. By the time he was in his mid-thirties, he was not only a multi-millionaire but also the boss of many college presidents.

There are hundreds of reasons that motivate people to strike out on their own, and it doesn't seem to make much difference what the reason is. If you have the drive, if this is what you really want to do, you can do it and become highly successful. However, there is good news and bad news. Not everyone is cut out to be an independent businessperson or an entrepreneur. There are other perfectly good ways that you can go through life and make a contribution to society. I tell you this because while there are many real rewards to being your own boss, there are also significant challenges. One basic principle of successful entrepreneurship and small business management or in building a giant corporation, if that is your ambition, is to do so with your eyes open. Sure running your own show is great, but there are disadvantages too, and I want you to know about them before you jump into the fray. So, at the end of this chapter there is a worksheet to help you understand what you are letting yourself in for to help you make an informed decision.

Once you are ready to accept the risks, the adventure, the highs and the lows, the rewards and the demands of being in business for yourself, this book can help—a lot. *The Entrepreneur and Small Business Problem Solver* is designed to give you the guidance you need to deal with the myriad of problems that every small businessperson and entrepreneur faces as they first enter business and build their business over the years. The first edition came out more than 20 years ago, and more than a hundred thousand entrepreneurs and small businesspeople have used it to help build their success. However, the solutions it provides are not mine alone.

You may have noticed that many who are most successful in these types of activities—Bill Gates, Donald Trump, Colonel Harland Sanders of Kentucky Fried Chicken fame, or Mary Kay Ash who built a billion-dollar cosmetic company while giving away Pink Cadillacs, and thousands of others whose names you know and others you don't—didn't make it by working an eight-to-five job for someone else, but rather by being on their own. Their real experiences are immensely valuable, and those who would show others the way would do well to ground themselves in the experiences of those who achieved outstanding success in the past.

This third edition of *The Entrepreneur and Small Business Problem Solver* is not only updated with the latest cutting-edge information regarding technology and the Internet but also with the collective wisdom of hundreds of successful entrepreneurs and small businesspeople who learned what works and what does not on the firing line while risking and making fortunes.

The Advantages of Having Your Own Business

I have already alluded to many of the advantages of having your own business, but let me list them and make them explicit:

- You are the boss.
- You have the opportunity to become far more successful financially than you ever could become working for someone else.
- You have the prestige of heading up a company and can have the title of CEO or president, a title that might take years to attain working for someone else or that you might never attain.
- You make the decisions regarding hours of work, vacations, and, within the framework of the law, who you do business with and what work you will do.
- As you work, you are building equity in an entity that can be sold later or passed on to your children.
- The government allows you to deduct certain expenses that contribute to making a profit from your income tax. We will discuss these further in the next chapter.

Your Contribution as an Entrepreneur or Small Business to Society

However, there is more. Being an entrepreneur or small businessperson does not mean stealing or cheating someone else or becoming a robber baron. In fact, I was recently reading a book by historian Stephen Ambrose.[1] In it, Dr. Ambrose was discussing the so-called robber barons who built the transcontinental railroad across the United States. He said that he was taught in school that these men took unconscionable profits out of the railroads, far more then they deserved, and exploited everyone they came in contact with. However, he discovered that this view was inaccurate and unfair. The U.S. government was unwilling to take the risks of building the transcontinental railroad. The American people wanted the railroad built, and they wanted it completed in just a few years. To accomplish the job, the investors had their arms twisted, first by President Lincoln and later by President Grant. These entrepreneurs took enormous risks in order to complete the job quickly. The quality was imperfect and there was corruption, however, they finished the job in just six years. No other country in the world was able to duplicate this feat. Using slave labor, it took Russia

---

[1] Stephen E. Ambrose, *To America* (New York: Simon and Schuster, 2002).

32 years to build a similar railroad. That's not to say there aren't bad-guy entrepreneurs, but the motivation of entrepreneurs is different than what many think.

Some years ago, famed Harvard social scientist David McClelland (see his book *Achieving Society of Human Motivation*) did some research into what motivated different groups of people. He found that the primary motivation for managers in large firms was a need for power. He thought that entrepreneurs would be motivated primarily by the desire for money. To his amazement, he discovered that the primary motivation for entrepreneurs and small businesspeople was not money but achievement. Entrepreneurs didn't spurn money, but it was used mainly as a measurement to determine how well or how poorly the entrepreneur was doing.

Many speak about big business and corporate jobs and the creation of jobs, but most new jobs come from small businesses not giant corporations. So, as an entrepreneur or small businessperson, you make a major contribution toward eliminating unemployment, too.

Did you think that with giant new product and research and development departments that most new innovations originate from within very wealthy companies? Even this isn't so, and it probably never was. It was two brothers who owned a bicycle shop and made the first flight after they invented the first workable powered airplane. Their name was Wright. Big business and government had previously sunk a lot of money into trying to develop an airplane powered by an engine, and they had failed.

The *second* company to introduce handheld electronic calculators was the giant Sears, Roebuck and Co. An entrepreneur by the name of Joe Sugarman headed the first. Sugarman made a million dollars selling handheld electronic calculators through the mail before Sears and others got interested. Sugarman is probably better known for his infomercials selling BluBlocker sunglasses. Over a 10-year period, he probably made another million dollars selling them, too.

Although today there are many big businesses, including IBM, turning out personal computers, IBM had previously done a study and determined that there was a market in the United States for a total of about 1,000 personal computers (PCs). As a result, IBM forgot about PCs and concentrated on giant computers for big business. Two college dropouts by the names of Steve Jobs and Steven Wozniak built the first commercial personal computer in Jobs's garage. It was called Apple II, and it got the eventual multibillion-dollar Apple Computers Corporation off the ground. IBM had to catch up later after Apple was well established. Amazing, but true: Most innovations seem to be thought up and introduced by entrepreneurs and small businesspeople, people just like you and me.

Entrepreneurship and small business built this country and is still building it today. So as a successful small businessperson, you not only have a tremendous opportunity to become wealthy and live your dream but also to help the U.S. economy and to help limit unemployment. Innovations or new products and ideas that you come up with will contribute to society. There are few other occupations where you can help so many other people at the same time that you help yourself.

The Drawbacks of Running Your Own Show

As I said earlier, the small-business life isn't perfect. There are drawbacks, and you had better recognize them right from the start. While you have work-hour flexibility as an entrepreneur, you are probably going to discover that to become successful, you are going to have to work harder than ever before. Sure, once you've really made it, you can hire professional managers to run your company and take dream vacations whenever you like. But, that's not how it's going to be at first. More than a few small businesspeople and entrepreneurs work seven days a week.

Did you think you had a high-stress level when you worked for someone else? Wait until you feel the pressure of meeting your bills with suppliers, creditors, and employees. Wait until you have to meet a payroll. Monthly or bimonthly you're going to have to come up with the money to pay each and every one of your employees.

And did I say that you could make a lot more money in your own business? Well, that's very true, but it's probably not true at first. Many small businesspeople make less money than they made working for someone else, at least at first.

Working for someone else, your biggest risk is getting fired and being out of work. Working for yourself, you can not only lose your business and be out of work, but you can also end up in debt at the same time. You are going to take risks of one kind or another every day you are in business.

What You Need to Make a Go of It

In 1979, Tom Wolfe wrote a book called *The Right Stuff* about American test pilots and the space exploration program. The heroes that Wolfe wrote about in his book had "the right stuff" to become test pilots and astronauts. If you would be a small businessperson or entrepreneur, you, too, must have the right stuff. While the right stuff that you require is not the same as that required for test pilots or astronauts, it is every bit as important for success. It includes a persistence and stubbornness to stick with projects and not to give up; an ability to tolerate uncertainty and risk or to handle high levels of stress for long periods of time; not to be intimidated by others or to always believe what others tell you is, or is not, possible; to have a strong belief in yourself and what you are trying to do; and to be able to balance the time demands of a business and personal life.

I have put together a worksheet to help you decide if you have the right stuff through a simple test. If you are honest with yourself, you will know right away whether you have the right stuff, or not. (See Worksheet 1.1 on p. 9.)

Full Time or Part Time?

Many situations do not constitute a conflict of interest with your present employment, and you can work part-time and ease into the business. This has the advantage of continuing your main source of income and taking a lot of pressure off. Sure, it's a little inconvenient, and you may not be able to concentrate on your own business. You may lose some sales and need to work a lot harder after your regular work hours and on weekends. Still, many start this way and, if the business you are contemplating fits into the category where you can do this, I recommend it until such time as the sales from your business can support you independently.

What Business Are You Most Likely to Become Successful In?

We all want to get into a business that is more likely to lead us to success. If you peruse any of the so-called opportunity seekers magazines, you will find hundreds of advertisements attempting to interest you in a business with high payoff and guaranteed and easy success. My advice is to resist the temptation. These advertisements are cleverly written, and I'm sure that they have had successes among their customers. However, if you want to know which business is most likely to lead to success, follow this advice: Select a business that you know something about and that you have a real passion for.

If you don't know anything about the business, you will have to spend time and money learning it. If you really don't care for the business, and you are simply attracted by the promise of high income, you will desert this business when times get tough and you run into problems. And even though this book helps solve many of those problems, you may eventually get frustrated and quit.

Consider the four entrepreneurs I mentioned earlier: Bill Gates, Donald Trump, Colonel Harland Sanders, and Mary Kay Ash. Computers fascinated Gates from the time he was in high school. He started a computer programming business even then. Donald Trump likes nothing more than building huge commercial buildings. He lives it. Colonel Sanders spent 40 years in the restaurant business before he ever started doing anything with his secret Kentucky Fried Chicken recipe. And Mary Kay Ash not only had more than 20 years experience with direct selling but also was as passionate about starting a business where women could make good money as Gates was about computers, as Trump was about his buildings, or as Colonel Sanders was about his secret recipe for fried chicken. The success they achieved was not accidental. They got into something they knew something about; something they loved to do and were passionate about.

If you are already in business, you know what I am talking about and can skip Worksheet 1.1 or the additional self-assessment tests listed and found on the Internet. Go right onto the subsequent chapters, as you need them.

If you aren't yet in business, take the time to use Worksheet 1.1 and some of the other self-tests listed to see whether you should be getting into your own business. Recently, I met a man who works for the company that cleans my windows. He works only eight months a year and travels around the world the other four months. He is perfectly happy not having the responsibility of running the business. So, making the decision of whether you want to run the show is not a trivial one, and it could save you a lot of money, time, anguish, and personal resources.

At the end of every chapter in the book, there are additional sources of information to help you, both in books and on the Internet. The Internet information alone will link you to dozens of free articles, magazines, and even books, which amounts to an additional library of information that you can consult for more detail on any subject. In addition, each chapter ends with one or more worksheets to help you develop and apply the material discussed in each chapter. The book has 20 chapters. After Chapter 1, the chapters are divided into three major subsections in which problems may be classified: Financial Problem Solving, Marketing Problem Solving, and Management Problem Solving. All are critical to your business. In addition, there is an Appendix that contain important references to help you.

I wish you all the luck in one of the greatest adventures of your life!

Sources of Additional Information: Self-Assessment Tests

Books

The Big Book of Personality Tests: 100 Easy-to-Score Quizzes That Reveal the Real You by Salvatore V. Didato, published by Black Dog & Leventhal Publishers.

How Do You Compare? 12 Simple Tests to Discover Hidden Truths About Your Personality by Andrew N. Williams, published by Peregee Books.

100 Best Retirement Businesses by Lisa Agnowski Rogak, published by Dearborn Trade.

The Psychologist's Book of Personality Tests: Twenty-Four Revealing Tests to Identify and Overcome by Louis Janda, published by John Wiley & Sons, Inc.

The Psychologist's Book of Self-Tests: 25 Love, Sex, Intelligence, Career, and Personality Tests Developed by Professionals to Reveal the Real You by Louis H. Janda, published by Peregee Books.

Psychometric Testing: 1,000 Ways to assess your personality, creativity, intelligence and lateral thinking by Philip Carter, Ken Russell, Ken Russell, and Philip Carter, published by John Wiley & Sons, Inc.

Test Your Management Skills: The Management Self-Assessment Test by Trevor Boutall, published by Butterworth-Heinemann.

Internet

Note: Because Internet sites frequently go down, multiple sites are listed for similar subject matter.

Starting a Business Test Sales Creators, Inc. developed this test located at http://www.salescreators.com/SCI/Sales_Consultants_for_New/New_Business/Starting_A_Business_TEST/starting_a_business_test.html.

The Entrepreneur Test. The Small Business Know-How Resource on the Internet developed this test at http://www.liraz.com/webquiz.htm.

The Self-Employment Test. The New York State Department of Labor developed this self-employment test at http://www.labor.state.ny.us/business_ny/entrepre/test.htm.

Self-Employed Attitude Test. Here's an attitude test developed by The Small Business Information Resource at the Business Bureau-U.K. in England. You can find it at http://www.businessbureau-uk.co.uk/new_business/attitude_test.htm.

SBA's Entrepreneurial Test. This test was developed by the U.S. Small Business Administration and their Online Women's Business Center. It is available at http://www.onlinewbc.gov/docs/starting/test.htm.

SBA Small Business Success Quiz. Here's another SBA self test at http://www.sbaonline.sba.gov/gopher/Business-Development/Success-Series/Vol1/Quiz/quizall.txt.

DOWNLOADABLE WORKSHEET 1.1
Do You Have "The Right Stuff" for Owning Your Own Business?

	True	False
When I run into a problem, I keep at it until I find a solution.		
When things don't go as planned, I find another way.		
I make mistakes; but I learn from them and go on.		
I frequently try to do things differently from others.		
I don't give up easily.		
I take chances for things I consider important.		
I'm willing to make sacrifices now to attain my long-term goals.		
Others think I am stubborn.		
I know something about the business I want to enter.		
I have or can get all the capital I need to start my business.		
I function well under pressure.		
I get along with other people very well.		
Money is not the most important motivator for me.		
I am a self-starter.		
I want to run my own business more than anything else.		
I have a strong need to accomplish something in life.		
I am willing to attempt new things that I have never done before.		
I like to be in charge.		
I can deal with setbacks.		
I have a lot of self-confidence.		
Totals		

Answer truthfully. The more "true" answers, the better chance of your being successful at running your own business. If your total is 10, or less, your chances of running your own business successfully is less than optimal. Still, it is your decision. If you have 15 or more true answers, you are in good shape to proceed.

To customize this document, download it to your hard drive from the John Wiley & Sons web site at www .wiley.com/go/cohenentrepreneur. The document can then be opened, edited, and printed using Microsoft Word or another popular word processing application.

FINANCIAL
PROBLEM SOLVING

CHAPTER 2

What You Need to Know about the Legal Aspects of Going into Business

In this chapter, we cover the essential legal aspects of going into business, including setting up the legal structure for your firm; obtaining business licenses and paying local taxes; dealing with the state board of equalization and resale permits; registering a fictitious name; setting up the books; and handling federal and state tax obligations; and records for income tax reporting.

Selecting the Legal Structure for Your Firm

There are several possible legal structures for you to consider when setting up your firm—sole proprietorship, partnership, corporation, and the subchapter S corporation. Each has its own particular advantages and disadvantages, depending on your situation. We look at each in turn.

The Sole Proprietorship

The sole or single proprietorship is a business structure for a firm that is owned and operated by one person. To establish a sole proprietorship, all you need to do is obtain whatever licenses are needed in your local area to begin operations. This means it is the easiest legal structure to set up, and it is also the most used form of small business legal structure.

Advantages of the Sole Proprietorship

- *Ease and speed of formation:* There are fewer formalities and legal restrictions with this form. A sole proprietorship requires little or no government approval and you usually need to spend only a few minutes with your city or county clerk to obtain a relatively inexpensive business license.

- *Reduced startup expenses:* There are minimal license fees and less legal help needed to set up this type of business organization.

- *Complete control:* Since there are no partners or other owners to consult with, you have total control over the business, and you can run it as you see fit. You make all the decisions. There is no board of directors or any other boss, except your customers, to direct you, tell you what to do, supervise the decisions you make, or criticize your errors. As a result, you can quickly respond to business needs on a day-to-day basis. Win, lose, or draw, you are the whole show and what you say goes.

- *Sole recipient of profits:* Because you are the sole proprietor, you are not required to share profits with anyone.

- *Relative freedom from government regulations and taxes:* For taxes, the government treats you and your sole proprietorship as one. If you actually end up losing money during the first year, then having this form of legal structure is an advantage since you may deduct those losses on your tax return against any other income that you may have earned. This can be especially valuable if you run your business part-time and you have a salary from a full-time position with another company. Naturally, the same advantage continues if you must run in the red for several years. However, the tax rules state that you must make money in three out of five years. If not, the Internal Revenue Service (IRS) classifies what you are engaged in as a hobby and not a business. For a hobby, your tax-deductible expenses are limited to the amount of income earned. Further, the expenses you can report are reduced by 2 percent of your adjusted gross income.

- *Termination:* Termination is also very easy with a sole proprietorship. You can liquidate your assets, pay your debts, turn out the light, and your entire operation is completely shut down. Or you can sell your business, if you wish to do so, with few restrictions. With a sole proprietorship, it is as easy to get out of business as it was to get into business.

Disadvantages of the Sole Proprietorship

- *Unlimited liability:* One major disadvantage of the sole proprietorship is that you have unlimited personal liability in your business. This means that you are responsible for the full amount of business debts. This could exceed your total investment in the business. This liability extends to all your assets, such as home and car. If your business fails while owing money to various creditors, those monies that you still owe can be collected from your personal assets. Of course, you can lessen the risk of liability in the case of physical loss or personal injury by obtaining proper insurance coverage.

This is discussed in Chapter 4. Also, these liabilities may not be of substantial importance in your situation. If you borrow money for your business, the bank will usually require that you personally guarantee your loan. As a result, even if you are incorporated, you may become personally liable. For many types of businesses, the chance of your being sued because of a failure of your product is very slim, for example, the manufacture and sale of greeting cards, personalized stationery, or costume jewelry. Therefore, even though you are totally responsible, your risks may be minimal.

- *Total responsibility:* In a sole proprietorship, you are essentially a one-person-band, therefore, you are limited to and by your own skills and capabilities. This means, for example, that you may not be able to take a long vacation, or that your enterprise could be put in serious jeopardy or even terminated by a serious illness or something that takes you away from your business for an extended period of time. The fact that only your skills and experiences are brought to the business means there are fewer resources available to your firm than to another firm in which more than one person is contributing experiences and personal resources.

- *Difficulties with capital:* Again, because you are one individual, it may be more difficult to obtain capital for your business than it is for other types of legal business structures with more than one individual involved. Also, it is difficult to get financing because you alone must make good a debt. As the average investor sees it, if you have a partner, this doubles the chances of getting his or her money back. The bottom line is that the sole proprietorship is the most difficult business structure for which to obtain financing.

The Partnership

The partnership is also fairly easy to get started, although written articles of partnership are customarily executed with the help of an attorney. Many states have adopted a uniform partnership act that defines a partnership as an association of two or more persons to carry on as co-owners of a business for profit. The contract or articles developed for use in your partnership may be very simple or fairly complex. They typically cover the following aspects:

- Absence and disability.
- Arbitration.
- Authority of individual partners in conduct of business.
- Character of partners including whether general or limited, active or silent.
- Contribution by partners both now and at a later period.
- Dissolution and winding up.
- Division of profits and losses.

- Draws and salaries.
- Duration of agreement.
- Employee management.
- Expenses and how to handle them.
- Name, purpose, and domicile of partnership.
- Performance by partners.
- Records and method of accounting.
- Release of debts.
- Required acts and prohibited acts.
- Rights of continuing partner.
- Sale of partnership interest.
- Separate debts.
- Settlement of disputes.

Characteristics That Distinguish a Partnership from a Sole Proprietorship
Certain characteristics distinguish a partnership from a sole proprietorship and
other business structures. These are as follows: (1) co-ownership of the assets,
(2) limited life of the partnership, (3) mutual agency, (4) share in management,
(5) share in partnership profits, and (6) unlimited liability of at least one partner.

Types of Partners   In a partnership, there can be different types of partners
that have different responsibilities to the business. An active partner is one who
works in the business. A dormant partner is inactive and not known or held out
as a partner.

- A limited or special partner is a partner who risks only his or her agreed investment in the business. A limited partner is usually not subject to the
same extent as a general partner to the liabilities of the firm, nor does he or
she participate in the management and control of the firm or in the conduct of the firm's business. The limited partner's obligations to the partnership are liable for partnership obligations only to the extent of the
original partnership investment, a share of any recourse debt, and a possible obligation to make future investments. Limited partnership interests
are treated as passive activities. Losses from passive activities are not deductible for alternative minimum tax (AMT) purposes and are being
phased out for regular tax purposes.

- A nominal partner is not a partner in the sense of being a party to the
partnership agreement. However, the nominal partner represents him- or
herself as a partner or permits others to make representation by the use of
his or her name. Therefore, under the law, a nominal partner is as liable as

if he or she were a partner to another party who has acted on the reliance on the truth of true partnership. An ostensible partner is an individual who is active and is known as a partner. A secret partner is a partner who is active but is not known or presented to be a partner. A silent partner is inactive but may be known to be a partner. A subpartner is an individual who is not a member of the partnership but contracts with one of the partners and participates in the interest of the partner in the firm's business and profits.

Advantages of the Partnership

- *Additional capital to start your business:* Your partner or partners are themselves sources of additional capital.

- *Help in decision making:* Two heads are better than one; your partners provide additional resources and help in decision making and the work of the business.

- *Relative ease of formation:* The legal formalities and expenses are not great. Although they are greater than those of a sole proprietorship, they are less than those of the development and creation of a corporation. Like a proprietorship, a partnership is easy to set up. Usually, you obtain a business license from your county clerk or city clerk, and the cost for the license is the same as for the proprietorship license.

- *Relatively stable business life:* In a partnership situation, you have double the resources to apply in solving problems or in handling mundane decisions such as when to go on vacation. There is more stability built into a partnership structure than into that of a sole proprietorship.

- *Relative freedom from government control and special taxation:* As with the sole proprietorship, there is a minimum amount of paperwork associated with a partnership as opposed to a corporation. There is a form that you must fill out each year for the IRS known as Form 1065, U.S. Partnership Return of Income, but basically the monies you receive from the partnership are treated as ordinary income just as are the monies you receive from a sole proprietorship. You can deduct losses in the partnership from other sources of income when you complete your income tax just as you can for a sole proprietorship.

- *Share in profits:* All partners, to a greater or lesser degree, are motivated to apply their best abilities and put in the time by direct sharing of the profits from the business.

- *Flexibility:* Like a sole proprietorship, a partnership is reasonably flexible in that it can respond rapidly to changing conditions of business. Alternatively, because more than one individual is involved, the decision-making process is less flexible than that of the sole proprietorship.

Disadvantages of the Partnership

- *All partners are bound by the actions of one partner:* This is perhaps the major disadvantage of a partnership: You are liable for the actions and commitments of your partners. A single partner can spend the company's resources on a business commitment and all partners are liable to that commitment, whether they agree or disagree.

- *Organizational problems:* Organizational responsibilities must be clearly written into the articles of partnership or you'll run into problems trying to figure out who's in charge of what and who has the final say on various business matters.

- *Unlimited liability of at least one partner:* By law, at least one partner has unlimited liability, just as with a sole proprietorship. Other partners may have similar liabilities, depending upon what's written into the articles of partnership.

- *Relative difficulty in obtaining capital:* For a partnership, you can obtain capital more easily than you can for a sole proprietorship. However, it is much more difficult to obtain capital for a partnership than it is for a corporation.

- *Disposing of partnership interests:* Buying out one partner may be very difficult unless the terms have been stated in the written agreement contained in the articles that formed the partnership.

The Corporation

Unlike the other business structures, the corporation is not a simple structure. Usually you must have the help of an attorney to incorporate, although you can set up your corporation by yourself. There are specific requirements for the state in which you want to incorporate. Frequently, there are books available with copies of forms for you to use. If you're interested, check a local bookstore and find out if such materials are available for your state.

Corporations that do business in more than one state must comply with the federal laws regarding interstate commerce and with the various state laws. These may vary considerably from state to state. In general, to form a corporation, subscriptions to capital stock must be taken and a tentative organization created. Then, approval must be obtained from the secretary of the state in which the corporation is to be formed. The approval is in the form of a charter for the corporation stating the powers and limitations of the particular enterprise.

Advantages of the Corporation

- *Limited liability:* Perhaps the major advantage that exists over the other two forms of business ownership and structure is limited personal liability. With a corporation, your liability is limited to the amount of your investment in the business. Accordingly, your creditors cannot take your personal holdings or assets should the corporation fail or be sued for more funds than are available in the corporation.

- *Ease in securing capital:* Various lenders, including banks, venture capitalists, and others are generally much more willing to make loans to a corporation that has been operating successfully than to a sole proprietorship or a partnership. Also, capital may be obtained through issuance of various stocks and long-term bonds.
- *Increased resources available:* Because a corporation generally includes more than one individual in its organization, the corporation has the ability to make use of multiple skills and resources.
- *Corporate benefits:* As a corporation, you and other members in your business are able to take advantage of fringe benefits such as pension plans, insurance, company cars, and so forth.
- *Permanence of existence:* A corporation has a life of its own and continues to exist and may do business even after the death or illness of the principal officer in the corporation.

Disadvantages of the Corporation

- *Paperwork:* There is a tremendous amount of paperwork associated with a corporation, for taxes and for other reasons. Getting this paperwork done takes time, effort, and money.
- *Government regulations:* Your activities in the corporation are limited by various laws of the government. In fact, of the three types of business structures, this is the one over which the government has the most control. You must make numerous reports to the federal, state, and local governments.
- *Inability to take losses as deductions:* As noted earlier, in both the partnership and the sole proprietorship, if you lose money in your business, these losses can be taken as deductions from other earned income at income tax time. However, this is not true with losses sustained by a corporation. Your corporation may lose money, but until such time as you sell your stock or the business fails, these losses cannot be taken against other earned income. (There is an exception to this in an S corporation, which is discussed later.)
- *Lessened control:* As pointed out earlier, corporations are very closely regulated by the state in which you are registered. This control can restrict your business activities. Furthermore, your corporation is required to have a board of directors and hold stockholders' meetings. Even though you can stack the board of directors in your favor so that you can still run the company, your control over your business and the decision-making process does suffer from this limitation.

- *Taxes:* Depending on your situation and the profits in your business, the fact that you are incorporated may be a disadvantage because of double taxation. Corporate profits are taxed once through the corporation itself as a taxable legal entity and a second time through your salary or when profits are distributed to you as a stockholder. You then pay tax on this as ordinary income. If profits are sufficiently high, this is of little consequence since you will be building your business and taking your money out later. However, if profits are not that high, you'll be losing money to Uncle Sam through taxation instead of saving it. Also, corporate tax rates are higher than individual tax rates. Again, an S corporation can help.

A Guide to Decision Making

In summary, in considering which form of legal structure to adopt, you should weigh the following factors:

- Cost.
- The value of partners in either a partnership or a corporation in both capital and personal resource contributions.
- Organizational flexibility.
- Stability of your business during illness or absence.
- Risks associated with each type of organizational structure.
- Your taxation situation.
- The impact of laws (federal, local, and state).
- The importance of other factors that are peculiar to your business.

How to Incorporate a Small Business

To incorporate a small business, you should either see an attorney or refer to one of the self-incorporation books. This section provides you with an overall view of the process and what is required.

Generally, the first step in incorporating is preparation of a certificate of incorporation. Many states require that the certificate be prepared by three or more individuals who are legally qualified, but the current trend is to require only one incorporator. Before a certificate of incorporation is filed, however, you must consider the location of the corporation since it has important bearing on taxation and other aspects of your business.

Most small and medium-size businesses obtain their charters from the state in which the greatest part of their business is conducted. However, sometimes there are advantages or benefits to be gained from incorporation in another state. To the state in which you are located, yours would be known as a "foreign corporation." Advantages may include lower state taxes, fewer restrictions on corporate powers and lines of businesses in which your company may engage, and lower capital requirements for incorporation. Alternatively, foreign incorporation may also have significant disadvantages. For example, under the laws in many states, you may be taxed twice, that is, by the state in which you incorporated and the state in which your business is located. Under the laws of some states, the property of a foreign corporation is subject to less favorable treatment than that of a corporation located in the state. Also, some states require a foreign corporation to obtain certification to do business in their state, and without this certification your corporation may be deprived of the right to sue in those states. Finally, there is no standard fee, and the fee for a corporation and the organizational tax charged for a corporation varies greatly from state to state.

Certificate of Incorporation

Many states have a standard certificate of incorporation form that you can use. You can obtain copies of this form from the designated state official who grants charters or, in some states, local stationery stores. Also, if you intend to incorporate by yourself, these forms will frequently be found in the book mentioned earlier. In most cases, the following information is required on these forms:

- *Corporate name of the company:* The name chosen cannot be so similar to the name of any other corporation authorized to do business in the state as to lead to confusion. Also, the name that you choose may not be deceptive; it may not mislead the public. To save yourself time, you can check out the availability of names through an official in your state whose job it is to handle such inquiries. You should do this prior to drawing up a certificate of incorporation. There are companies that perform this service that you can locate either through the state offices or the Yellow Pages. In many states, there are certain procedures that are used to reserve a name for your corporation. Again, the proper state official can supply you with this information.

- *Purposes for which the corporation is formed:* Most states require very specific information in this section. You must state in precise language the purposes of your corporation. However, several states allow the use of very broad language in stating the purpose of your corporation; the purpose can be written in such a way as to allow you to pursue virtually any lawful enterprise. There are advantages for stating the purpose of your corporation in either specific or general terms. The advantage in stating the purpose in general terms is that if the corporation decides to change its business, reincorporation will not be required. Alternatively, in dealing with financial institutions, a specific purpose gives a very clear picture of what you are doing. Also, a specific purpose prevents problems in qualifying your corporation to do business in other jurisdictions.

- *Length of time for which the corporation is being formed:* You may indicate a certain number of years or you may indicate that the length of time is in perpetuity.

- *Names and addresses of the incorporators:* This requirement is a simple one, although you should know that in some states one or more of the incorporators are required to be residents of the state within which the corporation is being organized. You should check and find out what is required in the state in which you intend to incorporate.

- *Location of the principal office of the corporation in the state of incorporation:* In those situations in which you decide to obtain your charter from another state, you will be required to have an office in that state. However, there is an alternative: You may have an agent in the state act for you. The agent is required to represent your corporation, maintain a duplicate list of stockholders, and receive or reply to suits brought against the corporation in the state of incorporation.

- *The maximum amount and type of capital stock that the corporation is authorizing for issue:* Under this paragraph, you indicate the capital structure of the corporation, including the number and the classification of shares and the rights, preferences, and limitations of each class of shares and stock.

- *Capital required at time of incorporation:* Some states require that a specific percentage of the par value of the capital stock be paid in cash and placed in a bank to the corporation's credit before the certification of incorporation is submitted for approval.

- *The names of the stockholders and the number of shares to which each stockholder subscribes.*

- *The names and addresses of persons who will serve as directors until the first meeting of stockholders or until their successors are elected and qualify:* For purposes of expediting the filing of the articles, sometimes dummy incorporators are employed. These dummy incorporators are usually associated with a service company or with an attorney for the organizers. Typically they elect their successors and resign at the first meeting of the incorporators.

Assuming that the name of the proposed corporation is satisfactory, that the certificate contains the information required and is properly executed, and that there is nothing in the certificate or in the proposed activities of the corporation that violates any law of the state or public policy, the charter is issued. The next step is an officers' and stockholders' meeting.

Officers' and Stockholders' Meeting

The officers' and stockholders' meeting is necessary to complete the incorporation process. This very important meeting is usually conducted by an attorney or someone familiar with corporate organizational procedures. Three basic things are accomplished during this meeting. First, corporate bylaws are adopted. Second, a board of directors is elected. And third, the board of directors elects the officers who will actually run the corporation on a day-to-day basis. It is possible in a small corporation for members of the board of directors to be elected officers of the corporation.

Bylaws of the Corporation

The bylaws of the corporation repeat some of the items already covered in the certificate of incorporation, but they also cover additional points. These include the following: (1) the location of the principal offices and other offices of the corporation; (2) the time, place, and required notice of annual and special meetings of stockholders, the quorum necessary at the meetings, and the voting privileges of the various stockholders; (3) the number of directors, their compensation, if any, their term of office, how to elect them, and the methods of creating and filling vacancies on the board of directors; (4) the time and place of regular and special directors' meetings, as well as notification and quorum requirements; (5) the process for selecting officers and their titles, duties, terms of office, and salaries; (6) the issuance and form of stock certificates, how to transfer them, and their control in the company books; (7) dividends, when they are declared, and by whom they may be declared; (8) the fiscal year of the corporation, the corporate seal, the authority to sign checks, and the preparation of an annual statement; and (9) the procedure for amending the bylaws that have been established.

S Corporations

S corporations were created by Congress to give tax relief to small companies. Specifically, the purpose of the S corporation is to permit a small business corporation to have its income taxed to the shareholders as if the corporation were a partnership, if it so desires. The advantages of an S corporation are twofold: (1) It permits you to avoid the double tax feature of taxation of corporate income; and (2) it permits you as a shareholder to have the benefit of offsetting business losses incurred by the corporation against your income. Thus, you have the advantage of the protection of incorporation as well as the tax advantage of a partnership.

It may not be to your advantage to have an S corporation if your corporation enjoys substantial profits under the tax laws because corporate tax rates are higher than personal tax rates. Therefore, even if you forecast profitability, it makes sense to take a closer look and to work closely with your accountant and tax attorney before passing up the S corporation.

To qualify as an S corporation, you must meet the following requirements: (1) the corporation has no more than 35 shareholders; (2) the corporation has only one class of stock; (3) all of the shareholders are U.S. residents, either citizens or resident aliens; (4) all of the shareholders are individuals (i.e., no corporations or other entities own the stock); and (5) the corporation operates on a calendar year financial basis. In an S corporation, no limit is placed on the size of the corporation's income and assets.

Obtaining Business Licenses

For most small businesses, you will need only a local business license. This may mean either a municipal or county license or both. These are payable at your city or county hall. To get the license, you may be required to conform to certain zoning laws and to meet building codes and other regulations set by the local health, fire, or police department. Permits may be required by these agencies for activities that are considered hazardous to the community. If you are required to have special permits, you will be informed at the time of the purchase of your business license.

State Licensing Requirements

Some states require licensing for particular occupations, and licenses are granted according to standards of professionalism and ability. Usually, the requirement for state licensing will be indicated at the time of your purchase of your local business license. However, for more specific licensing information, check with your state's department of commerce.

Federal Licensing Requirements

The federal government regulates interstate commerce and also requires federal permits or licenses for any enterprise involving preparation of meat products for transportation or sale, operation of a common carrier, construction of a radio or TV station, production of drugs or biological products, operation of an investment advisory service, and certain other businesses. Again, you are usually informed of the necessity of an additional license at the time of purchase of a local business license. However, to be certain, you can contact your local department of commerce, which is listed in the white pages of your telephone directory under "U.S. Government."

Dealing with the State Board of Equalization and Resale Permits

The state board of equalization is the government agency to which you pay the state taxes that you collect if your state has a sales tax. Usually, the same agency will enable you to secure a seller's permit, which allows you to buy tangible personal property that you intend to resell without paying sales or use tax to your vendor. To do this, you must give your vendor a signed resale certificate showing your seller's permit number.

To obtain a seller's permit, contact the sales and use tax department of your state. Again, contact your state department of commerce. If a fee is required for a seller's permit, the appropriate office listed will inform you. Sometimes this office requires some security from you for the payment of future tax because this office is the one to which you pay sales tax if applicable. If so, the amount is determined at the time you make your application for the permit required. If you fail to pay any sales tax due, the state can deduct the amount that you owe them from the security that you posted with them.

How much security is required, however, or whether any is required, depends on the information that you provide on the application form that they will give you to fill out. The security amount required may be less than $100. However, the requirement for security can vary from no deposit at all to several thousand dollars. In some cases, where the security deposit required is very high, installment payment arrangements can be made. The minimum is generally required if you own your own home and have substantial equity in it, if the estimated monthly expenses of your business are low, if your estimated monthly sales are low, if you are presently employed and this is a part-time business, if you have no employees, or if you have only one place of business. According to your specific situation, additional amounts may or may not be required.

Fictitious Name Registration

You may need fictitious name registration. Whether you must file a fictitious business name statement and get the required publicity depends on the law in your area of operations. Usually, you must file a fictitious name registration statement if the business name you select fits within the definition of a fictitious business name in your geographic area. This means that you are using a name in doing business other than your own or that of partners with whom you may be associated, that the name varies from the corporate name, that it does not include the surnames of all owners, or that it implies the existence of additional owners.

Obtaining fictitious name registration is usually very easy, and the fact that you must register it should not be considered an impediment to selecting a name that people will notice and associate with your business. To find out the law in your state, contact the appropriate city, county, or state agency for information regarding the requirements in your area. Typically, there will be a small registration fee and within a given period of the registration you must publish notice of the fictitious trade name in a general circulation newspaper in the area where the business is located. This may cost you another small fee. You then file an affidavit confirming such publication at the county clerk's office. In practice, this is a very easy matter. Frequently, the form can be obtained at the office of the newspaper in which you intend to publicize your notice, and they will handle everything for you, including filing the affidavit after publication. The form is usually a simple one, and filling it out will take you less than five minutes. Some states allow you to obtain more than one fictitious name on one form. For some types of businesses, such as certain types of consultancies or researchers, this is an advantage allowing you to legally use any of the fictitious names that are listed on the form. Usually, the fictitious name is good for about five years and then must be renewed. You are generally informed ahead of expiration. If you use your own name as that of your business, fictitious name registration is not required nor is it required if you use your corporate name in the business.

Setting Up the Books

Good records in your business are necessary for several purposes, including taxes, measurement of management effectiveness and efficiency, uncovering employee theft, material waste, and obtaining loans.

Essential records should include the following: (1) a periodic summary of cash receipts taken from sales receipts (this might be daily, weekly, or monthly, depending on your business); (2) an expense ledger tallying both cash and checks disbursed for expenses such as rent, payroll, and accounts payable; (3) an inventory purchase journal showing shipments received, accounts payable, and cash available for future purchases; (4) an employee compensation record listing hours, pay, and withheld deductions for both part-time and full-time workers; and (5) an accounts receivable record for credit sales. See Worksheets 2.1 through 2.6 provided at the end of this chapter.

Federal Tax Obligations

There are four basic types of federal taxes: income taxes, Social Security and Medicare taxes, excise taxes, and unemployment taxes. We discuss each in detail next.

Income Taxes

The amount of federal income taxes that you will owe depends on the earnings of your company, as well as the type of business or organizational structure you choose: sole proprietorship, partnership, or corporation. If you choose either the sole proprietorship or the partnership structure, your other income exemptions and nonbusiness deductions and credits will also be important factors. If you are a sole proprietor, your income tax is paid just as if you were working for someone else. The big difference is that your income is derived from the earnings of your business instead of from a salary or wage. You file the identical form that the individual taxpayer working for someone else files. The only difference here is that you file an additional form that in effect identifies items of expense and income from your business. That form is Schedule C of 1040, Profit or Loss from Business or Profession. If your business is a partnership, the partnership must file a return to reflect the income and expenses of the business, and you will report only your share of the profit on your return.

One important difference as an individual proprietor or a partner in a partnership is that you are required by law to pay federal income tax and self-employment tax as income received. You do this by filing a Declaration of Estimated Tax (Form 1040ES) on or before April 15 of each year. This declaration is an estimate of the income and self-employment taxes you expect to owe based on expected income and exemptions. You then make payment on this estimate each quarter, on or by April 15, June 15, September 15, and January 15. At the time of each payment, adjustments to the estimates can be made. As the owner of a new business, you may be required to file a declaration on a date other than April 15 if your expected income or exemptions change during the year. One example of this might be, if you stop working as an employee and your wages were subject to withholding. You would then be required to file a declaration as follows: If the change occurred after April 1 or before June 2, you must file by June 15. If the change occurred after June 1 and before September 2, you must file by September 15. If the change occurred after September 1, then you must file by January 15 of the following year.

If you are incorporated, your estimated payments are made on April 15, June 15, September 15, and December 15.

If your business is a corporation not filing as an S corporation, which was discussed previously, it pays taxes on its profits. Also, as an owner of the corporation, you pay an additional tax on the salary you receive or the dividends that your corporation pays to you.

Income tax rates for a corporation are currently set as shown in Table 2.1.

The income tax return for a corporation is due on the fifteenth day of the third month following the end of each taxable year. The corporation may select as its taxable year a period that does not coincide with the calendar year.

TABLE 2.1   Corporate Tax Rates

Taxable Income ($)	Tax Rate (%)
50,000 or less	15
50,001 to 75,000	25
75,001 to 100,000	34
100,001 to 335,000	39
335,001 to 10,000,000	34
10,000,001 to 15,000,000	35
15,000,001 to 18,333,333	38
Above 18,333,333	35

While income tax returns are typically filed annually, payment of the taxes is made quarterly on an on-account basis by most firms. Every corporation whose estimated tax is expected to be $40 or more is required to make estimated tax payments.

It is extremely important that you have the necessary funds to pay your income taxes on time. To assist you in paying income taxes as well as other taxes, it is recommended that you use Worksheet 2.7: Meeting Tax Obligations, which was developed by the Small Business Administration.

Withholding Income Taxes

By law, you must withhold federal income tax payments for your employees. These payments are passed on to the government periodically. This process begins when you hire a new employee. Your new employee must sign Form W-4, Employee's Withholding Allowance Certificate. On it, your employee lists the exemptions and additional withholding allowances that he or she claims. The completed Form W-4 certificate is your authority to withhold income tax in accordance with the withholding tables issued by the IRS. If an employee fails to furnish a certificate, you are required to withhold tax as if he or she were a single person with no withholding exemptions. Before December 1, you should ask your employees to file new exemption certificates for the following year if there has been a change in their exemption status since they last filed their certificates. At the end of the year, you are required to furnish each employee copies of Form W-2, Wage and Tax Statement, for him- or herself and each taxing jurisdiction, that is, the state and local government. The employee files a copy with his or her income tax return and keeps one. You, the employer, must also furnish a copy of Form W-2 to the IRS on or before February 28. For complete details of how to do this and to find the necessary forms, contact the local office of the IRS or go to the IRS web site at http://www.irs.gov.

Withholding Social Security and Medicare Taxes

In paying Social Security taxes, you also deduct the necessary tax that each employee owes. However, by law, you are required to match these deductions. If you are using Social Security for your own retirement, you must pay the tax for yourself. This must be accomplished on or before the tenth day of the following month. You then deduct the employee's Social Security income tax from wages due the employee. However, you are required to match only deductions you made on the employee's wages. You need not match the Social Security taxes you deduct on the employee's tips. You can get complete details of these taxes and how to pay them in Circular E, Publications 15, *Employer's Tax Guide,* and 15-A, *Employer's Supplemental Tax Guide,* from the IRS. Circular E describes employer tax responsibilities: withholding, depositing, reporting, and paying taxes. It is also available online at http://www.irs.ustreas.gov/pub/irs-pdf/p15.pdf.

Remitting Federal Taxes

To remit federal taxes, you take two actions: (1) You report the income and Social Security taxes that you withheld from the employee's pay, and (2) you deposit the funds that you withheld.

To report withholding and Social Security remittances to the federal government, use Form 941. A return for each calendar quarter is due on the last day of the following month, that is, April 30, July 31, October 31, and January 31. In many cases, remittances of taxes are required before the due date of the return. These dates depend on your situation.

To make deposits, you complete Form 501, Federal Tax Deposits, Withheld Income, and PICA Taxes. This form, along with a check, is sent to the Federal Reserve Bank that serves your district or to a commercial bank that is authorized to accept tax deposits. Your local bank or a Federal Reserve Bank can give you the names of such commercial banks. In general, the smaller the amount of your tax liability, the less frequently you are required to make a deposit.

Excise Taxes

Federal excise taxes are imposed on the sale or use of certain items or certain transactions and on certain occupations. Examples include occupational tax on retail dealers in beer, retail liquor dealers, and wholesale beer and liquor dealers. Diesel fuel and certain special motor fuels carry a retailer's excise tax. There are manufacturers' excise taxes on trucks and equipment and on petroleum products and firearms. If a business involves liquor, gambling, or firearms, it may be subject to an occupational excise tax. To determine whether you are subject to a federal excise tax, contact your local IRS office. Certain excise taxes are due without assessment or notice. With others, you must file a quarterly return on Form 720.

When you owe more than $100 a month in excise taxes, you must make monthly deposits of that tax in a Federal Reserve Bank or other authorized depository. Semimonthly rather than monthly deposits of excise taxes are required if you are liable for more than $2,000 in excise taxes reportable on Form 720 for any month during the previous quarter.

Unemployment Taxes

If you paid wages of $1,500 or more in any calendar quarter or you had one or more employees on at least some portion of one day in each of 20 or more calendar weeks, either consecutive or nonconsecutive, your business is liable for federal unemployment taxes. If your liability from deposits of federal unemployment taxes exceeds $100 for any calendar quarter and preceding quarter, you must deposit the tax with an authorized commercial bank or a Federal Reserve Bank within one month following the close of the quarter. Each deposit must be accompanied by a preinscribed Federal Unemployment Tax Deposit Form, Form 508. A supply of these forms will be furnished to you automatically if you have applied for an employer identification number. Alternatively, they can be obtained from the IRS where you file your return.

An annual return must be filed on Form 940 on or before January 31 following the close of the calendar year for which the tax is due. Any tax still due is payable with the return. You must file Form 940 on a calendar year basis even if you operate on a fiscal year basis. Form 940 may be filed on or before February 10 following the close of the year if all the required deposits are made on time, in full payment of the tax due, deposited on or before January 31. Usually the IRS will mail copies of Form 940 to you. However, if you fail to receive them, copies may be obtained from your local IRS office.

Obtaining an Employer's Identification Number

An employer's identification number is required on all employment tax returns to the federal government. You obtain this by filing a Form SS-4 with your regional IRS Center. Please note that this identification number is not the same as your Social Security number required on your individual income tax returns. At the time that you apply for an employer's identification number, you can request your business tax kit, IRS Publication 454. This tax kit has additional information on taxes pertinent to each particular business. You can also call the IRS at (800) 829-1040 to get one.

State Taxes

State taxes vary from state to state. However, the three major types are unemployment taxes, income taxes, and sales taxes. It is critical for you to know what your state taxes are and what your state requires you to pay, as well as what it requires you to collect as an agent of the state. In some states, if you fail to remit withheld state taxes, you can be charged with embezzlement.

Every state has state unemployment taxes. The rules and requirements vary state by state; however, they usually are based on the taxable wage base of a quarter, and the rate of tax charged is determined by your unemployment experience coupled with the unemployment experience of your state.

State income taxes are imposed by many states. If your state does so, you are required to deduct this tax from your employees' wages just as you deduct the federal tax. Sometimes these taxes are assessed in a fashion similar to that of the federal tax. If the requirements differ, make sure that your records allow you the necessary information for the state income taxes.

To meet the sales tax obligation, if your state has sales tax, you must act as if you were an agent. You collect the tax and pass it on to the appropriate state agency. This was discussed earlier in the section dealing with the state board of equalization and resale permits.

Local Taxes

Counties, towns, and cities impose various kinds of taxes. These include real estate taxes, personal property taxes, taxes on groceries, receipts of businesses, and unincorporated business taxes. A business license is also a tax, although you may not have thought of it as such. Local taxes may actually include income tax for very large cities. To ensure that you are paying the proper taxes, check with your local tax authorities.

Tax Credits

Tax credits are credits against the income tax that you pay and, as such, they are not deductions but account for much more. The laws have changed considerably under the new tax rules. Most tax credits have been eliminated.

In general, the regular investment credit has been repealed for property placed in service after December 31, 1985. However, there are some limited exceptions having to do with transition property, amortizable forestation and reforestation expenses, and qualified progress expenditures. Transitional property is generally any property you placed in service after 1985 if, on that date, you had a binding written contract for its acquisition, construction, or reconstruction.

Many old standby tax credits such as business energy credit, research credit, and target jobs credit have changed. They may be reduced, increased, or eliminated depending on what the government is trying to do. For the latest information on tax credits, go to URL: http://www.irs.gov/publications/p334/ch04.html. This is part of Publication 334, the *Government Tax Guide for Small Business.*

Outside Help

For help with the legal aspects of going into business, you may need an attorney and an accountant. Whenever there's a doubt about a legal question, an attorney's help should be sought. An accountant can help you determine what records to keep and advise on techniques, so you don't pay unnecessary tax. Both accountants and lawyers can advise on changes in tax laws that may require adjustments in the kind of facts necessary for tax reporting. Although use of attorneys and accountants will cost additional money, they may save you much more than their fees, not only in the long run but also in the short run.

Computer Programs

There are a number of computer programs that can help a great deal in the preparation of your taxes. One that I've found very useful is TurboTax published by Intuit Inc., 2632 Marine Way, MS2700, Mountain View, CA 94039. Their web site is http://www.intuit.com. Among other things, the program contains a large library of IRS tax forms. This will permit you to print out the forms yourself without having to go to one of the IRS offices. Also, the forms are linked, so that updating one form updates all.

Intuit also publishes a state tax supplement, so that once your federal forms are completed, interaction with their state program completes all of your state form requirements by punching a few buttons on your computer.

Items such as Estimated Tax Worksheets are automatically calculated, and a range of other options let you consider the consequences of various changes in your income tax planning for the coming year in just a few minutes.

The program can also be used to keep most of your business records for the coming year. This significantly reduces your tax preparation time.

Sources of Additional Information

Books and Online Publications

Drafting of Corporate Charters and Bylaws, by Kurt Pantzer and Richard Deer, published by the Joint Committee on Continuing Legal Education of the American Law Institute and the American Bar Association.

J. K. Lasser's Taxes Made Easy for Your Home-Based Business, 5th edition, by Gary W. Carter, published by John Wiley & Sons.

Legal Guide for Starting and Running a Small Business, 7th edition, by Fred S. Steingold and Ilona M. Bray, published by Nolo.com.

Tax and Business Organization of Small Business, by Jonathan Sobeloff, published by the Joint Committee on Continuing Legal Education of the American Law Institute and the American Bar Association.

Tax Guide for Small Business, Publication No. 334 by the Internal Revenue Service, published by the Superintendent of Documents, Washington, DC 20402 or at http://www.irs.ustreas.gov/publications/p334.

Internet

Note: Because Internet sites frequently go down, multiple sites are listed for similar subject matter.

Checklist for Going into Business. An online checklist published by the U.S. Small Business Administration (SBA), at http://www.sba.gov/library/pubs/mp-12.doc.

Government Regulations and Your Business. This SBA web site has links to all sorts of regulatory material required by the government. It is at http://www.sbaonline.sba.gov/starting_business/startup/guide4.html.

Legal Advice about Going into Business. Free Advice.com provides legal advice on starting a business written by lawyers and attorneys in a Q&A format at http://freeadvice.com/law/517us.htm.

Selecting the Legal Structure of Your Business. Booklet developed by the SBA at http://www.sba.gov/library/pubs/mp-25.doc.

Online Classroom. This complete online class on taxation is available through the Internal Revenue Service at http://www.irs.ustreas.gov/businesses/small/article/0,,id=97726,00.html.

FINANCIAL PROBLEM SOLVING

DOWNLOADABLE WORKSHEET 2.1
(Daily, Weekly, or Monthly) Summary of Cash Receipts

Date	Item Sold or Service Performed	Amount	Running Total
	Total amount received this period:		
	Total amount received prior to this period:		
	Total amount received to date:		

To customize this document, download it to your hard drive from the John Wiley & Sons web site at www.wiley.com/go/cohenentrepreneur. The document can then be opened, edited, and printed using Microsoft Word or another popular word processing application.

DOWNLOADABLE WORKSHEET 2.2
Expense Ledger

Date	To Whom Paid	Purpose	How Paid	Amount
			Total	

To customize this document, download it to your hard drive from the John Wiley & Sons web site at www.wiley .com/go/cohenentrepreneur. The document can then be opened, edited, and printed using Microsoft Word or another popular word processing application.

DOWNLOADABLE WORKSHEET 2.3
Expenditure Summary

Purpose	Total This Period	Total Up to This Period	Total to Date
Advertising			
Car and truck expense			
Commissions			
Contributions			
Delivery expense			
Dues and publications			
Employee benefits			
Freight			
Insurance			
Interest			
Laundry and cleaning			
Legal and professional services			
Licenses			
Maintenance			
Miscellaneous expense			
Office supplies			
Pension and profit sharing plan			
Postage			
Rent			
Repairs			
Selling expense			
Supplies			
Taxes			
Telephone			
Traveling and entertainment			
Utilities			
Wages			
Total			

To customize this document, download it to your hard drive from the John Wiley & Sons web site at www.wiley.com/go/cohenentrepreneur. The document can then be opened, edited, and printed using Microsoft Word or another popular word processing application.

DOWNLOADABLE WORKSHEET 2.4
Inventory Purchase Journal

Date	Inventory Ordered	Shipments Received/Date	Accounts Payable	Cash Available for Future Purchases
			Totals	

To customize this document, download it to your hard drive from the John Wiley & Sons web site at www.wiley .com/go/cohenentrepreneur. The document can then be opened, edited, and printed using Microsoft Word or another popular word processing application.

DOWNLOADABLE WORKSHEET 2.5
Employee Compensation Record

Date	Period Worked	Wage Rate per Period	Total Wages	Social Security Deducted	Federal Income Tax Deducted	State Income Tax Deducted	Net Paid
Totals							

To customize this document, download it to your hard drive from the John Wiley & Sons web site at www.wiley .com/go/cohenentrepreneur. The document can then be opened, edited, and printed using Microsoft Word or another popular word processing application.

DOWNLOADABLE WORKSHEET 2.6
Accounts Receivable for Credit Sales

Date	Customer/Client Name	Product/ Services	Amount Owed	Payments Made/ Dates

To customize this document, download it to your hard drive from the John Wiley & Sons web site at www.wiley .com/go/cohenentrepreneur. The document can then be opened, edited, and printed using Microsoft Word or another popular word processing application.

FINANCIAL PROBLEM SOLVING

DOWNLOADABLE WORKSHEET 2.7
Meeting Tax Obligations

Type of Tax	Due Date	Amount Due	Pay To	Date for Writing Check
Federal Taxes				
Social Security				
Employee Income				
Owner's/Corporation's income				
Unemployment				
State Taxes				
Income				
Sales				
Unemployment				
Franchise				
Other				
Local Taxes				
Sales				
Real Estate				
Personal Property				
Licenses				
Other				

To customize this document, download it to your hard drive from the John Wiley & Sons web site at www.wiley .com/go/cohenentrepreneur. The document can then be opened, edited, and printed using Microsoft Word or another popular word processing application.

CHAPTER 3

Sources of Capital and How to Get a Loan

The Best Source of Capital

The best source of capital for any new business is your own money. The reason it's best is that it's the easiest to use and it's the quickest to access. In addition, you don't need to worry about paying the money back and you don't have to surrender equity in your business. For relatively small sums, this is the easiest and best way.

If you need large amounts, you might have to borrow. However, you should recognize that many, if not most, outside sources of capital expect you to put up some of your own money. This assures these sources that you do not give up when the going in your business gets rough, and that you are willing to invest in your own idea.

Obtaining Money from Friends and Family

Friends and family are also good sources of money. This is the second fastest, easiest, and cheapest sources of cash that you need for your business, with fewer legal problems and with far less paperwork than outside sources. If you do raise money from friends and family, try not to surrender control of your business; that is, make this money a loan and do not give up ownership or partial ownership in your business.

If you become partners with friends or family, you may find it difficult to keep them out of day-to-day operations and decision making. Unless they have know-how to contribute, as well as money, there is no reason for their participation, and it can cause you complications in running your business with a free hand.

Borrowing from the Bank

There are various types of bank loans, and the difficulty of getting them varies considerably. Basically, the bank is a very conservative lender that insists on collateral and wants to be as certain as it can that it gets the money loaned to you returned with interest.

If you have money in a savings account, you can borrow against this money. The cost of such a loan is usually low, because the savings institution in which you have the money can use your savings as collateral until your loan is repaid. There is an advantage to this type of loan: The money you have in the savings account continues to draw interest while you have the loan, even while it is being held as collateral. So, if your money is normally earning 2 percent interest and if the loan is costing you 5 percent, the real cost of the loan is only 3 percent interest.

It might also be relatively easy to get a loan using your life insurance as collateral if your life insurance policy has cash value. You can generally obtain a loan up to 95 percent of the money that has been accumulated. With this type of life insurance loan, you don't actually have to repay the loan; you pay only the interest each year along with your premium. If you don't replace the money that you borrowed from your life insurance, that amount is deducted from the face value of the policy paid to any beneficiary.

Another type of bank loan that is relatively easy to get, if your credit is good, is a signature or personal loan for up to several thousand dollars. If you have dealt with the same bank for some time and they see you as a good risk, you may get an even larger loan. These types of loans are short term and must be paid off in several months to a few years. Depending on your negotiations with the bank, these loans may be paid off on an installment plan or in a lump sum at a specified time.

Types of Bank Loans

The commercial loan is a short-term loan from a bank that is usually paid off in a lump sum within a six-month period. Stocks and bonds, the cash value of life insurance, or a personal guarantee may be accepted as collateral for this type of loan. If the loan exceeds a certain amount, some banks require that the borrower maintain a reserve of cash known as a compensating balance in his bank account. The size of the reserve depends on a number of factors, but usually does not have to be more than 20 percent of the amount borrowed.

Accounts receivable financing is credit extended from the bank, unsecured, against money owed to you by your customers. Usually, the bank advances you up to about 80 percent of the receivable value. You are required to sign the receivables over to the bank. As the receivables are paid to you, you send payments to the bank crediting this amount against your loan along with the interest agreed on. Your customer is not involved in any way.

Inventory financing uses raw materials or finished goods in your inventory as collateral. You usually get a loan for 50 percent of the value of the inventory.

Loans against real estate can usually be made for up to 75 percent of the property value and amortized over a fairly long period, in some cases up to 20 years. A bank also provides residential mortgages and real estate refinancing.

If you intend to buy major equipment, banks make equipment loans for up to about 80 percent of the equipment's value. The maximum length of this loan is usually five years or the maximum life of the equipment.

Small Business Administration Loan Programs and Loans

The U.S. Small Business Administration (SBA) loan programs are a good source of capital; however, they are far from automatic and, like any loan, they require a completed loan package. Moreover, although the SBA offers numerous loan programs to assist small businesses, the SBA is primarily a guarantor of loans made by private and other institutions for borrowers who may not normally be able to get a commercial loan. Allow yourself as long a lead time as you can from the time you apply for the loan. Loans are far from instantaneous.

SBA Loan Program Eligibility

The SBA defines a small business as one that is independently owned and operated and not dominant in its field. A small business must also meet the employment or sales standards developed by the SBA and based on the North American Industry Classification System (NAICS).

In general, the SBA uses the following criteria to determine if a concern qualifies as a small business and is eligible for SBA loan assistance:

- *Wholesale:* Not more than 100 employees.
- *Retail or service:* Average (three years) annual sales or receipts of not more than $6 million to $29 million, depending on business type.
- *Manufacturing:* Generally not more than 500 employees, but in some cases up to 1,500 employees.

- *Construction:* Average (three years) annual sales or receipts of not more than $12 million to $28.5 million, depending on the specific business type.

There are various types of SBA loans, and their structures change from time to time. Therefore, you should check with the local office of your SBA. You can find it in your telephone directory's white pages under "U.S. Government" or on-line at http://www.sbaonline.sba.gov. Here are some of the types of loans offered:

The Basic 7(a) Loan Guaranty   The basic 7 (a) loan guaranty program is the SBA's primary business loan program to help qualified small businesses obtain financing when they might not be eligible for business loans through normal lending channels. It is also the agency's most flexible business loan program because financing under this program can be guaranteed for a variety of general business purposes.

Loan proceeds can be used for most sound business purposes including working capital, machinery and equipment, furniture and fixtures, land and building (including purchase, renovation, and new construction), leasehold improvements, and debt refinancing (under special conditions). Loan maturity is up to 10 years for working capital and generally up to 25 years for fixed assets.

The Certified Development Company, a 504 Loan Program   This 504 loan program provides long-term, fixed-rate financing to small businesses to acquire real estate or machinery or equipment for expansion or modernization. The maximum SBA debenture generally is $1 million (and up to $1.3 million in some cases). The loan is provided through certified development companies (CDCs). These are private, nonprofit corporations set up to contribute to the economic development of their communities or regions.

The Microloan, a 7(m) Loan Program   The microloan program provides short-term loans of up to $35 thousand to small businesses and not-for-profit child-care centers for working capital or the purchase of inventory, supplies, furniture, fixtures, machinery, and/or equipment. Proceeds cannot be used to pay existing debts or to purchase real estate. The SBA makes or guarantees a loan to an intermediary, who, in turn, makes the microloan to the applicant along with management and technical assistance.

Loan Prequalification Program

This allows business applicants to have their loan applications for $250 thousand or less analyzed and potentially approved by the SBA before they are taken to lenders for consideration, which enhances their chances for acceptance. The program focuses on the applicant's character, credit, experience, and reliability rather than assets. An SBA-designated intermediary works with the business owner to review and strengthen the loan application. The review is based on key financial ratios, credit and business history, and the loan-request terms. The SBA's Office of Field Operations and district offices administer the program. You can locate these in your telephone directory's white pages under "U.S. Government" or at http://www.sbaonline.sba.gov.

SBA Disaster Relief Loans

The SBA makes various types of loans for disaster relief. If you are in a declared disaster area and are the victim of a disaster, you may be eligible for financial assistance from the SBA, even if you don't own a business. As a homeowner, renter, or personal-property owner, you may apply to the SBA for a loan to help you recover from a disaster. Check with your local SBA office. Additional information, including questions and answers can be found at http://www.sbaonline.sba.gov /disaster_recov/loaninfo/property.html.

For example, you may also be eligible for physical disaster loans. Any business that is located in a declared disaster area and has incurred damage during the disaster may apply for a loan to help repair or replace damaged property to its predisaster condition. The SBA makes physical disaster loans of up to $1.5 million to qualified businesses. Additional information is at http://www.sbaonline .sba.gov/disaster_recov/loaninfo/phydisaster.html.

If your small business has suffered substantial economic injury, regardless of physical damage, and is located in a declared disaster area, you may also be eligible for financial assistance. Check with the local SBA office. Online information is at http://www.sbaonline.sba.gov/disaster_recov/loaninfo/ecoinjury.html.

There is also a special military reservist disaster program. The filing period for small businesses to apply for economic injury loan assistance begins on the date the essential employee is ordered to active duty as a reservist and ends 90 days after the essential employee is discharged or released from active duty. See http://www .sbaonline.sba.gov/disaster_recov/loaninfo/militaryreservist.html.

The Export Working Capital Program

The Export Working Capital Program (EWCP) was designed to provide short-term working capital to exporters. It supports export financing to small businesses when that financing is not otherwise available on reasonable terms. The program encourages lenders to offer export working capital loans, by guaranteeing repayment of up to $1.5 million or 90 percent of a loan amount, whichever is less. A loan can support a single transaction or multiple sales on a revolving basis. More information online is available at http://www.sbaonline.sba.gov/financing/loanprog/ewcp.html.

Export Express

SBA Export Express combines the SBA's small business lending assistance with its technical assistance programs to help small businesses that have traditionally had difficulty in obtaining adequate export financing.

Loan proceeds may be used to finance export development activities such as participation in foreign trade shows; translation of brochures; purchase of real estate and equipment to be used in production of goods or services, which are to be expanded; and to provide term loans and other financing to enable small business concerns, including export trading companies and export management companies, to develop foreign markets, acquire, construct, renovate, modernize, improve, or expand productive facilities or equipment to be used in the United States in the production of goods or services involved in international trade and more. For online information, see http://www.sbaonline.sba.gov/financing/loanprog/exportexpress.html.

International Trade Loans

If your business is preparing to engage in or is already engaged in international trade, or is adversely affected by competition from imports, an international trade loan may help. You must establish that the loan significantly expands or develops an export market, that you are currently adversely affected by import competition, that you may upgrade equipment or facilities to improve competitive position, or that you must be able to provide a business plan that reasonably projects export sales sufficient to cover the loan. For more information, see http://www.sbaonline.sba.gov/financing/loanprog/tradeloans.html.

Defense Loan and Technical Assistance Program

The Defense Loan and Technical Assistance program (DELTA) is designed to help eligible small business contractors transition from defense to civilian markets. The DELTA program provides financial and technical assistance to defense-dependent small businesses that have been adversely affected by defense reductions. The goal of the program is to assist these businesses to diversify into the commercial market while remaining part of the defense industrial base. Complete information on eligibility and other rules is available from each SBA district office and online at http://www.sbaonline.sba.gov/financing/loanprog/military.html.

U.S. Community Adjustment and Investment Program

Community Adjustment and Investment Program (CAIP) is intended to assist U.S. companies that are doing business in areas of the country that have been negatively affected by the North America Free Trade Agreement (NAFTA). Funds administered by the U.S. Treasury allow for the payment of fees on eligible loans. Additional information is available at http://www.sbaonline.sba.gov/financing /loanprog/caip.html.

Qualified Employee Trust Loan Program

The objective of this program is to provide financial assistance to employee stock ownership plans (ESOPs). The employee trust must be part of a plan sponsored by the employer company and qualified under regulations set by either the IRS code (as ESOP) or the Employee Retirement Income Security Act (ERISA). Applicants covered by ERISA regulations must also secure an exemption from the Department of Labor regulations prohibiting certain loan transactions. For more information, see http://www.sbaonline.sba.gov /financing/loanprog/trusts.html.

Pollution Control Loan Program

This program is designed to provide financing to eligible small businesses for the planning, design, or installation of a pollution control facility. This facility must prevent, reduce, abate, or control any form of pollution, including recycling. See http://www.sbaonline.sba.gov/financing/loanprog/pollution.html.

CAPLines Loan Program

CAPLines is the umbrella program under which the SBA helps small businesses meet their short-term and cyclical working-capital needs. A CAPLines loan, except the Small Asset-Based Line, can be for any dollar amount that does not exceed SBA's limit. Contact your local SBA office. Also, see http://www.sbaonline .sba.gov/financing/loanprog/caplines.html.

How to Apply for an SBA Loan

There are many companies that will carry out the entire SBA loan application procedure for a fee. In most cases, you will be able to do the same job for yourself at a much lower cost. You should be aware that no preparer can guarantee that you will get your loan approved. Be wary of any company that even implies that your loan approval is assured if they prepare your loan package.

Start by preparing a written loan proposal. Make your best presentation in the initial loan proposal and application because you may not get a second opportunity. Begin your proposal with a cover letter or executive summary. Explain who you are, your business background, the nature of your business, the amount and purpose of your loan request, your requested terms of repayment, how the funds will benefit your business, and how you plan to repay the loan. Keep this cover page simple and direct.

There are many different loan proposal formats. However, your prospective lender may have a preferred format, so always check first. When writing your proposal, don't assume the reader is familiar with your industry or your business. Always include industry-specific details, so your reader can understand how your particular business is run and what industry trends affect it.

The SBA recommends the following outline and information:[1]

- *Description:* Provide a written description of your business, including the following information:
  —Type of organization.
  —Date of information.
  —Location.
  —Product or service.
  —Brief history.
  —Proposed future operation.
  —Competition.
  —Customers.
  —Suppliers.
- Management experience: Resumes of each owner and key management members.
- *Personal financial statements:* SBA requires financial statements for all principal owners (20 percent or more) and guarantors. Financial statements should not be older than 90 days. Make certain that you attach a copy of last year's federal income tax return to the financial statement.
- *Loan repayment:* Provide a brief written statement indicating how the loan will be repaid, including repayment sources and time requirements. Cash-flow schedules, budgets, and other appropriate information should support this statement.
- *Existing business:* Provide financial statements for at least the last three years, plus a current dated statement (no older than 90 days) including balance sheets, profit and loss statements, and a reconciliation of net worth.

---

[1] "Applying for a Loan," U.S. Small Business Administration web site. Accessed July 13, 2004, at http://www.sbaonline.sba.gov/financing/basics/applyloan.html.

Aging of accounts payable and accounts receivables should be included, as well as a schedule of term debt. Other balance sheet items of significant value contained in the most recent statement should be explained. (See Chapter 5 of this book for information on preparation of financial statements.)

- *Proposed business:* Provide a pro forma balance sheet reflecting sources and uses of both equity and borrowed funds.

- *Projections:* Provide a projection of future operations for at least one year or until positive cash flow can be shown. Include earnings, expenses, and reasoning for these estimates. The projections should be in profit and loss format. Explain assumptions used if different from trend or industry standards and support your projected figures with clear, documentable explanations.

- Other items as they apply:
  —Lease (copies of proposal).
  —Franchise agreement.
  —Purchase agreement.
  —Articles of incorporation.
  —Plans, specifications.
  —Copies of licenses.
  —Letters of reference.
  —Letters of intent.
  —Contracts.
  —Partnership agreement.

- *Collateral:* List real property and other assets to be held as collateral. Few financial institutions provide noncollateral-based loans. All loans should have at least two identifiable sources of repayment. The first source is usually cash flow generated from profitable operations of the business. The second source is usually collateral pledged to secure the loan.

For additional information, the following SBA web sites are highly recommended:

- Applying for a loan at http://www.sbaonline.sba.gov/financing/basics/applyloan.html.
- Credit factors at http://www.sbaonline.sba.gov/financing/preparation/qualify.html.
- Preparing a loan proposal at http://www.sbaonline.sba.gov/starting_business/financing/loanproposal.htm.
- Loan package checklist at http://www.sbaonline.sba.gov/starting_business/financing/loanpackagechecklist.html.

Computer programs for preparing loan packages are available. For example, see the one from Business Development Specialists at 410 Park Ave., New York, NY 10022; Tel: (212) 656-1470 or at http://www.sbaeasystepkit.com/sba.

Obtaining Money from Factors

Obtaining money from factors means the outright sale of your accounts receivable to another party. Essentially, you get paid cash on delivery of your product or service while your customers receive credit on terms that they require. This differs from accounts receivable financing because factoring is not a loan. The factor actually purchases your accounts receivable for their full value, usually for up to 80 percent of their worth, at the time that you ship the goods. The remainder of their worth is given to you when your customers pay. The factor checks the credit of each of your customer's accounts and purchases these receivables from you without recourse, which means that the factor absorbs any bad debt losses. To compensate for these risks, factors typically charge a 1 to 2 percent fee for each invoice, plus interest, on the advance that they make to you. The total amount is usually greater than bank and commercial finance company rates for comparable loans. However, factors do not require as extensive a loan package as other lenders. Also, obtaining money from a factor can be fast. Sometimes once your credit references and other financial statements are supplied and the credit of the account has been confirmed, you can obtain money in as little as 24 hours.

Finance Companies

Finance companies assume a greater amount of risk in the loan than banks. Whereas a bank may deny you a loan if you have a high degree of debt or may be running into financial difficulties, a commercial finance company makes loans on the strength of your collateral rather than your track record or potential. Commercial finance companies make loans much as banks do to include equipment leasing and factoring. Naturally, you pay more money in interest for a commercial finance company loan than for a bank loan.

Loans from Suppliers

Your suppliers are a frequently overlooked source of a loan. Suppliers may be those selling you stationery and printing supplies, or various components or materials that are used in something that you manufacture. In effect, a loan exists if your supplier does not require payment until the delivery of supplies. In addition, sometimes suppliers grant you 30, 60, or 90 days, or even more time to pay for whatever material you have purchased from them. Clearly, the effect is that of a loan, even though a formal loan has not been negotiated. Usually, suppliers give a discount for early payment of purchased supplies; typically, this discount is 2 percent for payment within 10 days. This 2 percent savings should be weighed against your need for funds in the business. You should never be afraid to ask for credit to enable you to pay later if you need this money for some important business purpose.

Credit Card Loans

Everytime you use your credit card you are taking out a loan. Depending on the particular credit card and the amount of credit permitted with that card, you may be able to purchase supplies or materials for your business for several thousand dollars or more. This credit is easy to get and requires no special paperwork as long as you do not go above the amount that has been established for you with the particular credit card. Be careful of the interest rate on these, however. It can be extremely high, and you should weigh the easy acquisition of this money against the amount of interest charged.

Equity Capital Financing

Equity capital financing is selling off a portion of your business to another investor who contributes capital and may participate in the management of your business. Your business has no legal obligation for repayment of the amount invested or for payment of interest for the amount of the funds. The investor shares in the ownership of the business and is entitled to participate in any distribution of earnings through dividends in the case of corporations or any draw in the case of a partnership. How much the investor participates in the distribution of earnings depends on the number of shares that he or she holds; or in a partnership, the percentage of the business that the partnership owns. Because you do not have to pay a debt, equity financing may appear to be an easy way to obtain capital for your business. However, it has disadvantages. These include sharing your success with others and a loss of complete control of your business.

How to Value Equity Capital

A primary question once a decision has been made to use equity capital is how to value it. For example, in a start-up situation it is fairly typical for the individual with the idea or product innovation to get 50 percent equity and the investors to get the other 50 percent of equity. If the innovator also has capital to contribute, he or she is given the same proportion of equity for his or her additional capital as the investors are given for theirs. Although the 50-50 rule is fairly common, another way of doing this is to put some value on the contributions of the individual starting the company. For example, if a price tag can be put on patents that he or she is contributing, specific knowledge, and so forth, then this helps to place a value on the equity that is given to the investors in exchange for capital. All terms are negotiable and the valuation of the innovator's contributions versus capital contributions vary from situation to situation.

Venture Capital

Venture capital is generally used for relatively new businesses that are somewhat risky but that have both a successful track record and a clear potential for high growth and return on investment. Venture capital firms and individuals who venture their own capital are interested in many of the same factors that influence other lending organizations. That is, they want to know the results and ratios of past operations, how much money is wanted, what the money is wanted for, and financial projections. But venture capitalists look much more closely at the features of the product or service being offered and the potential in the market than do many other lending organizations. As a result, different venture capitalists frequently have definite preferences for certain types of industries, certain types of products, and certain locations.

Before you even consider this source, you should know that venture capitalists are interested in being owners. That is, they insist on an equity type of financing. Further, in most cases, venture capitalists insist on owning more than 50 percent of the business. However, this may not be as critical a factor as it seems. Although in theory, the venture capitalist controls the company by owning a majority of the stock, these companies are normally not interested in running the business on a day-to-day basis, or in exerting their control so as to interfere in your business management.

Despite the fact that venture capitalists insist on equity financing and owning a controlling interest in the businesses they finance, they are usually in a buyers' market. Typically, venture capital firms receive hundreds, if not thousands, of proposals during the course of the year. They may reject 95 percent or

more. To interest a venture capital firm in your business, you must sell them on
your business's worth. They are interested only in companies with some sort of
track record and invest only in firms that they believe can rapidly increase in
sales and generate substantial profits with the money they provide. Typically,
venture capital companies seek a return of three to five times their investment in
only five to seven years. And, also typically, venture capital firms are interested
in projects requiring fairly large investments.

Preparing the Venture Proposal

Because 90 percent or more proposals to venture capital firms are rejected, you
must do your homework and recognize what a venture capital firm is looking for
when you prepare your venture proposal. This proposal should emphasize the
market potential and competitive position of the company, along with its products, present and potential customers, suppliers, production costs, financial condition, and the character and competence of the management including
experience and background.

    The proposal should be upbeat without lying. Difficulties should be clearly
indicated, but each problem stated should also include a solution. The proposal
should be under 50 pages and should cover the following areas in detail: purposes and objectives of the project; the proposed financing, including the
amount of money that you'll need, how the money will be used, and how you plan
on structuring the financing; marketing, including the marketing segment that
you are after, competitors that are in the market and how you plan to beat them,
characteristics of the market, and costs of executing the marketing plan you are
proposing. You should also have a history of your firm including the significant
milestones since founding, prior financing, your success, company organization,
financial relationships with banks and other lending institutions, and a detailed
description of your product or service and the costs associated with it. As for financial statements, include balance sheets, income statements, and cash flows
for the past three years, as well as projections for the next three years that include the effect with the proposed project for which financing is being obtained.
You should include an analysis of key factors that may affect the financial performance, as well as the result if the level of sales projected is not attained. Include a list of shareholders in your company, the amounts invested to date, and
the form of capitalization equity per debt. Biographical sketches or resumes containing the qualifications and experience of key owners and managers of the
company should be included and emphasize experience and accomplishments
that have a bearing on the operation of your firm. Include a list of your main
suppliers and your main customers and problems that you anticipate or that are

possible, as well as actions that you would take in the event that these problems become a reality. Have a section detailing the advantages of your firm—its product, service, plans, personnel—and the project for which you need the money. Finally, you should emphasize why and how your unique advantages can only result in success for this project.

Capitol Vector publishes a CD ROM with all active venture capital companies listed. You can contact this company at info@capitalvector.com. The web site describing this CD-ROM is at http://www.capitalvector.com/capfinder.html.

Small Business Investment Companies

Small business investment companies (SBICs) are regulated and sponsored by the SBA. In fact, the government puts up a great deal of the capital for these firms to invest in young companies. SBICs exist to supply equity capital, long-term loans, and management assistance to qualifying small businesses. The privately owned and operated SBICs use their own capital and funds borrowed from the SBA to provide financing to small businesses in the form of equity securities and long-term loans. SBICs are profit-seeking organizations that select small businesses to be financed within rules and regulations set by the SBA.

There are also specialized SBICs that provide assistance solely to small businesses owned by socially or economically disadvantaged persons.

You can get a list of SBICs from your local SBA office or online at http://www.sbaonline.sba.gov/INV/ for SBICs.

State Business and Industrial Development Corporations

Many states have their own development corporations that are capitalized through funds from the state. These state business and industrial development corporations (SBIDCs), make long-term loans rather than equity investments, specializing in from 5- to 20-year loans for the expansion of facilities and the purchase of equipment. SBIDC interests and priorities vary from state to state. Some are particularly interested in making high-risk loans for businesses that cannot otherwise obtain loans from banks. Others only lend capital when the risk is minimal. To get more information on SBIDCs, check with your state business development office or chamber of commerce or the SBA office in your area.

Local Development Companies

Local development companies (LDCs) are resident organized and capitalized. However, they solicit SBA and bank loans to buy or build facilities for local small businesses. Typically, an LDC supplies only 10 percent of a project's cost; the remainder must be obtained through combined SBA and bank loans or one SBA guarantee bank loan. Also, an LDC can finance all of a company's facilities, but it cannot supply working capital or fund the purchase of inventory supplies or freestanding fixtures and equipment.

High-risk ventures are good candidates for an LDC loan because the LDC and not the small business is the actual loan recipient. Some LDCs are nonprofit corporations and therefore charge minimum interest on their 10 percent of the funds lent. Others that operate for a profit charge rates that are comparable with those of banks.

To use and get an LDC loan, you first submit a loan package to the LDC. You are then evaluated by the SBA and afterward by the participating bank. To find out the LDCs in your area, contact the SBA field office in your area.

Use of Finders in Locating Sources for Loans

Finders are individual financial consultants who are paid a percentage of the loan by you to locate a loan for you. These finders may be located by word of mouth from other entrepreneurs and small businesspeople or from your attorney, accountant, or banker. Sometimes finders place advertisements in financial papers or the classified section of your local newspaper or the *Wall Street Journal*. Finder's fees vary greatly. They may be as low as 1 percent or as high as 15 percent or more. Therefore, if you use a finder, make certain that you ask for enough money in the loan to include the fee.

Cashing in: Public Stock Offerings and Mergers

As you grow, you will need additional capital through professional finders, venture capitalists, SBICs, and other sources described earlier. However, as very high levels of capital are needed, you have basically two choices. One option is to merge with a larger company for an infusion of capital, and a second option is to sell shares through public offering. The public offering seeks to attract a large number of investors to purchase stock. Both stock offerings and mergers provide a way in which you can cash in on your business. For example, a merger may entitle you to stock from the larger firm that can be held or turned into cash, plus a management position and salary if you desire to continue managing the enterprise that you started, or a fee over a period of years as a consultant or as part of an agreement not to compete with the firm with which you've merged. Selling capital stock of a corporation is closely regulated and can fail. It is done through your local investment banker when your enterprise is a corporation. By using different types of stock, common versus preferred, you may retain your control over the corporation. Preferred stock has dividends as a priority, however, it does not have a voting privilege as does common stock. Therefore, by retaining the majority of common stock in a corporation, you can retain control.

The banker prepares a detailed study of your projections and plans for your firm that he or she issues in the form of an offering. The investment banker's charges depend on whether he or she guarantees sale of the full amount or whether the stock is sold on a "best efforts" basis. The first type of offering is usually reserved for large enterprises that have a strong track record. The investment banker can also analyze your business plan and loan package and prepare an offering of your company's stock to its investment contacts. This private placement may be in the form of stock equity or long-term debt but it is not intended for public trading, and therefore is not registered with the Securities and Exchange Commission (SEC).

Sources of Additional Information

Books

Anatomy of a Merger, by Robert Q. Parsons and John Stanley Baumgartner, published by Prentice-Hall.

Business Loans, by Rich Stephen Hayes, published by CBI Publishing.

Financing the Small Business, by Robert Sisson, published by Adams Media Corp.

Financing for Small and Medium-Sized Businesses, by Harry Gross, published by Prentice-Hall.

Going Public, by Daniel S. Berman, published by Prentice-Hall.

How to Borrow Your Way to a Great Fortune, by Tyler G. Hicks, published by Parker Publishing Co.

How to Finance a Growing Business, by Royce Diener, published by Frederick Fell Publishers.

How to Get a Small Business Loan, by Bryan E. Milling, published by Sourcebooks.

How to Negotiate a Business Loan, by Richard C. Below, published by Van Nostrand Reinhold Co.

Money Raising and Planning for the Small Business, by David L. Markstein, published by Henry Regnery Co.

The SBA Loan Book, by Charles H. Green, published by Adams Media Corp.

Winning the Money Game, edited by Donald Dible, published by the Entrepreneur Press.

Internet

Note: Because Internet sites frequently go down, multiple sites are listed for similar subject matter.

ABC's of Borrowing. A complete booklet by the SBA at http://www.sbaonline.sba.gov /library/pubs/fm-1.doc.

A Venture Capital Primer for Small Business. An SBA publication at http://www.sbaonline .sba.gov/library/pubs/fm-5.doc.

Bank Rate.com. This site enables comparison of borrowing rates for small business no matter what state you live in at http://www.bankrate.com/brm/biz_home.asp.

Borrowing for Your Small Business. This site sponsored by Eastern Bank has links to all sorts of loan categories at http://www.moneyfitness.com/mc3/topic.php?b =24550218&c=491.

Entrepreneur Capital Finance. Sponsored by BPPubs.com, the site has links to a variety of articles on borrowing at http://www.bpubs.com/SOHO_and_Small_Business /Financing.

Small Business Loans. A quick review by SmallBusinessNotes.com at http://www .smallbusinessnotes.com/financing/loans.html.

The ABC's of Borrowing. Another slant on borrowing by the Agora Business Center at http://www.agora-business-center.com/borrowing.htm.

DOWNLOADABLE WORKSHEET 3.1
Which Type of Funding Should You Use?

Step 1 Weigh the following factors on a scale of 1 to 5, 1 being not very important to you and 5 being very important to you.

Cost of capital—How important is the cost of capital and its effect on earnings? _____

Risk—How important is the risk imposed by the source of funding? _____

Flexibility—How important is it that you have flexibility in use of the money borrowed or your ability to borrow more in the future? _____

Control —How important is it to retain control over your business? _____

Availability—How important is it to attain the capital easily? _____

Amount—How important is the amount you can borrow? _____

Step 2 Note the potential sources you are considering for your loan. For each source and factor, assign a value of 1 to 5, 1 signifying that a source is not very attractive on a particular factor; 5 signifying that a source is very attractive on that factor.

Potential Source 1. _____

Cost of capital—How attractive is the cost of capital and its effect on earnings? _____

Risk—How attractive is the risk imposed by the source of funding? _____

Flexibility—How attractive is it on the flexibility in use of the money borrowed or your ability to borrow more in the future? _____

Control—How attractive is it in retaining control over your business? _____

Availability—How available is the capital from this source? _____

Amount—How attractive is the amount you can borrow from this source? _____

Potential Source 2. _____

Cost of capital—How attractive is the cost of capital and its effect on earnings? _____

Risk—How attractive is the risk imposed by the source of funding? _____

Flexibility—How attractive is it on the flexibility in use of the money borrowed or your ability to borrow more in the future? _____

Control—How attractive is it in retaining control over your business? _____

Availability—How available is the capital from this source? _____

Amount—How attractive is the amount you can borrow from this source? _____

Potential Source 3. _____

Cost of capital—How attractive is the cost of capital and its effect on earnings? _____

Risk—How attractive is the risk imposed by the source of funding? _____

Flexibility—How attractive is it on the flexibility in use of the money borrowed or your ability to borrow more in the future? _____

Control—How attractive is it in retaining control over your business? _____

Availability—How available is the capital from this source? _____

Amount—How attractive is the amount you can borrow from this source? _____

Potential Source 4. _____

Cost of capital—How attractive is the cost of capital and its effect on earnings? _____

Risk—How attractive is the risk imposed by the source of funding? _____

Flexibility—How attractive is it on the flexibility in use of the money borrowed or your ability to borrow more in the future? _____

Control—How attractive is it in retaining control over your business? _____

Availability—How available is the capital from this source? _____

Amount—How attractive is the amount you can borrow from this source? _____

Potential Source 5. _____

Cost of capital—How attractive is the cost of capital and its effect on earnings? _____

Risk—How attractive is the risk imposed by the source of funding? _____

Flexibility—How attractive is it on the flexibility in use of the money borrowed or your ability to borrow more in the future? _____

Control—How attractive is it in retaining control over your business? _____

Availability—How available is the capital from this source? _____

Amount—How attractive is the amount you can borrow from this source? _____

Potential Source 6. _____

Cost of capital—How attractive is the cost of capital and its effect on earnings? _____

Risk—How attractive is the risk imposed by the source of funding? _____

Flexibility—How attractive is it on the flexibility in use of the money borrowed or your ability to borrow more in the future? _____

Control—How attractive is it in retaining control over your business? _____

(continued)

Availability—How available is the capital from this source?   _____

Amount—How attractive is the amount you can borrow from this source?   _____

Potential Source 7. _____

Cost of capital—How attractive is the cost of capital and its effect on earnings?   _____

Risk—How attractive is the risk imposed by the source of funding?   _____

Flexibility—How attractive is it on the flexibility in use of the money borrowed or your ability to borrow more in the future?   _____

Control—How attractive is it in retaining control over your business?   _____

Availability—How available is the capital from this source?   _____

Amount—How attractive is the amount you can borrow from this source?   _____

Potential Source 8. _____

Cost of capital—How attractive is the cost of capital and its effect on earnings?   _____

Risk—How attractive is the risk imposed by the source of funding?   _____

Flexibility—How attractive is it on the flexibility in use of the money borrowed or your ability to borrow more in the future?   _____

Control—How attractive is it in retaining control over your business?   _____

Availability—How available is the capital from this source?   _____

Amount—How attractive is the amount you can borrow from this source?   _____

Step 3 Multiply the totals from the results from Step 1 and Step 2 for each source.

Potential Source 1. _____

	Step 1 Results	×	Step 2 Results	=	_____
Cost of capital	_____	×	_____	=	_____
Risk	_____	×	_____	=	_____
Flexibility	_____	×	_____	=	_____
Control	_____	×	_____	=	_____
Availability	_____	×	_____	=	_____
Amount					

Potential Source 1 Total   _____

Potential Source 2. _____

	Step 1 Results	×	Step 2 Results	=	_____
Cost of capital	_____	×	_____	=	_____
Risk	_____	×	_____	=	_____
Flexibility	_____	×	_____	=	_____
Control	_____	×	_____	=	_____
Availability	_____	×	_____	=	_____
Amount					

Potential Source 2 Total _____

Potential Source 3. _____

	Step 1 Results	×	Step 2 Results	=	_____
Cost of capital	_____	×	_____	=	_____
Risk	_____	×	_____	=	_____
Flexibility	_____	×	_____	=	_____
Control	_____	×	_____	=	_____
Availability	_____	×	_____	=	_____
Amount					

Potential Source 3 Total _____

Potential Source 4. _____

	Step 1 Results	×	Step 2 Results	=	_____
Cost of capital	_____	×	_____	=	_____
Risk	_____	×	_____	=	_____
Flexibility	_____	×	_____	=	_____
Control	_____	×	_____	=	_____
Availability	_____	×	_____	=	_____
Amount					

Potential Source 4 Total _____

(continued)

Potential Source 5. _____

	Step 1 Results	×	Step 2 Results	=	_____
Cost of capital	_____	×	_____	=	_____
Risk	_____	×	_____	=	_____
Flexibility	_____	×	_____	=	_____
Control	_____	×	_____	=	_____
Availability	_____	×	_____	=	_____
Amount					

Potential Source 5 Total _____

Potential Source 6. _____

	Step 1 Results	×	Step 2 Results	=	_____
Cost of capital	_____	×	_____	=	_____
Risk	_____	×	_____	=	_____
Flexibility	_____	×	_____	=	_____
Control	_____	×	_____	=	_____
Availability	_____	×	_____	=	_____
Amount					

Potential Source 6 Total _____

Potential Source 7. _____

	Step 1 Results	×	Step 2 Results	=	_____
Cost of capital	_____	×	_____	=	_____
Risk	_____	×	_____	=	_____
Flexibility	_____	×	_____	=	_____
Control	_____	×	_____	=	_____
Availability	_____	×	_____	=	_____
Amount					

Potential Source 7 Total _____

Potential Source 8. _____

	Step 1 Results	×	Step 2 Results	=	_____
Cost of capital	_____	×	_____	=	_____
Risk	_____	×	_____	=	_____
Flexibility	_____	×	_____	=	_____
Control	_____	×	_____	=	_____
Availability	_____	×	_____	=	_____
Amount					

Potential Source 8 Total _____

Step 4 Write in the eight totals below and compare. The highest totals are the best for your situation.

Potential Source 1 Total   _____

Potential Source 2 Total   _____

Potential Source 3 Total   _____

Potential Source 4 Total   _____

Potential Source 5 Total   _____

Potential Source 6 Total   _____

Potential Source 7 Total   _____

Potential Source 8 Total   _____

CHAPTER 4

Business Insurance—What You Need and What You Do Not Need

Business insurance is extremely important for your business because it provides a means of protection against many business risks. You pay a relatively small amount of money to insure your business against the loss of a far greater amount. It is not an understatement that the relatively small insurance fee that you pay may actually save your company from going under.

Risk Management

Insurance is really a way of managing risk in your business. This means identifying and controlling the exposure of your business or your personal assets to loss or injury. Proper risk management involves the following four-step process:

1. Identify the risks to which your business may be subjected.
2. Evaluate the probability of the occurrence of each risk that you have identified, along with the cost to you should it occur and the cost of insurance coverage protecting you against this risk.
3. Decide the best way to handle each risk: whether to accept all or part of the risk and whether to reduce it through insurance.
4. Control the risk by implementing what you have decided is the best method or combination of methods for each risk.

To identify each risk, you should think of everything that poses a threat to your business. This includes employee strikes or work stoppage; death or temporary ill health of key personnel; losses resulting from fire, earthquake, or some other natural calamity; through suit because of a product causing some injury; and so forth. You should list every threat that you can think of.

Now, you must assign a likelihood to each risk. If the event is likely, what might it cost you or your firm? For example, if you are sued because of a defect in your product that causes injury, how much are you likely to be sued for? If you have a fire, what is the fire likely to destroy and what is the monetary value of what could be destroyed? Now investigate how much insurance would cost to protect your business in each case.

You must then decide the best way to handle each of the risks to your business: You must make some decisions about each risk. In some cases, you may be able to avoid the risk entirely by having someone else perform the task that leads to the risk. For example, you can avoid certain fire risks and risks of injury to your employees by subcontracting the manufacture of your product to someone else.

Another alternative is spreading the risk. You can duplicate valuable documents, keeping them in two different locations, so that if a fire destroys one set, the other set is still available. Some risks may be prevented. Safety equipment may prevent injury; sprinkler systems and fire alarms minimize the potential for loss from fire. Another option is to transfer the risk. Transferring the risk is done through contracts with insurance companies. The insurance companies assume the risk of losses due to fire and so forth, in return for payment of a fee. This fee is called a *premium*. Finally, if the risk is slight, you may decide to accept it as a cost of doing business.

After weighing all alternatives, you must take action to implement the decision that you have made. In many cases, some type of insurance is the best course of action. Now, you need to develop an overall insurance program to implement this decision.

Developing an Insurance Program

Developing an insurance program requires (1) determining insurance costs, (2) developing an insurance plan for your business, and (3) getting professional advice. Let us look at each in turn.

Determining Insurance Costs

To decide how to handle the risk, it is necessary to obtain a rough idea of insurance costs. Before you actually purchase any insurance, you should investigate ways to reduce the cost of your coverage. These methods include:

- Use as high a deductible as you can afford.
- Make certain there's no duplication in the various insurance policies that you have.
- Buy your insurance in as large a unit as possible. Certain package policies covering differing risks are suitable for different types of small businesses.

- Review your insurance program periodically to ensure that your coverage is adequate and that your premiums are as low as possible and consistent with the protection that you seek.

Developing an Insurance Plan for Your Business

As with other aspects of business, you must plan ahead to manage your insurance program properly to receive the necessary coverage at the lowest possible cost. Some general principles help here.

Think through what you want to accomplish with your insurance program and write out clear statements of what you expect insurance to do for you and your firm.

Try to select only one agent to handle your insurance. This fixes responsibility on one individual or company. If you are not personally handling the insurance, make certain that whoever is handling it for your company understands the importance of his or her responsibility. Do not try to con your insurance agent. An insurance agent is like a doctor, attorney, or other professional: To give you maximum help, he or she should know everything possible about risks to your business and its exposure to loss.

Be careful about under insuring in areas that can cause major loss, even if the probability of the loss's occurrence is small. Premiums vary depending on probability. So, if the probability of occurrence is small, the premium is probably small as well.

Keep accurate and complete records of your insurance policies, including your premiums, losses, and loss recoveries. You can use this information to make better decisions about insurance coverage in the future as your business grows. Finally, make certain that independent appraisers appraise your property periodically. In this way, you will know what your exposure to risk actually is.

Getting Professional Advice

Insurance, like any other aspect of your business, can be complex. You cannot expect to master it by yourself unless you have very limited needs. Therefore, an agent who is professionally qualified, a broker, or some other consultant can be worth the fees for this service many times over. This is no different than the fees you pay for the services of an attorney or an accountant or any other business professional.

Basic Types of Insurance

There are three basic types of insurance for business: liability insurance, life and health insurance, and property insurance.

Liability Insurance

Any business is subject to laws governing negligence, and this includes negligence to customers, employees, or anyone else with whom you may happen to do business or with whom you have contact in the course of business, or who is on your property.

If you are negligent, you fail to do something. In the case of liability insurance, negligence refers to failing to exercise a degree of care that may be expected or required under your particular situation or circumstances. An example might be failing to clear snow properly from the walkway in front of the entrance to your premises, or permitting a hazard to exist because of the manufacturing processes that you employ. You may be liable through negligence even if you have signs posted specifically warning of this hazard or if you have cleaned the snow from the walkway to your own satisfaction. It may be that an accident occurs from carelessness on the part of the person injured. It doesn't make much difference. Many courts judge in favor of the plaintiff anyway; the business is assumed to be responsible for any accidents happening on the premises, even though the injured person's carelessness may contribute to the mishap.

But there are even more important kinds of liabilities to your business than accidents or mishaps that may occur on your premises. One example is product liability. You are liable for the effects of the product that you produce under almost every situation.

Some years ago, a firearm manufacturing company was successfully sued by someone injured by operating a firearm in a manner specifically noted in the manufacturer's manual provided with the gun, as being extremely hazardous. There is also liability as a result of an employee's automobile accident while on the job. The bottom line is that you may have to purchase separate liability protection against potential liabilities that are not included in a general comprehensive liability policy.

General Liability Coverage   Liability insurance covers the following types of losses:

- Payments that are required due to bodily injury or damage to the property of others that you cause accidentally.
- Medical services necessary at the time of the accident.
- Costs of defending lawsuits that allege bodily injury or property damage including expenses in investigation and settlement.
- The cost of any court bonds or other judgments during appeal.

There are various exclusions and limitations on most liability policies. Some policies may exclude obligations under workers' compensation laws because this is covered by special workers' compensation insurance, as discussed shortly. Also excluded may be damage to property of others that is in your care or control. This exclusion may be eliminated by payment of an extra premium. Finally, a major exclusion includes liability resulting from war, mishaps involving nuclear energy, blasting operations, and similar situations.

Limits to liability may be on a per-person or per-accident basis. For example, automobile liability insurance may limit you to $100 thousand per person injured or to a total of $400 thousand in any one accident. This means that if two persons are injured in a single automobile accident for which you are covered by liability insurance and the judgments are $200 thousand each, the policy pays only $200 thousand because of the limit of $100 thousand per person. Alternatively, if four individuals were injured and the judgment is $100 thousand each, the policy would cover the total amount.

Other limitations may include a single limit applying to bodily injury and property damage, or there may be a limitation on product liability that applies to a certain group of products. Be aware of all limitations before purchasing the insurance. Now, let's look at several types of liability insurance.

Automobile Liability Insurance   You are generally required to maintain insurance on all automobiles or other vehicles that you operate as a part of your business. You can be legally liable for accidents with vehicles owned by others, either employees, vendors, or even customers who are involved in these accidents while they are using their vehicles on behalf of your business.

Typical coverage for automobile liability insurance includes damages from collision, fire, theft, and other physical perils. Physical damage or perils can be subdivided into several types. These include collision damage, which can be insured separately from other types of losses. Collision insurance does not cover glass breakage and damage from falling objects, missiles, windstorms, hail, malicious mischief, and vandalism. With your automobile liability insurance, you can insure all types of physical loss except collision by taking out a comprehensive policy. A comprehensive policy generally excludes the following: losses from wear and tear; losses to tires unless owing to fire, malicious mischief, or vandalism arising from collision; loss from radioactive contamination; and loss from freezing or from mechanical or electrical breakdown. However, if any of these losses except for those covered by radioactive contamination result from theft, you are covered. The alternative to buying comprehensive insurance is to insure against each peril separately. You can imagine how complex this could become.

How much you pay for automobile insurance or physical damage insurance can vary widely depending on the vehicle, including its age, type, the territory including the location and distance traveled, and the age of the driver or drivers. Sometimes special physical damage rates can be obtained if you own more than one vehicle. These are called experience rates and give individual physical damage rates based on experience over a period of several years. Other special physical damage rates can be obtained under safe driver plans or merit rates for which an individual owner may qualify.

In these days of very high insurance rates, obtaining a policy that allows for a deductible amount permits you to save a significant amount of money on your collision coverage. This means that you assume the obligation for a certain amount of damage in the event of an accident. Let's say you agree to a $1,000 deductible coverage. If you suffer damage less than $1,000, you receive no reimbursement from the insurance. You are assuming the risk for that amount. Above $1,000, the policy covers your losses. Again, you must weigh your loss in the event of damage, the probability of occurrence, and other factors to develop a risk trade-off that helps you decide how much obligation you should assume in any given situation.

Product Liability Insurance   Product liability insurance is useful to you as a manufacturer or, in some cases, a retailer of products that may cause injury or damage to the user of the product. However, even though this is known as "product" liability insurance, services too can cause damage and may be subject to product liability laws. Today, judgments against physicians for incorrect or incompetent medical decisions are common, and in some cases so large that physicians have closed their practices because they could not afford the cost of the insurance. The insurance that physicians carry to protect themselves against lawsuits is a type of product liability insurance. Similarly, an automobile mechanic who does a repair job incorrectly could be liable for an injury caused due to the service performed.

Product liability insurance can be very expensive depending on the likelihood of your product causing injury or damage or even allowing it to happen, if your product is protective in nature. However, the awards in the event of an injury or death caused by your product may be so high as to make such insurance imperative.

Workers' Compensation Insurance   Workers' compensation insurance protects the employer against liability in the event of an accident to the employee. By law, you are required to provide employees with a safe place to work, hire only competent employees so they do not endanger one another, provide safe tools to work with, and warn employees of any existing dangers that may exist or develop while they are doing their job for you. If you fail to take any of these actions, you are liable for damage suits brought against you by your employees. The mere fact that you try to do these duties to the best of your ability is not sufficient. Under workers' compensation insurance, an employee can collect payment for doctors' bills and medications as well as hospital expenses and income payments for time lost beyond a specified minimum period. If injuries are received that result in permanent damage, the employee may collect a lump-sum payment to compensate for that loss.

These workers' compensation awards are not automatic and are made on the basis of a hearing by a special examiner or board. You have the right to be represented either directly or jointly with the insurance company. Awards made to the employee may be smaller in the case of carelessness by the employee or when the loss is the result of an injury caused by a fellow employee.

All-Inclusive Policies   You may also purchase insurance that can cover exceptionally large liabilities above and beyond your basic coverage. Such a policy may cover a multimillion-dollar lawsuit for the loss of life in an accident on your premises. Fortunately, these all-inclusive coverages, or umbrella policies, are not as expensive as you might think because the insurance company that provides them need only fulfill the few claims that exceed the basic insurance coverage. The result is that, for a relatively small cost, these all-inclusive policies can protect you against extremely severe losses. It is important to read the fine print carefully and take the time to have the insurance agent explain to you exactly what is covered and exactly what is not covered under the basic insurance policies that you purchase.

Life and Health Insurance

Life and health insurance provides extra compensation to employees, owners, or the business itself for losses that are sustained as a result of illness or death. The law does not usually require this, but most businesses do carry these policies for their employees today—in addition to the basic workers' compensation insurance. You probably have to carry life and health insurance policies for your employees to be competitive with other companies in your industry.

Typical coverage for this type of policy includes basic life insurance, basic health insurance, major medical insurance, dental insurance, and eyeglass insurance. Life insurance is used to provide financial protection to the employee's family in the event of the employee's death. Some group life insurance plans are tax deductible for the employer. Also, group coverage can frequently be obtained at lower rates even if your firm includes only one or two employees. Generally, a life insurance policy is offered in conjunction with some form of basic health or major medical insurance.

Health and medical insurance may include basic hospitalization and medical plans, major medical plans, and disability plans. Basic hospitalization medical plans pay the cost of hospitalization, medical care, and medication during hospitalization, and they also pay for medical care outside of hospitals and diagnostic services, such as blood tests, X-rays, urinalyses, and so forth. These policies, in some cases, may be split between medical and surgical, on one hand, and hospitalization, on the other. Usually basic medical insurance is less expensive in group plans, except in the case of small groups. If the group or firm has very few employees, it may be less expensive to cover them with individual policies. Again, that's a trade-off that you should calculate after speaking with your insurance agent.

Major medical or catastrophic plans are intended to meet the cost of catastrophic illnesses. They usually contain deductible clauses, so that they apply only after the payments covered by basic medical and hospitalization plans. For the same reason that all-inclusive policies are not expensive, major medical plans are not expensive, even for small companies.

In some states, the law requires disability plans. These plans pay the employees a proportion of their salary during temporary or extended absences due to illness or accidents that are work related.

It is possible to use life insurance annuities to provide pension benefits to your employees. Many large and small companies offer these pension and retirement plans, but they are complex and can be very expensive. You must be very careful about these plans to make sure that you do not have increasing premium payments and that your business has sufficient income to make pension payments over the long run. Pension plans are also subject to federal laws and IRS regulations. Therefore, they represent a major insurance decision for your firm, and you should be certain that the plan that you intend to adopt meets all federal requirements.

There is an alternative to pension/retirement plans. An Individual Retirement Account (IRA) is available for employees, and you may qualify for a Keogh Plan as an owner. The government has also instituted other types of plans for retirement. Because of tax deferments for various other reasons, these may be more advantageous to you than a very small pension plan. Check into these plans with your bank and insurance agent and again compute the trade-offs to yourself, your employees, and your firm.

Property Insurance

Property insurance protects against losses that may occur to your business property. This includes real property or buildings, personal property including machines, office supplies, and equipment, finished goods, and so forth. Property coverage that you may want to consider include the following:

- Automobile damage insurance.
- Comprehensive property insurance.
- Crime insurance.
- Fire insurance.
- Flood, hail, windstorm, and vandalism insurance.
- Inland marine insurance.

Automobile Damage Insurance   Automobile damage insurance is usually included as part of the automobile liability insurance policy discussed earlier. Therefore, it is usually excluded from all-purpose property policies.

Comprehensive Property Insurance   This is an all-risk policy that generally covers all perils except those that are specifically excluded and named in the policy. An all-risk policy has certain advantages:

- You avoid gaps in your coverage because you know that you are covered for all perils not specifically excluded.

- You are less likely to duplicate your coverage with additional policies than if you tried to get the same insurance by purchasing several different policies.

- In general, it is easier to obtain settlement for lawsuits with an all-risk policy. Owning several policies that cover a single loss may lead to a conflict as to how much each policy is to contribute toward coverage of the loss.

- The total premium on an all-risk policy is generally less than the same coverage obtained by several different policies.

The areas that all-risk policies do not usually cover include accounting records, automobiles, cash, jewelry, machinery, manuscripts, and like items, which are protected by other types of policies.

Crime Insurance   Some types of crime insurance can be included in comprehensive all-risk policies. However, other types of crimes such as off-premise robberies, disappearance of money, employee theft, and embezzlement are not included. Typical types of crime insurance include burglary insurance, which covers your safes and inventory of merchandise; robbery insurance, which protects you from loss of property, money, and securities by robbery either on or off the premises; comprehensive crime policies, which covers other types of theft loss in addition to burglary and robbery, including destruction or disappearance of property; and storekeepers' burglary and robbery policies, which are designed specifically for small businesspersons and cover up to a certain amount of loss for each occurrence of certain types of crime, such as inside robbery, outside robbery, stock burglary, or kidnapping of the owner.

Crime insurance rates are generally high. They do, of course, depend on many factors, including your type of business, the location, kinds of loss prevention measurements, such as safes and burglar alarms, and various other factors.

Fidelity bonds are a type of insurance that protect you against a serious potential loss that is caused by a special kind of crime: dishonesty of your own employees. For example, an embezzler may steal small amounts over a number of years, but the grand total may be quite high. A fidelity bond can insure you against this type of theft. Furthermore, the act of requiring an employee to be bonded may itself discourage stealing. Also, the character investigation performed by the bonding company may disclose unfavorable facts about an employee, enabling you to take preventive measures before a theft can occur.

Fire Insurance   Fire insurance is standardized in the United States. A standard policy covers three basic perils: fire, lightning, and losses to goods temporarily removed from their premises because of the fire. For any additional perils, you must pay extra. For example, a standard fire policy excludes theft and failure to protect the property after a fire. Also, a special policy that extends the standard fire policy is needed to cover loss by fire of accounts, bills, currency, deeds, evidence of debt, and securities.

Flood, Hail, Windstorm, and Vandalism Insurance   The perils of windstorm, hail, and vandalism are frequently covered under comprehensive all-risk property insurance policies discussed earlier. However, flood damage is not covered, and such a policy is usually purchased separately.

Inland Marine Insurance   The inland marine floater policy is designed for specialized types of retailers and wholesalers, including equipment dealers, furriers, jewelers, and launderers that are not covered by general all-risk commercial property insurance because their property is highly susceptible to loss. The type of insurance available may be all risk or there may be specifically named peril contracts.

Special-Purpose Insurance Coverages

Various additional coverages can be obtained to protect you against the potential of large losses. These include the following:

- Business interruption insurance.
- Credit insurance.
- Glass insurance.
- Key employee insurance.
- Power plant insurance.
- Profits and commission insurance.
- Rent insurance.
- Sprinkler leakage insurance.
- Surety bonds.
- Transportation insurance.
- Fair Access to Insurance Requirements Plan.

We'll look at each of these in turn.

Business Interruption Insurance

Your business loses money if you are shut down as a result of a major disaster including fire, earthquake, flood, or storm. Further, even after repairs have been made, you continue to pay expenses such as salaries of employees, taxes, and so forth, even though there may be little or no money coming in. Business interruption insurance can help you with this problem.

Credit Insurance

Credit insurance has several types. Retail firms that sell on credit generally use credit life insurance. It ensures that the outstanding debt of the customer is paid off in the event of his or her death. Commercial credit insurance enables you to have an open account of credit that you can extend to buyers of merchandise for commercial purposes. Installment sales floaters protect you against loss that has a potential for occurring when a purchaser has not insured goods bought on credit. In other words, they assure you of payments for goods that you have already sold.

Glass Insurance

Glass insurance protects you against breakage of large and expensive plate glass windows, signs, and showcases.

Key Employee Insurance

Key employee insurance protects you against losses resulting from the death or total disability of a key employee in your firm, including owners and partners. Thus, if a good deal of business depends on a single individual in your firm, this potential loss can be insured.

Power Plant Insurance

Certain types of machinery that can explode are not covered under all-risk or comprehensive property insurance. Therefore, these require separate policies. This category includes power plants, boilers, and other like machinery or electrical equipment.

Profits and Commission Insurance

This type of insurance enables you to insure profits or commissions you lose if some named peril destroyed the merchandise involved.

Rent Insurance

Rent insurance reimburses you if your tenant fails to pay.

Sprinkler Leakage Insurance

This insurance covers losses resulting from leakage from water sprinklers used in fire protection of your building.

Surety Bonds

Surety bonds enable you to compete on an equal basis with larger or better-known firms. Basically, surety bonds are a guarantee that you carry out work according to the contract. Typically, surety bonds are issued for persons or firms doing contract construction, for those connected with court actions, or for those seeking licenses or permits. The bond guarantees that you are honest and have the necessary ability and financial capacity to meet the obligations required. The surety bond also backs your credit and vouches for your ability to perform. As with a fidelity bond, the bonding firm requires extensive information about you. They also require you to put up collateral before the bond is issued. In the event of loss, sureties have the right to collect from you any amount they are required to pay to the person or company protected. You can see how such bonds put you on an equal footing with much larger firms because your ability to perform is guaranteed even though the individual paying for the job may not know you.

Transportation Insurance

Common carriers are not always liable for losses to the goods that they may be carrying for you. For example, common carriers are not liable for loss from floods, storms, earthquakes, or other perils or acts of God, which cannot reasonably be guarded against by the carrier. Therefore, transportation insurance is of some importance.

Two basic types of transportation insurance are inland transit policy and blanket motor cargo policy. Inland transit policy is most frequently used for land shipments. It covers those perils that are not the liability of the common carrier. The coverage includes collision, derailment, and acts of God. Pilferage is usually excluded, but theft of an entire shipping package or container can be covered. Typical exclusions for the inland transit policy are those arising from strike, riot, civil commotion, war, delay of shipment, or loss of market, and leakage or breakage—unless caused by one of the perils insured against. Certain types of property are also excluded, including accounts, bills, deeds, evidences of debt, money, notes and securities, and exports after arrival at seaport. Certain coverages in these provisions can be negotiated. Rates for an inland transit policy vary widely. You can save insurance costs by using a released bill of lading that makes the common carrier liable for a relatively low dollar value of damage. This can result in a reduction in transit rates more than enough to pay for the inland policy insurance.

A blanket motor cargo policy is issued to truckers and to those who ship by truck. All states require truckers to have certain minimum coverages, including their legal liability for loss of a shipper's goods. Federal laws also require interstate truckers to carry certain coverages. As a shipper, you may wish to obtain your own coverage rather than rely solely on the truckers because these minimums may not offer you full protection. Also, even if the trucker carries more than the minimum required by law, you have no assurance that the policy cannot be voided by breach of warranty or exclusions of various types. Finally, the trucker's policy does not cover acts of God. Therefore, blanket motor cargo policies can be obtained that cover fire, flood, collisions, explosions, and other perils. Typical exclusions for this type of policy are strikes, war, illegal trade, and civil commotion.

Fair Access to Insurance Requirements Plan

The Fair Access to Insurance Requirements (FAIR) plan started as a riot insurance program established by the U.S. Housing and Urban Development Act of 1968. In states accepting the plan, the state, the insurance industry, and the federal government cooperate to make property insurance available in certain high-risk areas at moderate rates. Some states have modified the basic plan to require other types of protection.

If your business is in an area generally known to be subject to riots or serious vandalism, and you are unable to get adequate insurance in the normal manner or cannot get insurance without paying excessively high premiums, this plan may help you out. In fact, you may not be turned down because of being located in a riot-prone area subject to vandalism. It is therefore in your interest to find out whether your state has a FAIR plan and where to apply if this situation applies to you. To do so, contact your state insurance commissioner.

How to Buy Insurance

There are basically two different types of insurance sellers: the *direct writer* and the *agent*. The direct writer is a commissioned employee of the insurer. The business he or she writes belongs to the insurance company itself, which may turn it over to someone else who is also an employee of the firm. The agent is an independent businessperson who has negotiated with the insurer to represent him or her in a given territory. The agent is also compensated on a commissioned basis.

There are advantages in dealing with either the agent or the direct writer. An independent agent may represent many different insurers. Therefore, such an agent is able to offer you a wide choice among a number of different coverages. Also, if this independent agent handles many different types of insurance, you need deal with only this one seller to obtain the same coverage that you otherwise have to obtain from several different insurance sellers. Because the insurance agent may deal with a variety of different coverages, he or she may have greater knowledge of the overall field than a direct writer, who is limited to the line of the employer insurance company. Finally, inasmuch as the business is all his or hers, the independent agent has a greater financial motivation to give you the best service possible.

Advantages in dealing with direct writers include lower costs because the commission paid to the direct writer by his or her own company is less than that paid to the independent agent. Also, the direct writer becomes a specialist in whatever area or line of insurance he or she is handling. Thus, whereas the independent agent has general knowledge, the direct writer has in-depth, specialized knowledge in one area. This may be advantageous to you, depending on the type of insurance that you are interested in and your business situation.

How to Pick an Insurer

The decision to pick one insurer over another generally is based on four factors: cost, type of insurance offered, flexibility in coverage, and financial stability of the firm.

Cost   To evaluate the cost factor, set up a matrix as shown in Table 4.1. Using this matrix, you can select the insurer who offers the lowest cost for the coverage and deductible that you decide on. There may be more than just the lower premium to consider. Some insurers charge a lower initial premium. However, another insurer, which charges a higher premium, may pay a dividend to its policyholders. Therefore, to make an accurate comparison, compare not only the initial premium involved but also the probable size of dividend, if one is being paid.

If the premium is extremely low, be particularly careful that this low premium is not made possible by extremely strict claim settlement policies, the setting aside of inadequate loss reserves, or such low commissions to their agents that the agents are not motivated to render quality service.

TABLE 4.1   Decision Matrix for Insurance Based on Cost and Deductibles

Insurance Company	Coverage ($)	Deductible Amounts			Required Premiums Less Dividends
		$500	$1,000	$2,000	
A	80,000	1,400	1,200	800	
	85,000	1,460	1,245	830	
	90,000	1,520	1,300	860	
B	80,000	1,525	1,300	835	
	85,000	1,580	1,335	910	
	70,000	1,670	1,410	960	

Type of Insurance Offered   Some insurers may specialize in certain types of insurance, and even in insurance for a specific industry. If you choose an insurer offering this sort of specialization, you obtain coverages that are specifically applicable to your business, and the cost of the coverages can be lower than that which other firms offer for a similar type of insurance.

Flexibility in Coverage   Various insurers are able to tailor their policies specifically to the type of buyers that they envision. Also, some enable you to insert certain provisions that may affect the final premium you pay or other factors. In some cases and with some insurers, you may negotiate depending on your situation and an insurance rating calculated according to the likelihood of the occurrence of the event for which you are to be insured. All of these factors can affect both the exact type of insurance coverage that you receive and the cost of the premiums.

Financial Stability of the Firm   In most cases, the agent representing the firm is your normal source of information about it, and generally you are not misled. In dealing with an unknown agent, you must also recognize that the agent could have an ulterior motive for recommending one insurance company over another. For example, one insurance company may pay him or her more. In this and similar situations, it is important that you know that the insuring company recommended has financial stability. Be especially careful when a policy is issued that has a provision that allows policyholders to be assessed additional premiums if the resources of the insurer are insufficient to pay claims against it. You should check to see whether the proposed policy is assessable or not. In general, you should purchase assessable policies only when non-assessable policies are not available and never if the insurance firm is unstable financially. To check on the financial stability of an insurance firm other than through the agent, consult a publication known as *Best's Insurance Reports,* published by the A.M. Best Company. The web site is at http://www.ambest.com.

This report publishes ratings that describe firms' reliability in their dealings with policyholders, their size of net worth, and other important factors. Most ratings fall in the three highest classes, A+, A, and B+. If the company that you are investigating does not fall into one of these three classes, you should look at it much more closely.

How Much Deductible?

You can decide on how much deductible or which policy and coverage to purchase by using the matrix method also. Let's consider the case of the deductibles in Table 4.1. Because of basic costs, we have already decided to do business with insurance company A, and now the question is how much deductible to take. First, we decide on how much insurance is adequate for our purposes. Let us assume that the answer is $80 thousand. Now we have three options: $500 deductible for a premium of $1,400, $1,000 deductible for a premium of $1,200, and $2,000 deductible for a premium of $800. Let us say we calculate that on average we suffer a $500 loss every two years, a $1,000 loss once every four years, and a $2,000 loss once every six years. We can then make the calculations shown in Table 4.2.

TABLE 4.2   CALCULATIONS FOR DEDUCTIBLE AMOUNTS

6 Years	$500 Deductible Amounts	
	Positive	**Negative**
Policy cost	6 × $1,400 = $8,400	
Losses	3 × $500 = $1,500	3 × $0 = $0
	6/4 × $500 = $750	1.5 × $500 = $750
	1 × $500 = $500	1 × $1,500 = $1,500
TOTAL	$11,150	$2,250
	$11,150 − $2,250 = $8,900	

6 Years	$1,000 Deductible Amounts	
	Positive	**Negative**
Policy cost	6 × $1,200 = $7,200	
Losses	3 × $500 = $1,500	3 × $0 = $0
	6/4 × $1,000 = $1,500	1.5 × $0 = $0
	1 × $1,000 = $1,000	1 × $1,000 = $1,000
TOTAL	$11,200	$2,250
	$11,200 − $1,000 = $10,200	

6 Years	$2,000 Deductible Amounts	
	Positive	**Negative**
Policy cost	6 × $800 = $4,800	
Losses	3 × $500 = $1,500	3 × $0 = $0
	6/4 × $1,000 = $1,500	1.5 × $500 = $750
	1 × $1,000 = $2,000	1 × $1,500 = $1,500
TOTAL	$9,800	$2,250
	$9,800 − 0 = $9,800	

Therefore, the best selection under the conditions cited is $500 deductible because $8,900 is less than either $10,200 or $9,800.

Sources of Additional Information

Books

Business Insurance, by Edwin H. White and H. Chasman, published by Prentice-Hall.

Enterprise Risk Management, by James Lam, published by John Wiley & Sons.

Fundamentals of Risk and Insurance, 9th ed., by Emmett J. Vaughan and Theresa M. Vaughan, published by John Wiley & Sons.

General Insurance, by John H. Magee, published by Richard D. Irwin.

General Insurance Guide, by B. G. Werbel, published by Werbel Publishing.

Group Insurance Handbook, edited by Robert D. Eilers and Robert M. Crowe, published by Richard D. Irwin.

Life and Health Insurance Handbook, edited by Davis W. Gregg and Vane B. Lucas, published by Richard D. Irwin.

Modern Life Insurance, by Robert W. Osier, published by Macmillan.

Risk and Insurance, by Mark R. Greene, published by Southwestern Publishing.

Risk Management and Insurance, by C. Arthur Williams Jr., and Richard M. Heins, published by McGraw-Hill.

Risk Management: Concepts and Applications, by Robert I. Mehr and Bole A. Hedges, published by Richard D. Irwin.

Risk Management and Insurance, by Etti G. Baranoff, published by John Wiley & Sons.

Internet

Note: Because Internet sites frequently go down, multiple sites are listed for similar subject matter.

Business Insurance. Business search engine and directory including company and industry profiles, news, financials, statistics, competitive analysis, and more at http://www.businessinsurance.com.

Business.Com. Information, resources, data and publications for insurance providers, actuaries, agents, and so on at http://www.business.com/directory/financial_services/insurance/index.asp.

Business Insurance Oracle. A practical guide to understanding and buying business insurance at http://www.insuranceoracle.com.

Free Advice on Legal Questions and Problems—Business Insurance. Free Advice's business insurance law information helps businesses to understand their legal rights through questions and answers at http://www.freeadvice.com/insurance_law /business_insurance.

Insurance for United States.com. Business insurance quotes. Fill out one form here and receive quotes from three agents in your area at http://www.insurance4usa.com /business-insurance.cfm?affiliateid=433.

Most Choice Business Insurance. Information about business insurance choices and how to get best values at http://www.mostchoice.com/business_insurance_overview.html.

My Own Business—Business Insurance. Provides free information about insurance for entrepreneurs at http://www.myownbusiness.org/s5.

DOWNLOADABLE WORKSHEET 4.1
Saving Money with Your Insurance

Possible Action to Help You Save Money	Check to Take Action on This
Get competitive bids on all of your policies, review them using the matrix system shown in Table 3.1, and compare the alternatives.	
Do not rely totally on your agent. Review your alternatives to be sure that your agent has not neglected to suggest the best possible coverage for your situation.	
Over a period of time, evaluate how your agent has performed in getting compensation for your losses.	
Make certain that you evaluate the use of deductibles in your insurance program.	
Check with your agent where you can reduce premiums through assuming certain obligations, for example, a sprinkler system, a burglar alarm system, and so forth.	

To customize this document, download it to your hard drive from the John Wiley & Sons web site at www.wiley .com/go/cohenentrepreneur. The document can then be opened, edited, and printed using Microsoft Word or another popular word processing application.

DOWNLOADABLE WORKSHEET 4.2
Insurance Checklist

The following insurance checklist is based on a checklist originally developed by Mark R. Greene, Distinguished Professor of Insurance at the University of Georgia and published by the U.S. Small Business Administration. This checklist will enable you to discover areas in which your insurance program can be improved, costs can be saved, and the effectiveness of your insurance can be increased. It will also serve as a guide on points to talk about with your insurance agent, broker, or other insurance counselor. Put a check by those items to look into or take action on.

Fire Insurance	Action
1. Add other coverages, such as windstorm, hail, smoke, explosion, vandalism, and malicious mischief to basic fire insurance.	
2. If you need comprehensive coverage, your best buy may be one of the all-risk contracts that offer the broadest available protection for the money.	
3. The insurance company may compensate you for your losses in three ways: (1) It may pay actual cash value of the property at the time of loss. (2) It may repair or replace the property with material of like kind and quality. (3) It may take *all* the property at the agreed or appraised value and reimburse you for your loss.	
4. You can insure property you don't own if you have a financial interest in the property when a loss occurs but not necessarily at the time the insurance contract is made.	
5. When you sell property, you cannot assign the insurance policy along with the property unless you have permission from the insurance company.	
6. Even if you have several policies on your property, you can still collect only the amount of your actual cash loss. All the insurers share the payment proportionately.	
7. Special protection other than the standard fire policy is needed to cover the loss by fire of accounts, bills, currency, deeds, evidences of debt, and money and securities.	
8. If an insured building is vacant or unoccupied for more than 60 consecutive days, coverage may be suspended unless you have a special endorsement to your policy canceling this provision.	
9. If, either before or after a loss, you conceal or misrepresent to the insurer any material fact or circumstance concerning your insurance or the interest of the insured, the policy may be voided.	
10. If you take any action that increases the hazard of fire, the insurance company may suspend your coverage even for losses not originating from the increased hazard.	
11. After a loss, you must use all reasonable means to protect the property from further loss or run the risk of having your coverage canceled.	
12. To recover your loss, you must furnish (unless an extension is granted by the insurance company) a complete inventory of the damaged, destroyed, and undamaged property within 60 days with complete details.	

Fire Insurance	Action
13. If you and the insurer disagree on the amount of loss, the question may be resolved through special appraisal procedures provided for in the fire insurance policy.	
14. You may cancel your policy without notice at any time and get part of the premium returned. The insurance company also may cancel at any time with a 5-day written notice to you.	
15. By accepting a coinsurance clause in your policy, you get a substantial reduction in premiums. A coinsurance clause states that you must carry insurance equal to 80 or 90 percent of the value of the insured property. If you carry less than this, you cannot collect the full amount of your loss, even if the loss is small. What percent of your loss you can collect will depend on what percent of the full value of the property you have insured it for.	
16. If your loss is caused by someone else's negligence, the insurer has the right to sue this negligent third party for the amount it has paid you under the policy. This is known as the insurer's right of subrogation. However, the insurer will usually waive this right upon request.	
17. A building under construction can be insured for fire, lightning, extended coverage, vandalism, and malicious mischief.	

Liability Insurance	Action
1. Beware of legal liability limits. $1 million or more is not considered high or unreasonable even for a small business.	
2. Most liability policies require you to notify the insurer immediately after an incident on your property that might cause a future claim. This is true no matter how unimportant the incident may seem at the time it happens.	
3. Most liability policies, in addition to bodily injuries, may cover personal injuries (libel, slander, and so on) if these are specifically insured.	
4. Under certain conditions, your business may be subject to damage claims even from trespassers.	
5. You may be legally liable for damages even in cases where you used "reasonable care."	
6. Even if the suit against you is false or fraudulent, the liability insurer pays court costs, legal fees, and interest on judgments in addition to the liability judgments themselves.	
7. You can be liable for the acts of others under contracts you have signed with them. This liability is insurable.	
8. In some cases, you may be held liable for fire loss to property of others in your care. Yet, this property would normally not be covered by your fire or general liability insurance. This risk can be covered by fire legal liability insurance or through requesting subrogation waivers from insurers of owners of the property.	

(continued)

Automobile Insurance	Action
1. When an employee or a subcontractor uses his own car on your behalf, you can be legally liable even if you don't own a car or truck yourself.	
2. Five or more automobiles or motorcycles under one ownership and operated as a fleet for business purposes can generally be insured under a low-cost fleet policy against both material damage to your vehicle and liability to others for property damage or personal injury.	
3. You can often get deductibles of almost any amount and thereby reduce your premiums.	
4. Automobile medical payments insurance pays for medical claims, including your own, arising from automobile accidents regardless of the question of negligence.	
5. In most states, you must carry liability insurance or be prepared to provide other proof (surety bond) of financial responsibility when you are involved in an accident.	
6. You can purchase uninsured motorist protection to cover your own bodily injury claims from someone who has no insurance.	
7. Personal property stored in an automobile and not attached to it (for example, merchandise being delivered) is not covered under an automobile policy.	
Workers' Compensation	Action
1. Common law requires that an employer (1) provide his employees a safe place to work, (2) hire competent fellow employees, (3) provide safe tools, and (4) warn his employees of an existing danger.	
2. If an employer fails to provide the above, under both common law and workers' compensation laws he is liable for damage suits brought by an employee.	
3. State law determines the level or type of benefits payable under workers' compensation policies.	
4. Not all employees are covered by workers' compensation laws. The exceptions are determined by state law and therefore vary from state to state.	
5. In nearly all states, you are now legally required to cover your workers under workers' compensation.	
6. You can save money on workers' compensation insurance by seeing that your employees are properly classified.	
7. Rates for workers' compensation insurance vary from 0.1 percent of the payroll for safer occupations to about 25 percent or more of the payroll for more hazardous occupations.	
8. Most employers in most states can reduce their workers' compensation premium cost by reducing their accident rates below the average. They do this by using safety and loss-prevention measures.	

Desirable Coverages	
Some types of insurance coverage, while not absolutely essential, will add greatly to the security of your business. These coverages include business interruption insurance, crime insurance, glass insurance, and rent insurance.	

Business Interruption Insurance	Action
1. You can purchase insurance to cover fixed expenses that would continue if a fire shut down your business—such as salaries to key employees, taxes, interest, depreciation, and utilities—as well as the profits you would lose.	
2. Under properly written contingent business interruption insurance, you can also collect if fire or other peril closes down the business of a supplier or customer and this interrupts your business.	
3. The business interruption policy provides payments for amounts you spend to hasten the reopening of your business after a fire or other insured peril.	
4. You can get coverage for the extra expenses you suffer if an insured peril, while not actually closing your business down, seriously disrupts it.	
5. When the policy is properly endorsed, you can get business interruption insurance to indemnify you if your operations are suspended because of failure or interruption of the supply of power, light, heat, gas, or water furnished by a public utility company.	

Crime Insurance	Action
1. Burglary insurance excludes such property as accounts, fur articles in a showcase window, and manuscripts.	
2. Coverage is granted under burglary insurance only if there are visible marks of the burglar's forced entry.	
3. Burglary insurance can be written to cover, in addition to money in a safe, inventoried merchandise and damage incurred in the course of a burglary.	
4. Robbery insurance protects you from loss of property, money, and securities by force, trickery, or threat of violence on or *off* your premises.	
5. A comprehensive crime policy written just for small businesspeople is available. In addition to burglary and robbery, it covers other types of loss by theft, destruction, and disappearance of money and securities. It also covers thefts by your employees.	
6. If you are in a high-risk area and cannot get insurance through normal channels without paying excessive rates, you may be able to get help through the federal crime insurance plan. Your agent or state insurance commissioner can tell you where to get information about these plans.	

(continued)

Glass Insurance	Action
1. You can purchase a special glass insurance policy that covers all risk to glass panels.	
2. The glass insurance policy covers not only the glass itself, but also its lettering and ornamentation, if these are specifically insured, and the costs of temporary plates or boarding up when necessary.	
3. After the glass has been replaced, full coverage is continued without any additional premium for the period covered.	

Rent Insurance	Action
1. You can buy rent insurance that will pay your rent if the property you lease becomes unusable because of fire or other insured perils and your lease calls for continued payments in such a situation.	
2. If you own property and lease it to others, you can insure against loss if the lease is canceled because of fire and you have to rent the property again at a reduced rental.	

Employee Benefit Coverages	
Insurance coverages that can be used to provide employee benefits include group life insurance, group health insurance, disability insurance, and retirement income. Key employee insurance protects the company against financial loss caused by the death of a valuable employee or partner.	

Group Life Insurance	Action
1. If you pay group insurance premiums and cover all employees up to a set amount, the cost to you is deductible for federal income tax purposes, and yet the value of the benefit is not taxable income to your employees.	
2. Most insurers will provide group coverages at low rates even if there are 10 or fewer employees in your group.	
3. If the employees pay part of the cost of the group insurance, state laws require that 75 percent of them must elect coverage for the plan to qualify as group insurance.	
4. Group plans permit an employee leaving the company to convert his group insurance coverage to a private plan, at the rate for his age, without a medical exam if he does so within 30 days after leaving his job.	

Group Health Insurance	Action
1. Group health insurance costs much less and provides more generous benefits for the worker than individual contracts would.	
2. If you pay the entire cost, individual employees cannot be dropped from a group plan unless the entire group policy is canceled.	
3. Generous programs of employee benefits, such as group health insurance, tend to reduce labor turnover.	

Disability Insurance	Action
1. Workers' compensation insurance pays an employee only for time lost because of work injuries and work-related sickness—not for time lost because of disabilities incurred off the job. But you can purchase, at a low premium, insurance to replace the lost income of workers who suffer short-term or long-term disability not related to their work.	
2. You can get coverage that provides employees with an income for life in case of permanent disability resulting from work-related sickness or accident.	
Retirement Income	**Action**
1. If you are self-employed, you can get an income tax deduction for funds used for retirement for you and your employees through plans of insurance or annuities approved for use under the Employees Retirement Income Security Act of 1974 (ERISA).	
2. Annuity contracts may provide for variable payments in the hope of giving the annuitants some protection against the effects of inflation. Whether fixed or variable, an annuity can provide retirement income that is guaranteed for life.	
Key Employee Insurance	**Action**
1. One of the most serious setbacks that can come to a small company is the loss of a key employee. But your key employee can be insured with life insurance and disability insurance owned by and payable to your company.	
2. Proceeds of a key employee policy are not subject to income tax, but premiums are not a deductible business expense.	
3. The cash value of key employee insurance, which accumulates as an asset of the business, can be borrowed against and the interest and dividends are not subject to income tax as long as the policy remains in force.	

CHAPTER 5

Financial Management

Financial management includes a number of different functions:

- Managing old and new assets so that every asset contributes to the maximum extent possible toward the profitable operation of your business.
- Ensuring the assets that you have are used to bring the maximum return possible on the money that you invest.
- Obtaining funds to finance additional assets.
- Evaluating the need for new assets.
- Repaying borrowed monies from profits that the same money has generated.

Because these functions impact on your profitability and your survivability, they are extremely important. One reason for owning and operating your own business is to make a good profit for yourself, and you need good financial management to reach this goal.

Methods to help you with these functions are discussed throughout the book, not only in this chapter. However, in this chapter we focus on items of particular concern for the small businessperson in handling financial management responsibilities. These include the definition and components of working capital, the tools of financial management necessary to accomplish any of the functions listed, analysis methods needed to find out whether you are performing adequately financially, and the break-even analysis, which must be used for many of your business decisions prior to an investment. Refer to this chapter again and again, and use it in conjunction with other chapters to enable you to analyze what is going on in your business at all times. This helps you correct deficiencies and make your business increasingly more profitable.

Working Capital

Small businesspersons are particularly concerned with the term *working capital*. It is the difference between your current assets and your current liabilities. It is the circulating lifeblood of your business. Lack of control of this lifeblood is a primary cause of business failure in firms of all sizes. To be alert for change or the opportunity for change, you must understand the components of working capital. A change in your business implies a change in the financial health of your company, either for better or worse. Monitor the following components to ensure that the end result in your company will be an improvement:

- *Cash and cash equivalents:* These comprise the most liquid form of current assets. This means they are the easiest to convert in form and to use. Cash equivalents are usually marketable securities or short-term certificates of deposit. You must maintain a well-planned cash budgeting system, so that you know whether the cash on hand, in the form of cash and equivalents, is adequate to meet current expenses as you must pay them—whether the timing relationship between cash inflow and outflow is favorable. Remember, it is fine that at the end of the year you might make a big profit but if, at any time during the year, you have a sufficiently large negative cash flow, you could end up bankrupt. You should also know when peak cash needs may occur and the magnitude of borrowing that might be required to meet cash shortfalls. And, of course, your system should enable you to see when and how repayment is accomplished.

- *Accounts receivable:* As explained in an earlier chapter, accounts receivable is one way your business extends credit to your customers or clients. However, this account must be closely watched, and you should note whether the amounts of accounts receivable are reasonable in relationship to your overall sales and the age of these accounts and, of course, what action you can take to speed up collections or whether such accounts should be eliminated in the future. It is for sales to be extremely high, if most of your cash is tied up in accounts receivable. Everyone may owe you money, but if no one is paying, you will not be able to stay in business.

- *Inventories:* Your inventory may make up better than 50 percent of your current assets. This is a significant amount and means that you must keep a close watch on this account. You should know whether the amount of inventory is reasonable in relation to sales and other operational characteristics of your business. A rapid turnover of inventory is important and should be compared with that of other firms in your industry. Also, you should note whether any amount of inventory is invested in items that are not moving or are slow to move. Alternatively, you may lose sales due to an inadequate inventory. Either situation implies action that you must take either to increase or decrease your inventory.

- *Accounts payable and trade notes payable:* One source of credit is trade credit. We mentioned this earlier, and about how the money you owe to suppliers is actually a form of a loan. But, unlimited amounts of credit are not good for your business, even if you could obtain them. In this respect, you should note the amount of credit and how it compares with your purchases. What is your payment policy and how does it affect your credit rating? This could be extremely important to you in the future, even if it is not now. Also, note the possible advantages of discount, such as the "2 percent if paid within 10 days" discussed in Chapter 6. Also of interest are the possible timing relationships between the payments on accounts payable and collections that you receive on accounts receivable.

- *Notes payable:* Notes payable to banks or perhaps even to individual lenders or the former owner of your business, are a major source of possible financing, and one that we discussed in Chapter 2. You must know whether the debt amount is reasonable in relationship to the other types of financing, such as equity financing, of your firm. Also, you must know when various payments fall due and whether funds are available to meet these payments on time.

- *Accrued expenses and taxes payable:* Accrued expenses and taxes payable represent obligations of the firm as of the date that you prepare the balance sheet. These accrued expenses represent items such as salaries, interest payable, bank notes, insurance premiums payable, and so forth. Taxes payable are self-evident. But in all cases, it is extremely important that the magnitude, timing, and availability of funds be looked into very carefully. Taxes not paid on time, for example, can result in your firm being closed down by the government until the taxes are paid and generally with a stiff penalty.

To help you monitor the elements of your working capital, various ratio analyses have been developed and are discussed in upcoming sections.

The Tools of Financial Management

Certain tools are available to help you with the financial management of your firm. These tools are as follows:

- *Accounting records:* These are the basis of your financial management. At this point, you may feel that keeping track of your business on a day-to-day basis and accounting for all transactions is too time consuming. Overall, you save time and money doing this. (Methods of keeping accurate and precise records are contained in Chapter 7.)

- *Financial records and reports:* These include the balance sheet and the profit and loss statement, which are discussed in Chapter 7. These two financial statements are the basis for all financial analyses and are used by bankers and other investors in making loan evaluations and investment decisions. For this reason, you must understand these two documents and be able to explain each item that may appear in them. State and federal laws pertaining to taxation also require reports that can be put together only from the use of profit and loss and balance sheets. Finally, these two documents are very helpful in accomplishing financial analyses.

- *Analysis techniques:* These tools include ratio analyses, return-on-investment guides, and break-even analysis. They are discussed next.

Ratio Analyses

Ratio analyses are indicators that have been developed to help you to determine the state of health of various financial aspects of your business. They provide indications as to weaknesses and strengths in your financial operation as well as clues to where and how to develop better financial performance. Such ratios also permit you to compare how you are doing with the performance of other similar businesses in your industry.

However, even with the important and considerable insight they provide, there are limitations to the use of ratio analyses. You must also consider the following limitations during your analysis:

- *Ratios are based on past performance:* Therefore, you must balance their indications with what is happening now and what is likely to happen in your business in the future.

- *Ratios are frequently calculated for specific dates:* If your business is seasonal, this factor must be considered.

- *Businesses are not perfectly comparable:* Different items may be stated in multiple ways on financial statements. As a result, the financial ratios computed for your business may differ from those of the average in your industry for reasons other than performance.

Despite these limitations, financial ratios and ratio analyses may be of great help to you. *Liquidity* is the ability to use the money available in your business. In general, the more liquid your money is, the better your financial health.

However, this is a bit oversimplified, as I demonstrate later. The ratios intended to measure liquidity in your business tell you whether you have enough cash on hand plus assets that can be readily turned into cash to pay debts that may fall due during any given period. The ratios also tell you how quickly assets can be turned into cash. Let's look at some of the measures of liquidity that are available to you.

The Current Ratio   The current ratio is possibly the best-known measure of financial health. It answers this question: Does your business have sufficient current assets to meet current debts with a margin of safety for possible losses due to uncollectible accounts receivable and other factors?

The current ratio is computed by using information from your balance sheet. You simply divide current assets by current liabilities. For example, if current assets are $155,000, and current liabilities are $90,000. Dividing $155,000 by $90,000 gives a current ratio of 1.7.

Is this a good current ratio? You cannot determine this from the numerical value of 1.7 by itself, even though there is a popular rule of thumb that says that a current ratio between 1 and 2 is okay. The current ratio very much depends on your business and the specific characteristics of your current assets and liabilities. However, one major indication is a comparison with other companies in your industry. I give sources for this information later in the chapter.

If after analysis and comparison you decide that your current ratio is too low, you may be able to raise it by the following actions:

- Increase your current assets by new equity contributions.
- Try converting noncurrent assets into current assets.
- Pay some of your debts.
- Increase your current assets from loans or other types of borrowing that have a maturity of at least a year in the future.
- Put some of the profits back into the business.

The Acid Test or "Quick" Ratio   You calculate this ratio as follows: cash plus government securities plus receivables divided by current liabilities.

The company shown in Figure 7.1 (in Chapter 7) has no government securities. Therefore, the numerator of this figure becomes $35,000 cash plus $55,000 in accounts receivable or $90,000. This is divided by current liabilities on the same balance sheet of $90,000 to result in an acid test ratio of 1.0.

The quick ratio concentrates on liquid assets whose values are definite and well-known. Therefore, the quick ratio answers this question: If all your sales revenue disappears tomorrow, can you meet current obligations with your cash or quick funds on hand? Usually, an acid test ratio of approximately 1.0 is considered satisfactory. However, you must also make this decision conditional on the following:

- There should be nothing in the foreseeable future to slow the collection of your accounts receivable.
- The receipt of accounts receivable collections should not trail the due schedule for paying your current liabilities. In evaluating this timing, you should consider payment of your creditors sufficiently early to take advantage of any discounts that are offered.

If these two conditions are not met, you need an acid test ratio higher than 1.0. However, it is erroneous to believe that either the current or the acid test ratio should always be as high as possible. Only those from whom you have borrowed money say this is so. Naturally, they are interested in the greatest possible safety of their loan. However, you do not want to have large sums of money lying idle and not earning you additional profits. If you do have idle cash balances and receivables and inventories that are out of proportion to your needs, you should reduce them. The key here is to be conservative enough to keep a safety pad and yet bold enough to take advantage of the fact that you have these resources, which can be used to earn additional profits for you. Before you decide what is the right amount of liquidity, you should consider the two ratios discussed next, average collection period and inventory turnover.

Average Collection Period The average collection period is the number of days that sales are tied up in accounts receivable. This number can be calculated by using your profit and loss statement or income statement as shown in Figure 7.2. First, take your net sales, which in Figure 7.2 are $1,035,000, and divide this figure by the days in your accounting period or 365. This equals $2,836, the average sales per day in the accounting period. Next, take your accounts receivable, which you obtain from the balance sheet, Figure 7.1. Accounts receivable are $55,000. Divide $55,000 by the figure you just calculated ($2,836): $55,000 divided by $2,836 equals 19. This is the average number of days sales are tied up in receivables. It is also your average collection period.

This tells you how promptly your accounts are being collected considering the credit terms you are extending. It also tells you (1) the quality of your accounts and notes receivable; that is, whether you are getting paid rapidly or not; and (2) how good a job your credit department is doing in collecting these accounts.

Now, the question is: Is the figure of 19 days good or bad? There is a rule of thumb that says the average collection period should not exceed one and one-third times the credit terms offered. Therefore, if your company offers 30 days to pay and the average collection period is only 19 days, you are doing very well. Alternatively, anything in excess of 40 days ($1\frac{1}{2} \times 30 = 40$) shows that you may have a problem.

Inventory Turnover   Inventory turnover shows how rapidly your merchandise is moving. It also shows how much capital you had tied up in inventory to support the level of your company's operations for the period that you are analyzing. To calculate inventory turnover, simply divide the cost of goods sold that you obtain from your income statement, Figure 7.2, by your average inventory. According to Figure 7.2, your income or profit and loss statement, the cost of goods sold equals $525,000. You cannot calculate your average inventory from Figure 7.1. You only know that for the period for which the inventory is stated, it equals $60,000. Let's assume that the previous balance sheet indicated that your inventory was $50,000. Then, the average inventory for the two periods is $60,000 plus $50,000 divided by 2, or $55,000. Now, let's see what inventory turnover is: Cost of goods sold again was $525,000 divided by $55,000 equals 9.5.

This means that you turned your inventory 9.5 times during the year. Put another way, through your business operations you used up merchandise that totals 9.5 times the average inventory investment. Under most circumstances, the higher the turnover of inventory, the better, because it means that you are able to operate with a relatively small sum of money invested in this inventory. Another implication is that your inventory is the right inventory. That is, it is salable and has not been in stock too long. But, even here, you must consider that too high a figure may be a sign of a problem. Very high inventory may mean that you have inventory shortages, and inventory shortages soon lead to customer dissatisfaction and may mean a loss of customers to the competition in the long run.

Is 9.5 a satisfactory inventory turnover? Again, the desirable rate depends on your business, your industry, your method of valuing inventories, and numerous other factors that are unique to your situation. And, once again, it is helpful to study and compare your turnover rate with that of similar businesses of your size in your industry. Once you have been working and operating for some time, past experiences with inventory turnover indicate what is good and what is not with less reliance on inventory comparisons.

Very frequently, it is helpful to analyze not just your total inventory but specific inventory turnover for different products or even groups of products or product lines. This shows you the items that are doing well and those that are not. You may also prepare turnover analyses for much more frequent periods than a year. Even monthly or weekly periods may be necessary or required for perishable items or items that become obsolete very quickly. Thus, you know to reorder those items that are truly "hot" items early and in plenty of time, and you also know which items you should not order and which items you must order before their value goes down to a point where you can no longer sell them at all.

Profitability Measures

Measures of profitability are essential in business if you are to know how much money you are making, whether you are making as much as you can, or if you are making money at all. There are several different ratios that assist you in determining this. These include asset earning power, return on the owner's equity, net profit on sales, investment turnover, and, finally, return on investment.

Asset Earning Power

Asset earning power is determined by the ratio of earnings before interest and taxes to total assets. From the income statement in Figure 7.2 we can see that total operating profit or income is $105,000. Total assets from the balance sheet, Figure 8.3, are $272,000. Therefore, $105,000 divided by $272,000 equals 0.39 or 39 percent.

Return on the Owner's Equity

Return on the owner's equity shows the return that you received in exchange for your investment in your business. To compute this ratio you usually use the average equity for 12 months, if it is available, or, if not, the average of figures from two different balance sheets, your latest and the one preceding. Return on the owner's equity equals net profit divided by equity. Net profit from Figure 7.2 is $55,000. Equity from Figure 7.1 is $115,000. Assuming the equity from the period before is also $115,000, we use this as an average. Therefore, return on the owner's equity equals $55,000 divided by $115,000, which equals 0.48 or 48 percent.

You can calculate a similar ratio by using tangible net worth in lieu of equity. Tangible net worth equals equity less any intangible assets such as patents and good will. If no intangible assets exist, then, of course, the two are equal.

Net Profit on Sales

The net profit on sales ratio measures the difference between what you take in and what you spend in the process of doing business. Again, net profit was determined to be $55,000. Net sales from Figure 7.2 are $1,035,000. Therefore, net profit on sales equals 0.053 or 5.3 percent. This means that for every dollar of sales the company has made a profit of $5.30.

The net profit on sales ratio depends mainly on these two factors: (1) operating costs and (2) pricing policies. Therefore, if this figure goes down, it could be because you have lowered prices or it could be because costs have been increasing at the same time that prices have remained stable.

Again, this ratio should be compared with figures from other similar businesses, and you should consider trends over a period of time. It is also useful to compare net profit on sales ratios for individual products to show which products or product lines should be given additional emphasis and which should be eliminated.

Investment Turnover

The investment turnover ratio is annual net sales to total assets. In this case, net sales of $1,035,000, divided by total assets of $272,000 from Figure 7.1, equals 3.8.

Once again, investment turnover should be compared and watched for trends.

Return on Investment

There are several different ways of calculating return on investment (ROI). It is a very useful method of measuring profitability. One simple way is to take net profit and divide it by total assets. In this case, the net profit equals $55,000. Total assets are $272,000. Therefore, $55,000 divided by $272,000 equals 0.20 or 20 percent.

It is desirable here to have the highest net profit for the smallest amount of total assets invested. You can use this rate of return on investment for intercompany and interindustry comparisons, as well as pricing costs, inventory and investment decisions, and many other measurements of efficiency and profitability. However you use it, always be sure that you are consistent in making your comparisons; that is, be sure that you use the same definitions of net profit and assets invested.

Here are some additional measures of profitability using ROI:

- Rate of earnings on total capital employed equals net income plus interest and taxes divided by *total* liabilities and capital. This ratio serves as an index of productivity of capital as well as a measure of earning power in operating efficiency.
- Rate of earnings on invested capital equals net income plus income taxes divided by proprietary equity and *fixed* liabilities. This ratio is used as a measure of earning power of the borrowed invested capital.
- Rate of earnings on proprietary equity equals net income divided by total capital including surplus reserves. This ratio is used as a measure of the yield on the owner's investment.
- Rate of earnings on stock equity equals net income divided by total capital including surplus reserves. This ratio is used as a measure of the attractiveness of common stock as an investment.

- Rate of dividends on common stock equity equals common stock dividends divided by common stock equity. This ratio is used to indicate the desirability of common stock as a source of income.
- Rate of dividends on common stock equity equals common stock dividend per share divided by market value per share of common stock. The ratio is used as a measure of the current yield on investment in a particular stock.

Sources of Ratio Analyses from All Industries

To compare your business with other businesses in your industry it is necessary to obtain pertinent data on other businesses. The following are sources of this information:

Dun & Bradstreet
Business Information Systems
99 Church Street
New York, NY 10007
This source publishes key business ratios in its monthly *Dun's Review* as well as in its annual publication *Cost of Doing Business.*

Accounting Corporation of America
The Research Department
1929 First Ave.
San Diego, CA 92101-2322
This organization publishes *Parameter of Small Businesses,* which classifies its operating ratios for various industry groups on the basis of gross volume.

National Cash Register Company
Marketing Services Department
Dayton, OH 45402
This firm publishes *Expenses in Retail Businesses,* which examines the cost of operations in over 50 kinds of businesses obtained from primary sources, most of which are trade associations.

Robert Morris Associates
Philadelphia National Bank Building
Philadelphia, PA 19103
Robert Morris has developed and published ratio studies for over 225 lines of business.

Small Business Administration (SBA)
Headquarters Office
409 Third St. SW
Washington, DC 20416
The SBA has a series of reports that provide expenses as a percentage of sales for many industries. Although the reports do not provide strict ratio information, a comparison of percentage expenses is very useful for your financial management.

Trade Associations

Many national trade associations publish ratio studies, including the following:

Air Conditioning & Refrigeration Institute (ARI)
4301 N. Fairfax Dr., Ste. 425
Arlington, VA 22203
Phone: (703) 524-8800, Fax: (703) 528-3816
E-mail: ari@ari.org
Web site: http://www.ari.org

Air Transport Association of America (ATA)
1301 Pennsylvania Ave., Ste. 1100
Washington, DC 20004-7017
Phone: (202) 626-4000, Fax: (202) 626-4166
E-mail: ata@air-transport.org
Web site: http://www.airlines.org/public/home/default1.asp

American Bankers Association
1120 Connecticut Ave. NW
Washington, DC 20036
Phone: (202) 663-5000, (800) 338-0626, Fax: (202) 663-7543
Web site: http://www.aba.com/default.htm

American Booksellers Association
828 S. Broadway
Tarrytown, NY 10591
Phone: (914) 591-2665, (800) 637-0037, Fax: (914) 591-2720
E-mail: info@bookweb.org
Web site: http://www.bookweb.org

American Electronics Association (AEA)
5201 Great American Pky., Ste 520
Santa Clara, CA 95054
Phone: (408) 987-4200, (800) 284-4232, Fax: (408) 986-1247
Web site: http://www.aeanet.org

American Forest & Paper Association (AF&PA)
1111 19th St. NW
Washington, DC 20036
Phone: (202) 463-2700, Fax: (202) 463-2785
Web site: http://www.afandpa.org

American Furniture Manufacturing Association (AFMA)
P.O. Box HP-7
High Point, NC 27261
Phone: (336) 884-5000, Fax: (336) 884-5303
Web site: http://www.afma4u.org

American Meat Institute (AMI)
1700 N. Monroe St., Ste. 1600
Arlington, VA 22209
Phone: (703) 841-2400, Fax (703) 527-0938
Web site: http://www.meatami.com

American Society of Association Executives (ASAE)
1575 I. St. NW
Washington, DC 20005-1168
Phone: (202) 626-2723, Fax: (202) 371-8825
E-mail: asae@asaenet.org
Web site: http://www.asaenet.org/main

American Supply Association (ASA)
222 Merchandise Mart, Ste. 1360
Chicago, IL 60654
Phone: (312) 464-0090, Fax: (312) 464-0091
E-mail: asaemail@interserv.org
Web site: http://www.asa.net

American Wholesale Marketers Association (AWMA)
1128 16th St.
Washington, DC 20036
Phone: (202) 463-2124, (800) 482-2962, Fax: (202) 463-6456
E-mail: davids@awmaner.org
Web site: http://www.awmanet.org

Association of American Publishers (AAP)
71 5th Ave.
New York, NY 10003-3004
Phone: (212) 255-0200, Fax: (213) 255-7007
Web site: http://www.publishers.org

Automotive Aftermarket Industry Association (AAIA)
4600 East-West Highway, Ste. 300
Bethesda, MD 20814-3415
Phone: (301) 654-6664, Fax: (301) 654-3299
E-mail: aaia@aftermarket.org
Web site: http://www.aftermarket.org

Bowling Proprietors' Association of America, Inc. (BPAA)
5301 South 76th Street
Greendale, Wisconsin 53129
Phone: (800) 514-Bowl (2695)
Web site: http://www.bowl.com/bowl/bpaa

Building Owners & Managers Association International (BOMAI)
1201 New York Ave. NW, Ste. 300
Washington, DC 20005
Phone: (202) 408-2662, Fax: (202) 371-0181
E-mail: info@boma.org
Web site: http://www.boma.org/Splash

Business Products Industry Association (BPIA)
301 W. Fairfax St.
Alexandria, VA 22314
Phone: (703) 549-9040, (800) 542-6672, Fax: (703) 683-7552
Web site: http://www.bpia.org

Carpet & Rug Institute (CRI)
310 Holiday Ave.
P.O. Box 2048
Dalton, GA 30722
Phone: (706) 278-3176, (800) 882-8846, Fax: (706) 278-8835
Web site: http://www.carpet-rug.com

Door & Hardware Institute (DHI)
14170 Newbrook Dr.
Chantily, VA 20151-2232
Phone: (703) 222-2010, Fax: (703) 222-2410
Web site: http://www.dhi.org

Food Marketing Institute (FMI)
800 Connecticut Ave. NW
Washington, DC 20006
Phone: (202) 452-8444, Fax: (202) 429-4519
E-mail: fmi@fmi.org
Web site: http://www.fmi.org

Food Service Equipment Distributors Association (FEDA)
223 W. Jackson Blvd. Ste. 620
Chicago, IL 60606
Phone: (800) 677-9605, Fax: (800) 677-9607
E-mail: ray@feda.com
Web site: http://www.feda.com

Healthcare Distribution Management Association
1821 Michael Faraday Dr., Ste. 400
Reston, VA 20190
Phone: (703) 787-0000, Fax: (703) 787-6930
Web site: http://www.healthcaredistribution.org

Independent Insurance Agents and Brokers of America
127 S. Peyton
Alexandria, VA 22314
Phone: (703) 683-4422, (800) 221-7917, Fax: (703) 683-7556
E-mail: info@iiaba.org
Web site: http://www.independentagent.com/eprise/main/CB_web site
/Affiliated/NationalAssociation/IIAA

Institute of Management Accountants (IMA)

10 Paragon Dr.
Montvale, NJ 07645-0000
Phone: (201) 573-9000, (800) 638-4427, Fax: (201) 573-8483
E-mail: ima@imanet.org
Web site: http://www.imanet.org/ima/index.asp

International Association of Plastic Distributors (IAPD)

4707 College Blvd., Ste. 105
Leawood, KS 66211
Phone: (913) 345-1005, Fax: (913) 345-1006
E-mail: iapd@iapd.org
Web site: http://www.iapd.org

International Fabricare Institute (IFI)

12251 Tech Rd.
Silver Spring, MD 20904
Phone: (301) 622-1900, (800) 638-2627, Fax: (301) 236-9320
E-mail: wecare@ifi.org
Web site: http://www.ifi.org

International Hardware Distributors Association (IHDA)

401 N. Michigan Ave., Ste. 2200
Chicago, IL 60611-4267
Phone: (312) 644-6610, Fax: (312) 527-6640
E-mail: ihda@sba.com
Web site: http://www.sba.com

Kitchen Cabinet Manufactures Association (KCMA)

1899 Preston White Dr.
Reston, VA 20191-5435
Phone: (703) 264-1690, Fax: (703) 620-6530
E-mail: dtitus@kcma.org
Web site: http://www.kcma.org

Laboratory Products Association (LPA)

225 Reineker, Ste. 625
Alexandria, VA 22314
Phone: (703) 836-1360, Fax: (703) 836-6644
Web site: http://www.lpanet.org

Material Handling Equipment Distributors Association (MHEDA)
201 Rte. 45
Vernon Hills, IL 60061
Phone: (827) 680-3500, Fax: (847) 362-6989
E-mail: connect@mheda.org
Web site: http://www.mheda.org

Mechanical Contractors Association of America (MCAA)
1385 Piccard Dr.
Rockville, MD 20850-4329
Phone: (301) 869-5800, (800) 556-3653, Fax: (301) 990-9690
E-mail: john@mcaa.org
Web site: http://www.mcaa.org

Motor & Equipment Manufacturers Association (MEMA)
10 Laboratory Dr.
P.O. Box 13966
Research Triangle Park, NC 27709-3966
Phone: (919) 549-4800, Fax: (919) 549-4824
Web site: http://www.mema.org

National Association of Electrical Distributors (NAED)
1100 Corporate Square Dr., Ste. 100
St. Louis, MO 63132
Phone: (314) 991-9000, Fax: (314) 991-3060
E-mail: info@naed.org
Web site: http://www.naed.org

National Association of Music Merchants, Inc.
5790 Arnada Dr.
Carlsbad, CA 92008
Phone: (760) 438-8001, (800) 767-6266, Fax: (760) 438-7327
Web site: http://www.namm.com

National Automatic Merchandising Association (NAMA)
20 N. Wacker Dr., Ste. 350
Chicago, IL 60606
Phone: (312) 346-0370, Fax: (312) 704-4140
Web site: http://www.vending.org

National Beer Wholesalers Association (NBWA)
1100 King St., Ste. 600
Alexandria, VA 22314
Phone: (703) 683-4300, (800) 300-6417, Fax: (708) 683-8965
E-mail: info@necanet.org
Web site: http://www.necanet.org

National Electrical Manufacturers Association (NEMA)
1300 North 17th St., Ste. 1847
Arlington, VA 22209
Phone: (703) 841-3200, Fax: (703) 841-5900
Web site: http://www.nema.org

National Grocers Association (NGA)
1005 North Glebe Road, Ste. 250
Arlington, VA 22201-5758
Phone: (703) 516-0700, Fax: (703) 516-0115
E-mail: info@nationalgrocers.org
Web site: http://www.nationalgrocers.org

National Home Furnishing Association (NHFA)
P.O. Box 2396
High Point, NC 27261
Phone: (336) 883-1650, (800) 888-9590, Fax: (336) 883-1195
E-mail: mail@nhfa.org
Web site: http://www.nhfa.org

**National Lumber & Building Material Dealers
Association (NLBMDA)**
40 Ivy St. SE
Washington, DC 20003
Phone: (202) 547-2230, (800) 634-8645, Fax: (202) 547-8645

National Paper Trade Association (NPTA)
500 Bi-County Blvd., Ste. 200E
Farmingdale, NY 11735
Phone: (631) 777-2223, (800) 355-NPTA, Fax: (631) 777-2224
Web site: http://www.gonpta.com

National Paperbox Assoc (NPA)
113 S. West Street, Third Floor
Alexandria, VA 22313
Phone: (703) 684-2212, Fax: (703) 683-6920
E-mail: boxmoore'paperbox.org
Web site: http://www.paperbox.org.

National Parking Association (NPA)
1112 16th St. NW, Ste. 300
Washington, DC 20036
Phone: (202) 296-4336, (800) 647-PARK, Fax: (202) 331-8523
Web site: http://www.npapark.org

National Restaurant Association (NRA)
1200 17th St. NW
Washington, DC 20036
Phone: (202) 331-5900, Fax: (202) 331-2429
E-mail: isal@restaurant.org
Web site: http://www.restaurant.org

National Retail Federation (NRF)
325 7th St. NW, Ste. 1000
Washington, DC 20004-2802
Phone: (202) 783-7971, (800) nrf-how2, Fax: (202) 737-2849
E-mail: nrf@nrf.com
Web site: http://www.nrf.com

National Retail Hardware Association (NRHA)
5822 W 74th St.
Indianapolis, IN 46278
Phone: (317) 290-0338, (800) 772-4424, Fax: (317) 328-4354
E-mail: nrha@iquest.net
Web site: http://www.nrha.org

National Shoe Retailers Association (NSRA)
7150 Columbia Gateway Drive, Ste. G
Columbia, MD 21046-1151
Phone: (410) 381-8282, (800) 673-8446, Fax: (410) 381-1167
E-mail: ingfo@nsra.org
Web site: http://www.nsra.org

National Sporting Goods Association (NSGA)
1601 Feehanville Dr., Ste. 300
Mt. Prospect, IL 60056
Phone: (847) 296-6742, Fax: (847) 391-9827
Web site: http://www.nsga.org/public/pages/index.cfm?pageid=1

National Tire Dealers & Retreaders Association (NTDRA)
11921 Freedom Dr., Ste. 550
Reston, VA 20190-5608
Phone: (800) 876-8372
Web site: http://www.tirestyres.com/assn/rs000149.html

North American Equipment Dealers Association (NAEDA)
1195 Smizer Mill Road
Fenton, MS 63026-3480
Phone: (636) 349-5000, Fax: (636) 349-5443
E-mail: naeda@naeda.com
Web site: http://www.naeda.com

North American Heating, Refrigeration, & Air-conditioning Wholesalers Association (NHRAW)
P.O. Box 16790
1389 Dublin Rd.
Columbus, OH 43216
Phone: (614) 488-1835, Fax: (614) 488-0482
E-mail: nhramail@nhraw.org
Web site: http://www.nhraw.org

North American Wholesale Lumber Association
3601 Algonquin Rd., Ste. 400
Rolling Meadows, IL 60008
Phone: (847) 870-7470, Fax: (847) 870-0201
Web site: http://www.lumber.org

Optical Laboratories Association
11096-B Lee Highway, Ste. 102
Fairfax, VA 22030-5014
Phone: (703) 359-2830, (800) 477-5652, Fax: (703) 359-2834
E-mail: ola@ola-labs.org
Web site: http://www.ola-labs.org

Paint & Decorating Retailers Association
403 Axminster Dr.
Fenton, OH 63026
Phone: (636) 326-2636, Fax: (636) 326-1823
E-mail: info@pdra.org
Web site: http://www.pdra.org

Petroleum Equipment Institute (PEI)
P.O. Box 2380
Tulsa, OK 74101
Phone: (918) 494-9696, Fax: (918) 491-9895
E-mail: pei@peinet.org
Web site: http://www.pei.org

Robert Morris Association/Association of Lending & Credit Risk Professionals
1 Liberty Pl.
1650 Market St., Ste. 2300
Philadelphia, PA 19103-7398
Phone: (215) 446-4000, (800) 677-7621, Fax: (215) 446-4101
Web site: http://www.rmahq.org

Shoe Service Institute of America (SSIA)
5024-R Cambell Rd.
Baltimore, MD 21236
Phone: (410) 931-8100, Fax: (410) 931-8111
Web site: http://www.ssia.info

Textile & Cleaners Allied Trades Association (TCATA)
271 U.S. Highway 46, No. 203-D
Fairfield, NJ 07004-2458
Phone: (973) 244-1790, Fax: (973) 244-4455
E-mail: info@tcata.org
Web site: http://www.tcata.org

United Fresh Fruit & Vegetables Association (UFFVA)
1901 Pennsylvania Ave. NW, Ste. 1100
Washington, DC 20006
Phone: (202) 303-3400, Fax: (202) 303-3433
E-mail: uffva@uffva.org
Web site: http://www.uffva.org

Urban Land Institute (ULI)
1025 Thomas Jefferson St. NW, Ste. 500W
Washington, DC 20007-5201
Phone: (202) 624-7000, (800) 321-5011, Fax: (202) 624-7140
E-mail: joinuli@uli.org
Web site: http://www.uli.org

Wine & Spirits Wholesalers of America (WSWA)
805 15th St. NW, Ste. 430
Washington, DC 20005
Phone: (202) 371-9792, Fax: (202) 789-2405
E-mail: juanita.duggan@wswa.org
Web site: http://www.wswa.org

Also recommended is the Small Business Network at http://www10 .americanexpress.com/sif/cda/page/0,1641,15657,00.asp.

Break-Even Analysis

The break-even analysis is an excellent technique for determining the ultimate success of any project before you begin. The break-even analysis tells you the following:

- How many units you must sell to start making money.
- How much profit you make at any given level of sales.
- How changing your price affects profitability.
- How expense reductions of different types affect profitability.

To accomplish a break-even analysis, you must first separate the costs associated with your project into two types: fixed costs and variable costs.

Fixed costs are those expenses associated with the project that you have to pay whether you sold one unit or 10,000 units or for that matter sold no units at all. For example, if you rented a garage to use in your business and the owner of the garage charged you $500 to rent the garage for the period of the project, then this is a fixed cost for that period. You have to pay the $500 whether you sell any products or many of your products. Research and development costs for a project or a product are also considered a fixed cost because this money has to be paid whether you sell any of the products.

Variable costs vary directly with the number of units that you sell. If it costs you $1.80 to manufacture a unit, then that $1.80 is a variable cost. If postage for mailing your product to a customer is $1, then $1 is a variable cost. If you sell 10 units, then your postage costs 10 times $1 or $10. If you sell 100 units, your total variable cost for postage is 100 times $1 or $100.

It is difficult to decide whether to consider some costs fixed or to consider them variable, and frequently there is no single right answer. You must make this decision by yourself as the owner of the business. As a general guideline, if there is a direct relationship between cost and number of units sold, consider the cost variable. If you can find no relationship, then consider the cost fixed.

Total costs of your project always equal total fixed costs plus total variable costs. Consider the following example for an item that you are going to sell:

Fixed Costs

Utility expense at $100 per month for 36 months	$3,600
Telephone at $200 per year for 3 years	600
Product development	1,000
Patenting expense	2,500
Total fixed costs	7,700

Variable Costs

Cost of product	$1 per unit
Cost of postage and packaging	50 cents per unit
Cost of advertising	$3 per unit
Total variable cost	$4.50 per unit

To calculate break-even, we start with profit. Profit is the number of units sold multiplied by the profit at which we are selling them less the number of units sold multiplied by the total variable cost minus the total fixed cost. Let's use an equation to make this a little easier to follow:

$$P = (U \times p) - (U \times V) - F$$

Or, we can simplify this to:

$$P = \{U \times (p - V)\} - F$$

where P = Profit
p = Price
U = Number of units sold
V = Variable cost
F = Fixed cost

Now, let's say we anticipate selling 1,000 units at $10 a unit. What are the results? Substituting the values we have in our sample, we have:

$$P = \{1,000 \times (\$10 - \$4.50)\} - \$7,700 = \$5,500 - \$7,700 = -\$2,200$$

What is the significance of the minus number? This means that instead of making a profit, we have lost money, $2,200 to be exact. Now, we may want to know how many units we must sell to make money, or at what point we stop losing money. The point at which we either make money or lose money is called *breakeven;* beginning at this point, we show a profit. To calculate this, we use the break-even formula with the same variables as before:

$$\text{Breakeven} = \frac{F}{p - V}$$

Because we know that F equals $7,700 and P equals $10 and V equals $4.50:

$$\text{Breakeven} = \frac{\$7,700}{\$10 - \$4.50} = 1,400 \text{ units}$$

This means if we don't change price or reduce expenses in any other way, we need to sell 1,400 units of this product before we start making any money.

However, there is an easier way to calculate this; we can use a break-even chart as shown in Figure 5.1. A break-even chart has a major advantage over the break-even and profit formulas. It shows us graphically the relationship of fixed and variable costs and total expenses to sales at all volumes of sales. This means that we can calculate profits at any level of sales right away.

To construct a break-even chart, follow these five steps:

Step 1: Get some graph paper and label the horizontal line on the bottom *Units Sold.* Label the vertical line at the left of the graph *Dollars* (sales and expenses). Divide each line into equal parts of dollars and units and label them appropriately.

Step 2: Analyze all of your costs for the project and decide whether each is fixed or variable. Decide on the period of sales for your project. Total your fixed and variable costs.

Step 3: Draw a horizontal line to intersect the proper point on the vertical line to represent fixed costs, as at point A in Figure 5.1.

Step 4: Calculate the dollar value of sales for any unit number. For example, if you sell 2,000 units, how much is this in sales dollars? For the example,

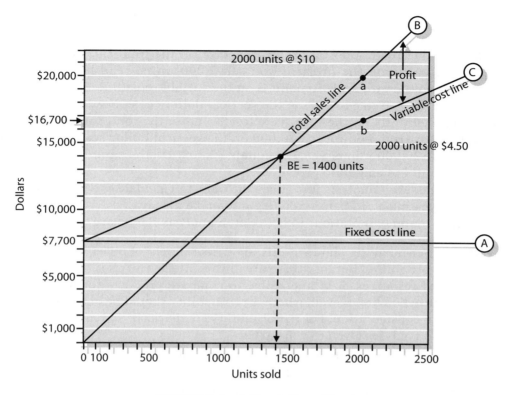

FIGURE 5.1   A Break-Even Chart

total sales volume is 2,000 times $10 or $20,000. Plot this point at 2,000 units at $20,000 on the chart as point A. Put one end of a ruler at the zero point in the lower left corner of the chart and the other end at the point you have just plotted. This is total sales line B in Figure 5.1.

Step 5: Calculate the dollar value for variable costs for any unit number. For example, in this case variable cost is $4.50 per unit. At 2,000 units, total variable cost is 2,000 times $4.50 or $9,000. Add $9,000 to the fixed cost, in this case $7,700, to come up with $16,700. Plot this on the chart as B in Figure 5.1. Lay one end of the ruler at the point where the fixed cost line, A, intersects with the vertical dollar scale, and the other at the point you just plotted. Draw a line to form the variable cost line, C, in Figure 5.1.

Now your break-even chart is complete. The point at which the total sales line or variable cost line intersects is a break-even point, which you read on the horizontal unit scale at the bottom of the chart in Figure 5.1 as 1,400 units, just as we calculated using the equation.

To calculate profit for any number of units you want, simply subtract the dollar value read opposite the profit point on the variable cost line, C, from the dollar value read opposite the profit point on the total sales line, B. For example, to calculate the profit if you sell 2,000 units, read right up from 2,000 units on the unit scale to point B on the variable cost line. Read straight across from point B to $16,700 on the vertical dollar scale. Now read straight out from 2,000 units on the unit scale to a point on the total sales line. Read straight across from point A to $20,000 on the vertical dollar scale. If you sell 2,000 units, $20,000 minus $16,700 equals $3,300. Do the same thing for any number of units to calculate profit.

Use break-even analysis any time you want to calculate the profit or how many units you must sell before you begin to make money.

There are some limitations to break-even analysis. These are as follows:

- Break-even analysis shows profit at various levels of sales, but does not show profitability. Because there are always alternative uses for your firm's financial resources, it is impossible to compare products for profitability solely based on break-even, whereas profitability should be one of the major points of consideration. For a profitability comparison, you must use one of the ratio analyses given to you earlier.

- Break-even analysis does not allow you examination of cash flows, and it is generally accepted that the appropriate way to make investment or capital-budgeting decisions is to consider the value of cash flows over a period of time and to discount this value using the cost-of-capital concept explained to you in Chapter 3. This cannot be done with break-even analysis, either.

Sources of Additional Information

Books

Accounting Handbook for Non-Accountants, by Clarence B. Nickerson, published by Cahners Books International.

Finance for the Non-Financial Manager, by Herbert T. Spiro, published by John Wiley & Sons.

Financial Handbook, edited by Jules I. Bogen, published by John Wiley & Sons.

Financial Management for the Small Business, by Colin Barrow, published by Kogan Page.

High Profit Financial Management for Your Small Business, by Suzanne Caplan, published by Dearborn Financial Publishing.

Managerial Finance, by J. Fred Weston and Eugene F. Brigham, published by Dryden Press.

The Barclays Guide to Financial Management for the Small Business, by Peter Wilson, published by Blackwell Publishers.

Profit Strategies for Business, by Robert Rachlin, published by Marr Publications.

Internet

Note: Because Internet sites frequently go down, multiple sites are listed for similar subject matter.

Basic Guide to Financial Management in Small For-Profit Businesses, by Carter McNamara. A complete guide on the basics at http://www.mapnp.org/library/finance /fp_fnce/fp_fnce.htm.

Financing for the Small Business. U.S. Small Business Administration, Overview of financing for small business at http://www.sbaonline.sba.gov/library/pubs/fm-14/.doc.

Business Finance Magazine. This is an online magazine with links to all sorts of information regarding business financing at http://www.businessfinancemag.com.

Financing Basics. A complete discussion with links provided by the U.S. Small Business Administration at http://www.sbaonline.sba.gov/financing/basics/basics.html.

Links to Hundreds of Business and Finance Journals. Look Smart Find Articles list more magazines than you can read on the subject matter at http://www.findarticles.com /p/articles/tn_bus.

Understanding and Controlling Cash Flow. This is an SBA sponsored booklet on the Internet at http://www.sbaonline.sba.gov/library/pubs/fm-4.txt.

Small Business Finance. Numerous links are broken down into categories at http://www.business.com/directory/financial_services/small_business_finance.

DOWNLOADABLE WORKSHEET 5.1
Attaining and Maintaining Profitability*

Part 1

Financial management boils down to one major consideration: Are you making a profit? Some businesses with excellent sales have suddenly found themselves bankrupt. The owners thought they were making lots of money. In fact, they were not. This worksheet is intended to help you with these critical calculations.

Place a checkmark in the appropriate block if you can answer the question satisfactorily. If not, leave the block empty until you have taken care of the discrepancy.

Fill in the blanks with actual figures when requested.

Analysis of Revenues and Expenses

Profit consists of revenues less expenses. Therefore, to determine what your profit is, you must first identify all revenues and expenses for the period you are analyzing.

1. **Have you chosen an appropriate period for profit determination?** ☐
   For accounting purposes firms generally use a 12-month period, such as January 1 to December 31 or July 1 to June 30. The accounting year you select doesn't have to be a calendar year (January to December); a seasonal business, for example, might close its year after the end of the season. The selection depends on the nature of your business, your personal preference, or possible tax considerations.

2. **Have you determined your total revenues for the accounting period?** ☐
   What is the amount of gross revenue from sales of your goods or service?
   (Gross Sales) _____
   What is the amount of goods returned by your customers and credited?
   (Returns and Rejects) _____
   What is the amount of discounts given to your customers and employees?
   (Discounts) _____
   What is the amount of net sales from goods and services?
   (Net Sales = Gross Sales − [Returns and Rejects + Discounts])

   _____

   What is the amount of income from other sources, such as interest on bank deposits, dividends from securities, rent on property leased to others?
   (Nonoperating Income) _____
   What is the amount of total revenue?
   (Total Revenue = Net Sales + Nonoperating Income) _____

---

* Based on *Checklist to Profit Watching* by Narendra C. Bhandari and Charles S. McCubbin, Jr. of the University of Baltimore and developed for the U.S. Small Business Administration.

To customize this document, download it to your hard drive from the John Wiley & Sons web site at www.wiley.com/go/cohenentrepreneur. The document can then be opened, edited, and printed using Microsoft Word or another popular word processing application.

Part 2

3. **Do you know what your expenses are?** ☐

   Expenses are the cost of goods sold and services used in the process of selling goods or services. Some common expenses for all businesses are:

   Cost of goods sold (Cost of goods sold = Beginning inventory + Purchases − Ending inventory)

   Wages and salaries (don't forget to include your own—at the actual rate you'd have to pay someone else to do your job)

   Rent

   Utilities (electricity, gas, telephone, water, etc.)

   Supplies (office, cleaning, and the like)

   Delivery expenses

   Insurance

   Advertising and promotional costs

   Maintenance and upkeep

   Depreciation (here you need to make sure your depreciation policies are realistic and that all depreciable items are included)

   Taxes and licenses

   Interest

   Bad debts

   Professional assistance (accountant, attorney, etc.)

   There are, of course, many other types of expenses, but the point is that every expense must be recorded and deducted from your revenues before you know what your profit is. Understanding your expenses is the first step toward controlling them and increasing your profit.

Financial Ratios

A **financial ratio** is an expression of the relationship between two items selected from the income statement or the balance sheet. Ratio analysis helps you to evaluate the weak and strong points in your financial and managerial performance.

4. **Do you know your current ratio?** ☐

   The **current ratio** (current assets divided by current debts) is a measure of the cash or near cash position (liquidity) of the firm. It tells you if you have enough cash to pay your firm's current creditors. The higher the ratio, the more liquid the firm's position is and, hence, the higher the credibility of the firm. Cash, receivables, marketable securities, and inventory are current assets. Naturally, you need to be realistic in valuing receivables and inventory for a true picture of your liquidity, since some debts may be uncollectible and some stock obsolete. Current liabilities are those that must be paid in one year.

5. **Do you know your quick ratio?** ☐

   Quick assets are current assets minus inventory. The **quick ratio** (or acid-test ratio) is found by dividing quick assets by current liabilities. The purpose is to test the firm's ability to meet its current obligations. It tells you if the business could meet its current obligations with quickly convertible assets should revenues suddenly cease.

Part 3

6. **Do you know your total debt to net worth ratio?** ☐
   This ratio (the result of total debt divided by net worth then multiplied by 100) is a measure of how the company can meet its total obligations from equity. The lower the ratio (the higher the proportion of equity relative) to debt then the better the firm's credit rating will be.

7. **Do you know your average collection period?** ☐
   You find this ratio by dividing accounts receivable by daily credit sales. (Daily credit sales = annual credit sales divided by 360.) This ratio tells you the length of time it takes the firm to get its cash after making a sale on credit. The shorter this period the quicker the cash inflow is. A longer than normal period may mean overdue and uncollectible bills. If you extend credit for a specific period (say, 30 days), this ratio should be very close to the same number of days. If it's much longer than the established period, you may need to alter your credit policies. It's wise to develop an aging schedule to gauge the trend of collections and identify slow payers. Slow collections (without adequate financing charges) hurt your profit, because you could be doing something much more useful with your money, such as taking advantage of discounts on your own payables.

8. **Do you know your ratio of net sales to total assets?** ☐
   This ratio (net sales divided by total assets) measures the efficiency with which you are using your assets. A higher than normal ratio indicates that the firm is able to generate sales from its assets faster (and better) than the average company.

9. **Do you know your operating profit to net sales ratio?** ☐
   This ratio (the result of dividing operating profit by net sales and multiplying by 100) is most often used to determine the profit position relative to sales. A higher than normal ratio indicates that your sales are good, that your expenses are low, or both. Interest income and interest expense should not be included in calculating this ratio.

10. **Do you know your net profit to total assets ratio?** ☐
    This ratio (found by multiplying by 100 the result of dividing net profit by total assets) is often called return on investment or ROI. It focuses on the profitability of the overall operation of the firm. Thus, it allows management to measure the effects of its policies on the firm's profitability. The ROI is the single most important measure of a firm's financial position. You might say it's the bottom line for the bottom line.

11. **Do you know your net profit to net worth ratio?** ☐
    This ratio (found by dividing net profit by net worth and multiplying the result by 100) provides information on the productivity of the resources the owners have committed to the firm's operations. Note: All ratios measuring profitability can be computed either before or after taxes, depending on the purpose of the computations. Ratios have limitations. Because the information used to derive ratios is based on accounting rules and personal judgments, as well as facts, ratios are not absolute indicators of a firm's financial position. Ratios are only one means of assessing the performance of the firm and must be considered in perspective with many other measures.

Part 4

Sufficiency of Profit

The following questions are designed to help you measure the adequacy of the profit your firm is making. Making a profit is only the first step; making enough profit to survive and grow is really what business is all about.

12. **Have you compared your profit with your profit goals?** ☐

13. **Is it possible your goals are too high or too low?** ☐

14. **Have you compared your present profits (absolute and ratios) with the profits made in the last one to three years?** ☐

15. **Have you compared your profits (absolute and ratios) with profits made by similar firms in your line?** ☐

Trend of Profit

16. **Have you analyzed the direction your profits have been taking?** ☐
    The preceding analyses report on a firm only at a single time in the past. It is not possible to use these isolated moments to indicate the trend of your firm's performance. To do a trend analysis, performance indicators (absolute amounts or ratios) should be computed for several time periods (yearly for several years, for example) and the results laid out in columns side by side for easy comparison. You can then evaluate your performance, see the direction it's taking, and make initial forecasts of where it will go.

Mix of Profit

17. **Does your firm sell more than one major product line or provide several distinct services?** ☐
    If it does, a separate profit and ratio analysis of each should be made:

    To show the relative contribution by each product line or service;
    To show the relative burden of expenses by each product or service;
    To show which items are most profitable, which are less so, and which are losing money; and
    To show which are slow and fast moving.

    The profit and ratio analyses of each major item help you find out the strong and weak areas of your operations. They can help you to make profit-increasing decisions to drop a product line or service or to place particular emphasis behind one or another.

Records

Good records are essential. Without them a firm doesn't know where it's been, where it is, or where it's heading. This is one of the most important functions of the owner-manager, his or her staff, and his or her outside counselors (lawyer, accountant, banker).

117

Part 5

Basic Records

18. **Do you have a general journal or special journals, such as one for cash receipts and disbursements?** ☐

    A general journal is the basic record of the firm. Every monetary event in the life of the firm is entered in the general journal or in one of the special journals.

19. **Do you prepare a sales report or analysis?** ☐

    (a) Do you have sales goals by product, department, and accounting period (month, quarter, year)? ☐

    (b) Are your goals reasonable? ☐

    (c) Are you meeting your goals? ☐

    If you aren't meeting your goals, try to list the likely reasons on a sheet of paper. Such a study might include areas such as general business climate, competition, pricing, advertising, sales promotion, credit policies, and the like. Once you've identified the apparent causes you can take steps to increase sales (and profits).

Buying and Inventory System

20. **Do you have a buying and an inventory system?** ☐

    The buying and inventory systems are two critical areas of a firm's operation that can affect profitability.

21. **Do you keep records on the quality, service, price, and promptness of delivery of your supply sources?** ☐

22. **Have you analyzed the advantages and disadvantages of:**

    (a) Buying from suppliers? ☐

    (b) Buying from a minimum number of suppliers? ☐

23. **Have you analyzed the advantages and disadvantages of buying through cooperatives or other such systems?** ☐

24. **Do you know:**

    (a) How long it usually takes to receive each order? ☐

    (b) How much inventory cushion (usually called safety stock) to have so you can maintain normal sales while you wait for the order to arrive? ☐

25. **Have you ever suffered because you were out of stock?** ☐

26. **Do you know the optimum order quantity for each item you need?** ☐

27. **Do you (or can you) take advantage of quantity discounts for large size single purchases?** ☐

Part 6

28. Do you know your costs of ordering inventory and carrying inventory? ☐

The more frequently you buy (smaller quantities per order), the higher your average ordering costs (clerical costs, postage, telephone costs, etc.) will be, and the lower the average carrying costs (storage, loss through pilferage, obsolescence, etc.) will be. Alternatively, the larger the quantity per order, the lower the average ordering cost and the higher the carrying costs. A balance should be struck so that the minimum cost overall for ordering and carrying inventory can be achieved.

29. Do you keep records of inventory for each item? ☐

These records should be kept current by making entries whenever items are added to or removed from inventory. Simple records on 3×5 or 5×7 cards can be used with each item being listed on a separate card. Proper records will show for each item: quantity in stock, quantity on order, date of order, slow or fast seller, and valuations (which are important for taxes and your own analysis).

Other Financial Records

30. Do you have an accounts payable ledger? ☐

This ledger will show what, whom, and why you owe. Such records should help you make your payments on schedule. Any expense not paid on time could adversely affect your credit, but even more importantly, such records could help you take advantage of discounts, which can help boost your profits.

31. Do you have an accounts receivable ledger? ☐

This ledger will show who owes money to your firm. It shows how much is owed, how long it has been outstanding, and why the money is owed. Overdue accounts could indicate that your credit granting policy needs to be reviewed.

32. Do you have a cash receipts journal? ☐

This journal records the cash received by source, day, and amount.

33. Do you have a cash payments journal? ☐

This journal will be similar to the cash receipts journal but will show cash paid out instead of cash received. The two cash journals can be combined, if convenient.

34. Do you prepare an income (profit and loss or P & L) statement and a balance sheet? ☐

These are statements about the condition of your firm at a specific time and show the income, expenses, assets, and liabilities of the firm. They are absolutely essential.

35. Do you prepare a budget? ☐

You could think of a budget as a record in advance, projecting future inflows and outflows for your business, usually prepared for a single year, and broken down into quarterly and monthly projections.

To customize this document, download it to your hard drive from the John Wiley & Sons web site at www.wiley .com/go/cohenentrepreneur. The document can then be opened, edited, and printed using Microsoft Word or another popular word processing application.

CHAPTER 6

Credit in Today's Economy: When to Give Credit and How to Collect Money Owed You

It is a fact of life in a modern economy that credit is necessary in most situations and for most businesses. This means that the basic problem is usually not whether to give credit, but how to manage the credit so that the following objectives are achieved:

- You have fewer dollars tied up in accounts receivable, allowing profitable application of these dollars in your business.
- Your credit losses are minimized.
- You have increased and maximized profits.
- Your customers or clients are encouraged to use your services or to buy your goods.
- Your company's investment in accounts receivable is protected to the maximum extent possible.

Credit Policy

To achieve these objectives, you must have a credit policy. This credit policy may or may not be written down, but it must be communicated to your employees and your customers or clients. Cooke O'Neal, a former vice president of the National Association of Credit Management, notes the following factors that influence your company's credit policy:

- Nature and size of business.
- Overall business objectives.

- General policy of business.
- Product or service requirements.
- Channels of distribution.
- Classes of customers.
- Conditions of competition.
- Price of product or service.
- Expectations of customers.

I add to this list: overall positioning and corporate strategy for achieving a competitive advantage over your competition.

Your credit policy may be characterized by either liberal or strict extension and collection of credit, or your policy may fall somewhere between these two sets of extremes. You have to decide by weighing stimulation of sales, on the one hand, with failure to collect or exposure to a larger bad-debt loss, on the other hand. You must also consider the amount in your accounts receivable and the working capital position of your business.

Basic Elements of Your Credit Policy Program

The basic elements of your credit policy program are:

- To whom credit is extended.
- Credit terms.
- Problem detection.
- Collection procedures.

To Whom Credit Is Extended

The extension of credit depends on several considerations, including personal judgment, investigation, credit applications, evaluation factors, the application evaluation, and applicant stability and information verification. Let us look at each in more detail.

Personal Judgment Judgment plays an important part in determining whether you should grant credit, and many potential problems can be eliminated simply by exercising good judgment. For example, if an individual or a firm owes you a great deal of money and has been slow to pay in the past, or has not paid, it doesn't take special insight to know that it is probably wise to refuse to give credit. If a firm or an individual appears low on cash, simply exercising good judgment may prevent a loss from bad debt. Remember that sales alone may not solve cash-flow problems in your business. In fact, building up sales but not collecting money may worsen your situation because it drains time and resources that may profitably be used elsewhere. Therefore, when making a credit decision, consider your likelihood of getting paid. If the likelihood is small, don't grant credit.

Investigation   Before making a decision on credit, you should get all of the facts. This means that for any sizable amount of credit you should do a thorough investigation. This helps protect you from an individual or a firm that really has no intention of paying at all, as well as those that are slow in paying. This may range from simply checking on a credit card number to be sure that the credit card has not been stolen, to a much more thorough probe involving the areas discussed in the following paragraphs.

Credit Applications   Much information can be gained from a credit application. For any sizable amount of credit, an application such as those developed in the worksheets at the end of this chapter should be required, and the information verified. In many cases, specific information may be required due to your situation, location, or industry.

Evaluation Factors   There are three basic factors to consider in evaluating a credit application. These are:

1. The applicant's *ability to pay*. This is based on income and obligations.
2. The applicant's *willingness to pay*. This is determined from the applicant's past credit history.
3. The *potential profitability* of the account. This is determined by your own analysis.

Remember that you lose the cost of your product or the service if you do not collect on any account where credit is granted. When the cost is very high relative to the selling price, you must be particularly careful and assess such risk with care.

Application Evaluation   To evaluate these factors, consider the following:

- Amount of credit desired.
- The bank balances of the applicant.

- Current credit standing.
- Current income.
- Current position.
- Employment history.
- Job security.
- Other obligations, including loan payments, rent, and so forth.
- Personal assets.
- Time on the job.

Applicant Stability and Information Verification   Whether you are dealing with an individual or a firm, the information contained on credit applications must be verified or it is worthless. You must be sure that it is current, that it is correct, and that it is complete with nothing left out. For individuals, their place of employment and other personal references (e.g., income or time on the job) can be verified easily by a letter or telephone request. Bank references can be verified in the same manner, even though banks may be somewhat restrictive in the information they provide. However, they usually confirm the existence of an account and give a broad, general range of the average balance. A bank may also indicate whether the account has been satisfactory. However, when checking out the facts concerning firms, additional sources may be necessary. The following sources of credit information are useful for both firms and individuals depending on the situation:

- *Mercantile credit agencies:* These are agencies that are privately owned and operated. They collect, analyze, and evaluate credit information on business firms on a continuous basis. For a fee, they provide credit ratings based on their observations. Perhaps, the best-known mercantile credit agency is Dun & Bradstreet. Dun & Bradstreet covers many fields and provides a reference book, credit reports, and other specific information to firms using its services. This information includes credit ratings, evaluation of financial strength, and other important credit information. Other mercantile agencies work in specialized areas; for example, the Lyon Furniture Mercantile Agency works with the furniture industry, and the Jeweler's Board of Trade deals with the jewelry industry. In addition, Dun & Bradstreet credit services reports on companies in every industry.

- *Credit bureaus:* Many credit bureaus are available for firms that need to check credit information on a frequent basis. Most local credit bureaus are affiliated with other national bureaus including the International Consumer Credit Association of the Associated Credit Bureaus of America. In this way, even if individuals have moved into your area recently, credit information is frequently available on them. Credit bureaus supply information including checks on newcomers in your area, written and telephone credit information on individuals, data on changes in customers' credit risk status, assistance in tracing customers who leave your area without providing forwarding information, and collection of poor risk accounts.

- *Suppliers:* Suppliers in credit departments frequently exchange information with you. This interchange can be extremely valuable to update your own records and warn you of situations where credit may negatively affect your business. You should also keep in touch with competitors and other firms who may be dealing with your customers. Frequently, an exchange of credit information can help out both sides, especially in a fluid situation where a customer's credit position may be changing rapidly.

- *Department of Commerce:* The Department of Commerce frequently provides assistance in checking out foreign firms that you may want to do business with. Check with the local office of the Department of Commerce. It can be located under the heading "U.S. Government" in your telephone book in the white pages, or on the Internet at http://www.commerce.gov.

Credit Terms

The credit terms that you extend may have a significant effect on your sales as well as your profits. You should be familiar with the terms used in business sales contained in Figure 6.1. These can be very important. For example, 2/10, n/30 means that the buyer gets a 2 percent discount if the bill is paid within 10 days. It usually is in the buyer's interest to pay within this time period, as this amounts to a 36.5 percent annual interest rate! You should also consider the following points:

- Insist on all or a portion of the money up front before you provide goods or services. In some industries, this may not be possible. But you can always ask. If you have an extremely poor credit risk, it may be the only way to protect yourself from severe financial losses.

- The use of credit cards is an excellent way to protect yourself, whether you are dealing with other firms or with individuals. Essentially, the credit card company, such as Visa or Master Card or others, grants the credit, and you get your money at once. The customer or client has his credit needs met without you taking any risk. Of course, you pay a percentage of your sales for this service, and this is a factor you must consider. However, a lot of trouble can be saved through the use of credit cards, and it is worth taking the time to see if you can use them.

Term	What It Means
3/10,	3 percent discount for first 10 days.
1/15,	1 percent discount for 15 days.
n/60	Bill due net on 60th day.
MOM (middle of month)	Billing is on the 15th of the month, including all purchases made since the middle of the previous month.
EOM (end of month)	Billing is at the end of month, covering all credit purchases of that month.
CWO or CIA (cash with order or cash in advance)	Orders received are not processed until advanced payment is received.
CBD (cash before delivery)	Merchandise may be prepared and packaged by the seller, but shipment is not made until payment is received.
COD (cash on delivery)	Amount of the bill is collected upon delivery of goods.
SD-BL (sight draft-bill of lading)	A negotiable bill of lading, accompanied by the invoice and a sight draft drawn on the buyer, is forwarded by the seller to the customer's bank. The bill of lading is released by the bank to the customer only upon his honoring the draft.
2/10, n/30, ROG (Receipt of goods)	2 percent discount for 10 days; bill due net on 30th day, but both discount period and 30 days start from the date of receipt of the goods, not from the date of sales.
2/10, n/30, MOM	2 percent discount for 10 days; bill due net on 30th day, but both periods start from the 15th of the month following the sales date.
2/10, n/30, EOM	Same as previous except both periods start from the end of the month in which the sale was made.
8/10, EOM	8 percent discount for 10 days; bill due net on 30th day. Both periods start from the end of the month following the sales date.

FIGURE 6.1 Common Business Sales Terms. *Note:* **Sales date is the day that the shipment was made. It will generally be the same date shown on the invoice. In consumer credit, the sales date is the day the sale was made. It may or may not be the same as the date of shipment.** *Source:* **Based on material from** *Managing for Profits* **by Harvey C. Krentzman, published by the Small Business Administration.**

- Remember that you are not obligated to grant credit. Therefore, never fool yourself into building up false sales when the chances of getting paid are poor. If you're not going to get paid later, or if the time when you'll get paid is so far in the future that the sale is worthless to you, the only solution is to refuse credit.

- Detecting problems must be an essential part of your credit and credit collection program. One way to do this is to calculate the average collection period. The average collection period is calculated by dividing your accounts receivable by the average daily credit sales. Let us say that your current outstanding accounts receivable are $10,000 and, on the average, your monthly credit sales are $3,000. First, you must calculate the average daily credit sales. This is the monthly sales of $3,000 divided by 30 days or $100. Now, divide the accounts receivable of $10,000 by the average daily credit sales of $100. This equals the average collection period in days. In this example, $10,000 divided by $100 equals 100 days. This means that on the average your customers are taking about 100 days to pay their accounts. There is another way of calculating the average collection period using net credit sales; subtract an estimated allowance for bad debts from your total annual sales.

Now that you have the average collection period for your accounts receivable, what do you do with it? You can make the following comparisons to determine whether a problem exists.

- *Payment terms:* How does the average collection period compare with the terms of sale that you offer? If you request payment within 100 days and the average collection period is not greater than this, it indicates that your debtors are complying with your terms. If the average collection period is greater than 100 days, they are not.
- *Past history:* How does your current average collection period compare with that which you had in the past? Are things getting better or getting worse?
- *Industry averages:* How does your average collection period compare with those of other companies in your industry? This indicates whether your credit and collection policies are as effective as other companies and your competitors in your industry.

Problem Detection

If the preceding comparisons using your average collection period indicate that you do have a problem, the next step is to determine how much of a problem you have. This can be accomplished by comparing the actual receivables with a target level. Let us say that your terms of sale specify payment within 30 days, which approximates the average within your industry as well. This, then, makes a suitable target for your receivables. If your average daily credit sales are $100 as in the previous example, you could then calculate a target for your receivables by multiplying your average daily credit sales by the collection period of 30 days, in this case $100 times 30 days equals $3,000.

You then compare this with your actual receivables. In the previous case, actual receivables are $10,000. You then know that you have a problem that amounts to $10,000 minus $3,000 or $7,000.

The implication of problem detection is problem solving. That is, you take immediate action to reduce the collection period, to speed conversion of the receivables to cash, to minimize the capital tied up in accounts receivable, and to reduce the risk of uncollectible accounts.

Collection Procedures

The fundamental rule of collection is to minimize the time between the sale or performance of the service and the collection of the money. For example, Dr. Robert Kelley, a consultant and teacher, states in his book, *Consulting*, that a former graduate student of his conducted research on the billing practices of professionals—doctors, dentists, and lawyers.[1] This student found that professionals who request payment before the client leaves the office have 90 to 100 percent collection rates, and those who send monthly statements average 65 percent collection rates. Therefore, to increase your collection rates, minimize the time between product delivery or performance and collection. Ask for the payment immediately after the services are performed or product sold.

Invoices   Invoice preparation is crucial to your collection procedures. Your invoices should be prepared promptly and accurately. Time is essential to eliminate one source of delay. Accuracy is necessary to eliminate another source: customer disputes over invoiced information. An invoice should clearly state the credit terms you decided on, as described earlier.

Statements   Statements keep customers advised of their account balances, and monthly statements should be submitted to all creditors with open accounts. The statement summarizes the amount owed previously as well as any additional activity in the account during the month.

Delinquency Charges   In some types of businesses, delinquency charges are applied against late payments to discourage customers from allowing their accounts to become overdue. This normally involves a finance or service charge of between 1 and 1½ percent per month on all balances more than 30 days past due. However, many companies may charge higher percentages, especially in times of high inflation.

---

[1] Robert E. Kelley, *Consulting*, Charles Scribner's Sons, New York (1981).

Lateness Follow-Up   When your customers or clients do not pay, you should initiate a follow-up immediately. The longer an account becomes dated, the less the chance of a collection. Never be afraid to initiate these follow-up actions. Some people are afraid to do so because they feel that a strict follow-up is a harassment of their customers and hurts their business. Again, remember that you have no business without payment, and a good customer is not a good customer unless he or she actually pays for what was received. Some individuals are also afraid of pursuing a rigid collection policy for fear that this hurts their reputation through negative word-of-mouth. This is highly unlikely. An individual who owes money hardly wants to advertise the fact that he or she hasn't been paying his or her bills.

A follow-up procedure for lateness in paying overdue or past-due accounts is generally a good idea. Such a policy makes it easier to implement the action required in an expeditious manner.

A typical follow-up procedure is a telephone call, a letter or series of letters, or some combination of these two instruments, usually with the letter coming first.

Collection Letters   An initial collection letter should be used when the account becomes approximately 15 days past due. At this time, the account is not considered seriously delinquent; therefore, the tone of the letter, while firm, should be moderate. If this letter is unsuccessful, a second letter should be sent approximately one month later. If this letter is unsuccessful as well, a third and stronger letter should be sent.

The worksheets at the end of this chapter can be used for developing an initial collection letter, a second collection letter, and a third collection letter. Note how the tone grows progressively stronger. The implication of action of a more serious nature is introduced as the letters progress. The exact wording to use depends on the situation in which you find yourself, including your relationship with this particular customer, your industry, and other factors. But the basics are clear. Send the letters in the sequence as indicated; starting 15 days after the account becomes due, and then at intervals of 30 days. A standard format greatly reduces the time you spend on this aspect of your business.

Use of the Telephone   The telephone can be used either with the letters or by itself. It can be even more persuasive since you get immediate feedback and can respond directly to the information given by the individual. However, the basic methodology is the same, and if you make more than one call, each call should be firmer than the last. The disadvantages of a telephone call are that it consumes your time and that it is a direct confrontation and can sometimes be tricky.

If you use the telephone technique, you should again attempt to find out what the problem is. If the entire amount cannot be paid, find out how much can be paid over a reasonable period and how soon the initial payment of that amount can be expected.

Again, your telephone call should indicate to the creditor that you are aware that the payment has not been made, and that you do not intend to allow the creditor to get away with nonpayment.

External Collection Procedures

There are two external collection procedures that are available should the letters or telephone calls fail: collection agencies and courts of law.

- *Collection agencies:* Collection agencies collect past due accounts receivable for you. Their advantages include experience, knowledge of persuasive collection techniques, and the additional emphasis that an outside agency gives to the collection procedure. While at first glance this may appear an easy way to take care of your problems, you should be aware of the fact that collection agencies usually insist on 25 percent to 50 percent of the amount that they succeed in collecting. Further, once you agree to work with a collection agency, you must make this percentage payment fee whether the debt is collected by you or through the agency.

- *Courts of law:* A court of law is the final recourse for collection. If the amount is small enough, you may be able to go through a small claims court that, except for your time, costs you nothing. However, for large amounts, you have to sue for collection. This takes considerable money and time. Before making such a decision, you should consider both your chances of collection and the cost in time and money. Check with your attorney on this.

Credit Insurance

Credit insurance is available, but it is available only to manufacturers and wholesalers that sell to other business firms. This is because it is difficult to analyze the risk involved in selling to ultimate consumers, and because a retailer's need for credit insurance is not as great because the retailer's risk is spread among a greater number of customers. It is possible to insure some specific business accounts rather than getting general coverage. This is desirable because higher percentages of coinsurance are required for accounts that are considered to be high risk to discourage reckless credit by firms that are insured. Accounts are usually classified according to their ratings by Dun & Bradstreet or similar agencies, and the premiums vary depending on the account ratings assigned. For export accounts, credit insurance is available from the Foreign Credit Insurance Association. Check with your local Department of Commerce office.

Use of a Factor   If you are using the services of a factor, you can avoid maintaining credit and collection systems. This is because a factor establishes a working procedure for clearing credit for new customers and setting up credit limits for old customers, and for collecting accounts receivable; then, the factor buys the accounts receivable outright from you. Naturally, this is going to cost something, so once again, consider the costs as well as the benefits.

Sources of Additional Information

Books

Complete Guide to Credit and Collection Law, 2nd ed., by Arthur Winston, and Jay Winston, published by Aspen Publishers.

Collection Letters Ready to Go! by Ed Halloran, published by McGraw-Hill.

Essentials of Credit, Collections, and Accounts Receivable, by Mary S. Schaeffer, published by John Wiley & Sons.

Credit and Credit Collection for Small Business, by Donald R. Kitzing, published by AMACOM.

Credit Management Handbook, edited by William B. Abbott et al., published by Credit Research Foundation.

Credits and Collections: Management and Theory, by Theodore N. Beckman and Ronald S. Foster, published by McGraw-Hill.

The Dun and Bradstreet Handbook of Credit and Collections, by Harold T. Redding and Guyon H. Knight III, published by Thomas Y. Crowell Co.

Using Credit to Sell More, by Donald E. Miller, Published by the National Association of Credit Management.

Internet

Note: Because Internet sites frequently go down, multiple sites are listed for similar subject matter.

ACA International web site. Association of Credit and Collection Professionals web site at http://www.collector.com.

Credit and Credit Collection. Links to important sites and resources at http://www.worldwidewebfind.com/sites/Business/FinancialServices/CreditandCollection.

Credit and Credit World. This is an online credit resource for professionals including daily news at http://www.collectionsworld.com.

Credit Guru.com. A newsletter about credit at http://www.creditguru.com.

Creditworthy. Offers information about credit and collection management, bankruptcy, credit reporting agencies and their reports, and other financial matters at http://www.creditworthy.com.

Lawdog Center. Covers all legal aspects, including laws, state by state at http://www.lawdog.com.

The establishment of credit and collection policies can be a major factor in your business's profitability or even its survivability. But, like any important aspect of business, these policies must be reevaluated periodically in order to determine and maintain their effectiveness. This checklist, based on one developed by the Small Business Administration, will help you to do this. If the answer on the item is "Yes," you are in good shape. If the answer is "No," you should examine that item more closely. If the item doesn't seem applicable to your situation, simply disregard.

Credit Approval	Yes	No
Is a written application required with every credit request?		
Do you have a standard form for credit applications?		
Is it completed personally by the applicant?		
Is it reviewed for completeness?		
Is all information verified for accuracy and timeliness?		
Are applicants checked out with a credit bureau?		
Does your evaluation consider income?		
Does your evaluation consider fixed obligations?		
Does your evaluation consider job stability?		
Does your evaluation consider residential stability?		
Does your evaluation consider credit history?		
Does your evaluation consider bank balances?		
Does your evaluation consider other assets?		
Invoices		
Are invoices prepared promptly?		
Is invoice preparation always accurate?		
Are payment terms clearly stated?		
Are customers' special instructions followed carefully?		
Terms of Sale		
Do you offer a cash discount?		
Do you use a late payment penalty?		
Is the time limit for payment clearly stated?		

To customize this document, download it to your hard drive from the John Wiley & Sons web site at www.wiley .com/go/cohenentrepreneur. The document can then be opened, edited, and printed using Microsoft Word or another popular word processing application.

(continued)

Statements	Yes	No
Are monthly statements submitted to all open accounts?		
Are statements prompt and accurate?		
Problems of Identification		
Do you recalculate your average collection period periodically?		
Do you compare your collection period with industry averages?		
Do you compare your collection period with past periods?		
Do you compare your collection period with payment terms?		
Do you have a monthly aging of all outstanding accounts?		
When you identify a problem, do you take action immediately?		
Follow-Up		
Do you have a follow-up procedure for slow accounts?		
Is there a standard sequence of follow-up letters?		
Is the tone of these letters progressively stronger?		
Do you use the telephone to contact delinquent accounts?		
Is your telephone technique effective?		
Do you have special arrangements for overdue accounts?		
Do you have a late-payment penalty?		
Do you put delinquent accounts on a cash-on-delivery basis?		
External Resources		
Do you have a working relationship with a collection agency?		
Are accounts turned over to an agency automatically after a specific time period?		
Do you refer the most serious delinquencies to an attorney?		

DOWNLOADABLE WORKSHEET 6.2
A Personal Credit Application

Date: _____ Name: _____ Age: _____

Address: _____ How Long: _____

Home Phone: _____ Business Phone: _____

Fax Number: _____ E-Mail:_____

Single: _____ Married: _____ Divorced: _____ No. of Dependents _____

Former Address: _____ How Long? _____

Employer: _____ Phone No.:_____

Address: _____ How Long? _____

Position: _____ Monthly Income: _____ Other Income: _____

Previous Employer: _____ Phone No.: _____

Address: _____ How Long? _____

Bank Account (Savings): _____ Phone No.: _____

Bank Account (Checking): _____ Phone No.: _____

Address: _____

Fax Number: _____ E-Mail:_____

Name of Spouse: _____ Where Employed:_____

Monthly Income: _____ Other Income:_____

Automobile Make and Model: _____ Date Purchased: _____

Nearest Relative with Whom You Are Not Living: _____

Address: _____ Relationship: _____

Real Estate Owned (Other Than Home): _____

Credit References:

Item	Creditor	Address	Payment	Balance Owed
Home	_____	_____	_____	_____
Car	_____	_____	_____	_____
Credit Card	_____	_____	_____	_____
Credit Card	_____	_____	_____	_____
Other	_____	_____	_____	_____
Other	_____	_____	_____	_____

If granted credit, I agree to pay all bills in accordance with the following terms:

_____

Signed: _____

_____

To customize this document, download it to your hard drive from the John Wiley & Sons web site at www.wiley
.com/go/cohenentrepreneur. The document can then be opened, edited, and printed using Microsoft Word or
another popular word processing application.

DOWNLOADABLE WORKSHEET 6.3
A Business Credit Application

Company: _____ Phone No.: _____

Address: _____

Types of Business and Organization _____

Bank: _____ Phone No.: _____

Address: _____

Trade References (Note: Do not use oil companies, credit cards, IBM, Xerox, or public utilities since these organizations will not confirm credit information.)

1. _____
   _____

2. _____
   _____

3. _____
   _____

Owners and/or Officers of Your Company

Name: _____ Title: _____

Name: _____ Title: _____

Name: _____ Title: _____

Person to Contact with Regard to Financial Commitments

Name: _____ Title: _____

It is understood that all purchases made during a given month are payable in thirty (30) days or no later than the end of the following month. Accounts not paid in accordance with these terms will be charged a 13.75% monthly service charge equivalent to 20% annual interest.

Date: _____ Authorized Signature: _____

Authorization for Bank Inquiry

I hereby authorize _____ to disclose credit information to

_____ for consideration of the establishment of trade credit.

Name of Account: _____ Account No.: _____

Authorized Signature: _____

Estimated Monthly Credit Requirements: _____

Sales Tax Status: _____ Taxable: _____ Exempt Resale Permit No.: _____

Individuals in Your Company Authorized to Place Orders

Name: _____ Title: _____

Name: _____ Title: _____

_____

To customize this document, download it to your hard drive from the John Wiley & Sons web site at www.wiley.com/go/cohenentrepreneur. The document can then be opened, edited, and printed using Microsoft Word or another popular word processing application.

DOWNLOADABLE WORKSHEET 6.4
Collection Letter 1

Dear _____:

    We know that it is probably an oversight, but the amount of _____ owed us for

_____ shipped to your company on _____ is overdue since

_____. Please send us your check immediately, so we can update our records and mark

you "paid in full . . . credit good."

                           Sincerely,

                           _____

DOWNLOADABLE WORKSHEET 6.5
Collection Letter 2

Dear _____:

    Unfortunately, _____, tells me that your account is in arrears in the

amount of _____ owed us for _____ and also that a previous letter was sent to

you pointing out this fact. If there is some mistake on this, please let me know at once, so we can get it

cleared up.

    We would like to maintain you as a customer and for you to maintain your good standing.
However, your past-due bill must be paid immediately or if there is some misunderstanding, we need
to get it straightened out. Otherwise, further action will be taken in accordance with our policy.

                           Sincerely,

                           _____

DOWNLOADABLE WORKSHEET 6.6
Collection Letter 3

Dear _____:

    This is the final notice we intend to send you before initiating legal action. Your account is in

arrears _____ for _____. If this amount is not received within ten days

to clear your account, we intend to initiate proceedings to recover this amount.

                           Sincerely,

                           _____

CHAPTER 7

Record Keeping Is Vital—What Records You Need and How to Keep Records Easily

Records are crucial to the success of your business. Even if you are successful initially, it is unlikely that you will be able to sustain this success without good records because you do not know what is making your business successful. You need records to ensure that your business is profitable, and they should be kept from the first day that you open your doors until you sell your business to someone else or retire. Good records and record keeping are needed to make future plans for your company and to evolve strategies that enable your business to grow rapidly and be successful in the future and to survive in the present. Without such records, your competition eventually evolves strategies that you cannot counter because you do not know your position in the market or what is going wrong. Unfortunately, despite its importance, many small businesspeople use the shoebox approach to record keeping. That is, the only record of a sale or a purchase they make is a piece of paper tossed in a shoebox. At the end of the year, someone attempts to analyze the contents of the box. This isn't record keeping. It cannot enable a business to respond successfully to the day-to-day demands, problems, and opportunities that appear.

This chapter helps you avoid the shoebox approach and shows you methods you can use not only to survive but also to make your business highly profitable. That these methods are made available to you does not mean that you shouldn't use the services of a good accountant. On the contrary, a good accountant can save you much additional money. A combination of using the methods described in this chapter and consulting an expert accountant saves you thousands of dollars or more throughout your business career. It may well make the difference between mere survival and tremendous growth and success.

Basic Requirements of a Record-Keeping System

The four basic requirements for a record-keeping system are:

1. Your system must be simple to use and to understand. If it's not simple to use, it takes too much time and trouble to keep updated; if it is not easy to understand, you and your accountant waste time trying to figure it out. Because time is money, make sure your system is easy to understand.

2. Your system should be accurate and relevant. Accurate means free of errors and conforming to whatever standards you set for the record-keeping system. Relevant means pertinent to your business; be sure you are not wasting time recording information that you do not need.

3. Your system should be consistent throughout. This means that whatever standards and structure you decide on are adhered to throughout the system. This is not to say that, if you find deficiencies in what you are doing, you cannot change. But it does mean that you should deviate from your standard methods only for good reasons and maintain only one method of doing things.

4. Your system should ensure that records are kept in a timely fashion. This means that you must keep them current. If you do not, you are not able to use this information effectively.

Basic Record Requirements

Just as there are four basic system requirements, there are four basic records that are required for any good small business:

1. Sales records.
2. Cash receipts.
3. Cash disbursements.
4. Accounts receivable.

   Let's look at each in turn.

Sales Records

Sales records should be subdivided into convenient categories, so that you can analyze them easily. For example, you may subdivide your sales records into wholesale and retail sales, or you may subdivide them by geographic areas or by some other market segmentation.

Cash Receipts

Cash receipts represent cash actually received in the form of sales and collection of accounts receivable from monies formerly owed to you.

Cash Disbursements

Cash disbursements are monies paid out by your business. In general, you should pay by check except for small items that you can pay out of a petty cash fund. In keeping track of cash disbursements, always list the date, the check number, the amount, and the purpose for which the disbursement was made. Also, you may break the heading into different categories, such as office supplies, advertising, rent, utilities, and so forth.

Simply drawing a check for a small amount, say $100, sets up the petty cash fund. The check is cashed and logged under the general heading of checks for the petty cash fund. The money is then placed in some convenient location, so that you can use it easily as required. As payments are made for small items, such as postage, bus fares, and supplies, each item is listed on a special form that again lists the date of expenditure, the amount, and the purpose for which the money was spent. When the fund is nearly spent, the items are summarized and a check is drawn to cover the exact amount. In this way, when the new check is cashed, the fund is replenished. Doing this also means that at all times the cash that you have on hand in the petty cash fund, plus listed expenditures, equals the amount of the fund.

Accounts Receivable

Accounts receivable are monies owed to you for services or goods supplied for which you have not yet been paid. To control the accounts receivable, be sure that all bills are sent when goods are shipped or services rendered and that they are mailed to correct addresses. Be especially careful of the larger accounts in your accounts receivable ledger. At the end of every month, age your accounts receivable. This means that you list accounts and enter amounts that are current, those unpaid for 30 days, and those unpaid for 60 days and longer. For those that are unpaid for 60 days or longer, find out exactly why these accounts are unpaid. In this way, your system helps in account control and collection. You should also pay attention to customer complaints about bills that are sent. If you feel the complaint is justified, perhaps you should negotiate and propose a special adjustment or in some other way reach agreement with your customer. Do not delay in doing this. If the customer has not paid and is delinquent in his or her payment, then try to get a promise of payment on a specific date. If the payment is not received by that date, then again contact the customer and ask the customer to explain why, and obtain a new promise if necessary. If funds are still not forthcoming, many states have provisions for a small claims court in which a lawyer is not required. By using the small claims court, it is fairly easy to take a delinquent account to task for nonpayment. You may try other means of getting the customer or client who owes money to pay. The action you take depends on the situation, the size of the account, future business anticipated with the same customer despite slowness in payment, whether you feel that you may ultimately be paid, and various other factors. See Chapter 6 for additional information.

You should establish a figure below which you do not bother going after monies owed. Let us say you have decided that this figure is $20. You ask twice for the amount from the individual owing this to you; then you drop it. You do this because the time and trouble spent collecting are worth more than this amount. Alternatively, if letting one customer get away with nonpayment may lead others to do the same thing, then maybe even a small account has to be pursued. Large accounts, of course, should be pursued vigorously to obtain payment.

Sometimes a new customer whom you do not know asks for credit. In this case, have your customer complete a credit application form such as Worksheet 6.2 in Chapter 6. For a small amount you can simplify this and just ask for basic information. Make sure that the credit is warranted before you grant it, especially with larger amounts. Obviously, You should think twice before granting additional credit or require a substantial amount up front.

General Rules for Tracking Your Finances and Your Bookkeeping System

Here are some general rules you should always follow no matter what system you adopt:

- Always pay your business bills by check or through your petty cash fund. Never make disbursements out of your daily cash receipts.

- Be certain that all incoming cash is recorded along with amounts, where the money came from, and the dates.

- Never take money out of your daily cash receipts for personal use, but instead, pay yourself a salary.

- Use a business bank account for all business funds and deposit all cash receipts in the account day by day as you receive them.

- Do not use your personal bank account for your business bank account, and keep personal cash separate from cash generated from the business.

- Periodically, have your record-keeping system checked over by a certified public accountant (CPA).

Should You Use Cash or Accrual Basis for Records?

Many small businesses use a simple cash basis for bookkeeping. Which basis is used depends on whether or not credit is granted to customers and the amount of inventory that is required. For example, if you are selling hamburgers, probably a credit system is not required, or is inventory extensive. In this situation, you would probably use a cash basis for your records. Alternatively, with credit granted to customers and a more extensive inventory, the accrual basis would probably be better. With the accrual basis, each item is entered as earned or as the expense is incurred without regard to when the actual payments are made or received. This means that sales made on credit are written down at once in your books as sales and also in your accounts receivable records. When the bills are actually collected, then your accounts receivable records are adjusted. Accruals are also made for expense items that are payable in the future. An example is yearly or periodic interest rates on loans. These accruals are made by entries explained later in this chapter.

Which Method of Depreciation Should You Adopt?

Depreciation is an expense of the business just as are rent, utilities, and salaries. Therefore, a charge to expenses should be made to cover depreciation of fixed assets other than land, which does not depreciate. Fixed assets may be defined as items that are normally in use for one year or longer. These may include buildings, equipment, tools, furniture, and other similar items. Most small businesses charge depreciation at the end of their fiscal year. However, if you have very substantial fixed assets such as a motel or hotel, you may want to calculate depreciation on a monthly basis. There are two basic methods of depreciation: (1) straight-line depreciation and (2) the declining balance method of depreciation.

Straight-Line Depreciation

Straight-line depreciation is based on the expected life of the items for book purposes. Therefore, it is first necessary to estimate the total life of the item being depreciated. Let us say that you own a new building. A reasonable period of depreciation for a building is 20 years. This means that to depreciate the building 100 percent, you would depreciate it 5 percent a year. Other assets may have shorter periods of depreciation. Machinery may have an estimated life of five years. In this case, the item should be depreciated at 20 percent per year. An example of a depreciation chart using the straight-line method is shown in Figure 7.1.

Estimated life = 20 years, so 1.0/20 = 5 percent. If the purchase date is other than January, first-year depreciation is less than the full amount.

Item	Date Purchased	Cost ($)	Estimated Life (Years)	Yearly Depreciation (%)	Accumulated Prior Depreciation ($)	This Year's Depreciation ($)	Total Accumulated Depreciation ($)
Office	January 2005	100,000	20	5	25,000.00	5,000	30,000.00
Auto	January 2005	20,000	5	20	12,000.00	4,000	16,000.00
Printing press	March 2005	5,000	10	10	1,416.67	500	1,916.67
Computer	July 2006	2,000	4	25	750.00	500	1,250.00

FIGURE 7.1 Sample Form for Straight-Line Depreciation of Assets

Example: Purchase in March 2005 (therefore, only 10 months depreciation in 2005). To adjust, if yearly depreciation is $500, then depreciation in 2005 is 10/12 × $500 = $416.67.

Declining Balance Method of Depreciation   The declining balance method of depreciation is used whenever quicker recovery of the investment is desirable. Using this method, your asset is depreciated by a certain percentage of the balance each year. However, if you use the declining balance method for tax-paying purposes, check with the latest IRS rules. The difference in using the declining balance method is that the yearly depreciation is taken not of the total cost of the asset but rather of the remaining value.

A comparison of the two methods is found in Table 7.1 on page 146. Note that using the declining balance method, the remaining value approach never reaches zero. In the example, in both cases the asset cost $1,000 and the estimated year life is five years. This means that yearly depreciation using the straight-line method is 20 percent, or, using the declining balance method, 40 percent of the remaining value of each year. The total depreciation after five years using the straight-line method is $1,000, but because in the declining balance method it never quite reaches $1,000 and the remaining value approaches but never equals zero, in this case it actually equals $922.24. To allow for this, the small businessperson should switch to the straight-line depreciation method near the end of the asset's useful life. Therefore, in the example shown (the fourth and fifth years of life depreciating at $86.40 and $51.84, respectively), the $216 remaining value in the fourth year should be split up to $108 each, and therefore at the end of the period the depreciation would be $1,000 instead of the $922.24 shown.

The declining balance method permits the businessperson to take a heavy depreciation in the early years of the equipment's life. This is very desirable when the asset has a high rate of obsolescence and its market value accordingly decreases very rapidly.

Up to now, we've assumed the salvage value of any equipment to be zero. However, this is usually not the case. That is, at the end of the depreciable period, the equipment is probably worth something either for resale, trade-in, or scrap. This salvage value should be estimated at the time that the estimated life figure is established. This scrap or salvage value is then subtracted from the original cost of the equipment to give the amount to be depreciated over the estimated life. For example, if the automobile shown in Figure 7.1 had a salvage value of $5,000 after the five-year period of estimated life, then only $15,000 should be depreciated rather than the $20,000 shown in the table. If you fail to use a salvage value in your depreciation calculations, then this amount is recoverable by the IRS at such time as you do receive money for trade-in, scrap, or salvage.

TABLE 7.1 Depreciation: Declining-Balance Method versus Straight-Line Method

Assumed Conditions:

Asset cost = $1,000

Estimated life = 5 years

Yearly depreciation (straight line) = ⅕ = 20%

Yearly depreciation (declining balance) = 40% of remaining value each year

Year	Straight Line	Declining Balance Remaining Value	Declining Balance Depreciation
1	(20% × $1,000) = $200	$1,000.00	(40% × $1000) = $400.00
2	(20% × $1,000) = $200	$600.00	(40% × $600) = $240.00
3	(20% × $1,000) = $200	$360.00	(40% × $360) = $144.00
4	(20% × $1,000) = $200	$216.00	(40% × $216) = $86.40
5	(20% × $1,000) = $200	$129.60	(40% × $129.60) = $51.84

Which Bookkeeping System Should You Adopt?

Specialized bookkeeping systems are available for almost every business and industry. To see what is available in your area of interest, you should contact the trade organization that serves your business. You may also check with stationery and office supply stores. Usually either a general bookkeeping system or even one designed especially for your business is available. You can also use the worksheets provided at the end of Chapter 2.

The Need for General Books and Journals

In addition to the basic records I've already discussed, you need books for different journal entries. These are called *general books*. General entries of this type are used to record business transactions that do not involve cash. Examples include accruals for depreciation and expenses that are due in the future.

Another book you should keep is called the *general ledger*. The general ledger is kept to record balances of assets, liabilities, and capital, and to accumulate sales and expense items. At the end of each fiscal year, your accounts are balanced and closed. Sales and expense account balances are transferred to the profit and loss account. The remaining asset, liability, and capital accounts provide the figures for the balance sheet. We discuss this shortly. A typical classification of accounts for the general ledger may include:

- Assets.
- Cash in banks.
- Petty cash fund.

- Accounts receivable.
- Materials and supplies.
- Prepaid expenses.
- Deposits.
- Land.
- Buildings.
- Tools and equipment.
- Automotive equipment.
- Furniture and fixtures.
- Reserve for depreciation (The reserve for depreciation is subtracted from the asset account. Technically this is known as a "credit" against the asset account.)
- Liabilities.
- Accounts payable.
- Notes payable.
- Sales tax payable.
- PICA taxes payable.
- FICA taxes payable.
- Federal withholding taxes.
- State withholding taxes.
- Unemployment taxes.
- Long-term debt and mortgages payable.
- Long-term debt SBA loan.
- Miscellaneous accruals.
- Capital accounts.
- Common capital stock.
- Preferred capital stock (for corporations only).
- Proprietorship accounts (for a proprietorship).
- Proprietorship withdrawals (for a proprietorship).
- Retained earnings.
- Sales accounts.
- Retail sales.
- Wholesale sales.
- Sales services.
- Miscellaneous income.

- Expenses.
- Salaries and wages.
- Contract labor.
- Payroll taxes.
- Utilities.
- Telephone.
- Rent.
- Office supplies.
- Postage.
- Maintenance expense.
- Insurance.
- Interest.
- Depreciation.
- Travel expense.
- Entertainment.
- Advertising.
- Dues and contributions.
- Auto expense.
- Contributions.
- Electricity.
- Heat.
- Trade dues.

Do not use too many different accounts. Tailor the accounts you use to your particular business. Sales should be broken down in a sufficient number of categories to provide a clear indication of your business. Different expense accounts should be used depending on the frequency of the individual expenses. Miscellaneous expenses are used for small, unrelated expense items.

Other Important Records

Several other important records should be maintained by your business. These include an equipment list, insurance records, and payroll records.

Equipment List

An equipment list consists of all the permanent equipment used in the business. Do not bother keeping track of the small items, but do keep track of any item that is useful for a period of a year or longer and has some appreciable value to it. On your list, show the date purchased, the name of the supplier, the description of the item, the number of the check with which the equipment was paid for, and the amount. This list is very useful for calculating depreciation, as described earlier, and for reorder information, insurance preparation, and business functions.

Insurance Records

Insurance records are an absolute must. See Chapter 4 concerning business insurance for more details.

Payroll Records

Use Worksheet 2.5 in Chapter 2 to assist you in preparing payroll records. Yearly and quarterly reports of individual payroll payments must be made to state and federal governments. You must supply each individual employee a W-2 Form at the year's end showing total withholding payments made for the employee during that calendar year. A special employment card should be kept for each individual employee showing the individual's Social Security number, as well as name, address, telephone number, name of next of kin, and current address. Also, on the form you should indicate whether the employee is married and the number of exemptions claimed. In this same file, a W-4 Form should be on record that is completed by the employee, as explained earlier in this book. A summary payroll should also be maintained showing the names, employee numbers, the rate of pay, hours worked, overtime hours if any, total pay, and the amount of deductions for FICA, PICA, withholding taxes, and deductions for insurance, pension or savings plan, and so forth. Use Worksheet 2.5 in Chapter 2 to maintain the records on individual employees. Enter the amounts for each pay period covering hours worked, gross pay, and the various deductions. At the end of each quarter, add up the amounts and the balance. These forms provide the needed information for quarterly and annual reports.

Preparation of Financial Statements

There are two basic, very important, financial statements that you must either prepare yourself or have an accountant prepare. One study showed that less than 7 percent of a group of failed businesses prepared these statements. These statements are (1) the balance sheet and (2) the income statement. Both forms are prepared using the records that you've already accumulated.

The Balance Sheet

The balance sheet records the condition of your company at a single point in time. Therefore, the information contained on it is true on one specific date and on one specific date only. It is prepared usually at the close of the last day of the month and it answers the question: How does your company stand financially at this point in time? The balance sheet has two main sections. One section shows the assets, and the other shows the liabilities and owner's equity, which together represent claims against the assets. On the balance sheet, the total assets always equal the combined total of the liabilities and the owner's equity. It is from this fact that this particular financial statement gets its name.

A sample balance sheet is shown in Figure 7.2. Note that the assets are grouped into various subsections. These include current assets, long-term assets, fixed assets, and other assets. Current assets are cash and resources that can be converted into cash within 12 months of the date of the balance sheet. These include cash, which includes both money on hand and deposits in the bank, accounts receivable, inventory, temporary investments expected to be converted

Balance Sheet		December 31, 200_
Current assets:		
Cash	$35,000.00	
Accounts receivable	55,000.00	
Inventory	60,000.00	
Temporary investments	3,000.00	
Prepaid expenses	2,000.00	
Total current assets		$155,000.00
Long-term assets:		
Bonds	$10,000.00	
Stocks	10,000.00	
		$20,000.00
Fixed assets:		
Machinery and equipment	$35,000.00	
Buildings	42,000.00	
Land	20,000.00	
Total fixed assets		$97,000.00
Other assets		
None	0	
Total other assets		$272,000.00
Current Liabilities:		
Accounts payable	$36,000.00	
Notes payable	44,000.00	
Current portion of long-term notes	4,000.00	
Interest payable	1,000.00	
Taxes payable	3,000.00	
Accrued payroll	2,000.00	
Total current liabilities		$67,000.00
Equity:		
Owner's equity	$115,000.00	
Total equity		$115,000.00
Total liabilities and equity		$272,000.00

FIGURE 7.2   Sample Balance Sheet for the XYZ Company

into cash in a year, and prepaid expenses. Long-term assets, which are also called long-term investments, are holdings that the business intends to keep for a year or longer, and typically yield interest for dividends including stocks, bonds, and savings accounts of a special type that are not to be touched for a term greater than a year. Fixed assets include the plant and equipment. These are the resources a business owns or acquires and uses in its operations, and are not intended for resale. Finally, we have other assets. These are resources that are not listed in any of the above categories. These include intangibles such as outdated equipment that is salable for scrap and trademarks or patents.

Now let's look at the liability section. Current liabilities are debts and obligations that are payable in 12 months. Typically they include accounts payable (amounts owed to suppliers for goods and services rendered in connection with business), notes payable (the balance of the principal due to pay off short-term debts for borrowed funds), interest payable, taxes payable, current portion of long-term notes that are payable, and payroll (salaries and wages currently owed). Long-term liabilities are those notes for other liabilities due over a period exceeding 12 months. The amount listed is the outstanding balance less the current portion, which is shown under current liabilities. Equity, which is also called net worth, is the claim of the owners on the assets of the business.

In a proprietorship or partnership, equity is each of the owners' original investment plus any earnings after withdrawal. Of course, in a corporation, the owners are the shareholders. The corporation's equity is the sum of the contributions plus earnings retained after paying dividends. The breakdown of equity includes capital stock, which is the total amount invested in the business in exchange for shares of stock, and retained earnings, which are the total accumulated net income less the total accumulated dividends declared since the corporation's founding. As noted earlier, the sum of the liabilities and equity must equal that of the assets. Note how this is true in Figure 7.2.

The Income Statement

The income statement, also known as the profit and loss statement, measures costs and expenses against sales revenues over a definite period of time, such as a month or a year, to show the net profit or loss of the business for the entire period covered by the statement. A sample income statement is shown in Figure 7.3. The first entry is sales or revenue.

This is all the income coming into a business for services rendered or for goods sold. In addition to actual cash transactions, it reflects the amounts due from customers on accounts receivable, as well as equivalent cash values for merchandise or other tangible items if used as a payment. From this figure is subtracted the value of returned merchandise and allowances made for defective goods. The result is net sales. The next major column is cost of sales. Cost

Income Statement	For the year ended December 31, 200_	
Sales or revenue:	$1,040,000.00	
Less returns and allowances	5,000.00	
Net sales		$1,035,000.00
Cost of sales:		
Beginning inventory, January 1, 200 _	250,000.00	
Merchandise purchases	500,000.00	
Cost of goods available for sale	750,000.00	
Less ending inventory, December 31, 200_	225,000.00	
Total cost of goods sold		525,000.00
Gross profit		$510,000.00
Operating expenses: Selling and general and administrative		
Salaries and wages	180,000.00	
Advertising	200,000.00	
Rent	10,000.00	
Utilities	5,000.00	
Other expenses	10,000.00	
Total operating expenses		405,000.00
Total operating income		$105,000.00
Other revenue and expenses		0
Pretax income: $105,000.00		
Taxes on income	50,000.00	
Income after taxes but before extraordinary gain or loss		$55,000.00
Extraordinary gain or loss		0
Net income (or loss)		$55,000.00

FIGURE 7.3 **Sample Income Statement for the XYZ Company**

of sales equals the total amount of goods available less the inventory remaining at the end of the accounting period for which the income statement is constructed. Generally, service businesses such as a medical practice or a consultancy have no cost of sales. From the foregoing, the gross profit or gross margin is calculated. It is the difference between the cost of goods sold and the net sales. It is the business's profit before expenses and before taxes.

Operating expenses are the expenses of doing business. They generally fall into two major categories: (1) selling and (2) general and administrative expenses. Selling may include such things as salaries and wages, commissions, advertising, and depreciation. General and administrative expenses include salaries and wages of owners or senior managers, employee benefits, insurance, depreciation, and similar items.

The total operating expenses just calculated are now subtracted from the gross margin to show what the business earned before financial revenue and expenses, taxes, and extraordinary items.

Other revenue and expenses are income and expenses that are not generated by usual operations of the business. Typical items in this category are interest from investments and various financial expenses.

Total financial revenue less the expenses is now added to the total operating income. The result is pretax income. Taxes are then subtracted to develop income after taxes but before extraordinary items.

Extraordinary items are listed separately on the income statement. These are occurrences that are extremely unusual, cannot be foreseen, and are not generally expected to recur that generate either an income or a loss. Damage due to a storm or an earthquake, for example, might be considered an extraordinary loss. Adding in this final item results in the net income or net loss for the period of the income statement.

The balance sheet and the income statement are extremely important tools for you as a small businessperson. They are intended to represent a true and fair picture of the condition of your company for a specific time period. However, because they are drawn up under conditions of uncertainty and some transactions are not complete at the time they are prepared, they should be used with caution and the judgment of both yourself and your accountant who may prepare them. (You should bear this in mind when you use some of the financial tools presented in Chapter 5.)

Specialized and Computerized Record-Keeping Systems

Most industries have companies that have developed and sell specialized record-keeping systems for the particular industry in which you do business. Many are computer software, and some may be expensive, but if needed they can save you much time and effort, and, consequently, money. To locate what is available in your industry, consult your industry trade association, or the advertisements in magazines devoted to your industry. Or you can do a search on the Internet.

For example, I recently used a search engine with the words "small business record-keeping software" and got over a million hits, so you have quite a variety of record-keeping programs to choose from. There are also general small business software programs. Here are a few to try:

- *Quicken* is one of the best-known. Intuit also produces the *TurboTax* federal and state income tax program. The web site can be found at http://www.quicken.com/small_business.
- *ACCPAC BPI* offers a full-function accounting system. The URL for their financial/accounting software is http://www.accpac.com/products/finance/bpi.
- *Global Business Software* is published by H. T. Parks, Inc. in Georgia. The URL is http://www.htparks.com.

- *EZ Small Business Software* offers several prices for more powerful options. The URL is http://www.elwoodsoftware.com.

Clearly, this isn't even the tip of the iceberg. Many companies offer specialized types of software record-keeping programs. With many, you also have the capability of downloading a trial program first. I highly recommend this approach.

Sources of Additional Information

Books

Bookkeeping Made Simple, revised edition, by Louis W. Fields, Richard R. Gallagher, published by Made Simple Books.

Financial Recordkeeping for Small Stores, Small Business Management Series No. 32, by Robert C. Ragan, published by the Small Business Administration.

Keeping Financial Records for Business, 8th ed., by Burton Kaliski, published by Southwestern Educational Publishing Co.

Keeping Records in Small Business. Small Marketers Aids No. 155, by John Cotton, published by the Small Business Administration.

Keeping the Books: Basic Record Keeping and Accounting for the Successful Small Business, 6th edition, by Linda Pinson, published by Dearborn Trade.

Record Keeping Systems Small Stores and Service Trade, Small Business Bibliography No. 15, by Nathan H. Olshan and Office of Management Information and Training staff, published by the Small Business Administration.

Internet

Note: Because Internet sites frequently go down, multiple sites are listed for similar subject matter.

Businesstown.com—Basic Accounting. Basic accounting steps you need to run your small business and keeping track of your finances using the standard accounting tools at http://www.businesstown.com/accounting/basic.asp.

BuyersZone.com. FREE Accounting and Bookkeeping Services Quotes from Multiple Suppliers at http://www.buyerszone.com/professional_services/accounting/qz _questions_694.jhtml?requesteid=15628.

Powerhomebiz.com. Basic Business: Good Record Keeping, by "Wild Bill" Montgomery. An article on the basics at http://www.powerhomebiz.com/vol11/recordkeeping.htm.

Setting Up a Record Keeping System, by Cheryle Jones Syracuse. Part of a Ohio State University small business series at http://ohioline.osu.edu/cd-fact/1152.html.

The Small Business Advisor: Accounting and Record Keeping. Covers the basics with links to resources and additional information at http://www.smallbusinessadvice.com/acct.html.

Starting a Business and Keeping Records, by the Internal Revenue Service. U.S. Government record keeping requirements at http://www.irs.ustreas.gov/pub/irs-pdf/p583.pdf.

DOWNLOADABLE WORKSHEET 7.1
Small Business Financial Status Checklist

The following is a checklist of what every owner/manager should keep track of on a daily, weekly, and monthly basis. It is based on one originally developed by John Cotton, a retired utility executive in Albuquerque, New Mexico, and published by the Small Business Administration.

Daily	Complete	Incomplete
Cash on hand		
Bank balance		
Summarize sales and cash receipts		
Reconcile any errors in recording collections		
Record of all monies paid out, by cash or check		

Weekly	Complete	Incomplete
Check accounts receivable and take action on slow payers		
Look over accounts payable and take advantage of discounts		
Review payroll (rate, hours worked, deductions, net pay, etc.)		
Prepare taxes and reports for state and federal government		

Monthly	Complete	Incomplete
Ensure journal entries are classified according to like elements		
Check profit and loss statement for the month		
Check over the balance sheet		
Reconcile the bank statement		
The petty cash account		
Make federal and state tax deposits		
Check that accounts receivable are aged (i.e., 30, 60, 90 days, etc.) past due and take action on all bad and slow accounts.		
Inventory control: remove unmoving stock, order new stock, analyze what is moving fast or slow and take action		

To customize this document, download it to your hard drive from the John Wiley & Sons web site at www.wiley.com/go/cohenentrepreneur. The document can then be opened, edited, and printed using Microsoft Word or another popular word processing application.

CHAPTER 8

Doing Marketing Research: Easily, Quickly, and Profitably

Marketing research is the gathering, recording, and analyzing of information about problems relating to marketing. It helps identify who your market is as well as which methods best satisfy the needs of your market. But it encompasses many other aspects of marketing, including new product introduction, pricing, advertising, and consumer behavior, among others. So important is marketing research that certain basic marketing strategies, such as market segmentation, in which you identify a specific portion of the market and concentrate your resources on selling to that one segment, or product differentiation, in which you differentiate your product from a competitor so as to best appeal to potential buyers, are absolutely impossible without it.

Among the many things that marketing research tells you are the following:

- Who are your customers and potential customers?
- What kind of people are your customers? This includes demographic categories, such as age, income, and education, and psychographic categories, such as your customers' interests and preferences.
- Where do your customers live?
- Why do your customers buy?
- Do they have the ability to pay?
- Are you offering the kinds of goods and services that your customers want?
- Are you offering your products or services at the right place, at the right time, and at the correct amount?
- Are your prices consistent with the value your customers place on the product or service that you are selling?
- How are your promotional programs working?

- What do your customers think of your business and its image?
- How do your business and your business procedures compare with those of your competitors?[1]

Correct use of marketing research can mean amazing profits for your business and tremendous advantages over your competitors. A famous example of correct use of marketing research took place in the early 1960s. It was the product that gave famed automotive icon Lee Iacocca his big chance and resulted in the introduction of a model and category of cars still in existence today. Ford, along with two other major American motor companies, had developed cars to compete with foreign cars, such as Volkswagen. Ford's entry had been the Falcon, introduced in 1959. As the years passed, the numbers of Ford Falcons that were sold began to decrease as a percentage of Ford's total sales. This was also true for the competing cars offered by the two other American companies. Ford might simply have concluded that American small cars were not wanted. Instead, Ford did marketing research to find out more about the falling off of Falcon sales. During this research, Ford discovered an interesting and important fact: While sales of the Falcon were declining, sales of sporty options, such as bucket seats, stick shift, and padded dash, were increasing. This was due primarily to the greater numbers of young adults who were purchasing the vehicle. Ford's careful study of the market research findings led the company to put out the Ford Mustang, which was introduced in 1965. This sports car-like vehicle demolished all previous records for sales and developed a new market that competitors followed as best they could, some two to three years behind. The head of Ford's Mustang project was none other than a young engineer by the name of Lee Iacocca.

But successful use of marketing research is not limited to major companies such as Ford. Thousands of small firms and entrepreneurs have used marketing research successfully to carve out huge shares of their respective markets. An optical firm totally turned its company around and doubled sales within a year by identifying its customers. A mail-order entrepreneur sold $10 million worth of a single product through marketing research techniques. A small computer firm successfully took on IBM for a segment of the total computer market and won through the correct application of marketing research.

In this chapter, you learn the same techniques used by these and other firms so successfully.

---

[1] Adapted from J. Ford Laumer Jr., James R. Harris, and Hugh J. Guffer Jr., *Learning About Your Market*, Small Business Administration (1979).

Three Important Categories of Marketing Research

Three categories of marketing research important to any small business are: internal information, secondary research, and primary research. Let's look at each in turn.

Internal Information

Internal information is extremely useful because it is generally close at hand and costs you little or nothing to obtain. Therefore, before thinking about expensive field experiments or surveys, look at your own records and files. These include: sales records, receipts, complaints, all of the records noted in the record-keeping section of this book, and anything else that tells about your customers and what they are interested in and what they buy. One source of information is your customers' addresses. This alone tells a great deal about your customers, including where they live, their income, and their lifestyles. This information can be of great assistance to you in determining what your customers are interested in buying. The most successful mail-order firms make millions not by selling a single product once to a customer but by selling numerous products to their customer list again and again.

Secondary Research

Secondary research concerns information already available outside your company. The key here is its availability. It has already been put together by someone else. This information may have been collected by other firms, by government agencies, and may be found in books, newspapers, and a host of other sources. But the important fact is that this information is already available. Someone else has done the work; that is why it's called "secondary" research. It also costs you little or nothing to obtain. You don't have to design the survey method. You don't have to do the interviewing. And you don't have to spend time and resources collecting this information. Where can you find this information? At the end of this chapter, there are over 100 sources of statistics, studies accomplished, and secondary research that you can analyze to obtain more facts regarding your customers. Also, you can obtain tremendous material, for free, on the Internet. We look at some of those sources also. You can also purchase completed marketing research reports from some firms.

Primary Research

Perhaps you have already looked at the cheaper and easier research methods—your internal records and secondary sources of information—and found that the specific information that you need simply isn't available. In this case, you must do the research or hire someone else to do it for you. This means of getting information, specifically tailored to your needs, is called primary research.

Exploratory versus Specific Research

There are two basic types of research to consider once the decision is made that primary research is necessary: exploratory research and specific research. Exploratory research is aimed at helping you to define the problem. It is typically done through in-depth interviews with a relatively small number of people. It tends to be open-ended: Questions are asked that invite detailed, lengthy answers from the respondents. These interviews tend to be nonstructured and freewheeling. Here is one example of exploratory research and how it solved a problem for a soup company.

A promotion for a new soup product had failed. The basic promotion had been a free pair of nylons if the customer would try the soup. The general question was: Why had the promotion failed? In-depth interviews were conducted with a limited number of customers to discover the answer. From this limited research, the result was found that an image of "feet in soup" had resulted. This error in consumer behavior psychology caused the failure.

Specific research is used when the basic problem has already been defined. It focuses on ways of solving the problem. Specific research typically uses much larger samples than exploratory research, and because of this it tends to be much more expensive. The interviews used with specific research are very structured, complete, and formal. Using the example from the soup company, specific research could be conducted to find out what to do about the soup promotion; that is, what premium, if any, should be given to consumers for trying the new soup. The respondent might select his or her preference from a number of choices.

The Marketing Research Process

The marketing research process can be divided into the following steps:

1. Define the problem.
2. Decide whether marketing research is needed.
3. Identify objectives.
4. State specific data to be obtained.

5. Design the research instrument to be used.
6. Decide on the sample.
7. Collect the data.
8. Tabulate and analyze.
9. Draw conclusions and decide on courses of action.

Define the Problem

You cannot proceed until you have a good definition of what your problem is; for example, a new product introduction, or identification of customers for a certain market. This first step of the research process seems obvious and for this reason many people tend to overlook it. Yet, experts tell us that it is the most important step. When defining the problem, look beyond the symptoms. Symptoms may be declining sales, declining profits, and so on. But you must ask yourself: Why are sales declining? Why are profits down? List every possible reason. Could your customers be changing? Is there new competition? List all the possibilities, but focus on those that can be measured. These are the ones that you can do your marketing research on. Problems that cannot be measured are not candidates for marketing research.

Decide Whether Marketing Research Is Needed

If you cannot measure the influence on the problem, you cannot do marketing research. But even if measurement is possible, before you decide to invest your time and treasure in marketing research, you should consider several factors: (1) Is internal or secondary research available? (2) What is the estimated cost in money, resources, and time to do the research? If the research has already been done and is available free, it makes little sense to do it over. If the research can be obtained, but at too high a cost, higher than the increase in sales or profits that may result, the research is clearly not worthwhile. The same thing is true if it takes so long to get the information that you are not able to use it. If the potential actions of a competitor are important, maybe you should assume increased risks and proceed without research, or just minimal research. Always recognize that doing marketing research may not be the answer to the problem that you have defined. However, if thinking through the situation shows that you can accomplish research that is of assistance in solving the problem, then proceed to the next step.

Identify Objectives

Understand everything you can about the problem and the information you are seeking before proceeding. This enables you to specify clearly the objective or objectives of the study that you are undertaking. You may have a single objective or you may have several. But, either way, you must state it or them in the clearest possible terms. For example, "The objective of this study is to determine who is buying memberships in health clubs within 10 miles of my location."

State Specific Data to Be Obtained

Now, you must decide on exactly what information you want to obtain. If you want to know who is purchasing memberships in health clubs in a 10-mile area, you may wish to know them by (1) income; (2) education; (3) age; (4) sex; (5) occupation; (6) employment; (7) precise geographical location; or (8) what type of media they read, see, or listen to. All the desired information should be specified in this section.

Design the Research Instrument to Be Used

It is time to decide how to do the research. First, you must decide whether you wish to do exploratory or specific research. Then, you must decide where and how the information is to be obtained. Your questionnaire must motivate the respondents to supply the information you want, sometimes concealing the reasons for obtaining it so as not to introduce extraneous factors into the results. It can have several different forms: It may be a set of questions designed to be asked over the telephone or in a personal interview, or a survey going through regular mail or by e-mail. Each form has advantages and disadvantages, and which one to use depends on your situation. For example, a mail or e-mail survey must be as short as possible, or many people won't respond. The same is true for the telephone interview. But a personal face-to-face interview can be as long as an hour or more. You must also consider the complexity of the questions to ask. For most complex questions, a personal interview is necessary. If you are handling a touchy subject, the telephone interview may be extremely difficult because the respondent may hang up. Also, the personal interview may be risky because the individual making the interview may bias the reply. In a mail or e-mail interview, because you are not there to obtain feedback, you must strongly motivate the individual to answer. A self-addressed, stamped envelope is almost a necessity with mail, to enable the respondent to send the survey back to you easily. But don't use a postage stamp. You waste money if the person does not answer. Instead, use a special reply permit indicia that you can obtain at your local post office. Even with this, responses by mail are far fewer than with other survey means. You must allow for this in the number of samples that you attempt to obtain.

One survey that compared all three methods had comparative responses as follows: mail, 15 percent; telephone survey, 70 percent; and personal interview, 80 percent. There are also trade-offs regarding cost. Mail is the cheapest, with e-mail cheapest of all. This is followed by telephone. Personal interview is three times as costly as phone because an individual must go from place to place and must be compensated for his time. Use Figure 8.1 for a means of comparing the three methods in detail.

Once you've decided the type of questionnaire to construct, you must then begin to design it. Usually, the questionnaire should be divided into several sections. The first section contains the basic classification data, including the name of the respondent, the address, and so forth. Frequently, the interviewer can fill in this information prior to the interview.

The introductory statement is usually the second section. It establishes rapport with the interviewee. Although it may be structured into the questionnaire section itself, if this is a personal or phone interview it should be put in the interviewer's own words so as not to sound stilted. Establishing this early rapport makes the difference between success and failure of the interview.

The next section describes the product or service if the research has to do with your wares directly. Be careful of overselling the product here, so as not to bias the results. The description should be complete and it should be factual. Generally, initial impression questions should appear first. They should be neither complicated nor personal. If the questionnaire is exploratory in nature, the questions should be open-ended without leading to any specific answers. If specific, the questions should give the respondent a choice of alternative answers.

It is important with products to determine buying intentions because sometimes individuals like a product but do not want to purchase it. If you can determine the reasons for this attitude, you may be able to make the changes necessary to make the product or service successful. Product appeals are necessary to determine how to promote the product effectively. This information helps you to determine what is important to emphasize and what is important to de-emphasize. Pricing is also a very important aspect, and here you should attempt to determine a selective demand curve for your product or your service. That is, by asking your potential customers about the likelihood of their purchase of the product at different prices, you can later tabulate the results and know at which price the product is demanded more than at any other. It may be difficult to get exact answers for this question, but it certainly helps to give you a general idea of the price range. You should also determine distribution channels by asking the consumer where he or she would expect to find the product. Determine the advertising medium in which he or she would expect to see, hear, or read about the product or service advertised.

Certain information of a personal nature, such as age, education, income, and the like, should be left to the end of the questionnaire. Be careful never to ask for a person's specific age or income or other information of this type, but rather indicate a range. Finally, at the end of the interview, deliver a friendly thank you. Your subjects are deserving of this.

Survey Aspect	Mail/E-Mail	Telephone	Personal Interview
Questionnaire			
Length	The shorter the better	Short (15 minutes or less)	Longer (up to one hour or more, possible follow-up by mail), usually maximum of 30 minutes
Complexity of questions	Can be moderately complex	Must be simple	Can be more complex
Flexibility	Poor to no feedback	Fair	Best
Ability to probe deeper	Not possible due to no feedback	Fair	Best
Handling sensitive subjects	Good	Could be difficult	Could be difficult
Ability to change order of questions	Cannot change	Excellent	Excellent
Sample			
Sample bias	A problem, respondents usually better educated	Both very low income (no phone) and high income (unlisted numbers) may be under-represented	Lowest bias
Sample of non-respondents	May be needed	Usually not needed	Usually not needed
Geographic Clustering	Controllable	Controllable	Controllable
Interview			
Response rate	Low—typically 15 percent or less	High—70 percent typical	High—80 percent typical
Interviewer bias/cheating by interviewer	None	Can occur	Can occur
Identity of respondent	Usually confidentiality promised	Known	Known
Cost and Administration			
Cost	Low	Moderately expensive	Highest cost
Administration load	Light	Heavier	Heaviest

FIGURE 8.1   Comparison of Data Collect Methods Adapted from William A. Cohen and Marshall E. Reddick, *Marketing Your Small Business Made Easy* **(Deerfield Beach, FL: Made E-Z Products, 2000, Fig 4-1, p. 65).**

Be certain that the information you want is contained in your questionnaire. In some cases it may be necessary to conceal what you are actually after to obtain unbiased responses. For example, if you are trying to determine which one of a number of products is favored by the consumer and your product is one of these, it may be important to conceal the fact that you are representing one of the products indicated in the survey. Always consider:

- Whether your respondent has the information that you're asking for.
- Whether he or she has the necessary experience to provide you with an accurate answer.
- Whether it is likely that he or she remembers to provide you with an accurate answer.
- Whether he or she has to work hard to get the information.
- Whether he or she is likely to give you the information.
- Whether he or she is likely to give you the true information.

There are many different types of questions that you may use in your questionnaire, for example:

- *Open-ended:* This is where you ask the question and allow the respondent to talk at some length. The question is not structured and there is no one specific answer.
- *Multiple choice:* Here you give a number of different choices to your respondent. Each choice may be a different product or a different description of some information that you are trying to obtain. Or, in the case of demographics, it may simply be a different age group.
- *Forced choice:* You give two choices, one or the other. Sometimes it is very difficult for a respondent to give a specific answer, but you may wish to have him or her choose one of two. An example is, "Do you primarily eat ice cream (1) at home, or (2) at an ice cream parlor?"
- *Semantic differential:* Allows for an intensity of feelings about some statement. For example, if we are talking about ice cream, you might ask a question such as this: "The XYZ brand of ice cream is . . . ?" You then have an adjective scale ranging from delicious to terrible. In between these two extreme points are other adjectives, such as fair.

By analyzing a number of responses, you can develop an average answer for each question.

The sequencing of your questions is extremely important. In general, your opening questions should motivate and not challenge the respondents psychologically. As pointed out earlier, identification items fit easily into this classification. Think of easing your respondent into the questionnaire.

Difficult questions should come in the body or at the end of the questionnaire. Why? First, your respondents are more at ease after they've answered some of the questions. Second, they are more accustomed to answering your questions and are less likely to hesitate in answering.

Another important point is that earlier questions influence questions that follow. For example, the mention of a product in one question may influence the answer to a following question. Consider this question: "ABC Soap has recently changed its formulation to be even more cleansing. Have you used this new formulation?" Let's say your next question is: "What do you think of the new ABC Soap?" You can see how the first question influences the next question.

These guides to questionnaire preparation are provided in Worksheet 8.1 at the end of this chapter. Worksheet 11.1 is a consumer profile questionnaire that has a number of different questions to ask regarding demographics, psychographics, lifestyle, social class, media use and interest, and other information. You can incorporate important questions from Worksheet 11.1 into your marketing research questionnaire as well.

Decide on the Sample

Deciding on the sample means defining whom you survey as well as how many people you survey. Whom you survey depends on your objectives and on the method of selection of your sample subjects. For example, you may use either random or nonrandom sampling. If you use random sampling, every individual from the population surveyed has an equal chance at being selected. If you use nonrandom sampling, you may include groups containing certain specific individuals you wish to be sampled or surveyed, or you may simply obtain respondents by availability.

The sample size decision depends on how much confidence you have or wish to have in your results. For 100 percent confidence, you would need to sample everyone. But this isn't always possible or desirable. If you can't sample randomly or sample everyone, you may try systematic sampling. That means you sample every nth element in the total population. Let's say that you are sampling customers; perhaps, you talk to every twenty-fifth or every fiftieth customer. Another way of handling this problem is to subdivide the total universe of people that you want sampled into a few groups that are mutually exclusive. You then randomly sample these smaller groups. Or you could divide the total number of people into many groups and randomly choose some of the groups for sampling.

Determining how many responses you need to reflect the nature of the total universe of individuals you are sampling depends on the standard deviation or dispersion of the responses. For most of the research done in small business, estimating the sample size need, within reasonable bounds, is probably better than attempting complicated statistical methods. If a greater degree of accuracy is needed, it's probably better to hire a marketing research firm to do the work.

Collect the Data

Once the sample size has been decided, you can then begin to use the research tool that was designed to actually collect data. Remember to be neat, courteous, and professional if you are doing this, either in person or by telephone.

Tabulate and Analyze

In this step, tabulate the collected data according to the specific questions that were developed. This data can then be analyzed on a percentage basis to reveal answers to the questions. For example, demographic analysis may show that the majority of customers are ages 18 to 24 and single. It may also show that most customers have graduated from high school and taken some college courses and are mostly white-collar workers. This information can be extremely important. One local CD shop had been carrying large stocks of classical recordings for years, when most of its buyers were teenagers. A dress shop that was doing poorly was offering racks of expensive dresses, which most of its customers could not afford.

Draw Conclusions and Decide on Courses of Action

At this point, draw conclusions based on your analysis of the data about your customers, the product, or whatever you are researching. You shouldn't stop with conclusions, but should initiate changes to increase your profits based on these conclusions.

Examples of Research You Can Do   The kind of marketing research you do is really limited only by your imagination. Some research can be done, even of the primary type, at very little cost except for your time. Here are some examples of simple research done by small businesses that greatly increased sales suggested in a booklet *Learning About Your Market,* published by the SBA.

- *License plate analysis:* In many states, license plates give you information about where car owners live. Therefore, simply by taking down the numbers of cars parked in your location and contacting the appropriate state agency, you can estimate the area from which you draw business. Knowing where your customers live can help you in your advertising or in targeting your approach to promotion. Through the same method you can find who your competitors' customers are.

- *Telephone number analysis:* Telephone numbers can also tell you the areas in which people live. You can obtain customers' telephone numbers from sales slips, credit card slips, or checks. Again, knowing where they live gives you excellent information about their lifestyles.

- *Coded coupons:* Coding coupons that can be used for discounts or inquiries about products can easily check the effectiveness of your advertising vehicle. You can find out the areas that your customers come from, as well as which vehicle brought them your message.

- *People watching:* Simply looking at your customers can tell you a great deal about them. How are they dressed? How old are they? Are they married or single? Do they have children? Many owners use this method intuitively to get a feel about their customers. However, a little sophistication with a tally sheet for a week can provide you much more accurate information simply, easily, and without cost. It may confirm what you've known all along, or it may change your picture of your typical customer completely.

Sources of Additional Information

Books

Business Competition Intelligence, by William L. Sammon, Mark A. Kurland, and Robert Spitalnic, published by John Wiley & Sons.

Competitor Intelligence, by Leonard M. Fuld, published by John Wiley & Sons.

Business Research: Concept and Practice, by Robert G. Murdick, published by Richard D. Irwin.

Do-It-Yourself Marketing Research, by George E. Breen, published by McGraw-Hill.

Honomichl on Marketing Research, by Jack J. Honomichl, published by NTC Business Books.

A Manager's Guide to Marketing Research, by Paul E. Green and Donald E. Frank, published by John Wiley & Sons.

Market and Sales Forecasting, by F. Keay, published by John Wiley & Sons.

Marketing Research: A Management Overview, by Evelyn Konrad and Rod Erickson, published by AMACOM.

Market Research Made Easy, 2nd ed., by Don Doman, Dell Dennison, Margaret Doman, published by Self-Counsel Press.

The Handbook of Online Marketing Research, by Joshua Grossnickle and Oliver Raskin, published by McGraw-Hill.

Research for Marketing Decisions, by Paul E. Green and Donald S. Lull, published by Prentice-Hall.

Successful Marketing Research, by Edward L. Hester, published by John Wiley & Sons.

Internet

Note: Because Internet sites frequently go down, multiple sites are listed for similar subject matter.

Free Marketing Research Sources. ResearchInfo.com provides numerous links to marketing research resources at http://www.researchinfo.com.

PJ Marketing Research. Provides links to worldwide marketing research experience, including how to write a market research report at http://www.pj-marketing.com.

Market Research and Internet Marketing Research. KnowThis.com provides links to articles at http://www.knowthis.com/research.

Marketing Research Home Page. This is an online supplement that accompanies Donald R. Lehmann, Sunil Gupta, and Joel H. Steckel's *Marketing Research*, a textbook. This site provides you with access to a multitude of marketing research information sources and links, arranged by topic at http://www.prenhall.com/lehmanngupta.

Quirk's Marketing Research Review. Quirk has a great deal of information, articles, and so on at http://www.quirks.com.

DOWNLOADABLE WORKSHEET 8.1
Designing Your Own Marketing Research Questionnaire

Very basic classi-fication data can usually be completed by the interviewer before the interview. Complicated or very personal data should go at the end of the questionnaire.	Name of Interviewer: _____ Date: _____ Name of Respondent: _____ Date: _____ Address: _____ Other (nonpersonal) relevant data: _____

The introductory statement establishes rapport with the interviewee. It should not be read, but rather put in the interviewer's own words. This introduction will make the difference between success and failure for the interview.	Good morning, my name is _____ , and I am conducting a market study for a new product (or service) called _____ _____. The answers you give me to the following questions will help determine whether or not to introduce this new product (or service) idea, and what features to incorporate into the product. May I have a few minutes of your time?

Product description tells the interviewee about the product or service. It should be a complete description of the product. Do not try to oversell the product; that may bias the results.	The benefits of this product are: • _____ • _____ • _____

_____

To customize this document, download it to your hard drive from the John Wiley & Sons web site at www.wiley.com/go/cohenentrepreneur. The document can then be opened, edited, and printed using Microsoft Word or another popular word processing application.

Initial impression questions should appear first. They should be non-complicated, non-personal, closed-end questions. Attitude scales are used to determine the intensity of the respondents' feelings. Open-ended questions are useful for determining why the person feels the way he or she does.

1. What is your immediate reaction to this idea?

Positive	Negative
Great ____	So-so ____
Like it very much ____	I do not particularity like it ____
Like it somewhat ____	I do not like it at all ____

Why do you say that? Please explain. _____
_____
_____

Buying intentions are important to determine. A person may like the idea, but not want to buy it. If one can determine why he would not, perhaps the product can be revised to meet more with his demands.

2. Which of the following best expresses your feeling about buying this product if it were available to you?

Positive	Negative
I'm absolute sure I would buy it ____	I probably would not buy it ____
I'm almost sure I would buy it ____	I am almost sure I would not buy it ____
I probably would buy it ____	I am absolutely sure I would not buy it ____

Why do you say that? Please explain. _____
_____
_____

(continued)

Product appeals must be determined, so as to be able to effectively promote the product. Such information will indicate what to emphasize and what to de-emphasize.

3. Tell me, all things considered, what is there about this product idea that appeals to you most. What do you consider its most important advantages?

    Appeals to Most   **Advantages**

    1.   1.

    2.   2.

    3.   3.

Pricing is an important aspect. Here one can determine a relative demand curve for the product. It is difficult for the consumer to answer this question precisely, but it should at least give the entrepreneur an idea of the price range.

4. How much do you think such a product would cost?

The retail outlet, where the product would be most likely to be found, is important.

5. Where would you expect to buy such a product?

The advertising medium to use must also be determined. Sometimes consumers do not like a product for minor reasons, and when these reasons are eliminated, they will buy. The more difficult, tiring questions should be placed at the end of the interview.

6. Where would you expect such a product to be advertised?

Not infrequently the person you are interviewing will come up with good ideas and concepts you may have missed in your questionnaire.

7. Are there any suggestions you would care to make that you think might improve this product?

Classification data of a personal nature should be asked at the end of the interview. Never ask for a person's specific age or income directly, because he could resent it, feeling this information is too personal. Always use a range.

Classification data:

1. In what category does your age fall?
   19 or below ___
   20–29 ___
   30–39 ___
   40–49 ___
   50–59 ___
   60–69 ___
   70 or older ___

2. In what category does your family income fall?
   19,000 or below ___
   20,000–39,999 ___
   40,000–59,999 ___

(continued)

        60,000–79,999 ___
        80,000–99,000 ___
        100,000 or more ___

3.   Check one: female married ___   single ___
                  male married ___   single ___

Thank you for your cooperation!

Always close with a friendly thank you. It's the right thing to do, and also you may want to interview them in the future.

DOWNLOADABLE WORKSHEET 8.2
Appraising Your Primary Research Study

Follow this checklist to ensure your marketing research study will be complete. If you use it, your research should provide you with excellent results.

	Yes	Needs Work
1. Review of research objectives		
a. Research objectives are consistent with overall problem or question.		
b. Objectives consider prior research done and secondary research available.		
2. Overall study design		
a. The concept of the research is relevant to what you want to find out.		
b. The terminology you use is easily understandable.		
c. The design of your study is a clear bridge from question to solution.		
d. You have eliminated biases in your questions that may influence results.		
e. If necessary, you have preserved the anonymity of respondents.		
f. Ethical considerations have been taken into account.		
g. Your organization for administrating the study is clear.		
3. Methods used		
a. The right populations (market segments) will be sampled.		
b. The data collection methods planned are unbiased.		
c. You have anticipated potential errors or mistakes in data collection and eliminated them.		
d. If sampling was used, the sample is representative of your target market.		
e. The plan for processing the data is clear.		
f. The categories used in tabulation are meaningful for the results.		
g. The statistical methods you selected for the analysis are appropriate.		
4. Actions and follow-up		
a. You have thought through potential results and how this will affect your actions or recommendations for actions to others.		
b. All action possibilities will be considered.		
c. There is no information needed for action that is lacking in your planned study.		
d. Potential actions that will be taken as a result of your study are within your organization's capability of being performed.		

To customize this document, download it to your hard drive from the John Wiley & Sons web site at www.wiley.com/go/cohenentrepreneur. The document can then be opened, edited, and printed using Microsoft Word or another popular word processing application.

MARKETING PROBLEM SOLVING

CHAPTER 9

How to Find and Introduce a New Product or Service

I t is an unfortunate fact that 8 out of 10 new products fail in the marketplace. Yet, new product introduction is absolutely essential. Why is this so? Without new products, your business cannot survive. You cannot continue to produce the old products that have made your company successful because of the product life cycle. The product life cycle shows that every product goes through the stages of introduction, growth, maturity, and decline. In this final phase, while sales may continue to be made, the product becomes more and more unprofitable. Life cycles are of different lengths for different products. Some life cycles are extremely long, such as those for the safety pin or the hairpin. Others, such as those for electronic calculators, computers, digital cameras, and other electronic products, are extremely short. However, no product or service can be offered in one form forever.

A company does not introduce a new product only because it is forced to do so. Some of the possible reasons for a company's decision to offer something new follows:

- Your product has become noncompetitive because improvements in competitive products have rendered yours obsolete.

- The use for which your product was created has either disappeared or has gone into decline.

- Your product may be related to some phase of the national or local economy. Nationally, this may be war or peace; locally, this may be heavy industry, the military, energy, agriculture, or any other facet of economic life.

- A new product may be desirable to take up excess capacity in your manufacturing plant.

- You may have surplus capital that you wish to utilize for additional profits.

- You may find the opportunity to utilize by-products and materials in the manufacture of other products.

- You may want to make maximum use of your sales organization and have additional products that allow you to amortize these overhead costs over a broader base.

- You may be in a business that has cycles, known as peaks and valleys, either due to seasonal fluctuations or ordering phases. Sometimes down turns can be leveled out by the use of new products that sell during the valleys.

- You may wish to make use of marginal or partly used manpower or other facilities.

As noted earlier, the mortality of new product ideas is extremely high. Alan A. Smith, of the consulting firm of Arthur D. Little, Inc., of Cambridge, Massachusetts, researched the experience of 20 companies concerned with successful new product development. He found that there were 540 possibilities in the idea stage that were considered for research. Of these, 448 were eliminated during initial screening of items that should be pursued. This left 92 products that were selected for preliminary laboratory investigation. Only 8 of the 92 appeared sufficiently promising to warrant development, and 7 of the 8 were dropped as nonsalable, or unprofitable, as determined during some process of development or introduction into the marketplace. Only 1 of these 7, or 1 out of the original 540 idea possibilities, was placed in regular production.

While many possibilities for new ideas and new products should be considered, you can see that 92 to 1 or even 8 to 1 is not a terrific success ratio, and much money was wasted finding the one product that was successful. In this chapter, you see how to increase your new product's success ratio dramatically. The worksheets provided at the end of this chapter should help you to do this.

Sources for New Products

How can you find new products? Any of these sources may give you a new product idea to make you a fortune:

1. *Currently successful products:* Look at currently successful products, but be careful not to copy them. Copy only the concept. If you copy the idea exactly, you may be in violation of the law if the idea is covered by a patent or copyright. But, even if you don't copy an idea exactly, if your product is very much like another one, the individual who has introduced the product into the market has already captured a fair share, and you are in the position of trying to take away that share. A currently successful product may also give you an idea for an entirely new product, which satisfies the same need, but is even better.

2. *Inventor shows:* Many inventors are not good marketers. In fact, most inventions that are patented never actually go into production, or if they do, they fail in the marketplace. At inventor shows, you see hundreds of new products that the inventors offer to license for someone else to manufacture for a royalty, or they may even sell the invention outright. You can find the inventor shows in your area by contacting your local chamber of commerce. Or you can go to http://inventors.about.com/od/eventsconventions/index_a.htm for a listing of the major inventor shows worldwide.

3. *Foreign products:* Foreign products are not always available in the United States, and frequently these products, which are unfamiliar here, may have a large market and sell quite well. Every country likes to see the number of its exports increase. This points to a primary source of foreign products: the commercial attachés of foreign consulates and embassies. If you live in or near a large city, you can find the numbers of foreign consulates or embassies in the telephone book. Another source is the *Directory of United States Importers* (Piers Publishing Group 400 Windsor Corporate Park, 50 Millstone Road, Suite 200, East Windsor, NJ 08520-1415; 877-203-5277). In your local library, you may find various directories of importers and exporters for various countries. Check in the reference or business section of your library.

4. *Newspapers:* Read the business opportunity section of your local paper as well as publications such as the *Wall Street Journal.* Frequently, individuals who have a product to sell may advertise. You can contact them to negotiate the best deal possible for a product that may be successful. In addition, you may consider advertising in these publications yourself, or in trade magazines, stating that you are interested in acquiring certain types of new products.

5. *Local manufacturers:* Many manufacturers have created a product at one time or another that was not successful for his or her particular line of work or business, but which you may be able to make very successful. Simply call the president of each company and ask whether any old tooling exists for discontinued products from your line. Sometimes you can buy this tooling very cheaply, for perhaps only a couple hundred dollars, even though it may be worth $40,000 or more. This is one of Joe Cossman's secrets that helped to make him a multimillionaire. He frequently purchased old tooling from manufacturers, turned the product around, and made a fortune with it. Among the products acquired in this way were his famous Potato Spud Gun and Flippy the Frogman, both toy products that made him money all over the world.

6. *National Aviation and Space Administration's Tech Briefs:* This information is released periodically by the National Aviation and Space Administration (NASA). The briefs describe new ideas, concepts, and patents for by-products of the space program. All of these are available for licensing from NASA. Nowadays, NASA partners with industry to disseminate this information. Visit these web sites: http://technology.nasa.gov/ and http://www.nasatech.com.

7. *Patent abstracts bibliography:* This semiannual publication lists NASA- and government-owned patents and applications for patents as a service to those seeking new licensable products for the commercial market. This may be ordered from the NASA Center for Aerospace Information, 7121 Standard Drive, Hanover, MD 21076-1320. Their telephone number is (301) 621-0390. You can also order online at http://www.sti.nasa.gov/Pubs/Patents/Patents.html.

8. *New products from corporations:* You can write or contact major U.S. corporations. Most have research and development divisions that develop products the corporation has no interest in producing or selling. As a result, many have established special offices to market the licensing of their patents to individuals outside of their company. The titles of these individuals vary; however, you can usually get in touch with them by contacting any corporation that is large enough to have a research and development division and asking for the director of patent licensing.

9. *Distress merchandise:* Every retailer has been in a situation where certain merchandise could not be sold. Under these circumstances, he cuts the price tremendously and then attempts to sell it at a bargain rate. This material is called *distress merchandise.* When you see distress merchandise, if you think that you have a market for it, look at the product and see if there is a patent number on it. If there is, you can locate the inventor by purchasing a copy of the patent from the patent office. Or, if you live close to a depository for patents, you can look at the patent and find out the inventor's name and address at no cost. As mentioned earlier, inventors are frequently poor marketers, and the fact that this is distress merchandise indicates that if the inventor still controls the patent, he or she may well be interested in licensing or outright selling. Write to get patent information at U.S. Patent and Trademark Office Mail Stop USPTO Contact Center, P.O. Box 1450, Alexandria, VA 22313-1450, or go to their web site at http://www.uspto.gov.

10. *The Official Gazette of the U.S. Patent Office:* This bulletin is published weekly and lists all the patents granted by the patent office. Annual subscriptions are available from the Superintendent of Documents, U.S. Government Printing Office, 732 N. Capitol Street, NW, Washington, DC 20401. The gazette contains a section that lists one-time-only patents available for sale or licensing. Many libraries also subscribe to the *Official Gazette* of the U.S. Patent Office or are a federal depository of U.S. patents. You can also view weekly patents issued online at http://www.uspto.gov/web/patents/patog. Also, patent attorneys in your area may know of new products recently patented and available for licensing.

11. *Expired patents:* In the United States, a patent is good for only 17 years. The only exception is an ornamental design patent, which is good or 3½,

7, or 14 years. After that period, the patent is in the public domain and may be produced and sold by anyone. Also, you can look at the entire technology of any general product area by writing the patent office and asking for a list of all the patent numbers falling into a specified product area. The patent office charges you for this service, but once you have the list of umbers you can go to a federal depository of patents, which is usually located in a major library. All you need to do then is look up the patent number and you can get the full information. If the patent on the invention has expired, you are free to do as you want. If it has not expired, you may approach the inventor outright (getting his name and address from the patent) about licensing or purchasing the idea. See the earlier addresses and web sites to do this.

12. *Trade shows:* Like inventor shows, trade shows have hundreds of products, many of which may be of interest to you. The U.S. Department of Commerce lists trade shows both domestic and international at http://www.export.gov /tradeevents.html. Or you may ask your local chamber of commerce about upcoming trade shows. Your library may have directories of trade shows in the reference section. Also, see Chapter 13.

13. *Old items from magazines:* If you look through an old Sears or Montgomery Ward catalog, you notice that many of the products described therein are still of tremendous interest. You can also get good ideas from old magazines. Old mail-order products are especially well suited for reissue. An afternoon spent in the library looking at old magazines may give you an idea, which you may use as is or one to which you can give a new twist. Some of these products look to be on the "cutting-edge," yet are 50 years old or older!

14. *Personalizing items:* People like to see items and like to buy items that have their names on them. This idea has been used again and again, every single day, to sell products of all sorts: From brass business card cases sold through the *Wall Street Journal* to briefcases, wallets, address labels, paperweights, and even cookies, sold through all media types. Do some research, because the field is far from exhausted. If you can find a product on which you can imprint someone's name, you probably have a profitable product.

15. *Commercial banks:* If you acquire all or part of another business, you may also acquire the products that that business controls. Many small companies find outstanding products that may need the strength that your company can provide to become successful. This strength may have to do with personnel, facilities, equipment, know-how, marketing, or capital. Frequently, commercial banks know of such a situation and can arrange the meeting between you and someone with a product that you might be interested in. The bank does this for no charge with the expectation of receiving banking business that might ensue from some sort of an arrangement.

16. *Small Business Investment Companies (SBICs) and investment bankers:* These companies are continually examining potential businesses, all of which have products of one sort or another. If you contact SBICs and investment bankers, they might well lead you to new products or an equity position in a business that has products, which are desirable for your firm. You can obtain the latest list of SBICs from your local SBA office or go to http://www.sbaonline .sba.gov/INV on the Internet.

17. *Licensing brokers:* A licensing broker is a type of consultant having a wide range of contacts in the licensing field. They represent companies seeking licenses; that is, companies with products that they wish to license, as well as companies searching for products to license. They often have considerable experience in developing fair and reasonable licensing arrangements and can advise you or their client along these lines. You can locate licensing brokers through patent attorneys, in the telephone book, and sometimes in your local newspapers under the "Business Opportunities" heading.

18. *The Thomas Register of Manufacturers:* This publication consists of several volumes listing manufacturers of all types of items in the United States. There are several such directories, and you can find them at your local library. You may find not only the names and addresses of the individuals running these companies but also products that are available and the individuals to write to about obtaining them. Every single page is a source of another potential product for your business. You can also access them online at http://www.thomasregister.com.

How to Decide Which New Product to Develop or Introduce

As you begin thinking about new product introduction and development, you will discover that there are many products among which to choose. Of course, you can't develop them all; the problem then is deciding which products are best for your company. You may think that this is fairly easy; you simply introduce those products that bring you the most profit. However, the choice is not easy. You may have limited financial resources and a more profitable product has to be passed over in favor of one that you can afford. Or, it may be important to you to recoup your investment rapidly. Then, too, you must consider the particular background and experience you have, either with the type of product or with marketplaces. For these reasons, the worksheets that follow this chapter are extremely important before you commit money and time to a particular product or service.

In general, the worksheets list the following factors that you must consider in comparing potential new products for development and for which you must obtain factual information or forecasts:

- Total profit.
- Profitability.
- The cost to develop.
- The market for the product.
- The life cycle, including estimated length.
- The cost of research and development.
- The plant overcapacity or undercapacity.
- The synergistic effect with other products in your product line.
- The cost of putting the product on the market.
- Technical know-how required.
- Labor skills required.
- Availability of raw materials.
- By-products that may be sold from the manufacture of this product.
- Goodwill.
- Marketing know-how available.
- Physical distribution facilities.
- Available distribution channels.

Deciding which product or service to introduce is no five-minute task, but the time and effort invested is worthwhile. You want the product or service you select to be a success. Now, we are getting down to the serious assessment of spending money for one project over another. The end results are those potential products you introduce and those you do not. First, list what factors you plan to use for comparison, those that you think are most important: high return on investment, a proprietary position, a large market share, low risk of failure in development, low risk of failure in marketing, huge demand, and so forth. Certain quantitative methods of comparison are also recommended. For example, you can calculate the total profit of a particular project if you can estimate its life cycle by using either the present value or internal rate of return methods shown you for comparison in the financial section of this book. You can compare the return for each investment or each project, by dividing the projected return by the investment and choosing those projects that have the larger return. If time to recoup your investment is important, compare using the payback formula, investment divided by the return per year. All of these various quantitative and nonquantitative comparisons need to be considered. You can use Worksheet 9.4 to do this.

How to Beat Your Competition in New Product or Services

You may feel that because you are a small firm you have little or no chance to beat your larger competitors, especially in introducing a new product or a new service. This is wrong, and very frequently a small firm can win out over its competition. Here's how.

Ability to Make Decisions Fast

A small company, where one person or a few people make decisions, has an extremely big advantage in terms of time. Larger companies act slowly, because of a bureaucracy and many levels in the managerial chain of command, when making even simple decisions, while you can operate much more rapidly and efficiently. It is not unusual for a small firm to make a decision in one day that takes a large firm several months or a year or more to make.

Lower Break-Even Point

Because a smaller firm carries a much lower overhead, the break-even point for your introduction of a new product or a new service is much lower than that of a larger firm. Also, because as a smaller firm you can be more efficient, your break-even point can be lower than that of a larger competitor. As a result, many large firms cannot introduce certain new products or services unless the volume is sufficiently large. Alternatively, you are able to introduce products or services to service a smaller market. A volume that is tremendously profitable for you may be unprofitable for a larger company.

Regional Sales

For the same reason, many small firms can serve a specific region in their locality and provide much better customer service and a far more effective and efficient promotional effort than can their larger competitors. This is the reason that many local areas have their own brands of beer and other commodities. Further, in this local area, the small company frequently outsells the larger competitor many times over.

Custom-Made Products

Large firms, because of their volume requirements, frequently cannot do custom work. And for the same reason, quality sometimes suffers. This leaves a nice niche for the smaller company that can do custom work with individuals or other companies that desire this type of product or service. Because of this, some small companies absolutely monopolize the custom-made quality markets in their industries. They charge high prices and make huge profit margins because they have developed this market, a market their bigger competitors cannot reach.

Sources of Additional Information

Books

Corporate Strategy and New Product Innovation, edited by Robert R. Rothberg, published by Free Press.

Creativity in Product Innovation, by Jacob Goldenberg and David Mazursky, published by Cambridge University Press.

Developing New Products in Half the Time, 2nd ed., by Preston G. Smith and Donald G. Reinertsen, published by John Wiley & Sons.

Handbook of New Product Development, by Peter Hilton, published by Prentice-Hall.

Innovation, by Milton D. Rosenau Jr, published by Lifetime Learning Publications, a division of Wadsworth.

Innovation, by Richard Foster, published by Summit Books, a division of Simon & Schuster.

Lateral Marketing: New Techniques for Finding Breakthrough Ideas, by Phillip Kotler and Fernando Trias de Bes, published by John Wiley & Sons.

New Product Development Strategies, by Frederick D. Buggie, published by AMACOM.

Planning New Products, by Philip Marvin, published by Penton Publishing Co.

Product Planning, edited by A. Edward Spitz, published by Auerbach Publishers.

Internet

Note: Because Internet sites frequently go down, multiple sites are listed for similar subject matter.

New Product Development. Wikipedia provides this free article of new product development at http://en.wikipedia.org/wiki/New_product_development.

New Product Introduction (NPI). Better Product Design provides a complete discussion with links pertaining to management of the new product development process at http://www.betterproductdesign.net/npi.

Product Development Forum by DRM Associates and PD-Trak Solutions. New Product Development, concurrent engineering, IPD, QFD, target costing, and DFM information, best practices, resources and links at http://www.npd-solutions.com/pdforum.html.

Product and Service Management by Carter McNamara. Discussion and many links pertaining to activities necessary in the development of new products at http://www.mapnp.org/library/prod_mng/prod_mng.htm#anchor1332959.

Product Development and Management Association. The PDMA organization's web site is devoted to the study and practice of new product development. Also, provides the "PDMA Glossary for New Product Development" at http://www.pdma.org/library/glossary.html.

DOWNLOADABLE WORKSHEET 9.1
Important Questions to Ask Yourself Before Developing a New Product[1]

Your Company Strengths	Yes	No
Is manufacturing your company's strength?		
Are your production personnel highly skilled?		
Do you prefer a product with a high ratio of labor to production costs?		
Do you have skilled industrial design expertise available?		
Do you have production equipment currently available?		
Is your production equipment currently underutilized?		
Do you currently have a strong sales force?		
Is your current product line too limited?		
Do you have a competitive advantage in a particular technology?		
Do you have significant cash or credit resources available?		
Do you have a reputation for high quality?		
Do you have a reputation for low cost or high value?		
Market Preference		
Do you prefer a particular industry?		
Do you prefer a product sold to retail consumers?		
Do you prefer a product sold to industrial users?		
Do you prefer a product sold to the government?		
Do you prefer a product with long usage?		
Do you prefer fad products?		
Do you prefer a consumable item?		
Do you prefer a particular method of distribution?		
Would you consider a product limited to a particular locality?		
Do you prefer a product for a specialty market?		
Do you prefer a product sold through mass merchandising?		
Do you intend to sell your product abroad?		
Have you determined the break-even point for this new product?		
Have you determined the return on investment (ROI) for this new product?		
Have you determined the payback period (how long it will take to recoup your investment for this new product)?		

[1] Based on a checklist originally developed by John B. Lang and published in *Finding a New Product for Your Company,* by the U.S. Small Business Administration.

To customize this document, download it to your hard drive from the John Wiley & Sons web site at www.wiley .com/go/cohenentrepreneur. The document can then be opened, edited, and printed using Microsoft Word or another popular word processing application.

(continued)

	Yes	No
Is price range important to be consistent with your present or planned business?		
Have you set sales volume objectives over the next three years?		
At what sales volume does a product exceed your company's capability?		
Product Status		
Is the source of the new product idea important to you?		
Will you accept a product that cannot be protected through patent or copyright?		
Are you willing to license a patent, process, etc., from someone else?		
Are you willing to develop an idea or concept to a patentable stage?		
Are you willing to accept a product that has previously failed in the marketplace?		
Are you willing to enter a joint venture with another company?		
Would you merge with or buy a company that has good products but needs your company's strengths?		
The Product Configuration		
Are there any maximum size limitations to a product you can manufacture?		
Are there any weight or size limitations?		
Is production time a factor?		
Do you prefer a product made of a certain material?		
Are there any manufacturing processes important to the type of product you select?		
Is quality control a significant factor?		
Finance		
Have you established an overall budget for this product?		
Have individual budgets been established for finding, acquiring, developing, market researching, manufacturing, and marketing the new product?		
Has a time period been established by which a new product must become self-supporting, profitable, or capable of generating cash?		
Does the new product require a certain profit margin to be compatible with your financial resources or company objectives?		
Has external long-range financing been explored for your new product?		
Have you determined average inventory to sales ratio for the new product?		
Have you determined average aging of accounts receivable for your new product?		
Does the product have seasonal aspects?		

Screening questions act as a filter to eliminate products that you shouldn't even consider before you waste a lot of time, money, or other resources. Your answers to these questions can lead to a well thought-out guide for the acceptability of any potential new product. A short, condensed profile helps communicate your needs. Such a profile also indicates a high degree of professional management that sources of new products will welcome.

Company Operations

- How compatible is the product concept with the current product lines? _____
- Does it represent an environmental hazard or threat to your production facility and to the facilities of your neighbors? _____
- Would it unreasonably interrupt manufacturing, engineering, or marketing activities? _____
- Could you meet the after-sale service requirements that would be demanded by customers? _____

Potential Market

- What is the size of the potential market? _____
- Where is the market located? _____
- What would be your potential market share? _____
- How diversified is the need for the product? Is it a one-industry or multiindustry product? _____
  _____
- How fast do you anticipate the market for the concept to grow? _____
- How stable would such a market be in a recession? _____

Concept Marketability

- Who would be your competitors? _____
- How good is their product? _____
- How well capitalized are potential competitors? _____
- How important is their product to the survival of their business? _____
- How is your product differentiated from the competition's? Will the differentiation provide a market advantage? _____
  _____
- Could you meet or beat the competition's price? _____
- Is the product normally sold through your current distribution channels or would you have to make special arrangements? _____
- Do you have qualified sales personnel? _____
- Do you have suitable means by which to promote the product? _____
- What would you anticipate to be the life expectancy of the product? Is it going to move through the various life cycle stages in six months, six years or sixty years? _____
  _____
- Will the product be offensive to the environment in which it will be used? _____

---

[1] Adapted from Tom W. White, "Use Variety of Internal, External Sources to Gather and Screen New Product Ideas," *Marketing News,* September 10, 1983, p. 12.

To customize this document, download it to your hard drive from the John Wiley & Sons web site at www.wiley .com/go/cohenentrepreneur. The document can then be opened, edited, and printed using Microsoft Word or another popular word processing application.

(continued)

Engineering and Production

- What is the technical feasibility of the product? _____
- Do you have the technical capability to design it? _____
- Can it be manufactured at a marketable cost? _____
- Will the necessary production materials be readily available? _____
- Do you have the production capabilities to build it? _____
- Do you have adequate storage facilities for the raw materials and completed product? _____
- Do you have adequate testing devices for proper quality control of the product? _____

Financial

- What is your required return on investment (ROI)? _____
- What is your anticipated ROI for this product? _____
- Do you have the available capital? _____
- What would be the pay-back period? _____
- What is your break-even point? _____

Legal

- Is the product patentable or is some other means of protecting your exclusivity available? _____
  _____
- Can we meet legal restrictions regarding labeling, advertising, shipment, etc.? _____
- How significant are product warranty problems likely to be? _____
- Is the product vulnerable to existing or pending legislation? _____

DOWNLOADABLE WORKSHEET 9.3
Quick Go-No-Go Checklist

1. Does this product or service fit your needs, interests, background, and abilities? _____

2. What is your realistic assessment of the chance of success? _____

3. Do you know where to obtain the services of everyone needed to complete this project? _____

4. What advantage(s) will this product or service have over the competing products or services?

   _____

   _____

   _____

5. Is there a real market for the new or improved product or service? _____

6. Is this market profitable and will you be able to defend it easily against competitors? _____

   _____

7. Do you really know how you will sell and distribute this product or service? _____

   _____

8. Does the product or service fit with your present line, or if you are not currently in business, can you easily expand this product or service into a full line? _____

   _____

9. Will the product fill a permanent or long-term need, or will it be a fad product or service? (Note: You can make money either way, but it is important that you know up front.) _____

   _____

10. Can the product be made with the your present equipment? If not, what will be the tooling cost and how soon and how easily will you be able to recoup your investment? _____

    _____

DOWNLOADABLE WORKSHEET 9.4
Selecting Products or Services from Many Opportunities

Step 1. Decide the relative importance of the factors listed. Assign a percentage value of importance to each. The total percentages for all factors must equal 100%. You may assign a value of 0% for factors that are completely unimportant. You may also add to the list of factors.

Step 2. Look at each factor individually. For each factor assign 0 to 10 points. Those products that seem very good in relation to a particular factor receive 10 points. Those that are very poor receive 0 points. Complete a separate sheet below for each product.

Step 3. Multiply the relative importance percentage by the points assigned for each factor. Put the results in the final value column.

Step 4. Add the final values for each factor and arrive at a total product/service value for that product or service.

Step 5. Repeat this process for each product or service being compared.

Step 6. Compare total product/service values for all products and services. That product or service with the highest total product/service value is the one that you should introduce.

Product or Service _____

Factors	Relative Importance Percentage	Point Value	Final Value
Demand for product			
Strength			
Period			
Need			
Market			
Size			
Location			
Competition			
Product			
Compatibility with current line			
Uniqueness of features			
Price			
Protection			

Factors	Relative Importance Percentage	Point Value	Final Value
Company strengths			
Marketing			
Location			
Special facilities			
Production			
Financial considerations			
Capital budgeting			
Return on investment (ROI)			
Payback			
Cash flow			
Product development			
Technical risk			
Producibility			
Scheduling			
Totals	100%	⇐	**Total Product/ Service Value**

Things to Consider if a New Product/Service Introduction Is Failing

If things are going wrong, action should be taken as soon as possible to correct the problem. If any of the following occur as you begin new product introduction or development, stop, heed, and take action as soon as possible.

Source of Warning Signal Feedback	Feedback	Action to Take	Action Notes
Consumer	Price	Find out if price is too low or too high and adjust price	
Consumer	Hard to use product	Modify product or educate	
Consumer	Not convinced of value	Modify advertising/promotion	
Retailer or Wholesaler	Low rate of turnover	Increase consumer advertising/ promotion	
Retailer or Wholesaler	Fear of loss of current sales	Increase trade advertising and address issue	
Retailer or Wholesaler	Potential servicing problems	Modify product or address through promotion/person	
Retailer or Wholesaler	Field already crowded	Increase trade advertising and promotion to address issue	
Retailer or Wholesaler	Hard to ship or display in store	Redesigning packaging or store display	
Retailer or Wholesaler	Product needs demonstration	Consider demonstration alternatives	
You	Difficult to get right materials for production	Focus on this issue	
You	Raw materials subject to price fluctuations or scarcity	Buy in larger quantities	
You	Production could slow down other products	Analyze alternatives and make decision	
You	Patent protection may not be possible	Consider alternative means of protection including getting to market first and establishing position	
You	Product difficult for person to demonstrate	Modify/change demonstration	
You	Competitor dominates market	Consider a niching strategy where you will dominate a small segment	

CHAPTER 10

How to Price Your Products and Services for Maximum Profits

It is important to realize that it is the market, and not your costs, that ultimately determines the price at which you can sell your product or service. Your costs only establish a floor below which you cannot sell your product or service and make any money. Therefore, in determining the price for your product or service, the relevant price is somewhere between the price floor that you established with your cost data and the price ceiling that is the maximum amount for which you could possibly sell your product or service.

The Importance of the Pricing Decision

The decision of what price to charge for your product or service has a major influence in several important areas, which include the following:

- *Profit:* The price you select determines how much profit you make.
- *Recouping your investment:* The price at which you decide to sell your product or service determines how quickly you are able to recover the investment you made in developing and marketing your product or service.
- *Resources available for promotion:* Your price helps determine the amount of financial resources you have at any given time to compete in the marketplace.
- *Ability to penetrate a new market:* The price you select determines whether you are successful in getting your product introduced into a new market.
- *Image:* The price you select creates an image of the product and of your business. A high price usually implies status and quality. A low price may imply economy or value, but be careful as it could also imply low quality.

The Emphasis on Nonprice Competition

Because price is important in determining the success of a business, you would think that every single business owner and manager devotes a great deal of thought to pricing. However, this is not true. One reason is that, even in today's economy, many consumers have much larger disposable incomes than in the past. Therefore, price may be of less importance, depending on what you are selling. Also, with the sophisticated marketing techniques that are available today, many marketers feel that they don't need to use price to attract consumers. Some businesspeople give little thought to price because they are simply unaware of the sensitivity of demand in the marketplace to making changes in price, either upward or downward.

Perhaps, those most aware are dealing in direct-response marketing, or testing of all types, including the testing of different prices. Along these lines, I once sold a four-volume set of booklets on how to become published as a writer through the mail for $19.95. During testing I reduced the price to $14.95, wondering whether the increased number of sales would make up for the loss in contribution of each individual set sold. I assumed that sales would go up as price was reduced. The results were quite surprising. Not only did I lose money because of the $5 differential in price for each unit sold, but the total number of sales actually went down. When I increased the price to $19.95, sales went up and returned to their former level.

Some businesspeople avoid serious pricing decisions because they feel there are fewer worries if they maintain a single stable price. This way they don't have to change the prices of the items in their literature or catalog, they don't have to reevaluate inventories for accounting, and they don't have to renegotiate contracts. To them, price just isn't worth the worry. I hope to convince you that this is not a good way to handle pricing. The fact that many business owners do not seriously price their products or services gives you an opportunity to make a great deal of money and win out over your competition by doing so. Therefore, it is always in your interests to consider price an important weapon in your marketing arsenal.

When Should You Consider Pricing or Repricing?

You should consider pricing or repricing what you are selling at any time, but especially in the following circumstances:

- When you are introducing a new product or products.
- When there is an interrelated addition to your product line which may affect the pricing of older items already in the line.

- When you wish to penetrate a new market.
- When the competition has changed its price.
- During periods of inflation.
- During periods of depression.
- When you are about to change your strategy.
- When you are testing to find the correct price.
- When the product is in a different part of its life cycle.

The Economic Theory of Pricing

Now it is useful to know a little pricing theory. According to economic theory, price is determined according to the downward-sloping demand curve as shown in Figure 10.1. As prices increase, a smaller quantity of the product or service is demanded by potential customers. The implication of the downward slope of the demand curve is that it takes a lower price to sell more. Now, look at the demand curve, D + 3, which is higher than the other demand curves, D + 2 and D + 1. If you started with a lower demand curve, for the same price, now you can sell more products. To get this new demand curve, you must take some additional action. This could be increased advertising or

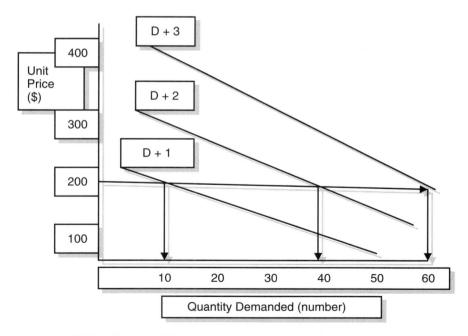

FIGURE 10.1   The Downward Shopping Demand Curve

a sweepstakes or some other form of promotion. However, at the same price you may also sell fewer products if the demand curve drops to D + 1 as shown in Figure 10.1. This can happen, for example, if the introduction of a new technology causes obsolescence of your product. When the slide rule was first replaced by the handheld calculator, the demand curve shifted to successively lower and lower demand curves. Eventually the slide rule could no longer be sold at a profit.

Now, even though this is true, a firm can sometimes charge more and sell more product; this is what happened with the mail order product mentioned earlier. This is true because of selective demand for a specific product and the way the product is perceived. Some factors here are distinctive features, perceived value, and status.

How to Price a New Product

Let us look first at perhaps one of the most difficult pricing tasks that any manager of a small business or even a giant business faces: the pricing of a new product that is not yet in the market. To price a new product, there are three steps that you must take. These are as follows:

1. Determine your objective in pricing.
2. Find the demand versus the price.
3. Determine your basic pricing strategy.

Determining Your Objective   In any pricing decision that you make, you should think about what your overall objective is. Research in the United States showed that pricing decisions were made primarily for the following five business objectives:

1. To see a return on investment.
2. To stabilize price and profit margin.
3. To capture a target market share.
4. To meet or prevent competition.
5. To maximize profit.

These pricing objectives show that your pricing decision should be based on a combination of goals which are internal to your company and the external market environment.

How to Estimate Demand versus Price   Now that your basic objectives have been established, you must find some way to estimate the demand versus the price. The following methods have all been found effective in estimating this demand.

- *Ask customers:* From asking a sufficient number of customers about various potential prices, you get some idea of how much of your product can be sold at each price. You may also learn the percentages of your potential customers who buy at each price. For example, a survey may show that 80 percent of your customers would buy the product if the price were $5, 20 percent if $7, and 10 percent if $10. This information also gives you some indication of the profits that you might expect. The drawback here is that people do not always respond truthfully. See Chapter 8 on marketing research for more details about this.

- *Comparison with substitutes or a replacement item:* We may compare the item that we are going to introduce with similar items that are on the market today—what their prices are and how many are selling at those prices. If the product is totally new, then we may try to find a product, which it is replacing. For example, if we are introducing a new type of electronic watch, we may derive some initial price demand curves from the old design.

- *Cost savings:* Sometimes, especially with industrial products, a price can be calculated based on the cost savings possible with the adoption of a new product. If you are going to price in this fashion, it is important for you to promote the cost savings to your prospective customers.

- *Test marketing:* Test marketing of the product is an outstanding way to derive demand versus product price. All that is necessary is that the product be offered at various prices to the same market. Because this type of testing requires the customer actually to put money on the barrelhead for the product, it is much more accurate than simply asking the potential customer whether he or she would purchase your product.

Once quantitative figures can be established for demand at various prices that we may set, we consider the various pricing strategies that may be adopted.

Determining Your Pricing Strategies   For a new product, there are three basic pricing strategies:

1. A high-price strategy, or a skimming strategy.
2. A low-price strategy, or a penetration strategy.
3. A meet-the-competition price strategy.

SKIMMING PRICE STRATEGY   This strategy is used when the product is so new that there is little or no competition, or when you wish to give the product status through the price. You can skim the market using the high price, and later on, when competition enters the market, you reduce the price to meet the competition. Such a strategy also enables you to have more resources available to meet the competition when that day comes.

PENETRATION STRATEGY   This strategy is used to get into a new market by going in at a very low price. Some people try your product simply because your price is significantly lower than the price that the competition is charging. Naturally, you must be very careful when using this strategy because of the implications regarding quality and the possibility of getting stuck with a low status image. Also, maintaining the low price with a lower contribution to profit margin means very, very high volume sales, which cannot always be achieved. Many companies using this strategy do so only to get the product tried by prospective customers, and then, once a sufficient number has adopted it, the price is raised and the strategy changed to a meet-the-competition price or an even higher price.

A MEET-THE-COMPETITION STRATEGY   According to this strategy, you are going to price your product or service at the same price as the competition. If you are going to do this, you must have something else unique or people do not switch from the competition to your company unless they are thoroughly dissatisfied with the competition for some other reason. For example, perhaps you set the same price as your competition, but the quality of your product is much higher and the reliability of your product is better; or your service is better and your employees more friendly. The point is that you must offer something different, something more than your competition, or people have no reason to switch.

Second Phase Pricing

After you have introduced a new product or service and it is established in the marketplace, you may want to change it. Perhaps you introduced a product that was totally new and for which you have no patent or other protection. After some time, the competition enters the market with its new products, which are similar to yours. Perhaps they are using a penetration price, or some price that is lower than the one that you are offering. How do you react to this tactic, which could result in a potential loss of your market? As mentioned earlier, perhaps your product has gone rapidly through the life cycle. Let us say you are selling a PDA, computer, or digital camera that technology has now rendered obsolete. You may make the decision to do a remainder sale and sell everything out at a fraction of its initial high price, perhaps even at or below your cost. Whatever second phase strategy you work out, you must begin to think ahead even as you introduce a new product. What can you do as the product becomes obsolete?

Here is an excellent example of a second phase strategy. The individual who used it actually increased his price when the competition entered with a penetration price. During one summer season, marketing genius Joe Cossman introduced the now common garden sprinkler—a hose with hundreds of tiny holes placed in a flexible tubing to allow water to sprinkle the grass or flowers in any desired pattern. This unique plastic hose was easily duplicated in production. Moreover, no patent protection was possible. Therefore, Cossman expected and had many competitors during the second summer season. However, Cossman's method of distribution was not to sell direct but instead to sell through supermarkets to which he gave a 50 percent discount from retail price. Instead of reducing his price when the competition came in, Joe actually increased his retail price. He passed the increased profit margin on to his distributors, the supermarkets. This increased their profits, and at the same time the image of the Cossman sprinkler was that it was of higher quality than the competitors' products. Added to that, the supermarkets had dealt with Cossman and his product the previous year. They knew he was reliable. Cossman's innovative price strategy extended the time that he controlled the market, and he made more profit the second year with competition than he did the first year without it. Always think through your situation regarding distribution and other important factors in developing an innovative pricing decision.

What to Do If No One Buys

If the market does not take your product or your service at the price you have established to cover your costs and to allow you to make a desired profit, you have five alternatives:

1. *Lower the price:* This means you are accepting less profit in the hope that more of your product or service is purchased.
2. *Increase the price:* This means that you are repositioning your product as compared with that of the competition, so your product is perceived by your potential customers as being of higher quality or better in some other fashion.
3. *Reduce your costs:* In this way, you can maintain the price and still be profitable with the amount that you are selling.
4. *Drop the product completely:* This may sound drastic, but sometimes it is the wisest course.

5. *Differentiate your product from that of your competition:* This is the same sort of thing you must do if you establish a meet-the-competition price for a new product. That is, you emphasize quality, service, product performance, delivery time, financing arrangements, discounting, or some other aspect of importance to your customer.

Pricing Policies

There are three basic pricing policy categories:

1. *Single price:* You have one price for all buyers regardless of timing, quantity, and other factors.
2. *Variable price:* Price is always open to negotiation.
3. *Nonvariable price:* You offer the same price to all under similar conditions. Of course, under different conditions a different price is offered.

A single price has few advantages. The single price policy is used most frequently when selling to consumers or when selling to other small-purchase customers. The policy is easy to administer, and the emphasis then is always on nonprice appeals including all types of promotion such as face-to-face salespeople. This policy is not attractive to individuals or businesses who buy in large quantity.

When selling to customers who make quantity purchases, it is important to understand when it is best to have a nonvariable pricing policy or a variable pricing policy.

As noted earlier, a variable price can be negotiated. This means, you can make adjustments to your price instantly during the process of negotiation. Also, you can be flexible in your dealings. Whatever the competition does can be countered immediately, and you can easily respond to other changes in the marketplace during the negotiation process. Finally, you can vary your appeal to be based on price or nonprice promotionals according to the situation.

However, a variable pricing policy also has disadvantages. Because the resulting price charged is different from one customer to another, the potential exists for bad feelings on the part of those customers who pay more for the same product or service. Also, for very large contracts, it takes time to negotiate. It is often said that time is money, and when your own time or the time of valuable people resources in your firm is spent, costs could be significant. Sometimes having a variable price means that you are not be able to negotiate yourself, in which case you must delegate the pricing decision to someone working for you.

This means loss of your control over the pricing in your firm to a certain degree. The potential also exists for abuse in this delegation because some of your people may resort to what amounts to price-cutting instead of actually selling. Finally, there are some legal complications which may result, growing out of a law known as the Robinson-Patman Act. We discuss the implications of this act for a variable pricing policy shortly.

A nonvariable price has advantages as well. Clearly, it simplifies the selling process because no one except you has any authority to vary the prices. There is an ease of administering such a policy, and it is clearly fair to all buyers. Naturally, you avoid any legal complications of having a variable price, and you, of course, maintain control over the pricing decision.

Discount Policies

Discount policies can also affect sales in a very dramatic fashion. One entrepreneur, the inventor of a unique item used by pilots, lost thousands of dollars in potential orders from the government because he had no discount policy. Discount policy may be classified in the following ways:

- A *promotional discount:* This means special discounts to the consumer or perhaps within your distribution or organization to promote your product or your service.
- A *trade discount:* This is a discount on the basis of the position in the distribution channel, such as a discount offered to a retailer or a wholesaler if you are a manufacturer, or anyone between you and the ultimate consumer of your product or service.
- A *quantity discount to encourage large orders:* There are two types of quantity discounts. One is a noncumulative type, which is based purely on the quantity ordered at a specific period of time. Another is the cumulative discount, which is increased depending on quantities ordered by the same buyer over an indefinite period of time. Cumulative discounts tend to tie the buyer to the seller.

The Robinson-Patman Act of 1936

The Robinson-Patman Act deals with price discrimination. Its intent is to regulate any tendency to injure competition. The implication is clear for any of your pricing policy decisions, and either the Federal Trade Commission or a private complainant can initiate action against you for your pricing policies if you sell at different prices to two or more competing customers engaged in interstate commerce and your acts have a tendency to injure competition. Now, there are certain defenses against these accusations. For example, it is not a violation of the act if you are selling at different prices because of cost differences, or if you have to lower the price to one customer to meet the competition, or if you have to lower the price because of changing market conditions. When in doubt, consult your attorney.

Sources of Additional Information

Books

Power Pricing, by Robert Doan and Hermann Simon, published by Free Press.

Price and Price Policies, by Walton Hamilton, published by McGraw-Hill.

Pricing Decisions in Small Business, by W. Warren Haynes, published by University of Kentucky Press.

Pricing for Profit, by Curtis W. Symonds, published by AMACOM.

Pricing for Marketing Executives, by Alfred R. Oxenfeldt, published by Wadsworth.

Pricing for Profit and Growth, by Albert U. Bergfeld, James S. Barley, and William R. Knobloch, published by Prentice-Hall.

Pricing Strategies, by Alfred R. Oxenfeldt, published by AMACOM.

Pricing Strategy, by Morris Engleson, published by Joing Management Strategy.

A Robinson-Patman Primer, by Earl W. Kintner, published by Macmillan.

The Strategy and Tactics of Pricing, 3rd edition, by Thomas T. Nagle, Reed K. Holden, and Reed Holden, published by Prentice-Hall.

Internet

Note: Because Internet sites frequently go down, multiple sites are listed for similar subject matter.

Pricing Introduction. Tutor2u provides definitions and theories with links to notes and key pricing terms at http://www.tutor2u.net/business/marketing/pricing_introduction.asp.

Pricing New Products by Michael V. Marn, Eric V. Roegner, and Craig C. Zawada at *Inc.com*. Reprint from *The McKinsey Quarterly*. Article originally published by the famed consulting firm for clients at http://www.inc.com/articles/2003/07/pricing.html.

Small Business Pricing Strategies by Sharon Senter at WebMarketing Articles.com. Article on some interesting pricing tactics at http://www.webmarketingarticles.com/Pricing_Strategies.htm.

Strategies for Pricing a Product or Service Optimally. Ideas for Marketing provides an article discusses pricing strategies and link to a manual on pricing at http://www.ideasformarketing.com/pricing.html.

The Pricing Strategy by Ken Evoy at Easy Home Business. Article discusses pricing strategies and tactics and has a link to free five-day pricing course at http://www.easy-home-business.com/better-business-price.html.

DOWNLOADABLE WORKSHEET 10.1
Establishing Costs, Sales Volume, and Profits[1]

For questions for which your answer is "no," decide whether you must carry out the action to establish your price. Disregard those questions not applicable to your business.

Question	Yes	No
Costs and Prices If you set the price by applying a small markup, you may be overlooking other cost factors that are connected with that item. The questions in this section will help you to collect the information to determine pricing on specific types of items.		
Do you know which of your operating costs remain the same regardless of sales volume?		
Do you know which of your operating costs decrease percentage wise as your sales volume increases?		
Have you ever figured out the break-even point for your items selling at varying price levels?		
Do you look behind high gross margin percentages? (For example, a product with a high gross margin, may also be a slow turnover item with high handling costs. Thus is may be less profitable than lower margin items which turn over fast.)		
When you select items for price reductions, do you project the effects on profits? (For example, if a food marketer considers whether to run canned ham or rump steak on sale, an important cost factor is labor. Practically none is involved in featuring canned ham; however, a rump-steak sale requires the skill of a meat cutter and this labor cost might mean little or no profits.)		
Pricing and Sales Volume An effective pricing program should also consider sales volume. For example, high prices might limit your sales volume while low prices might result in a large, but unprofitable volume. The following questions should be helpful in determining what is right for your situation.		
Have you considered setting a sales volume goal and then studying to see if your prices will help you reach it?		
Have you set a target of a certain number of new customers for next year? (If so, how can pricing help you to get them?)		
Should you limit the quantities of low-margin items that any one customer can buy when they are on sale? (If so, will you advertise this policy?)		
What is your policy when a sale item is sold out before the end of the advertised period? Do you allow disappointed customers to buy the item later at the sale price?		

[1] This worksheet is based on material originated with Joseph D. O'Brien, professor of marketing at Boston College.

To customize this document, download it to your hard drive from the John Wiley & Sons web site at www.wiley .com/go/cohenentrepreneur. The document can then be opened, edited, and printed using Microsoft Word or another popular word processing application.

Question	Yes	No
Pricing and Profits Prices should help bring in sales that are profitable over the long pull. The following questions will help you think about pricing policies and their effect on your annual profits.		
Do you have all the facts on costs, sales, and competitive behavior?		
Do you set prices to accomplish definite objectives? (Example: a 1 percent profit increase over last year).		
Do you have a goal of a certain level of profits in dollars and in percent of sales?		
Do you keep records that will give you the needed facts on profits, losses, and prices?		
Do you review your pricing practices periodically to make sure that they are helping to achieve your profit goals?		
Judging the Buyer, Timing, and Competitors Questions in this part are designed to help you check your practices for judging the buyer (your customers), your timing, and your competitors.		
The Buyer and Pricing Strategy After you have your facts on costs, the next point must be the customer—whether you are changing a price, putting in a new item, or checking out your present price practices. Knowledge of your customers helps you to determine how to vary prices in order to get the average gross margin you need for making a profit. (For example, to get an average gross margin of 35 percent, some retailers put a low markup—10 percent, for instance—on items that they promote as traffic builders and use high markup—sometimes as much as 60 percent—on slow-moving items.) The following questions should be helpful in checking your knowledge about your customers.		
Do you know whether your customers shop around or buy impulsively and for which items this is true?		
Do you know how your customers make their comparisons? (Example: newspaper ads, television, the Internet, hearsay?)		
Are you trying to appeal to customers who buy on price alone? To those who buy on quality alone? To those who seek the best value for their money?		
Do your customers tell you that your prices are comparable with those of your competitors, or higher or lower?		
Do you know which item (or types of items) your customers ask for even if you raise the price?		
Do you know which items (or types of items) your customers no longer buy when you raise the price?		

(continued)

Question	Yes	No
Do certain items seem to appeal to customers more than others when you run sales?		
Have you used your individual sales records to classify your present customers according to the volume of their purchases?		
Will your customers buy more if you use multiple pricing? (For example, 3 for 39 cents for products with rapid turnover.)		
Do your customers respond to odd prices more readily than even prices, for example, 99 cents rather than $1?		
Have you decided on a pricing strategy to create a favorable price image with your customers? (For example, a retailer with 8,000 different items might decide to make a full margin on all medium or slow movers while featuring—at low price levels—the remaining fast movers.)		
If you are trying to build a quality price image, do your individual customer records, such as charge account statements, show that you are selling a larger number of higher priced items than you were 12 months ago?		
Do your records of individual customer accounts and your observations of customer behavior in the store show price as the important factor in their buying under general or special conditions?		
Time and Pricing Effective merchandising means that you have the right product, at the right place, at the right price, and at the right time. All are important, but timing is the critical element for the small retailer. The following questions should be helpful in determining what is the right time for you to adjust prices.		
Are you a "leader" or a "follower" in announcing your price reductions? (The follower, even though he matches his competitors, may create a negative impression on his customers.)		
Have you studied your competitors to see whether they follow any sort of pattern when making price changes? (For example, do some of them run clearance sales earlier than others?)		
Is there a pattern to the kinds of items that competitors promote at lower prices at certain times of the month or year?		
Have you decided whether it is better to take early markdowns on seasonal or style goods or to run a clearance sale at the end of the season?		
Have you made regular annual sales, such as Anniversary Sales, Fall Clearance, or Holiday Cleanup, so popular that many customers wait for them rather than buying in season?		
When you change a price, do you make sure that all customers know about it through price tags and so on?		
Do you try to time price reductions so they can be promoted in your advertising?		

Question	Yes	No
Competition and Pricing		
When you set prices, you have to consider how your competitors might react to your prices. The starting place is learning as much as you can about their price structures. The following questions are designed to help you check out this phase of pricing.		
Do you use all the available channels of information to keep you up to date on your competitors' price policies? (Some useful sources of information are: things your customers tell you; the competitor's price list and catalogs, if he uses them; his advertising; reports from your suppliers; trade paper studies; and shoppers employed by you.)		
Should your policy be to try always to sell above or below competition or only to meet it?		
Is there a pattern to the way your competitors respond to your price cuts?		
Is the leader pricing of your competitors affecting your sales volume to such an extent that you must alter your pricing policy on individual items (or types of items) of merchandise?		
Do you realize that no two competitors have identical cost curves? (This difference in costs means that certain price levels may be profitable for you but unprofitable for your competitor or vice versa.)		
Practices That Can Help Offset Price		
Some small businesspeople take advantage of the fact that price is not always the determining factor in making a sale. They supply customer services and offer other inducements to offset the effect of competitors' lower prices. Delivery service is an example. A comfortable shopper's atmosphere is another. The following questions are designed to help you take a look at some of these practices.		
Do the items or services that you sell have advantages for which customers are willing to pay a little more?		
From personal observation of customer behavior in your store can you tell about how much more customers will pay for such advantages?		
Should you change your services so as to create an advantage for which your customers will be willing to pay?		
Does your advertising emphasize customer benefits rather than price?		
Are you using the most common non-price competitive tools? (For example, have you tried to alter your product or service to the existing market? Have you tried stamps, bonus purchase gifts, or other plans for building repeat business?)		
Should policies on returned goods be changed so as to impress your customers more favorably?		
If you sell repair services, have you checked out your guarantee policy?		
Should you alter assortments of merchandise to increase sales?		

DOWNLOADABLE WORKSHEET 10.2
Checklist for a Small Retailer[1]

Question	Yes	No
General Questions Is the relative price of a particular item very important to your target customers? The importance of price depends on the specific product and on the specific individual. Some shoppers are very price conscious; others want convenience and knowledgeable sales personnel. Because of these variations, you need to learn about your customers' desires in relation to different products. Having sales personnel seek feedback from shoppers is a good starting point.		
Are prices based on estimates of the number of units that consumers will demand at various price levels? Demand-oriented pricing such as this is superior to cost-oriented pricing. In the cost approach, a predetermined amount is added to the cost of the merchandise, whereas the demand approach considers what consumers are willing to pay.		
Have you established a price range for the product? The cost of merchandise will be at one end of the price range, and the level above which consumers will not buy the product at the other end.		
Have you considered what price strategies would be compatible with your store's total retailing mix that includes merchandise, location, promotion, and services?		
Will trade-ins be accepted as part of the purchase price on items such as appliances and television sets?		
Supplier and Competitor Considerations This set of questions looks outside your firm to two factors that you cannot directly control—suppliers and competitors.		
Do you have final pricing authority? With the repeal of fair trade laws, "yes" answers will be more common than in previous years. Still, a supplier can control retail prices by refusing to deal with nonconforming stores (a tactic which may be illegal) or by selling to you on consignment.		
Do you know what direct competitors are doing price wise?		
Do you regularly review competitors' ads to obtain information on their prices?		
Is your store large enough to employ either a full-time or part-time comparison shopper? The three questions emphasize the point that you must watch competitors' prices, so that your prices will not be far out of line—too high or too low—without good reason. Of course, there may be a good reason for out-of-the-ordinary prices, such as seeking a special price image.		

[1] This worksheet was developed by Bruce J. Walker, a professor of marketing, Arizona State University, and published by the Small Business Administration.

To customize this document, download it to your hard drive from the John Wiley & Sons web site at www.wiley.com/go/cohenentrepreneur. The document can then be opened, edited, and printed using Microsoft Word or another popular word processing application.

Question	Yes	No
Developing a Price Level Strategy Selecting a general level of prices in relation to competition is a key, perhaps the most important, strategic decision.		
Should your overall strategy be to sell at prevailing market price levels? The other alternatives are an above-the-market strategy or a below-the-market strategy.		
Should competitors' temporary price reductions ever be matched?		
Could private-brand merchandise be obtained to avoid direct price competition?		
Calculating Planned Initial Markup In this section you will have to look inside your business, taking into account sales, expenses, and profits before setting prices. The point is that your initial markup must be large enough to cover anticipated expenses and reductions and still produce a satisfactory profit.		
Have you estimated sales, operating expenses, and reductions for the next selling season?		
Have you established a profit objective for the next selling season?		
Given estimated sales, expenses, and reductions, have you planned initial markup? This figure is calculated with the following formula: $$\text{Initial markup percent} = \frac{\text{Operating expenses} + \text{Reductions} + \text{Profit}}{\text{Net sales} + \text{Reductions}}$$ Reductions consist of markdowns, stock shortages, and employee and customer discounts. The following examples use dollar amounts, but the estimates can also be percentages. If a retailer anticipates \$94,000 in sales for a particular department, \$34,000 in expenses, and \$6,000 in reductions, and if the retailer desires a \$4,000 profit, initial markup percentage can be calculated: $$\text{Initial markup percent} = \frac{\$34,000 + \$6,000 + \$4,000}{\$94,000 + \$6,000} = 44\%$$ The resulting figure, 44% in this example, indicates what size initial markup is needed on the average to make the desired profit.		
Would it be appropriate to have different initial markup figures for various lines of merchandise or services? You would seriously consider this when some lines have much different characteristics than others. For instance, a clothing retailer might logically have different initial markup figures for suits, shirts, and pants, and accessories. (Various merchandise characteristics are covered in an upcoming section.) You may want those items with the highest turnover rates to carry the lowest initial markup.		

(continued)

Question	Yes	No
Store Policies Having calculated an initial markup figure, you could proceed to set prices on your merchandise. But an important decision such as this should not be rushed. Instead, you should consider additional factors, which suggest what would be the best price.		
Is your tentative price compatible with established store policies? Policies are written guidelines indicating appropriate methods or actions in different situations. If established with care, they can save you time in decision making and provide for consistent treatment of shoppers.		
Will a one-price system, under which the same price is charged every purchaser of a particular item, be used on all items?		
Will odd-ending prices, such as $1.98 and $44.95, be more appealing to your customers than even-ending prices?		
Will consumers buy more if multiple pricing, such as 2 for $8.50, is used?		
Should any leader offerings (selected products with quite low, less profitable prices) be used?		
Have the characteristics of an effective leader offering been considered? Ordinarily, a leader offering needs the following characteristics to accomplish its purpose of generating much shopper traffic: used by most people, bought frequently, very familiar regular price, and not a large expenditure for consumers.		
Will price lining, the practice of setting up distinct price points (such as $5.00, $7.50, and $10.00) and then marking all related merchandise at these points, be used?		
Would price lining by means of zones (such as $5.00-$7.50 and $12.50-$15.00) be more appropriate than price points?		
Will cent-off coupons be used in newspaper ads or mailed to selected consumers on any occasion?		
Would periodic special sales, combining reduced prices and heavier advertising, be consistent with the store image you are seeking?		
Do certain items have greater appeal than others when they are part of a special sale?		
Has the impact of various sale items on profits been considered? Sale prices may mean little or no profit on these items. Still, the special sale may contribute to *total* profits by bringing in shoppers who may also buy some regular-price (and profitable) merchandise and by attracting new customers. Also, you should avoid featuring items that require a large amount of labor, which in turn would reduce or erase profits. For instance, according to this criterion, shirts would be a better special sale item than men's suits that often require free alterations.		

Question	Yes	No
Will "rain checks" be issued to consumers who come in for special-sale merchandise that is temporarily out of stock? You should give particular attention to this decision since rain checks are required in some situations. Your lawyer or the regional Federal Trade Commission office should be consulted for specific advice regarding whether rain checks are needed in the special sales you plan.		
Nature of the Merchandise In this section, you will be considering how selected characteristics of particular merchandise affect a planned initial markup.		
Did you get a good deal on the wholesale price of this merchandise?		
Is this item at the peak of its popularity?		
Are handling and selling costs relatively great due to the product being bulky, having a low turnover rate, and/or requiring much personal selling, installation, or alterations?		
Are relatively large levels of reductions expected due to markdowns, spoilage, breakage, or theft? With respect to the preceding four questions, "yes" answers suggest the possibility of or need for larger-than-normal initial markups. For example, very fashionable clothing often will carry a higher markup than basic clothing such as underwear because the particular fashion may suddenly lose its appeal to consumers.		
Will customer services such as delivery, alterations, gift wrapping, and installation be free of charge to customers? The alternative is to charge for some or all of these services.		
Environmental Considerations The questions in this section focus your attention on three factors outside your business, namely economic conditions, laws, and consumerism.		
If your state has an unfair sales practices act that requires minimum markups on certain merchandise, do your prices comply with this statute?		
Are economic conditions in your trading area abnormal? Consumers tend to be more price conscious when the economy is depressed, suggesting that lower-than-normal markups may be needed to be competitive. Alternatively, shoppers are less price conscious when the economy is booming, which would permit larger markups on a selective basis.		
Are the ways in which prices are displayed and promoted compatible with consumerism, one part of which has been a call for more straightforward price information?		
Adjustments to Prices It would be ideal if all items sold at their original retail prices. But we know that things are not always ideal. Therefore, price adjustments should be considered and may be necessary.		
Are additional markups called for, because wholesale prices have increased or because an item's low price causes consumers to question its quality?		

(continued)

Question	Yes	No
Should employees be given purchase discounts?		
Should any groups of customers, such as students or senior citizens, be given purchase discounts?		
When markdowns appear necessary, have you first considered other alternatives such as retaining price but changing another element of the retailing mix or storing the merchandise until the next selling season?		
Has an attempt been made to identify causes of markdowns so that steps can be taken to minimize the number of avoidable buying, selling, and pricing errors that cause markdowns?		
Has the relationship between timing and size of markdowns been taken into account? In general, markdowns taken early in the selling season or shortly after sales slow down can be smaller than *late* markdowns. Whether an early or late markdown would be more appropriate in a particular situation depends on several things: your assessment of how many consumers might still be interested in the product, the size of the initial markup, and the amount remaining in stock.		
Would a schedule of automatic markdowns after merchandise has been in stock for specified intervals be appropriate?		
Is the size of the markdown just enough to stimulate purchases? Of course, this question is difficult—perhaps impossible—to answer. Nevertheless, it stresses the point that you have to carefully observe the effects of different size markdowns so that you can eventually acquire some insights into what size markdowns are just enough for different kinds of merchandise.		
Has a procedure been worked out for markdowns on price-lined merchandise?		
Is the markdown price calculated from the off-retail percentage? This question gets you into the arithmetic of markdowns. Usually, you first tentatively decide on the percentage amount the price must be marked down to excite consumers.		
Has cost of the merchandise been considered before setting the markdown price? This is not to say that a markdown price should never be lower than cost; on the contrary, a price that low may be your only hope of generating some revenue from the item. But cost should be considered to make sure that below-cost markdown prices are the exception in your store rather than being so common that your total profits are significantly affected.		
Have procedures for recording the dollar amounts, percentages, and probable causes of markdowns been set up? Analyzing markdowns is very important since it can provide information that will assist in calculating planned initial markup, in decreasing errors that cause markdowns, and in evaluating suppliers.		
Final Question Have you marked the calendar for a periodic review of your pricing decisions? However, this is just to make certain you review your pricing periodically. Pricing is always a work in progress, and you should rethink your pricing strategies and tactics frequently.		

CHAPTER 11

How to Build Your Business with Advertising and Publicity

Millions of dollars are spent on advertising every single year. You were exposed to about two million advertising messages from the time you were born until you reached the age of 21. To prove the strength of these messages, see if you can answer these questions. What is a Timex? What is a Gillette? What is Tylenol? What is a Big Mac? What is Ivory? What is a Mustang? What is an Apple? What is a product that Sony makes? Unless you never read, watch television, or listen to the radio, you probably answered the majority of the questions without difficulty. Now, let's try one a little more difficult. What do the letters LSMFT stand for? Research has shown that a significant number of people can answer this question, even those who are now in their early twenties. Yet, the advertising message that used these letters has not been used for almost 50 years. LSMFT stands for "Lucky Strike Means Fine Tobacco," and the message hasn't been on the air since 1958! Think about that.

Advertising is used for three basic purposes:

1. To promote awareness of a business and its product or service.
2. To stimulate sales directly.
3. To establish a firm's image or modify a firm's image.

You Can Compete with the Big Companies

Amazingly, even though some firms spend millions of dollars on their advertising every year, you can compete with them, and you can compete with them successfully if you get your money's worth for your advertising dollar. Why is this so? It is so because many firms, even large firms, do not advertise in a very efficient manner.

Let's look at some examples. For years, cigarette manufacturers fought to keep television advertising. When cigarettes were finally banned from advertising on television, tobacco companies predicted doom and stocks plunged. Yet, what happened to cigarette sales without television advertising? Sales went up! This showed that for more than 50 years, much of the million dollars that had been spent had largely been wasted through ineffective television advertising.

Some years ago, a major company, Lestoil, developed a new spray cleaner. This new cleaner was a disinfectant that cleaned so well that household germs were killed instantly. To convey this message, this new product was advertised under the name "Clean and Kill." The result, however, was that the product was killed before the household germs. The advertising campaign was totally ineffective. Why? Possibly housewives, the buying agent for this product, thought that the product was some type of poison.

Just as there have been major disasters in advertising, there have been tremendously successful campaigns. Can you imagine a company bragging about not being first? Well, that's what Avis Rent-A-Car did some years ago. Their message was "We're No. 2," and, therefore, "We try harder." This made it very difficult for Hertz. How could Hertz retaliate without appearing to be the giant villain? The campaign was tremendously effective, and Hertz lost much of the power that it should have had from being in first place while Avis gained even though it was not the largest company in the industry.

Years ago, Mercedes Benz produced its first diesel car of modern times. This was long before the time of the energy crunch. In fact, the diesel engine seemed to offer very few advantages since gasoline was relatively cheap in those days. Moreover, diesel fuel cannot be purchased everywhere. Also, diesel engines are very noisy compared with the standard gasoline engine. In despair, Mercedes Benz prepared to junk the production of the diesel-engined car. But as a last resort, they turned the project over to Ed McLean, a direct marketing expert in the United States. Ed McLean wrote a direct sales letter targeted to individuals who had the money and might be persuaded to buy a Mercedes Benz. This sales letter turned the supposed disadvantages of the diesel engine around and made them advantages. The fact that diesel fuel couldn't be found everywhere meant that the automobile was exclusive. The noise of the engine was promoted as positive evidence that the engine was running. This letter was sent out to consumers on well-chosen mailing lists. The campaign was so successful that Mercedes Benz actually had to reopen the production line and manufacture more diesel engine automobiles! This advertising success won Ed McLean the Golden Mailbox Award from the Direct Mail Marketing Association.

How to Develop an Advertising Program

Advertising works as well for a small firm as for a major multibillion-dollar corporation, if you use it correctly. To use advertising correctly, you must have an advertising program. To develop an advertising program, you must take the following steps:

1. Analyze the market.
2. Set concrete goals and objectives.
3. Set a budget.
4. Develop a creative strategy.
5. Choose your medium or media.
6. Evaluate the results.

Analyze the Market

To analyze the market, you've got to view your own product or service in terms of who can use it. That "who," whether male or female, child or senior citizen, or all of the above, is your target consumer. Now, how are you going to reach him and/or her? Worksheet 11.1 of this chapter helps you do this.

Marketing and advertising experts have developed a very useful concept called *market segmentation*. If you use the market segmentation concept, instead of trying to sell to the entire market, you zero in on a specific segment of the population who are most interested and can best be served by your product or service. The segmentation concept makes sense. You cannot satisfy the entire market with one specific item, and further, you always have limited resources with which to advertise and promote your products or services.

Advertisers use segmentation through their application of strategy: positioning strategy, media strategy, and creative strategy. Positioning strategy refers to how your product is positioned in comparison to the competition. For example, Colonel Sanders' Kentucky Fried Chicken first became successful when advertising was aimed at housewives with a contemporary state of mind, busy, active, finding it hard to prepare meals for their family on a daily basis. Yet, at first, Kentucky Fried Chicken was a failure when positioned mainly as a countrified, folksy product. Note that this target market has changed over the years. Nothing is forever.

Use of media strategy by advertising means selecting the appropriate medium or media to reach the segment that is most interested or would be most interested in buying your product. For example, why are beer, razors, and similar male-oriented products advertised on television during sporting events? Because this is when and where the main user of these products is available as an audience for the advertising.

Creative strategy concerns the copy in the advertisement, the graphics, pictures, or photographs, and the ideas that combine these into an effective ad. For example, Mark O. Haroldsen wrote a book called *How to Wake Up the Financial Genius Within You*. His message for the opportunity-seeker's market in magazines, such as *Salesman Opportunity, Spare Time Opportunities,* and the like, used the title of the book as the headline. Yet, in advertising in the *Wall Street Journal,* Haroldsen used an entirely different advertisement. The headline read: "How to Avoid Paying Taxes Legally." Why did he use this different creative strategy for the *Wall Street Journal*? In the first case, he was appealing to individuals who wanted to make money. In the *Wall Street Journal,* he was appealing to professional managers and entrepreneurs who were already making money and were interested in reducing their considerable taxes.

Nowadays, advertisers segment the market in many ways. Here are just a few categories that you might consider for your product or service:

- *Age:* Advertisers tend to spend the most money trying to gain the attention of individuals in the age group 18 to 34. Why do they do this? Because, statistically, this group spends the most money on consumer products. However, this is certainly not true for all types of products or services. For example, record manufacturers go primarily to the age group 12 to 19, and those who sell luxury items appeal to the age group 34 to 49. Older consumers buy other products in higher numbers.

- *Sex:* Here again you can see a segmentation. Mennen's Speed Stick underarm deodorant is sold to men. But women buy an entirely different brand, although the chemical composition may be almost identical to that of Mennen's Speed Stick. Or, more obviously, men may buy *Playboy* magazine, while women buy *Vogue.*

- *Income, education, and occupation:* Income, education, and occupation are frequently considered together because they are related. For instance, a medical doctor has a high income and an advanced education. However, this type of correlation is not always true. Many blue-collar workers earn as much as or more than white-collar workers. In fact, one problem Robert Oppenheimer had when he headed the Manhattan Project to develop the atomic bomb, was that his electricians made as much as his scientists and engineers. When his professionals discovered this, they complained bitterly about this perceived inequity. Many tradespeople, such as plumbers, certain mechanics, and others, may make relatively high salaries. And, of course, if you are self-employed you have the potential for making much more money than salaried professionals.

- *Geographic location:* Here again, winter weather implies certain types of products, such as heavy clothing, just as sunny weather implies other types of clothing or products. Even if you are selling disco clothes, your product directs you to the location of your potential sales.

- *Marital status and family size:* Certain types of products and services are segmented according to these factors. Video dating services, travel and tour services, singles bars, and nightclubs, are all segmented depending on marital status. Certain types of products are segmented by family size, when a giant economy size is offered.

- *Ethnic group:* Segmentation is accomplished by ethnic group because some groups prefer certain types of products over others. Soybean products, for example, such as tofu or soybean milk, are sold mainly to Asian communities. Certain types of delicatessen products are sold mainly to Jewish, Italian, or German communities. Other types of foods, cosmetic products, or luxury items must also be segmented by ethnic group.

- *Subculture:* Subcultures, such as "recent college graduates" or "over 65," can also be effectively segmented from the mass market and therefore advertised to. For example, for the over-65 group, market research has shown a greater tendency to do comparison shopping, to buy mainly nationally known name brands, and to shy away from shops that are felt to cater exclusively to older customers. Some years ago, a nationally known food company lost millions of dollars in sales because it introduced a special line of senior foods, which was ignored by its intended market.

- *Social class:* Different social classes tend to prefer and read different types of publications. For example, *Reader's Digest* and *Ladies' Home Journal* are in one class; *Time* and *Sports Illustrated* in another; *New Yorker* and *Vogue* magazine in yet another.

Of the categories previously discussed, age, sex, marital status, family size, income, education, and occupation, and geographical location are all known as *demographic* factors. Subculture, ethnic group, and social class are known as *social culture* factors. There is also more and more segmentation done for advertising in psychographics and lifestyle categories. These include activities, interests, and opinions, product usage, new product adoption behavior, and family decision making. To accomplish segmentation by psychographics or lifestyle factors, special research is done, which measures aspects of human behavior including what products or services are consumed, the activities, interests, and opinions of respondents, special value systems, personality traits and conception of self, and attitudes toward various product classes.

Recently, additional special groups have been identified as being especially good targets for segmentation. Some of these new groups are as follows:

- *College students:* There are more than 13 million college students. Individuals selling to this market have made million of dollars, for example, computer dating, which originated with a college student in 1966. The student who invented this concept became a millionaire prior to graduation through market segmentation.

- *The Hispanic market:* This is a viable market, which has become so strong that special courses in marketing have been offered at some of the nation's largest universities. The Hispanic market includes almost 40 million people in the United States.

- *Divorces:* While divorce may not be desirable in any society, it is a fact in ours. The average marriage lasts less than six years and there are almost a million divorces a year in the United States.

- *Individuals living together:* Today, individuals who are living together constitute a major segment. They number greater than two million.

- *The working woman:* More than two-thirds of women work today, and more than 50 percent of mothers are working; this is a truly gigantic segment.

- *Health:* There is a tremendous interest in health in the United States. Vitamin sales have doubled in 10 years and continue to explode. The readership of magazines pertaining to health, such as *Prevention*, is steadily growing, with new magazines and newsletters appearing every day. According to the U.S. Census Bureau, more than half of the U.S. population is overweight. As a result, diet books and other products and services are of continual interest to this segment. There is almost always at least one diet book on the *New York Times* Best Seller List.

- *Children:* Many children ages 6 through 11 receive allowances, which, on average, approach more than $100 a year. The result is more than 2.5 billion dollars in spendable income, making this segment a tremendous buying force.

- *Sports enthusiasts:* Jogging, tennis, bicycling, swimming, and even the martial arts are nosing out more traditional sports, such as football and basketball, in popularity. There is a tremendous interest in all sports and a tremendous market segment to be served.

- *Spiritualness and mind power:* Recent popular interest in subjects such as yoga, mysticism, Transcendental Meditation, Scientology, and Silva Mind Control has made this a leading and increasingly large segment of the population. Further, this group constitutes a segment that is completely separate from religion in the traditional sense.

To learn how best to reach your customer, some sort of market research is necessary. One way of doing this is with your own survey of your customers or potential customers. Worksheet 11.1, Developing Profiles of Your Target Market, helps you to do this.

Set Concrete Goals and Objectives

Once your analysis is completed, your job is to establish the goals and objectives of your advertising program. What do you want to happen? You should answer the question in precise, concrete terms so that you can measure your results at a later time. By when do you want it to happen? Give a specific time frame. For example, a suitable advertising objective might be to increase the number of males ages 15 to 25 who walk into your retail establishment and make a purchase by 20 percent over the next three months. That says precisely who, what, and when.

Set an Advertising Budget

Once goals and objectives have been established, you must look to your advertising budget. In some cases, your budget is established before goals and objectives due to your limited resources. It is a given, and you may have to modify your goals and objectives. If money is available, you can work the other way around and see how much money it takes to reach the goals and objectives you have established.

The professionals use different methods of establishing an advertising budget. These are as follows:

- Percentage of anticipated or past year's sales.
- The arbitrary approach.
- Quantitative models.
- Objective and task approach.
- Affordable approach.
- Competitive approach.

Of these methods, most surveys indicate that the most popular method used is that of percentage of anticipated sales. This means that you must forecast your sales for the future period and then allocate a fixed percentage of money to your advertising. This fixed percentage is usually found by comparing other firms advertising in your industry that are of your size and have a similar product. Obviously, this method has an advantage over taking a fixed percentage of a past year's sales since you are looking to the future. Alternatively, it says little about the advertising program and has nothing to do with the objectives and goals that you have established.

The arbitrary approach means simply that you pull a figure out of the air and decide that this is how much money is devoted to advertising. This method has little to recommend it.

Quantitative models can be extremely sophisticated. However, their complexity and the fact that so many factors must be considered mean that it is little used and probably not desirable or even workable for a small firm. As a matter of fact, major firms use the quantitative model method very little.

With the objective and task approach, you relate your budget to the goals and objectives you have established. While the percentage of sales or profits or percentage of any approach first determines how much you spend, without much consideration of what you want to accomplish, this method establishes what you must do to meet your objectives—only then do you calculate its cost. For a small firm, it must frequently be used with the affordable approach because in some cases, and as mentioned previously, you may set objectives that can only be reached at a much higher budget than you can afford. In this case, you must scale down your objectives.

To use the objective and task method, you break down the cost of your budget by calendar periods, by media, and perhaps by sales areas. Breakdown by calendar periods means that you divide the advertising plan on a monthly or weekly basis. Media breakdown denotes how much money you place in each advertising medium, such as television, radio, newspaper, direct mail, and so forth. Sales areas are the areas in which you spend your advertising budget. That is, if you are going after different market segments simultaneously under one advertising program, you have to decide how much money each market segment gets. Use Worksheet 11.2 to assist you in preparing your advertising budget.

With the affordable approach, you don't go for the optimal, but only what your firm can afford.

Finally, we have the competitive approach. With this approach, you analyze how much the competitor is spending and spend more, the same, or less depending on your objectives.

Develop a Creative Strategy

A creative strategy involves what you say in your advertising message, how you say it, and any artwork that is included. Unless you are a professional in this area, or your ad is very simple, it is better to get expert, professional help in preparing creative work. You can find these professionals fairly easily in your phone book. For artwork, look under "Artists—Commercial or Advertising Artists." Do the same for photography and for copywriters.

If you intend to write your own copy, I recommend the book *How to Write a Good Advertisement,* by Victor O. Schwab (Wilshire Book Company).

If you are going to write your own copy, follow the following guidelines: First, make the headline appeal to self-interest, offer exciting news, or rouse interest in your consumer. The headline should be positive, not negative. The headline should suggest that the reader could obtain something easily and quickly. Make the headline stress the most important benefit of your product or your service, and write it so that it grabs the reader's attention and causes him or her to read farther. Also, be sure that the headline is believable and, of course, when you begin to write the body of the copy, make sure that the headline does in fact tie in with what you write later.

In the copy content itself, you should try to gain interest immediately. If you have enough room in your copy, use a story or a startling or unusual statement or quote; use news if you don't have enough room. Show the benefits and advantages that appeal to emotional needs to such an extent that your offer and what you say are made irresistible. If you can, add credibility to your copy through the use of testimonials. These are statements made by other people who have used your product or service and are happy with it.

When you are writing copy, always remember that you are writing to communicate, and therefore write it in a conversational tone. Use short words, short sentences, short paragraphs, and lots of subheadings throughout. If you want your copy to be read, make it interesting and make it easy to read. I have found that Rudolf Flesch's book, *The Art of Readable Writing* (HarperResource) to be of considerable help here.

These principles in copywriting should apply whether your advertisement is to appear in print or on radio or television. Only minor modifications should be necessary depending on limitations of these different media.

Choose Your Medium and Media Vehicle

Each of the different advertising medium categories (print, electronic, etc.) include several media: magazine or newspaper, Internet, and so on. The specific radio or television show, magazine, and so forth is known as a *vehicle*. For example, *Time* magazine is a specific vehicle of magazine media.

There are four major considerations when you make your selection of medium (assuming you're using just one) and vehicle:

1. *Budget match:* Which medium and vehicle you use must be consistent with the money that you have available in your budget.

2. *Medium and vehicle and target consumer match:* The medium and vehicle that you select must be seen, heard, or read by your target consumer market.

3. *Medium and vehicle market mix relationship:* The medium and vehicle you select must also reflect the emphasis that you give to the marketing mix. The marketing mix is made up of various inputs of product, price, distribution method, and promotional factors. What is the relationship between medium and vehicle and market mix? Let us take a new product, which requires a demonstration for prospects to understand its function. For this kind of product, you may choose to use TV as your medium because prospects can actually see the product demonstrated. Also, the product must fit the atmosphere of the vehicle.

   Some years ago, entrepreneur Joe Cossman sold over one million shrunken heads made out of rubber. As a novelty, they were affixed to rearview mirrors in automobiles. Obviously, *Vogue* magazine, an upscale magazine for women, was never considered as a vehicle for this particular product. High price denotes a certain vehicle, as does low price. Similar matching must be followed with distribution and promotional factors.

4. *Creative medium and vehicle marriage:* Certain appeals are best for certain media and vehicles, as mentioned previously using the example of Mark O. Haroldsen's book, *How to Wake Up the Financial Genius Within You.* To reach prospects interested in moneymaking opportunities of this sort, the vehicle selected was *Specialty Salesmen* and similar magazines. To reach those interested in tax shelters, the vehicle selected was the *Wall Street Journal.*

The Categories of Media   The categories of media should also be considered as you plan for your advertising campaign. These include:

- Print (newspapers, magazines).
- Broadcast (radio, TV).
- Direct mail (letters addressed directly to lists of potential buyers in your target consumer market group).
- Specialty items (pens, pencils, or other gadgets with the name of your firm embossed on them).
- Directories (Yellow Pages advertisements, advertisements in association membership directories, and so forth).
- Outdoor (billboards, transit posters).
- Movie theater advertisement.
- The Internet.
- Various others, such as matchbook covers.

Audience   One publication that greatly assists you in planning your campaign is the Standard Rate and Data Service (SRDS). The SRDS publishes updated information in many categories for advertisers including: consumer magazines, farm publications, business publications, newspapers, weekly newspapers, network radio and TV, spot radio and TV, transit, mailing lists, and more. While major advertisers and advertising agencies are the usual subscribers to SRDS, many libraries carry these volumes. You may find them extremely useful in matching your target audience and selecting the media and vehicles that you can use. You might also want to visit their web site at www.srds.com.

Making Intermediate Comparisons   Each medium has its advantages and its disadvantages for your particular situation. For example, television, which has a broad reach and offers opportunities for a dynamic demonstration, is expensive and does not allow for demographic selectivity to any great extent. Newspapers may be relatively cheap; however, they offer little secondary readership, limited color facilities, and little demographic selectivity possibilities. To assist you in making intermedia comparisons, consider Table 11.1, which compares various media. It is based on a comparison developed originally by Bank of America for their small business borrowers.

Advertising Planning Concepts   Some of the concepts to consider in your planning, in addition to cost, are reach versus frequency; continuity; target market, marketing and advertising objectives; the marketing mix of product, price, promotion, and distribution, and promotional variables; competitive advertising activity; the size of your budget; and your creative strategy. All of these have been discussed previously except for reach versus frequency and continuity.

Reach versus Frequency

Reach is the total number of households that are exposed to an advertising message in a particular vehicle or medium over a certain period of time. It is expressed as a percentage of the total universe of households. Frequency is the number of exposures to the same message each household receives. Therefore, average frequency equals the total exposures for all households sampled, divided by the reach. Even at tremendous expense, you cannot reach 100 percent of your target market. Therefore, the key is trying to estimate the point at which additional dollars should go into frequency after the optimal reach has been achieved. Some pointers to assist you in making this decision are as follows:

Go for Greater Reach

- When you're introducing a new product to a mass market and want as many people as possible to know about it.
- When your advertising message is so compelling that most people react to the initial exposure.
- When your product or service message is in itself newsworthy and demands attention.

Go for Higher Frequency

- When your competitor is going for high frequency against the same segment as you.
- When you are seeking direct response; that is, when you want individuals to order the product or respond to the service directly from the ad.
- When you want your target consumer to act within a certain limited time period.

TABLE 11.1 Media Comparison

Medium	Market Coverage	Type of Audience	Costs	Specialized Suitability	Major Advantage	Major Disadvantage
Daily newspaper	Single community or entire metro area; zoned editions sometimes available.	General; tends more toward men, older age group, slightly higher income and education.	Relatively inexpensive	All general retailers.	Wide circulation.	Nonselective audience.
Shopper papers or magazines	Most households in a single community; chain shoppers can cover a metro area.	Consumer households.	Relatively inexpensive	Neighborhood retailers and service businesses.	Consumer orientation.	This is a freebee and is not always read.
Telephone directories	Geographic area or occupational field served by the directory.	Active shoppers for goods or services.	Relatively inexpensive	Services, retailers of brand-name items, highly specialized retailers.	Users are in the market for goods or services.	Limited to active shoppers.
Direct mail	Depends on mailing; controlled by the advertiser.	Controlled by the advertiser through use of segmented list.	Costs more per audience unit.	New and expanding businesses, those using coupon returns or catalogs.	Personalized approach to an audience of good prospects.	Relatively expensive on a cost per prospect basis.
Radio	Definable market area surrounding the station's location.	Selected audiences provided by stations with distinct programming formats.	Usually more expensive than print advertising, but not per audience unit.	Businesses catering to identifiable groups: teens, commuters, housewives.	Can select market and attain wide market coverage.	Must be used consistently over time to attain maximum value.

	Coverage	Audience	Cost	Typical Users	Advantages	Disadvantages
Television	Definable market area surrounding the station's location.	Varies with the time of day and other factors.	More expensive for regular TV, less with cable.	Sellers of products or services with wide appeal.	Visual impact with wide market coverage.	High costs for both advertising and production of ad.
Transit	Urban or metro community.	Transit riders and pedestrians.	Relatively Inexpensive.	Businesses along transit routes, especially those appealing to wage earners.	Repetition and length of exposure.	Limited audience.
Outdoor	Entire metro area or single neighborhood.	General; especially auto drivers.	Medium.	Amusements, tourist businesses, brand-name retailers.	Dominant size, frequency of exposure.	Clutter of many signs reduces effectiveness of each one.
Internet Website	Consumers using the Internet.	Browser of particular information.	Low, but outside promotion generally needed.	As an adjunct to other advertising.	Low cost.	Need for means of driving prospects to website.
E-mail	E-Mailbox owners.	Controlled by advertiser with segmented lists.	Very low.	Maintaining contact with established customers.	Low cost.	Perception as spam if not used carefully.

- When there isn't too much to differentiate what you are offering from what your competition is selling.

CONTINUITY   Continuity has to do with the length of time that your medium schedule should run. You can run a medium schedule continuously or periodically; once a day, once a week, or even more infrequently. Here again, you should consider the various factors that may influence success as a trade-off against cost and limited resources. For funding optimal frequency, experts have developed something called the "three-hit theory." The basis of the theory is that there is an optimal range after which you are wasting money. According to the theory, this range has three receipts of your message or "hits." Three hits ensure that the customer learns of your product or service through your advertising message. To get the three hits, you need 11 to 12 potential advertising exposures. Therefore, the average potential frequency should be 11 to 12 times. Once you have decided on the medium (or media), you must then decide on the vehicle(s). To do this, you can use demographic or other research, which describes the prospect who is the target market for your product or service, against that supplied by the vehicle in question. And in this regard, every magazine or television or radio show can offer a current demographic profile of its readership or listenership. It is therefore a question of matching up their information with your research of your target customer.

Negotiating and Special Discounts   Many small business advertisers don't realize that they could advertise for much less than they are now, if they only knew about the special negotiating possibilities and discounts that are offered. These include the following:

- Mail-order discounts.
- Per inquiry deals.
- Frequency discounts.
- Stand-by rates.
- Help if necessary.
- Remnants and regional editions.
- Barter.
- Bulk buyers.
- Seasonal discounts.
- Spread discounts.
- An in-house agency.
- Cost discounts.

For example, if you are a mail order advertiser, many magazines realize that you must make money directly from your ad or you cannot stay in business and advertise again. In addition to this, with this type of advertising, it is easy to know immediately whether you are doing well and the ad made money. Accordingly, many magazines give special mail-order discounts, sometimes up to 40 percent, to mail-order advertisers. Therefore, if the advertisement normally costs you $200, you need only pay $120. This is a big discount and certainly nothing to pass by. Even for many national mail-order advertisers, it may spell the difference between a profitable ad and failure.

A per inquiry (PI) deal is one in which you agree to pay the publication only for those inquiries or sales that the ad itself brings in. This may be on the radio, television, or in a magazine. As a result, in return for this agreement, the magazine runs your advertisement with no money from you up front. Certainly, this is a major advantage for a small businessperson. Usually, the mail is sent to the vehicle, which sorts it and keeps the records for you. At other times, the ad is keyed and the mail sent directly to you. You must turn a percentage of each order over to the vehicle at fixed periods that you agree on. If the orders go to the vehicle, they send you the names of those who order so that you can respond and send the product to the customer. They also send the amount owed you for each product. A typical PI deal usually costs something like 50 percent of the selling price to the publication vehicle.

Frequently, it is difficult to locate PI deals, and you need to talk to the salesperson representing the vehicle. Few magazines, radio stations, or television stations like their regular advertisers to know that they accept PI deals, so don't expect them to be advertised much. They are not easy to find, but they are worth looking for.

Most media offer frequency discounts. Therefore, if you advertise more than once or more than what is standard, you can expect a lower cost than what you might otherwise achieve. Be careful, however, in committing yourself to long-range advertising programs until you know whether the campaign is going to work.

Most vehicles are committed to publication or broadcast on a regular basis. At certain times, all advertising may not be sold outright up to the last minute. The vehicle therefore has a choice: it can either sell this advertising at a greatly reduced amount—stand-by rate—or put in some sort of editorial content which does not generate additional profits. To get the stand-by rate, you first let the different vehicles know that you are interested in this type of a deal, and they must be able to get hold of you quickly by telephone. Sometimes a stand-by rate is available only after you advertise with this publication or station for some time, because they then know and trust you. This is important because the deal is closed verbally—no money in advance. The advantage of the stand-by rate is well worth it. Again, you may pay as little as 40 to 50 percent of the normal cost of advertising.

Help, if necessary, is applicable usually to mail-order advertisers and recognizes the fact that the mail-order advertiser must make money from the ad to stay in business. If the ad is not profitable, the publication may agree to run the ad and repeat it if necessary until you at least breakeven. Help may not assist you in making additional money, but it can prevent you from losing money.

Therefore, you should always check into the possibility of help-if-necessary deals, if you are a mail order advertiser.

Many national magazines allow advertisers to buy space only in certain regional editions, rather than in every edition that appears nationally. This situation works to your advantage in reduced advertising costs. Sometimes the regional editions are not sold out in advertising space and may go begging. You can get remnants in regional editions at a discount of as much as 50 percent. To locate remnant advertising possibilities, talk to salespeople representing the advertising vehicle.

Sometimes a publication or station may be willing to barter; that is, to take products or services in exchange for advertising. This occurs when the vehicle has an interest other than publishing or broadcasting. Barter is a great way to go because it allows you to increase sales without using up capital resources.

Bulk buyers are purchasers of huge amounts of advertising from advertising media. Because of the quantity in which it is bought, they pay much less. The bulk buyer then resells the advertising space. The price you pay to a bulk buyer varies greatly and it is negotiable. Toward the end of the advertising period, if this space isn't sold, you may be able to get discounts as large as 50 percent.

Some media do not do well during certain seasons of the year. As a result, during these periods they offer substantial seasonal discounts over their normal rate. If your product or service sells well during that season, you should seriously consider seasonal discounts in your advertising. On the same principle, your product may cost a great deal to sell during prime time on television or radio. However, there may be no need to sell during prime time. In fact, your product may sell better in other than prime time. Therefore, you should consider non-prime time discounts much in the line of seasonal discounts.

If you are a big advertiser and advertise on two or three pages or more in a particular issue of a magazine, you may be able to get a special spread discount. This may or may not be on the vehicle's rate card, which describes its advertising costs, so you must ask about it. Again, discounts can run as high as 50 percent of the normal cost.

Advertising agencies get an automatic 15 percent discount from any vehicle in which they place your ad. This is one way they have of making money. As a result, many small businesspeople form their own in-house agency to take advantage of the 15 percent discount for themselves. Most vehicles say they do not deal with in-house agencies and do not accept advertising from them at the 15 percent discount. However, what they are really saying is that they do this as long as you're not obvious about the fact that you are an in-house agency. Therefore, for the cost of registration of a name other than that of your regular company, and some specially printed stationery with this name, you can get a 15 percent discount every single time you advertise. To recapitulate:

- Select a name for your in-house advertising agency, which is different from the name of your regular firm.
- Have special stationery printed up with the in-house agency's name.
- Do not volunteer the fact that you are an in-house agency. Merely indicate that you're placing the ad for the company indicated and give other instructions in accordance with the rate card or the Standard Rate and Data Service Publication.

Many advertisers overlook the fact that most vehicles give a 2 percent discount for payment of cash within the first 10 days. However, if you do not take this discount, very few vehicles automatically return your money. So look for this information in materials supplied in the information on the rate card, which you request from the vehicle. If you can get a 2 percent discount, you can save a lot of money. Even small firms are saving as much as $50,000 a year this way, once they become large advertisers.

Evaluate the Results

Unless you know how well your advertising is doing, much or all of your money could be totally wasted. Therefore, it is important to establish some measurements of the effectiveness of your advertising. There are several methods of doing this. They are:

- Direct response.
- Involuntary methods.
- Recognition and awareness tests.
- Recall tests.
- Focus group tests.

Direct Response This is probably the best means of measuring the effectiveness of your advertising, because you measure actual responses to your ad. To do this, all you need do is code the advertisement so that you know which response is from which advertisement. A typical code uses "Suite," "Room," "Drawer," or sometimes even different initials before the name of the company, or different initials after the box number. For example, a letter can stand for the vehicle in which the advertisement appears, and a digit following the letter can denote the month. Let us say that you advertised in *Outdoor Life* magazine in January. "A" could stand for *Outdoor Life,* and the digit "1" could stand for advertisement in January. The simple addition to your address of "Suite A-l" or "Room A-l" would tell you immediately the vehicle and the exact advertisement.

Involuntary Methods These methods of measuring advertisement effectiveness usually involve pretesting. They record involuntary responses over which neither the subject nor the researcher has control. They are objective, but they are also expensive. They are also done in an unnatural setting. One device, called a pupilometer, measures the dilation of the pupil while the individual is observing advertising. The device is unwieldy and uncomfortable, and it certainly isn't the way that the reader usually sees advertising. One very simple involuntary method is called the "down the chute" test. It consists of having someone read advertising copy while you watch his eyes. If there are no problems with comprehension or readability, it is presumed that the individual's eyes keep moving from left to right, left to right, as he goes line by line down the page. But if the pupils stop moving, there could be a problem, and at this point you should ask the reader what he is reading. You note the problem and then continue the procedure.

Recognition and Awareness Tests   In recognition and awareness tests, consumers who have read or seen an advertisement are asked whether they remember the ad. One limitation is the possibility of confusion of your ad with similar ads, and the sample size used is usually small compared to the total number of readers.

The oldest type of recognition test is a readership test called the "Starch." In the Starch system, the interviewer shows the magazine to the subject, and if the subject says he or she has read it, the interviewer goes through the magazine ad by ad with the subject indicating whether he or she has "noted the ad," which means he or she has seen it; "associated it," which means he or she remembers the brand name; or "read most," which means that he or she has read at least half of the copy. The Starch system reports the percentage of ads "noted," "associated," and "read most" for each subject.

Awareness tests measure the cumulative effect of advertising. Test subjects are consumers in the target consumer group for the ad. First, demographic information is gathered to determine if they are likely customers. Then, they are asked the question: "Have you seen the ads lately for (name of product)?" The problem with this type of test is that there are too many variables, which can affect the response.

Recall Tests   In a typical recall test, the prospects are first screened and asked questions about their attitude. They are then asked to watch a program, while those in a control group are asked similar questions but do not watch. The effectiveness of recall is determined later when brand awareness is measured in both groups and the results are compared.

Focus Group Tests   The focus group has grown as a method of pretesting in recent years. It is relatively low budget in that 8 to 10 representative consumers are invited in. It is therefore not a quantitative measure but rather a qualitative measure of reactions to help you decide whether to run one ad or another.

The small businessperson and entrepreneur can adopt many of these methods to help in determining the effectiveness of advertising. The key is to keep your methods simple, hold down costs, and be careful about drawing inferences if you use a very small sample size.

Should You Employ an Advertising Agency?

Whether to employ an advertising agency depends a great deal on how large a company you have and what an advertising agency can do for you. Many of the things that an advertising agency can do, such as media selection, copywriting, supplying artwork, and so forth, you may do for yourself, in which case, it may be better to establish your own in-house agency as described earlier and save 15 percent. Alternatively, all these activities take up your resources, and an agency can tie everything together and can probably do a more professional job for you. The problem here is that many of the best agencies only work for your firm when you become a major advertiser. If you are big enough, the services provided by an agency may cost you nothing since the agency receives 15 percent commission from the medium or media used. If you are not a major advertiser, the agency bills you for services rendered on an hourly, daily, or project basis.

If you do decide to employ an advertising firm, do not engage the first one that you contact. First, talk to the principals of the agency and get some definite information about them. This should include: the size of the agency; that is, last year's billing, how long the principals have been with the agency, their general philosophy of positioning, whether they deal mainly with industrial accounts or with consumer accounts, and what some of their accounts are. You should also query them to find out in which areas of your business they would like to become involved. Some agencies handle everything for you. Others develop and place your ads, and that's it. Ask who at the agency is working directly on your account and his or her title, and who is responsible for supervision on a day-to-day basis. You should also ask for representative accounts, accounts similar to yours with which the advertising agency has experience, so that you may contact those firms. You should ask about compensation arrangements: If you are going to be spending $10 thousand or more on advertising, it is perfectly legitimate to ask for a speculative presentation by the agency. In fact, you should ask for a proposal from several different agencies. During these speculative presentations, you can get a feel for what the agency can do and whether you like or do not like the people and services you are paying for. There are, however, certain disadvantages to asking several agencies for proposals. They have competitive information on your firm, and some agencies see this as exploitive as they must pay for this proposal even if they do not get your business. In general, it is better not to ask for a speculative proposal unless the agency is a serious candidate.

As mentioned earlier, one of the problems that you may have as a small firm is getting an agency to work with you. One way to do this is to stress your tremendous growth potential. If you don't have much cash, try barter. That is, trade your product or services for their services. Finally, you could offer stock in your company in exchange for their services.

How to Get Free Advertising through a Publicity Release

Every magazine is constantly looking for new ideas, new news, and new information to tell its readers. So, whenever you have a new product or service or something different happens with regard to your current product or service that might be of interest to a magazine's readers, many magazines are happy to publicize it and charge you nothing. This has an additional advantage. Editorial coverage of your product or service is usually more effective than your own advertising. You should understand that magazines do not run every single idea or product publicity release that you submit. To reach those that do, you must run a direct-mail campaign. Your campaign package should consist of three basic elements:

1. A sales letter to the editor.
2. A release or suggested editorial material about your new product or service.
3. Either the product itself or a 4-by-5-inch glossy photograph of the product (generally a photograph is just as good, unless your product is a book or a booklet).

How to Get Newspapers All over the Country to Give You Free Publicity

Another type of promotion is one that I did for my book *Building a Mail Order Business* (John Wiley & Sons). I wrote to editors of the family or general interest sections of newspapers all over the country. I offered each exclusive use in their geographic area of a short article I had written called "Can Anyone Make a Million Dollars in Mail Order?" Naturally, I mentioned my book. This got me free newspaper coverage all over the country and eventually led to numerous appearances on radio and TV. As a result, we sold thousands of books that we would not otherwise have sold.

Sources of Additional Information

Books

Guerrilla Publicity, by Jay Levinson, Rick Frishman, and Jill Lublin, published by Adams Media Corporation.

Hey Whipple, Squeeze This, by Luke Williams, published by John Wiley & Sons.

How to Advertise: A Handbook for Small Business, by Sandra Linville Dean, published by Enterprise Publishing, Inc.

How to Advertise and Promote Your Business, by Connie McClung Siegel, published by John Wiley & Sons.

How to Be Your Own Advertising Agency, by Herbert J. Holtje, published by AMACOM.

How to Get Big Results from a Small Advertising Budget, by Cynthia S. Smith, published by Hawthorne Books, Inc.

How to Write a Good Advertisement, by Victor O. Schwab, published by Wilshire Book Co.

Risk Free Advertising, by Victor Wademan, published by John Wiley & Sons.

Tested Advertising Methods, by John Caples, published by Reward Books.

The Small Town Advertising Handbook, by Tom Egelhoff, published by smalltownmarketing.com.

The Successful Promoter, by Ted Schwarz, published by Contemporary Books.

Internet

Note: Because Internet sites frequently go down, multiple sites are listed for similar subject matter.

Advertising: Basic. Businesstown.com provides links to numerous articles on advertising and promotion at http://www.businesstown.com/advertising/basic.asp.

Advertising for Your Small Business, by Ian White. Links to numerous articles and free guides at http://www.access2000.com.au/Guides/Advertising/advertising.htm.

Advertising Media, by Hairong Li. A good general article on advertising media with statistics on various advertising methods at http://www.admedia.org.

Publicity.com, by Bill Stoller. Free sample issue of free publicity newsletter with many good ideas at http://www.publicityinsider.com.

Small Business Advertising. Numerous links to articles and advertising web sites at http://www.boiseadvertiser.com/smadv.htm.

Word of Mouth Advertising. Market Navigation, Inc. provides a collection of articles through links with a number of articles regarding what some consider one of the most effective methods of promotion at http://www.mnav.com.

Your First Job Is to Get Them to See Your Advertising, by Noel Peeples. A lot of good information and a link to a free minicourse on advertising. Accessed at http://www.marketleadersltd.com/Advertising_Of_Small_Business.htm.

DOWNLOADABLE WORKSHEET 11.1
Developing Profiles of Your Target Markets

Note: Complete a separate profile for each market you intend to pursue. Check all that apply for each profile.

Personal Demographic Information

1. Sex: Male _____ Female _____

2. Age: Under 6 _____ 6 to 11 _____ 12 to 17 _____ 18 to 24 _____ 25 to 34 _____
35 to 44 _____ 45 to 54 _____ 55 to 64 _____ 65 and over _____

3. Martial Status: Married _____ Single (never married) _____ Widowed _____
Divorced or Separated _____

4. Education: Grade school or less (Grades 1–8) _____ Some high school (grades 9–12 _____
Graduated from high school _____ Some college _____ Graduated from college _____
Some postgraduate college work _____ Masters Degree _____ Doctoral Degree _____

5. Principal Language Spoken at Home: English _____ Spanish _____ Other _____

6. Ethnicity: _____

7. Employment: Unemployed _____ Not employed, looking for work _____
Self-employed at home _____ Self-employed outside the home _____
Employed, working for someone else _____
Employed full-time (30 hours per week or more) _____
Employed part-time (less than 30 hours per week) _____

8. Occupation: Professional and technical _____
Managers, officials, and proprietors, except farm _____ Clerical _____ Sales _____
Craftsman _____ Foreman _____ Nonfarm laborers _____ Service workers _____
Private household workers _____ Farm managers _____ Farm laborers _____
Farm foreman _____ Armed forces _____ Retired _____ Student _____
Other _____

9. Geographic Region: Northeast _____ Metropolitan New York _____ Mid-Atlantic _____
East Central _____ Metropolitan Chicago _____ West Central _____ Southeast _____
Southwest _____ Metropolitan Los Angeles _____ Remaining Pacific Rim _____

10. Geographic Type: Central City _____ Urban Fringe (suburbs) _____ Town _____
Rural _____

---

11. Population of City or Town: 25,000 or less _____ 50,000 to 25,000 _____
    100,000 to 50,001 _____ 250,000 to 100,001 _____ 500,000 to 250,001 _____
    1,000,000 to 500,001 _____ 5,000,000 to 1,000,001 _____ 5,000,001 or more _____

Household Demographic Information

12. Household Size: 1 member _____ 2 members _____ 3 members _____
    4 members _____ 5 members _____ 6 or more members _____

13. Number of Children: None _____ One _____ Two _____ Three or more _____

14. Children in Household by Age: Under 2 years _____ 2 to 5 years _____
    6 to 10 years _____ 11 to 13 years _____ 14 to 18 years _____ 19 years or older _____

15. Other Dependents in Household by Sex: Male _____ Female _____

16. Household Income: Under $15,000 _____ $15,001 to $25,000 _____
    $25,001 to $50,000 _____ $50,001 to $100,000 _____ $100,000 or greater _____

17. Income Earners in the Family: Male _____ Female _____ Children _____

18. Residence Ownership: Own _____ Rent _____

19. Dwelling Characteristics: House (unattached) _____ Attached home _____
    Apartment _____ Mobile home or trailer _____ Other _____

20. Type of Work of Primary Wage Earner: Unskilled _____ Blue-collar worker _____
    Self-employed business owner _____ Self-employed professional _____
    Employed professional or manager _____ Independently wealty/unemployed _____
    Unemployed _____ Other _____

Psychographic Information

21. Typical Member of Target Market Is: Very competitive _____ Usually follows others _____
    Want things arranged, organized, secure, and predictable _____ Self-centered _____
    Seeks independence _____ A joiner _____ Analyzes self and others _____
    Seeks aid, help, and advice from others _____ Desires to control and/or lead others _____
    Feels inferior _____ Wants to help others _____ Seeking new occupations _____
    Sticks to a task and works hard to complete a job _____ Enjoys social activities _____
    Ambitious _____ Self-confident _____ Stressed _____

(continued)

Life-Style Preferences and Attitudes

22. Leisure activities: Entertaining _____ Movies _____ Plays _____ Concerts _____
Opera _____ Dinner _____ Reading _____ Listening to music _____
Watching television _____ Internet activities _____ Playing games _____
Watching sporting events _____ Cooking _____ Other _____

23. About the Family: Thinks the man should be the boss and run the family _____
Thinks the woman should be the boss and run the family _____
Believes marriage should be a partnership with no bosses _____
Thinks children should be an important part of most family decisions _____

24. Regarding Dress: Likes to wear casual, comfortable clothes most of the time _____
Wants to look fashionable and stylish most of the time _____
Is concerned about a professional appearance most of the time _____

25. Physical Condition and Health: Is concerned about health _____
Is unconcerned about health _____ Has a health problem _____
Has a weight problem _____ A frequent user of nonprescription drugs _____
A frequent user of vitamin, mineral, or herb supplements _____
Exercises regularly _____ Desires to exercise regularly, but does not do so _____

26. Finances: Is financially secure _____ Concerned about finances _____
Habitually in debt _____

27. Risk Preference: Conservative and does not take chances _____
Willing to take calculated risks _____ Frequently takes chances _____

28. Buying Less Expensive Products: Picks the same brand habitually in most cases _____
Looks for bargains, deals, premiums _____ Wants quality, will pay extra to get it _____
Rarely takes chances on unknown products or manufacturers _____
Likes to try new and different products and services _____
Plans shopping carefully with a list of needs and makes an excursion out of the trip _____
Analyzes ingredients, weight, and package size _____
Never reads the information on a package to find out what it contains _____
Relies heavily on the opinion of others prior to purchase _____
Relies heavily on advertisements for information _____

Media Use

29. Primary Sources of Information on Products or Services: Word-of-mouth from friends _____
    Newspaper ads _____ Radio ads _____ Television ads _____ Direct mail _____
    Telephone solicitation _____ Ads on buses and transit vehicles _____ Billboards _____
    E-mail _____ Internet _____ Other _____

30. Uses media at these times: 6 A.M. to 10:00 A.M. _____ 10:00 A.M. to 3:00 P.M. _____
    3:00 P.M. to 7:00 P.M. _____ 7:00 P.M. to 12 A.M. _____ 12 A.M. to 6:00 A.M. _____
    Pays particular attention to these types of stories or programs: Local news _____
    National news _____ Weather _____ Sports _____ Business and finance _____
    Editorials and interviews _____ Classified _____ Daytime serials _____
    Comics or comedy shows _____ Crime news or programs _____ Adventure _____
    Quizzes or game shows _____ Movies _____ Self-help stories _____
    How-to-do-it _____ Theater, arts, and entertainment _____ Editorials _____
    Interviews _____ Travel _____ Drama _____ Soap operas _____
    Reality show _____ Dramas _____ Situation comedies _____ Science fiction _____
    Cooking and homemaking _____ Cartoons _____ Beauty contests _____
    Documentaries _____ Other _____

DOWNLOADABLE WORKSHEET 11.2
Establishing an Advertising and Publicity Budget

Project	Month		Year to Date	
	Budget	Actual	Budget	Actual
Media				
Newspapers				
Radio				
TV				
Internet				
Literature				
Direct Mail				
Other				
Promotions Associated				
Exhibits				
Displays				
Contests				
Sweepstakes				
Premiums				
Discount Coupons				
Other				
Advertising Expense				
Salaries				
Supplies				
Stationery				
Travel				
Postage				
Subscriptions				
Entertainment				
Dues				
Other				
Totals				

To customize this document, download it to your hard drive from the John Wiley & Sons web site at www.wiley .com/go/cohenentrepreneur. The document can then be opened, edited, and printed using Microsoft Word or another popular word processing application.

CHAPTER 12

How to Sell and Build Your Own Sales Organization

As a method of promotion, personal selling of your product is a major consideration. Unlike other methods of promotion, including advertising, publicity releases, contests, and sweepstakes, personal selling involves face-to-face communication and feedback. That gives it a tremendous edge over any other method and leads to six primary advantages.

The Six Primary Advantages of Personal Selling

There are six primary advantages that personal selling has over other promotional methods:

1. *More flexibility:* Your salespeople can vary and tailor their sales presentations depending on the prospects' needs, behavior, motives, special situations, and environment at the time of the presentation.

2. *Immediate feedback:* Salespeople can vary their presentation and approach depending on the reaction as they proceed.

3. *Market pinpointing:* Much advertising is wasted because you pay for sending your message to individuals who may be readers or viewers of a vehicle but are not real prospects for your goods or service. With face-to-face personal selling, greater pinpointing of the target consumer is possible than with other means of promotion because you can immediately eliminate prospects who are not real candidates for purchase.

4. *On-the-spot sales:* Personal selling is the only method of promotion with which you can sell the product and receive money immediately.

5. *Not just sales:* Your salespeople can perform other necessary services while making sales calls. For instance, they can do customer research,

relay customer complaints, develop credit information, and verify the reality of customer prospects.

6. *No time limit:* An advertisement gets read. It either does its work or is disregarded. But until they get thrown out, your salespeople can keep trying to make the sale.

The Big Disadvantage of Personal Selling

Face-to-face selling has one single disadvantage, and it is a big one: high cost. The cost of recruiting, motivating, training, and operating a sales force is not low. Finding the caliber of people necessary to do the job may be extremely expensive. As energy costs have skyrocketed, so has the cost of each individual sales call. In many parts of the country today, a single sales call may cost $200 or more.

Because of this major limitation, sales forces and face-to-face selling must be used wisely and efficiently. This chapter shows you how to accomplish this.

What Different Sales Jobs Do Salespeople Do?

Salespeople do a variety of different types of sales jobs. Some sales jobs simply require order taking rather than actually persuading an individual to buy something. Others require the sale of complicated, sophisticated, and expensive machinery or technology. The different sales jobs are sometimes placed into seven groups:

Group 1: Product delivery persons. With this type of sales position, selling is actually secondary to delivering the product, be it milk, fuel oil, or soft drinks. This type of salespeople rarely originates sales. Therefore, a persuasive personality is not required, although an individual who performs good service and is reasonably pleasant may ultimately increase sales over a period of time.

Group 2: Inside order-takers. Inside order-takers are salespeople who generally work inside, behind retail counters. In this case, and in the majority of situations, the customer entered the store to buy. These salespeople primarily service the customer. Sales can be increased by the order-taker's helpful attitude, but usually not significantly so.

Group 3: Outside order-takers. Outside order-takers are salespeople who work in the field outside of the store. Their job generally involves calling on retail food establishments. They do little or no selling, but, like the sales-people in the first group, are primarily delivery people.

Group 4: Missionary salespeople. The primary job of missionary salespeople is to build goodwill while performing promotional activities or providing other services to a customer. Examples of these types of salespeople are those detail men and women who service physicians and the pharmaceutical industry. They may be expected or even permitted to solicit orders.

Group 5: Technical salespeople. Technical salespeople such as sales engineers don't need persuasive powers so much as they need technical, in-depth knowledge of the product or service, which they can display when dealing with the customer. No matter how persuasive, a technical sales-person cannot be successful without this technical background. Therefore, technical knowledge is the foremost trait required for salespeople in this group.

Group 6: Creative sellers of tangibles. These are salespeople who must sell tangible products through creative selling. That is, they must actually persuade people to purchase. Now, we are getting into a more difficult sales job because the customer may not be aware of a need for the product or how the product can satisfy his or her needs better than other products or services he or she is currently using. The creative seller may sell a product that is also technical; however, in this case, persuasiveness and other sales traits are absolutely required. Creative sellers of tangible products sell everything from encyclopedias to airplanes.

Group 7: Creative sellers of intangibles. This is probably the most difficult of sales positions. Not only must the salesperson be persuasive and be able to sell, but he or she must sell a product that is not easily demonstrated and cannot be shown to or touched by the customer. Products that fall into the intangibles category include insurance, consulting services, and advertising.

Knowing what kind of salesperson you want is very important. If you get the wrong type for your sales job, you either fail to get sales or waste money on individuals who meet qualifications and have abilities you do not need.

Three Keys to Developing a Superior Sales Force

Your sales force can do a poor, mediocre, or terrific job in selling for you. It all depends on you and your ability to develop your sales force. Here are three keys to success:

1. *Selection:* You've got to find the best salespeople for the job. It is a challenging problem, but if you succeed, the best salespeople make a major contribution to the overall sales ability of your organization.

2. *Training:* Once you have superior people, they must be given the correct training to maximize and build on the use of their sales ability.

3. *Compensation:* Compensation plans depend on many factors. They are critical in sales because compensation is what motivates your salespeople and makes them perform. Performance cannot be measured simply in terms of sales volume. While the importance of sales volume cannot be overemphasized, other factors may be very important to your organization. These factors may include service, providing information to customers and creating goodwill.

Sources of Salespeople

Salespeople present some unique recruiting challenges. For example, a research study in the insurance industry revealed that there were four primary sources for prospective insurance salespeople:

1. Salespeople personally known by the hiring sales manager.
2. Individuals with influence.
3. Individuals selected from the present sales force and given new geographical territories or sent to new locations.
4. Salespeople recruited through direct-mail advertising.

Which of these groups do you think did best? Those salespeople recruited from the present sales force did five times as much business the first month as those recruited cold through direct-mail advertising. Also of interest is that it took six times as long to complete negotiations and start the new sales recruits doing business from groups 3 and 4 as it did to start those from groups 1 and 2.

Other sources of salespeople that you should consider in your sales force recruiting are as follows:

- *Those working for you who are not currently in sales:* Be alert for the bright, persuasive individual with a sales-type personality who is interested in selling. Such an individual may be moved from another position in your company to become very effective for you in a sales position.

- *Recommendations from present customers:* Your current customers may assist you by recommending effective salespeople who they know and have worked with personally. Do you think a customer is more likely to buy from someone he recommended? You better believe it!

- *Local schools and universities:* New graduates are always looking for opportunities, and working in sales is a great way to start a career. If you have such an opportunity, schools and colleges may assist you in finding candidates from among their students.

- *Recommendations from your present sales force:* Your present sales force frequently comes in contact with other salespeople from other companies and in other industries. They may have some excellent recommendations for new recruits.

Selecting Good Salespeople

To begin the selection process, you must identify what type of salesperson you need. Next, establish a job description and list of specifications that you want the salesperson to possess. Armed with a job description and these specifications, you can search for sources of available salespeople and finally implement your selection system.

Critical Elements of a Sales Force Selection System   The six critical elements of your selection system are as follows:

1. Application forms.
2. References.
3. The interview.
4. Intelligence and aptitude tests.
5. Physical examination.
6. Field observations of candidates.

While application forms, references, and interviewing are discussed in detail in Chapter 17, it is important to realize that, for salespeople, the most important quality in a candidate is his or her readiness and ability to sell. Therefore, you should not hesitate to emphasize this aspect, especially in checking on references and in the personal, face-to-face interview.

To make the personal interview more objective, some interviewers of potential salespeople use a form having a semantic differential intensity scale to note differences. Various attributes can be more or less objectively rated immediately through judgment. Worksheet 12.1 has been developed for your use in interviewing potential sales personnel.

Keep in mind the importance of doing your own thinking about the kind of salesperson you need. Then, develop procedures that help in selecting individuals who meet the requirements of your situation. In selecting salespeople, there is always the question: How do you tell whether the candidate is really qualified? How do you determine whether the candidate has: initiative, reliability, mental ability, and other requirements for the job?

You have to make a judgment based on what you can learn about the candidate. His or her application gives you some information. You get additional facts and impressions about his or her past performance and personal style in a personal interview and by talking at length with him or her. Sometimes you may test him or her by asking critical questions about your industry and its customers. Or you might use tests, which are prepared by firms that specialize in their preparation.

Tests, physical examinations, and field observations are particularly important for sales positions. Because the sales job itself may require considerable fieldwork, good health and personal appearance may have a direct bearing on success or failure. Therefore, if the job is at all demanding physically, a physical examination should be required prior to hiring. There are types of intelligence and aptitude tests for selling that became extremely popular after World War II. Most are controversial today because it was found that they are far from perfect and may eliminate a few excellent candidates while allowing some poor candidates to get through. However, psychological testing eliminates candidates who are totally unsuited for selling. Administering these tests has one additional advantage: It impresses the potential employee with the importance that you place on the sales position. This can have a motivational effect on the candidates you hire.

However, be very careful with psychological testing. Have a professional evaluate the results. You can find such psychological testers listed in the Yellow Pages under "Aptitude and Employment Testing" or through an Internet search. It may be dangerous to purchase the test and attempt to evaluate the results on your own. One firm that tried this eventually discovered that candidates it hired who scored well on a test were in reality much poorer performers than those who scored less well.

For some very important positions, on-the-job observation may be necessary to determine whether the salesperson is suitable or not. This can be done through a conditional hire over a relatively short period, usually of several weeks or months. An acceptable performance under personal observation is made one of the criteria for changing this temporary hire to permanent employee status.

Above all, it is important to check references before making a decision. Use the telephone or a face-to-face contact because a former employer may be too busy, or reluctant, to express himself freely in writing. Also, you can tell a lot by voice inflections and intonations about what the former employer really thinks about the candidate.

Training Salespeople

There are four main areas in which training contributes to the success of your sales force regardless of the type of selling in which they are engaged.

1. Knowledge.
2. Work habits.
3. Selling skills.
4. Attitude.

Knowledge   A salesperson must have knowledge of the product or service, knowledge of the company, knowledge of the sales environment, and knowledge of the entire environmental situation in which he or she is operating. Only with knowledge can the sales individual best explain the product or the service to the customer.

Work Habits   The salesperson's work habits are responsible for great success as well as great failure stories. An individual's work habits can also spell the difference between sales success and failure in your company. With sales calls as expensive as they are, a salesperson who makes few calls can ruin you in short order. Making calls is a matter of mental attitude and selling work habits. Some applicants with little or no sales experience take jobs as salespeople simply to tide them over while they look for something else. I have known situations where such individuals, unsupervised by small business owners made no sales calls at all, but spent all of their time looking for another job.

Selling Skills   There are so-called natural salespeople. But, while some individuals may be naturally better suited for selling than others, sales skills can be learned and mastered by many people. Part of your challenge is judging what the sales candidate already brings to the table and what needs to be learned and developed.

Attitude   A critical factor of performance in selling is attitude. It is so important that most books by successful salespersons emphasize this single factor above all others. If a salesperson has a positive attitude and the desire to succeed, he or she is probably going to succeed. I have seen hundreds of determined salespeople who started off poorly, but went on to become sales stars. It is the salesperson's attitude that ultimately spells the difference between success and failure.

METHODS OF TRAINING SALESPEOPLE   There are several methods that you can use to help to train your salespeople to become sales superstars:

- *Indoctrination training:* With indoctrination training, you give your salespeople basic orientation on the sales job and show them how it is done. In many cases, your sales manager accompanies the new salesperson to help him or her learn the job through observation. As the salesperson gets more and more experience, he or she takes over more and more of the job, and finally the manager backs off entirely and the salesperson is on his or her own.

- *Job rotation training:* Job rotation training is generally for larger companies. A salesperson spends a certain amount of time in a variety of jobs, which may include positions in the factory, in production, in research and development, in the office, and in a sales branch. This way he or she gets a better idea of how the salesperson's job fits into other company operations.

- *In-class training:* When field experience cannot be easily given, or sometimes even if it is, classes can be conducted to train salespeople how to do their job. This training is particularly effective for providing new information on products, the company, the market, and so forth. The classroom can also be used for motivation. Moreover, selling skills can be taught and experienced through various types of role playing. However, in-class training is time consuming. In a very small company, extensive classroom training may take too many of your resources. Even so, many successful smaller companies begin with full-time training for new salespeople lasting from several days to a week or more. They have found that it is worth the investment.

- *Sales meetings:* Sales meetings act as a training ground for new salespeople as well as for salespeople who have been with the firm. In sales meetings, they can trade experiences and build friendly competition. You can also give additional or new training to help salespeople increase their job effectiveness.

- *Seminars:* Many training or seminar companies around the country offer training programs especially designed to train new salespeople. My own company, The Institute of Leader Arts (www.stuffofheroes.com), offers a variety of customized programs for all types of organizations. There are many training organizations, both national and local, that can provide training needs for your salespeople. These companies can be located in the Yellow Pages under "Training—Sales or Sales Training" headings. You can also find many organizations by doing a similar search over the Internet. An investment of this type can pay off tremendously in the effectiveness of all your sales employees.

Compensating the Salesperson

The compensation plan for salespeople is particularly important, and it has definite aims. These aims include encouraging the highest volume of sales for your most profitable items while at the same time providing motivation and incentive for your salespeople to work harder at selling your product or service. Specifically, your compensation plan must have objectives both for you and for your salespeople.

Objectives for your salespeople include:

- To receive compensation in direct proportion to sales accomplishments.
- To be compensated for time spent with the customer that does not directly result in sales, such as "missionary" work and service to the customer.
- To have provisions for security, retirement, and possible seasonal or other slumps in selling.
- To receive compensation on a par with what could be earned selling for other companies or for other lines of products or services.
- To have a sense of esprit de corps and accomplishment, not only within the sales force but with other employees.

Your objectives may include:

- To motivate and inspire your salespeople to increase sales.
- To encourage your salespeople to sell high-profit items.
- To enable your firm to maintain the maximum of profit consistent with other factors including compensation for your salespeople that meet all criteria listed as objectives.
- To maintain the maximum control possible over your sales force and your salespeople's activities.
- To encourage cooperation among your salespeople and with other functional areas and people in your company.
- To encourage esprit de corps both in the sales force and your company.

Three Basic Means of Compensating a Sales Force There are three basic ways to compensate the sales force: (1) salary, (2) commission, and (3) combination plans. Each has its advantages and its disadvantages.

With a salary plan, you have an arrangement whereby you pay a defined amount of money, weekly, monthly, or annually, in return for whatever work is required by the sales force. It has the following advantages:

- It is easy for the company to budget and administer.
- Because the compensation is guaranteed so long as the salesperson works for you, it allows for the greatest amount of control over your sales force.
- It is generally easier to recruit salespeople for this type of compensation plan.
- Because compensation is guaranteed, extravagant promises or overselling by your salespeople is discouraged.
- It is easier to arrange for your salespeople to accomplish nonselling activities because their "time is not money."
- The system encourages the maximum cooperation among salespeople and other members of your company.
- It is easier to transfer salespeople to other territories using this plan.

However, this compensation plan also has disadvantages:

- There is a lack of incentive for high sales.
- Salary is a fixed cost unrelated to sales revenue.
- So-called super salespeople are rarely attracted by a straight salary because they can make much more money on a commission system.
- If business activity is declining, it is very difficult to adjust salaries. You generally are forced to discharge some of your salespeople. This means morale problems and additional costs for training and hiring when business conditions improve.
- Salaries must be paid whether there are any sales.

Straight salary plans are usually most useful under any of four conditions:

1. For compensating new salespeople who are not yet ready to assume their full responsibilities.
2. For compensating missionary salespeople whose duties are not to make an immediate sale, but whose work eventually leads to sales over a period of months or even years.
3. For opening new territories in which you have not formerly been selling.
4. For sales of sophisticated or technical products requiring lengthy negotiations.

A compensation plan using sales commissions alone is simply an agreement on your part to pay the salesperson a percentage of each dollar of a product or service sold. In such a plan, the salesperson is usually entirely on his or her own. A successful salesperson can make a lot of money. An unsuccessful salesperson makes nothing. In some states, the straight commission plan has been modified because minimum wages must be paid. However, the basic principle is the same. The amount earned is directly related to sales made. Advantages of the commission plan are as follows:

- A company with limited capital can fully staff its sales force without high overhead commitments.
- This method provides direct incentive for high sales.
- A commission plan attracts more aggressive and persuasive salespeople because these are the only ones that can make it work successfully.
- The costs of sales are automatically reduced if and when sales decline.

The commission plan has its disadvantages, although at first it may appear that the system is absolutely ideal for any company. The disadvantages of the commission system of compensation are:

- There is a great deal of difficulty getting salespeople to devote time to sales tasks that may be important to your company but for which no commission is paid.
- There is great danger in overselling the customer and possibly incurring customer ill will.
- There is a great deal of bookkeeping involved.
- There is potentially greater difficulty in recruiting.
- There is less cooperation within the company among salespeople and other functional areas.

Because of the potential difficulties with straight commission plans, some modifications have been made. For example, with the commission against draw modification of the straight commission, a salesperson is allowed to draw a certain amount of money ahead of his or her sales against commissions that are earned later. This sales advance or draw allows the salesperson to at least make living expenses even during a slump. As soon as the first commissions are earned, they are used to pay the draw that the salesperson has already been advanced.

With the modified commission scale, a commission rate is established by a series of steps. It is frequently used with the draw to help the salesperson pay off the money advanced as rapidly as possible. To do this, a higher commission may be paid on the first sales until the money advanced is covered; then the commission rate may drop to lower levels or steps depending on the scale that is constructed. This is also advantageous to the company if sales are greater than anticipated because the commission is less on the higher amount of sales. The approach, however, does have a disadvantage; some companies take the opposite tactic and increase commission percentage for higher amounts of sales. In some cases, this increase is exercised through a bonus plan, a bonus being paid for effort resulting in increased sales or sales above a certain set goal or quota.

Let us say that you are paying 10 percent commission and have established the quota for salespeople of $20,000 in sales per month. The bonus comes into play if this $20,000 per month is exceeded. Perhaps you offer an additional 5 percent bonus for sales exceeding the quota. Thus, if a salesperson only met this quota, he or she receives $20,000 times 10 percent or $2,000 commission. But for sales of $30,000 a month, your salesperson receives $30,000 times 10 percent or $3,000, plus an additional 5 percent of the $10,000 difference between $20,000 and $30,000, or an additional $500. Therefore, the total amount of compensation is $3,000 plus $500 or $3,500.

Commission plans work well under the following circumstances:

• Where considerable incentive and motivation are needed to get high sales.

• Where very little missionary work or other sales assistance that does not have to do with closing out a sale is required.

• Where the company is not so strong financially that it can afford large amounts of overhead to compensate salespeople whether any sales are made.

• Where salespeople can operate independently.

Combination plans offer a fixed compensation element plus a variable element made up of a commission on sales or a bonus based on volume. In combination plans, the fixed portion is a salary. The variable portion is used to motivate sales and to achieve many of the benefits of the commission type of compensation plan. The variable element of the combination plan may include payments on sales volume, payments on a performance evaluation, a combination of volume and a performance evaluation, or some type of bonus. The advantages of combination plans are:

• Flexibility in dealing with the overall job of selling the company's product or service.

• Flexibility in making changes in territory assignment or assignment of customers.

• Choice among the various factors that motivates the salespeople to work independently to achieve high sales.

• Ability to group salespeople for team selling situations of major products while applying direct incentive as well as salary compensation to motivate this performance.

The disadvantages of combination plans are:

- Complexity in construction of the plan.
- Amount of time required for administration and bookkeeping.
- Difficulty of explaining the plan to salespeople.
- The need for constant review to be sure the factors that are being used as part of the overall compensation are doing what they are supposed to be doing.

The combination plan can work well for many companies, but to use it you must balance the best features of the salary plan and the commission plan, while at the same time trying to eliminate their disadvantages. This isn't always easy and requires considerable thinking and planning ahead of time. It should be used when (1) a complex selling task is to be rewarded, and (2) factors other than volume are considered important and yet an incentive element is definitely required.

How to Measure the Performance of Your Sales Personnel

Until you know how your sales force is performing, you have no way of making meaningful changes that improve performance. Therefore, it is necessary to develop a means of evaluation. In general, this is done through two methods: judging quantitative factors and judging qualitative factors. Quantitative factors generally are easier because they are specific and objective. Sales volume either goes up or it does not. You see the results in black and white. Qualitative factors must rely much on subjective judgment. However, in many types of sales operations, qualitative factors must be considered because of the importance of their influence on company objectives.

Quantitative Factors

The following are factors in sales that are useful in comparing quantitative performance:

- Sales volume segmented as to areas, products, customer groups, and so forth.
- Sales volume as a percentage of a predetermined quota or calculated territorial potential.
- Gross profit.
- Sales that may be segmented by number of orders, average size, or similar factors.

- Closing ratio (a ratio of the number of sales closes divided by the number of calls made).
- Percentage of new accounts sold.
- Number of new accounts sold.
- Number of new accounts sold divided by number of new accounts called on.

Qualitative Factors

The following are factors that should be considered in evaluating your sales force on a qualitative basis:

- Analytical ability.
- Company knowledge.
- Competition knowledge.
- Customer relations.
- Decision-making ability.
- General attitude.
- General knowledge of sales environment, the customer, legal aspects, and the product.
- Health.
- Organization and management of time.
- Personal appearance.
- Personality.
- Preparation for presentations and sales calls.
- Product knowledge.

Should You Use Sales Territories?

A sales territory is a geographical area in which a salesperson does his or her business. His or her activities may be limited in certain areas or may not be. Further, he or she may not have an exclusive over a certain area. Establishing sales territories has the following advantages:

- It fixes precise performance responsibilities.
- It helps a salesperson to organize his or her time.
- It helps maximize customer service.

- It cuts down on overlapping of sales efforts.
- It fosters competition and comparison among salespeople in different territories.
- It helps equalize opportunities in various territories among different salespeople.
- It makes for adaptation of certain background personality factors and desires of salespeople to their customers.
- It helps control the overall sales operation.
- It ensures that all of your salespeople have ample opportunities to sell.
- It helps maintain total and efficient coverage of your entire market.

Despite these advantages, in certain circumstances, it is better not to limit your salespeople to distinct territories. This may be true if you don't have sufficient salespeople to cover all the territories that might be available, or if certain of your salespeople seem to operate better when they are freewheeling, and maybe you can get the best results out of all of them if you do not establish territorial rights. Sometimes you are not able to establish territory divisions fairly. In this case, it is better not to establish them at all. And in some industries, such as executive recruiting, it may make sense not to establish territories on a geographical basis but rather to group your salespeople around functional areas of business. Finally, if you are introducing a new product and you want to saturate the market as quickly as possible, the restrictions of sales territories may slow the process down because some of your salespeople cover their territories more rapidly than others.

How to Establish Sales Territories

If you're going to establish sales territories, it is important first to establish them fairly. Therefore, there must be some basis of comparison. Usually, select a market index or indices relating to the product or the service that you are selling. These indices are usually based on one or more demographic factors, such as income, which would represent buying power or segments of the population interested in the product or the service. For example, if you were selling a high-priced automobile, how many families in the area or the potential area, which would constitute a geographical territory, could afford such a car? Or, if you had a product that went in the home, how many homes are in the territory that use such a product? Sometimes a combination of different factors is used with a weighting system applied depending on the relative importance of the factor. In this fashion, territories are divided with indices resulting in approximately the same sales potential.

Next, determine how wide an area a salesperson can handle. Factors such as distance, call frequency, as well as numbers that a salesperson can process must all be considered. This impacts the size of the different territories that are divided, and also lets you know how many salespeople you need to cover a particular area.

At this point, you may begin allotting the various territories based on market potential to salespeople. Various adjustments may be necessary depending upon local conditions, demand, competition, transportation factors, the product, and other strategic and environmental variables. For example, if a newer product is being sold, the territory may be expanded to give the salesperson having to sell this new product greater opportunity to sell a profitable volume. Each factor for adjustment should be considered on an individual basis so that the net result is territories that have essentially identical market potential and number of accounts that can be serviced by the salesperson. Territory allotment should be done so that the servicing of the territories is profitable to you and profitable to the individual doing the selling.

Sources of Additional Information

Books

How I Raised Myself from Failure to Success in Selling, by Frank Bettger, published by Fireside.

How to Hire and Develop Your Next Top Performer, by Herbert Greenberg, published by McGraw-Hill.

How to Master the Art of Selling, by Tom Hopkins, published by Warner Books.

How to Sell Anything to Anybody, by Joe Girard, Stanley Brown, and Robert Casemore, published by Warner Books.

Sales Management, by Robert J. Calvin, published by McGraw-Hill.

Soft Sell, by Tim Connor, published by Sourcebooks.

The Lacy Techniques of Salesmanship, by Paul J. Micali, published by E. P. Dutton.

The Sales Managers Handbook, by Joseph C. Elders, published by Authorhouse.

Internet

Note: Because Internet sites frequently go down, multiple sites are listed for similar subject matter.

Ambassador of Selling. This site contains many articles on selling at http://www.sellingselling.com/articles.html#Anchor-Article-59579.

Market News Magazine. This is a free online course on salesmanship published for the Canadian electronic industry at http://www.marketnews.ca/training_sales.cgi.

Positive Results. Numerous articles on selling plus newsletter at http://www.positiveresults .com/sen/archives/index.asp.

Sales Dog.com. Offers a free weekly newsletter with lots of articles and advice at http://www.salesdog.com.

Sales Vault. Many articles on salesmanship and selling at http://www.salesvault.com.

DOWNLOADABLE WORKSHEET 12.1
Sales Interview Objective Assessments

Objectively rating potential sales personnel during job interviews is particularly challenging because salespeople are trained to sell—a product, service, and themselves. Therefore, the more objective we can be regarding rating potential new hires, the better. One way of doing this is to use the semantic differential scales provided in this worksheet. This allows a good assessment both of the individual potential hire, as well as a comparison with other candidates who may interview at a later time. Just circle the number that best represents your impression and then total these numbers. If you have special criteria to consider, just add it to the list.

1. General appearance

Poor   1   2   3   4   5   6   7   8   9   10   Excellent

2. Dress

Poor   1   2   3   4   5   6   7   8   9   10   Excellent

3. Verbal communication

Poor   1   2   3   4   5   6   7   8   9   10   Excellent

4. Technical knowledge

Poor   1   2   3   4   5   6   7   8   9   10   Excellent

5. Persuasiveness

Poor   1   2   3   4   5   6   7   8   9   10   Excellent

6. Flexibility

Poor   1   2   3   4   5   6   7   8   9   10   Excellent

To customize this document, download it to your hard drive from the John Wiley & Sons web site at www.wiley .com/go/cohenentrepreneur. The document can then be opened, edited, and printed using Microsoft Word or another popular word processing application.

7. Attitude toward work

_____

Poor   1   2   3   4   5   6   7   8   9   10   Excellent

8. Intelligence

_____

Poor   1   2   3   4   5   6   7   8   9   10   Excellent

9. Ability to sell himself or herself

_____

Poor   1   2   3   4   5   6   7   8   9   10   Excellent

10. Overall impression

_____

Poor   1   2   3   4   5   6   7   8   9   10   Excellent

Total Point Score _____ points

DOWNLOADABLE WORKSHEET 12.2
Information Required from Potential Salespeople

It is important that you thoroughly know your sales candidate's prior sales experience and motivation. Therefore, always obtain the maximum information possible before you make the hire decision. This should include the following information:

Company _____ Address _____

Supervisor _____ Tel. No. _____ E-mail Address _____

Product or Service _____ Company Annual Sales _____ Number of Salespeople _____

Sales Productivity: Upper 25% _____ Middle 50% _____ Lower 25% _____

Annual Sales Produced _____ Reason for Leaving _____

Time Employed in Months _____

Company _____ Address _____

Supervisor _____ Tel. No. _____ E-mail Address _____

Product or Service _____ Company Annual Sales _____ Number of Salespeople _____

Sales Productivity: Upper 25% _____ Middle 50% _____ Lower 25% _____

Annual Sales Produced _____ Reason for Leaving _____

Time Employed in Months _____

Company _____ Address _____

Supervisor _____ Tel. No. _____ E-mail Address _____

Product or Service _____ Company Annual Sales _____ Number of Salespeople _____

Sales Productivity: Upper 25% _____ Middle 50% _____ Lower 25% _____

Annual Sales Produced _____ Reason for Leaving _____

Time Employed in Months _____

Company _____ Address _____

Supervisor _____ Tel. No. _____ E-mail Address _____

Product or Service _____ Company Annual Sales _____ Number of Salespeople _____

Sales Productivity: Upper 25% _____ Middle 50% _____ Lower 25% _____

Annual Sales Produced _____ Reason for Leaving _____

Time Employed in Months _____

To customize this document, download it to your hard drive from the John Wiley & Sons web site at www.wiley .com/go/cohenentrepreneur. The document can then be opened, edited, and printed using Microsoft Word or another popular word processing application.

Three things I most liked in working as a salesperson:

    1. _____

    2. _____

    3. _____

Three things I most disliked in working as a salesperson:

    1. _____

    2. _____

    3. _____

CHAPTER 13

How to Make Money with Trade Shows

Trade shows have been held since medieval times, providing sellers with an opportunity to display their products. It has been estimated that there are more than 35,000 trade events in the United States every year, and more than 7,800 trade shows. Taking proper advantage of the unique potential offered by a trade show can make you a great deal of extra money and boost your sales. Alternatively, incorrect use of this promotional opportunity wastes money, time, and other limited resources.

Advantages of Trade Shows

Trade shows offer unique advantages over other means of promotion. Here are a few:

- You can meet with many of your customers and potential customers at one time.
- You can demonstrate your products and give your customers an opportunity to see and handle them.
- You can meet with your salespeople and bring them up to date on your latest products, techniques, and plans.
- You can locate new salespeople or other sales representatives to sell your products.
- You can promote your company image in a certain business or industry.
- Because the trade show itself is promoted to interest a target group of potential customers, you are furnished with a preselected audience having interests matched with your products or services.
- You can rapidly test new products to see whether there is interest from customers, salespeople, and other sales representatives.

- You can distribute additional information regarding your products or services to qualified buyers, potential buyers, sales representatives, and other interested people.

- You are able to reach some people who ordinarily are not accessible.

- Other companies in your industry, both competitors and suppliers, are often demonstrating their products at the same trade show. This gives you a look at your competition as well as the opportunity to talk to the top people in firms important to your business.

- You are able to develop inquiries and leads for expanding your list of prospects into new markets, which you haven't yet entered.

- You are able to make large numbers of potential contacts in a relatively short interval of time.

- You are able to complement your other promotional activities through your trade show participation.

Please note that this list of objectives is not all-inclusive. There may be other goals or objectives that are unique to your situation, and which you should identify prior to trade show participation.

How to Find Trade Shows to Attend

With the large number of trade shows being held worldwide every year, it is clear that you cannot attend them all. It is therefore extremely important that those that you do attend are the most beneficial in boosting your sales and accomplishing other objectives that you establish. To make your plans, you must first know what shows are going to be held. The following are sources of information:

- *Successful meetings:* Magazine publishes conference and trade show information. You can subscribe by calling (847) 763-9050. Also see their web site at http://www.successmtgs.com/successmtgs/index.jsp.

- *BizWiz:* Publishes an online resource guide "Convention/Trade Show" at http://www.bizwiz.com/resource/ConventionTradeShow.htm.

- *Trade show week:* Publishes an online directory at http://directory .tradeshowweek.com/directory/index.asp.

- *Family shows:* Publishes a listing of trade shows and conventions at http://www.familyshowpromotions.com/trade_shows/convention-trade -show.html.

- *Check trade or industry magazines:* Frequently a calendar of upcoming trade shows and conventions is furnished.

From any of these sources, make a list of shows that interest you and seem to be right for your business. Then, write the management of each show and ask for the literature about the show.

Once you have the literature, look for the following specific information:

- Who has attended in the past and who are the people that these shows attract.
- How many attend.
- The geographical areas from which the attendees come.
- The industries and markets the attendees represent.
- The job titles and responsibilities held by the attendees.
- Seminars, workshops, and events that may be offered at the show.
- The physical location of various exhibit booths available and the location relative to other events going on, entrances, exits, and so forth.
- Other services provided by the show sponsors.

You should keep in mind that the information provided to you is a sales document and presents everything in the best possible light. Therefore, one additional source of information obtained from this document, which you can and must put to use, is the list of prior exhibitors. If you contact these individuals, you can ask directly whether they were able to reach their objectives and whether they think the trade show in question meets your need. Ask a lot of questions. The more you can learn about the show, the more information you have to make your decision.

Focus Your Efforts on the Objectives for Attending

To maximize the benefits that you receive, it is necessary that you set definite objectives prior to your participation. That is, you should sit down and work out exactly what you wish to accomplish by your participation in the trade show you are going to attend. Then you must allocate time and resources toward getting ready to achieve those objectives at the show. Read the list that follows to determine which objectives are applicable in your case. Then go to Worksheet 13.2 at the end of this chapter to help you focus on the objectives you want to achieve. For example:

- To test market a new product.
- To recruit new sales personnel or new sales representatives or dealers.
- To develop new sales territories or new distribution channels.

- To encourage your customers to bring their technical problems to you for solutions.
- To introduce new products or new services or policies.
- To make sales.
- To demonstrate equipment that could not otherwise be shown easily to a customer.
- To bring together your representatives, internal sales, and marketing people, and other key executives for conferences during the trade show.
- To expand your list of potential customers.
- To check on your competition and what they are offering.
- To increase the morale of your sales personnel and representatives and encourage them to work together.
- To build your company's image in the industry.
- To demonstrate your interest in and support of the sponsoring association.

How to Calculate the Space You Need for Your Exhibit

To calculate how much space you need, you must consider your objectives and what goes into your exhibit. Every display, exhibit, or piece of furniture requires a certain amount of square footage. In addition, you probably have salespeople on duty in the booth, and they too require space. Therefore, you must decide how many salespeople you should have and how much footage you should allow for this.

Robert B. Konikow, public relations counsel for the Trade Show Bureau in New York City, recommends first finding out how many of the people visiting the trade show are likely prospects. Do this by analyzing the prospectus that you received in the mail from the trade show. Try to ascertain the number of visitors with meaningful titles or groups that you are interested in talking with. You won't be able to get all of these people to your booth, but you should aim at enticing at least half of them for a visit. Take the total number of prospects you are seeking and divide by two. Divide this number by the total number of hours the show is open. From this calculation, you can obtain the average number of visitors per hour.

A salesperson can typically handle approximately 15 prospects per hour. This is a good figure to use for your next calculation unless your own experience has shown that your salespeople handle more or less. Take the hourly visitor rate you have calculated previously and divide it by 15. From this you get the average number of salespeople you should have on duty in your booth to handle the number of visitors you expect.

For each sales representative you have on duty, you must allow approximately 50 square feet of space. With less than 50 square feet of space, the visitor has a feeling of being crowded. But with more space, the visitor gets a feeling of isolation and is unwilling to intrude on your salespeople. So, multiply the number of salespeople that you have calculated by 50 and you get the amount of clear space that you need. Add this to the space that you've calculated previously for your demonstration equipment and furniture and you come up with how large a booth you are likely to need in square feet.

Let's look at an example: Assume that your furniture and equipment which you are going to display occupy 5 square feet of space. Let us say that you have decided from the prospectus that 1,200 prospects are likely to attend the show. Dividing this figure by 2 gives you 600, the number likely to visit your booth. Further, the show is open a total of 20 hours. Dividing 600 by 20 gives you 30 visitors per hour. Dividing the 30 visitors per hour by the 15 prospects that a salesperson can see per hour on the average gives us 2 salespeople who should be on duty. Multiply 50 by 2 to get 100 square feet of space necessary for your salespeople. One hundred plus 5 for the furniture and equipment you're going to display equals a total of 105 square feet necessary. Most standard booths are 10 by 10, or 100 square feet. The extra 5 square feet can be easily absorbed and a standard booth fills your bill. If the amount of space you need is much larger then the standard size, perhaps you should consider either two standard booths or an irregularly sized booth.

How to Design Your Display

You must design your display to meet your own requirements and to conform to the requirements of the trade show. You should also consider the following factors:

- You cannot show more than your budget allows.
- You want to attract only good prospects who meet the objectives you have established.
- You want to demonstrate the uniqueness of whatever it is that you are selling.

You must consider your booth just as you would an advertisement. It must first attract attention, then gain interest, then create a desire to step in, and encourage action by your prospect, whether he or she is a potential customer or potential sales representative.

Remember that just as the headline in a good display or space advertisement attracts a reader to a specific ad, your trade show booth should, by its appearance, attract the people you want to see to your products. If you can, use live demonstrations and other displays that are different from those of your competition and demonstrate benefits to your customers or to the prospects you are trying to attract. Participation demonstrations provide added interest and are much better than static exhibits or presentations that prospects merely watch.

Demonstrations can be very simple and yet still carry the message across to the audience you wish to reach. A manufacturer of a new safety lens, much more protective than the ordinary safety lens, developed a simple but highly effective demonstration. He arranged a table like a small shooting gallery with a pellet gun mounted in a transparent, protective case. The handle and trigger of the gun were exposed so that it could be fired. A regular safety lens and this manufacturer's lens could be shot by interested prospects. The regular safety lens shattered easily. This manufacturer's new safety lens did not. This was the hit of this particular trade show and resulted in numerous sales. Go to other trade shows in your area even if you are not exhibiting and check out the exhibits that are attracting large numbers of prospects. This gives you many good ideas when you design your own exhibit.

Things to Do before the Show

After you have selected your trade show (or shows), designed your exhibit, and made other arrangements, you can greatly increase your ability to capitalize on a trade show's advantages if you venture into some of the following preshow activities:

- *Feature a unique item:* Focus the activities around a unique item brought in especially for the show. Naturally, the unique item should support the objectives that you have established previously.

- *Contact local media for publicity:* Write letters to newspapers, radio and television stations, and other media in the city where the trade event is held. With the letter, send a publicity release as described in Chapter 11. Feature the unique item you have developed for the show and ask to have your publicity release printed. Make yourself available for personal interviews.

- *Publicize to your industry:* Send the publicity release on your unique item to all trade magazines in your field. Promote this product or service to the maximum extent possible by asking to have your publicity release printed.

- *Mail special letters with the publicity release to your customers, sales representatives, and others who may be interested:* Give them a special invitation to see your booth and the item you are promoting. Be sure that you indicate the exact location of your booth.

- *Send letters with the publicity release and with your invitation to other interested parties who might not normally attend a trade show for your particular industry or association:* For example, if you were a small book publisher exhibiting a special health food diet cookbook at a certain exhibit, you might also do a mailing to all the health food stores in the city in which the show is being held. These individuals might not normally attend a book or publisher's trade show, but a special invitation promoting an item they are interested in might get them there and to your booth.

- *Obtain and prepare additional promotional material, such as posters in your store windows or stickers to affix to your normal correspondence, which announce the fact that you are in a certain trade show:* This has the additional advantage of promoting your image to your customers and suppliers even if they do not go to the show.

- *Prepare brochures or other information about your products or services to distribute to prospects at the show:* Make sure this information is to the point, directly relates to your product or service, and, of course, is interesting. However, unless your product is highly technical and is an expensive item, do not go overboard on this. Remember, many show attendees do nothing more than collect brochures and throw them away later.

You should also be concerned with the following tasks. Many of these details were probably covered in the prospectus sent to you by the trade organization or were necessary for registration. However, they are important, so don't neglect them even if omitted from the information sent to you by the organization sponsoring the trade show:

- Be sure that you have insurance covering your trade show activities.
- Prepare and prefabricate as much of your booth as possible prior to shipping. Labor costs at shows are expensive.
- Be sure you've timed your packing and shipping so everything arrives well ahead of time.
- Select your booth location early. The better locations sometimes cost more money and may go quickly. Many experts say that the location of the booth is a major factor in trade show success.
- Be sure that you have your hotel reservations and also a rental car reserved if you need it.
- Have an emergency plan in case your booth is lost or delayed in shipment. You might be able to fall back on displays put up through your local repre-

sentatives or other equipment that you might carry with you. However, always remember, "Expect the best but be prepared for the worst."

- Have certain items duplicated and carry them with you in case they are lost or damaged in shipment, and have a tool kit for emergency repairs.

Things to Do during the Show

To maximize the benefits of a trade show, you should not simply go and have a good time. You should make a list of specific things that you intend to do, including the following:

- Contact the local media if they haven't already contacted you after a mailing. Try to get additional exposure through interviews, appearing on television and radio talk shows, and so forth.

- Contact local customers, suppliers, and other interested prospects. If you cannot do this face-to-face, use your telephone. Personal contact while you are in town is of considerable assistance to your business.

- Meet and talk with other exhibitors. Sell to them, if possible. Think creatively about ways in which other exhibitors may help you in your business. One exhibitor made thousands of dollars in sales simply by noting that his product fit naturally as a lead-in item to a higher-priced item sold by another exhibitor. His proposal was to give this other exhibitor exclusive sales rights in his industry, which was totally different from the industry for which the product was usually sold. Be alert to opportunities at exhibits.

- Use your local sales representatives to the maximum extent possible. They are able to profit heavily from the fact that you are exhibiting in their city. They can help you prepare your booth and be your local contact point.

During the exhibit, you meet many people and obtain business cards from many. It is a sad fact that when you talk to many people, one after the other, you don't remember later what these business cards are for. One way of dealing with this problem is to write what the individual wants on the back of the business card as soon as you receive it. An even better way is to use a pocket tape recorder and record this information. Also, don't be at a trade show without a cell phone and your address list of important contacts including your employees and salespeople, customers, suppliers, and so on. Much comes up that you want to take care of on the spot.

Things to Do after the Show

The trade show itself generates many potential sources of business for you. But you must follow up immediately so that all this potential business does not get lost. Consider the following suggestions:

- Write up a post-show publicity release and mail it to all prospects that you met during the show. If the show provides a registration list of the names of companies and other persons attending the show, use this and add it to your mailing list.

- Mail this publicity release to all your sales representatives throughout the country to promote your participation at the show. If you got good results during the trade show, let your sales representatives know about it. It stimulates them to do better work for you.

- Go over the business cards that you obtained and make certain that each one is individually handled and that whatever the prospect wanted is furnished.

- Go over the objectives you established for the trade show and ask yourself whether these objectives were met. This provides you with important information as to whether the trade show was worthwhile and whether you should attend next year. If you decide that this trade show was worthwhile, start planning immediately. Make reservations right away.

- Review the material you gathered at the show and the list of actions that you deferred until you returned, immediately on your return. I can't tell you the amount of business that has been lost because after the show the individual responsible put this off. Also, if you didn't go to the show yourself, insist on an update from the person who did go, and go over the material he or she brought back immediately.

- Build an e-mail list of prospects from trade show contacts that you can update periodically with news of new products or services, special deals, and so on.

Sources of Additional Information

Books

Creative Selling Through Trade Shows, by Al Hanlon, published by Hawthorne Books.

Exhibitions and Trade Shows: The Step-by-Step Guide to Making a Profit From Exhibiting, by Ivan Jurisevic, published by Pearson Education.

The Exhibit Medium, by David Maxwell, published by *Successful Meetings* magazine.

Guerrilla Trade Show Selling, by Jay Levinson, Mark Smith, and Orvel Wilson, published by John Wiley & Sons.

How to Design a "Wow!" Trade Show Booth Without Spending a Fortune, by Steve Miller and Robert Bjoquist, published by Hikelly Productions.

How to Get the Most Out of Trade Shows, by Steve Miller, published by McGraw-Hill.

How to Participate Profitably in Trade Shows, by Robert B. Konikow, published by Dartnell Corp.

Trade Show Exhibit Planning Guide, published by Guideline Publishing Co.

Trade Show Survival Guide, by Matt Hill, published by Hill Group.

Internet

Note: Because Internet sites frequently go down, multiple sites are listed for similar subject matter.

Federation of International Trade Associations. Directories, member associations and how to join, newsletter and more at http://www.fita.org.

Trade Shows and Missions. Information on international trade shows and how to get involved with them at http://www.fas.usda.gov/agexport/shows/tsopage.html#why percent20participate.

How Trade Shows Work is an article provided by howstuffworks.com with plenty of information at http://money.howstuffworks.com/trade-show.htm.

Trade Show Week. Contains lists of shows, industry reports, and more at http://www.tsnn.com.

Trade Show Quotes. Provides competitive quotes for putting various aspects of shows together for small to mid-sized companies at http://www.trade-shows.org.

DOWNLOADABLE WORKSHEET 13.1
Determining Your Objectives and Focusing Your Resources

To determine your objectives for going to a particular trade show in order of their importance, look at the list. In the second column, rank each objective by its order of importance. In the third column, check off each objective when the resources have been allocated and you are fully prepared for the trade show. Work on the most important objectives, according to your ranking, first.

Objective	Your Ranking	Preparation Complete
To test market a new product		
To recruit new sales personnel or new sales representatives or dealers		
To develop new sales territories or new distribution channels		
To encourage your customers to bring their technical problems to you for solutions		
To introduce new products or new services or policies		
To make sales		
To demonstrate equipment, which could not otherwise be shown easily to a customer		
To bring together your representatives, internal sales, and marketing people, and other key executives for conferences during the trade show		
To expand your list of potential customers		
To check on your competition and what they are offering		
To increase the morale of your sales personnel and representatives and encourage them to work together		
To build your company's image in the industry		
To demonstrate your interest in and support of the sponsoring association		
Other		
Other		
Other		

To customize this document, download it to your hard drive from the John Wiley & Sons web site at www.wiley.com/go/cohenentrepreneur. The document can then be opened, edited, and printed using Microsoft Word or another popular word processing application.

How to Decide Which Trade Shows to Attend

It will not be possible for you to attend all trade shows. It would cost too much money and take too much of your time and other resources. To make a decision about which, or which not, to attend, use this worksheet. First, look at each factor in column one. In column two, assign an importance percentage for each factor, so that no matter how many factors you have listed, the total is exactly 100%. For example, if the number of people attending is very important, you might assign an importance percentage of 40%. Let's assume that the geographical area was of very little importance and you assigned an importance percentage of only 1%. What you are saying is that the importance of the number attending the tradeshow is 40 times as important as the geographical area that these people come from. Of course, for some, the opposite could be true and the geographical area of the show attendees might be the most important factor. In column three, assign a numerical value to each factor from 1 to 5 according to how well each criteria is met. For example, if this show had very high attendance, you would want to assign a "5." If it had low attendance, assign only a "1." Now, multiply column two and column three and put the numerical result in column four. Total these up and repeat the process on a different sheet using the same system. By comparing the total values, you can see the high value shows that you should attend, and the lesser value shows that you should skip.

Important Factors (Column 1)	Importance to You in Percent (Column 2)	How Well Criteria Is Met (Column 3)	Value of Each Factor (Column 2 × Column 3)
Who has attended in the past and who are the people that these shows attract?			
How many attend?			
The geographical areas from which the attendees come.			
The industries and markets the attendees represent.			
The job titles and responsibilities held by the attendees.			
The topics of seminars, workshops, and events that may be offered at the show.			
The physical location of various exhibit booths available and the location relative to other events going on, entrances, exits, and so forth.			
Other services provided by the show sponsors.			
	100%	Total Value ⇨	

To customize this document, download it to your hard drive from the John Wiley & Sons web site at www.wiley .com/go/cohenentrepreneur. The document can then be opened, edited, and printed using Microsoft Word or another popular word processing application.

DOWNLOADABLE WORKSHEET 13.3
Determining the Size of Booth You Need

Calculate the number of prospects for your product or service likely to attend the show:	A.
Divide this number by 2	B.
Number of hours the show will be open	C.
Divide B by C to get the number of visitors per hour	D.
Divide D by 15 prospects, the average number of prospects a salesperson sees in an hour	E.
Multiple E by 50 (square feet) to get the number of square feet necessary for the salespeople	F.
The square footage required for your display, furniture, and equipment	G.
Add F and G to get the total square footage required **Total Square Footage Required**	

To customize this document, download it to your hard drive from the John Wiley & Sons web site at www.wiley .com/go/cohenentrepreneur. The document can then be opened, edited, and printed using Microsoft Word or another popular word processing application.

CHAPTER 14

Making Money with E-Commerce

Computers, technology, and the Internet have revolutionized business. Company research that once required multiple telephone calls and interviews, trips to the library, and the purchase of various directories now takes only a few minutes. Product information that took hours of expensive research time is now at your fingertips. Brochures, catalogues, color photographs, pictures, and other material, once so expensive, can now be made available instantaneously to prospective customers at a small cost. A direct-mail campaign to prospects that took weeks of preparation, hours of envelope stuffing, and several days or more in the mail, plus money for printing, envelopes, and postage, now costs next to nothing and can be sent to hundreds or thousands of prospects in a few seconds. You can collect money, take orders, and give instructions to fulfill orders in a few minutes. All of this spawned e-commerce as a unique business as well as an adjunct means of sales and marketing to businesses of every type.

However, there are some very strong cautionary tales. So impressive is the power and the future potential of business conducted by computers and over the Web, that big money from investors was drawn to e-commerce businesses like a magnet. Recently graduated students who mastered the basics were able to attract amazing amounts of money from what was thought to be sophisticated investors.

No one seemed to notice that while these new e-commerce businesspeople had mastered the technical side of conducting business through the Internet, they did not necessarily know anything about conducting a business. Consequently, while profits were nonexistent, investors sunk more and more into businesses whose potential bankruptcies ticked away like time bombs. In many cases, the businesses had many customers, but no profits. Cybermalls attracted many would-be entrepreneurs. Not recognizing that the psychology of purchase over the Internet was entirely different from that of brick and mortar malls, many were convinced to put their hard-earned money into these ventures.

When the crash came, it came big time, and the number of former Internet senior executives out on the street looking for jobs probably numbered in the tens of thousands. Yet, with good business acumen, they and you can survive and make a profit on the Internet. Moreover, with knowledge, you can use the Internet as a profitable adjunct to whatever business you have established and are already growing. However, to do this, you need a lot more than simply a web site with your name on it.

The Basis of E-Commerce Is the Internet

The Internet is nothing more that an electronic line linking you with other parties simultaneously. The significant aspect is the number and location of these parties. The parties on this line are located all over the world. The estimate of the numbers of individuals on this party line range up to 500 million or more and it is growing by the millions every month. One source says a billion people are already on these lines. With a billion people seeking products and information, and having needs and wants in their lives and businesses, and making information, news, and advertising available, that's a lot of potential for reaching any target audience, including someone interested in your products or services.

What Do You Need to Get Online?

To get online, you need your computer, a modem, a connection to the Internet, and a Web Browser, such as Microsoft Internet Explorer or Netscape Navigator. The connection comes from a company like America on Line (AOL) or Prodigy or numerous others. These folks are constantly competing for your business, and that's why you may have received free disks or a CD ROM in your mailbox, which offers you free hours and an automatic connection when you use the disk or CD ROM. When you buy a new computer, it has a modem, and you probably have both a browser and a connection company all loaded up on your hard disk and ready to go. All you have to do is agree to their terms (you pay extra for the service) and follow the directions provided, and you're online. You probably also want a separate phone line, otherwise your time online interferes with your phone calls and visa versa. You can also connect by cable and some of the newer telephone line connections, whereby your computer is always connected to the Internet without a modem. These connections are so fast nowadays that the old connection types via telephone and a modem are barely competitive.

Researching on the Internet

In the chapter on research, I mentioned the library. In a library, you use the library's catalog index, which may be on a card or on a computer terminal. You can search catalog indexes on the Internet as well. These catalog indexes are called *search engines*. However, where your library's catalog index may list 40,000 entries, a search engine may have a billion!

There are many search engines: Some are specialized for certain areas of interest; some search the whole Web. Even with a billion or more entries, what one search engine can't locate for you, another frequently can.

The Search Engines

Here are a few of these search engines:

- AltaVista: http://www.altavista.digital.com.
- Archie: http://www.alpha.science.unitn.it/cgi-bin/archie.
- Galaxy: http://www.galaxy.com.
- Google: http://www.google.com.
- HotBot: http://www.hotbot.com.
- Internet Sleuth: http://www.isleuth.com.
- Lycos: http://www.lycos.com.
- MetaCrawler: http://www.metacrawler.com.
- UltraSeek: http://www.ultra.infoseek.com.
- WebCrawler: http://www.webcrawler.com.
- Yahoo!: http://www.yahoo.com.

As a test, I typed in "search engines" in the search function in Yahoo! I got over 23 million entries!

How to Use the Search Engines

The best way to find out about these search engines is to do a search, so let's try one. There are four easy steps:

1. Type the Internet address into your Web browser software.
2. Enter a word or word group having to do with your research topic into the entry box on the engine.

3. Click the button on the engine that begins your search.

4. Review your results and further investigate those matching documents (listed as electronic links, which you can inspect by clicking with your mouse) that look good. If you received no "hits" repeat steps 2 through 4 with some new words.

Let us go through the process with a search and try it out. We can use the Yahoo! engine. First, type in Yahoo's electronic address: "http://www.yahoo.com." Then hit the "ENTER" key on the computer. That opens the Yahoo! home page.

Let us say we want to research massage products. In Step 2, enter the word "massage." Then hit the search button using the monitor indicator controlled by the mouse. This takes you to another screen with the entries. When I did this, I got 560,000 entries. Using your mouse again, point and click on each entry sequentially to take you to that particular web page.

Now, if these results weren't what you want, you can do a more advanced search. Go back and point to and click on the words "advanced search" at the top of the Yahoo! page. This takes you to another screen on your computer and some options for different search methods, help, and so on.

From this example, you can see how easy it is to find and research products, prospects, or the competition on the Internet. Just type in your target market and see what comes up.

Evaluating and Using Your Results

That is all there is to it. You can print out things you find. You can also copy information with your computer and electronically paste it into other documents. Of course, you should be careful to credit anything you use by footnoting and also be careful not to run afoul of copyright laws protecting others' intellectual property. Material on the Internet is protected just like printed material in this respect.

Sometimes you have to work with different but related words to find what you want. Sometimes you need to try different search engines. But there is so much information out there that I've come to believe that you can get just about anything; it is just a matter of doing the research. No wonder government security agencies were concerned a few years ago when they located accurate instructions on how to build an atomic bomb!

Some Books on Researching on the Internet

For an in-depth look at researching on the Internet, try the following:

- *The Information Specialist's Guide to Searching and Researching on the Internet,* by Ernest Ackermann and Karen Hartman, published by Abt Content.
- *The 10 Minute Guide to Business Research on the Net,* by Thomas Pack, published by Que Education and Training.
- *The Internet Research Guide,* revised edition, by Timothy K. Maloy, published by Watson-Guptill Publications.

Marketing on the Internet

In the summer of 1999, a movie that cost $50,000 to make beat out *Star Wars Episode I* in per screen average sales, taking in an average of $26,500 at every screening. The movie was *The Blair Witch Project.* Made by Hollywood nobodies with no name actors and actresses, the movie became a blockbuster and grossed millions of dollars. What was the secret? Believe it or not, as of this writing more than 5 years later, you can still find this web site on the Internet: Try http://www.blairwitch.com, the web site and Internet marketing.

If the Internet can do this for a film, what can it do for you in advertising your product or service? Plenty, but you've got to be smart about it and know what you're doing.

The Main Internet Freeways for Marketing

At the present time, there are three main Internet freeways, which are useful in marketing for the consultant. These are:

1. The World Wide Web.
2. The Usenet.
3. E-mail.

Let us look at each in turn.

The World Wide Web   The World Wide Web (www) consists of a giant freeway of homepages, catalogues, and electronic stores; you name it. It is in color, has graphics, sound, and even video.

To place a color advertisement of multiple pages in a magazine and to run it continuously, month after month, would cost you a fortune. Never mind that a magazine does not have the flexibility of sound or video. Only the largest of corporations can afford such advertising, and even they are very selective. But on the World Wide Web, even you and I can afford to do it and can compete with the giants of our industry. In fact, I'm going to show you how you can do this for only a couple of hundred dollars a year.

HOW TO BUILD YOUR OWN WEB SITE   You can pay thousands of dollars for someone to build your web site for you, and they can do a really professional job. However, there are alternatives to paying someone to develop your site. One way of developing your own web site is to do it yourself. No, you don't need to be a computer programmer with years of technical know-how or a room full of experts. There are computer programs available that walk you through the steps and are easy to use. Some computers may even have programs like Microsoft's FrontPage® already loaded for you. That is what I did.

Several years ago, Anchor Recruitment International in Perth, Australia, sponsored my professional seminar on leadership in Perth. Before going to Australia, I visited and admired Anchor's web site on the Internet at http://www.anchor-recruit.com.au. I was surprised to learn that Paul Marcoux, the president of Anchor had developed his own web site using FrontPage. With his encouragement, I developed my own web site at www.stuffofheroes.com.

However, there are many programs available besides FrontPage. Most programs I've seen recently cost from a little under a hundred to several hundred dollars, but some are free or are free if you use other services of the company offering them. Here are a few sources on the Internet as of this writing:

- http://www.buildyoursite.com.
- http://www.coolpage.com/cpg.html.
- http://www.easywebeditor.com/?vov_web_page_software.
- http://www.homestead.com.
- http://sitebuilder.serveryard.com.
- http://www.virtualmechanics.com/index.html.
- http://www.webbuild.net/?Source=Overture.
- http://www.webpage-maker.com.

Many universities also conduct courses in this subject. Several years ago, I attended a four-hour course during which the instructor walked us through step-by-step, and we actually built our own site during the course. You may also find a student or professor willing to build a web site for you at a university at a cut-rate price.

How to Get Noticed by Search Engines Once You Have Your Site

Your next step is to pick a name and get someone, called an internet service provider or ISP to put your site up on the World Wide Web. Pick a name that's easy to remember and to get to. However, if you depend on search engines as your sole method of marketing, you're likely to be disappointed.

That said, there are things you can and should do to improve your opportunities through search engines. Just don't think that your search engine program by itself is going to do it. It won't. Here are some of the main issues that determine placement in the search engines:

- Keywords in URL domain name.
- Keywords in the title on the web page.
- Keywords and phrases in headings.
- Keywords and phrases in the body text.
- Meta tags "description" and "keyword"—Tags are hidden words in the programming that are used to help describe your site.
- Keywords in "alt" tag, "comment" tag, and "title" attribute.
- Keywords in any text links.
- Links from other sites to yours, including number and frequency of contact (your site's popularity).
- Consistency of the theme throughout your site.

While it is generally desirable to repeat keywords and phrases in your title, headings, and body text, if you do this too frequently, some search engines actually penalize you in their rating of your site in their list. The rule of thumb is not to repeat keywords or phrases more than five times in your title, headings, or first paragraph, or more than 10 times on a page. You can see that this is far from simple. For a site with a complete discussion of search engines and many links, see http://www.monash.com/spidap.html.

For free information, newsletters, and more regarding what to do and how to do it on search engines, go to:

- http://www.addpro.com.
- http://www.highrankings.com.
- http://searchenginewatch.com.
- http://selfpromotion.com.
- http://www.seoinc.com.

PICKING A NAME   I suggest a domain name that's short and easy to remember. That way, whenever you give it out, face-to-face in casual conversation or more formally in a speech, people remember it, whether they write it down or not.

Registering Your Domain Name

Once you have a name, you must register it with what is called InterNIC. They also give you a domain address called a universal resource locator (URL). Among other things, registration prevents duplication in domain names. I registered with Network Solutions, Inc. at P.O. Box 17305, Baltimore, MD 21297-0525. Their toll-free number is (888) 771-3000. You can also register electronically at http://rs.internic.net. At the time I registered, the cost was $70 for two years.

Now, as to that ISP—there are hundreds, and you can locate them through a search. My ISP is Solo Web Hosting services at http://www.websolo.com. You can register on the Internet and they advertise that they can activate you in 10 minutes. They offer a free domain name check at their site and register your name for you with InterNIC. Their current charges are $9.95 per month for their basic package in Windows, which includes various other services. Prices are always subject to change and there are many ISPs out there, which you can easily find by an Internet search using "ISP" as your search term.

There are other services that may be of interest to you. For example, if you sell a product, you want your customer to have the ability to order using a credit card. If you sell written information, giving your customer the opportunity to download the information on the spot saves you postage and printing costs, and lets your customer get the material instantly. These and other services are all available at a nominal additional cost to you. You just have to check with the potential ISP and see what they provide.

WHY YOU SHOULD STAY AWAY FROM MOST CYBERMALLS   Cybermalls or virtual malls have been heavily promoted with full-page newspaper advertisements on weekends, free seminars, videotapes, and you name it. The idea sounds good on the surface. Just like regular shopping malls, you open a store on a cybermall. The cybermall develops your site and you pay yearly rent for it. Most offer some sort of training, really consulting, to help you with marketing questions. And most cybermalls bundle various services together: e-mail boxes, free virtual banners advertising your service, and so on. Costs are high in comparison with an ISP—as much as a thousand dollars or more a year, compared with $100 to $200 per year for an ISP.

Is it worth the additional costs? For most entrepreneurs, I would say "no." The mall theory is that: (1) People come to visit the mall and stop in to buy your products or services just like a regular shopping mall, and (2) customers come to the mall for one product or service and see your listing. According to the theory, they go to visit your site, too. This is called "spillover."

Unfortunately, the psychology of visiting the regular shopping mall, is not the same as the virtual mall. People go to a regular mall partly for a good time. They go to see what's new, they socialize, they have lunch, and they may even go to a movie. For many, it's a day at the mall and they shop until they drop. Those that visit a cybermall are usually looking for something specific. Few have the interest or time to spend all day at a cybermall without the socialization of their friends, spouse, or girlfriend/boyfriend that goes along with shopping. So even though the cybermall may be well promoted, and most are not, you're not going to get much business due to walk-in business and the fact that you are in a mall.

Regarding spillover, it's more of the same. Unlike the thrill of the chase in a day of buying, cybermall buyers probably get what they want and get out. You have to be pretty lucky for someone to see the business listing on their way out and start looking for your particular business on the spot. Buying most products or services on the Internet is usually not an impulse purchase. Prospects usually are looking for something.

How Should You Market on the World Wide Web?

The key to World Wide Web marketing is promotion, both online and offline. You have to get people to your web site. You can't rely on the search engine to do it for you. Remember the 560,000 entries of massagers when we researched this product earlier in the chapter? There is so much competition on the Web for any business or service, that trying to build a business based on a search engine alone is more just a hope than good business planning.

A BIG SECRET OF MARKETING ON THE WEB   HotHotHot! was a web site, which sold salsa over the Internet. The owners sold out a couple years ago. They began back in 1994, so HotHotHot! was one of the first businesses to attempt to sell anything online. It became hugely successful and is one of the folk heroes of the Internet. As it happens, the salsa business was located in Old Town, Pasadena, near my home, and I participated in some consulting for the owners of HotHotHot! in a new business they started. They told me that half of their salsa business came from their web site, the other half from their storefront.

The key, even in those days with a tiny percentage of those marketing on-line now, was not the search engine. I mean, let's face it. How many people go to a computer to buy salsa? This business's secret was publicity. One of the owners had majored in public relations in college. She tirelessly promoted the business and their web site through articles she wrote and interviews she gave to newspapers and magazines about the uniqueness of the business and what was then the uniqueness of their web site marketing.

You have to do the same thing today, because publicity is still a major secret of Internet selling. Make your web site marketing synergistic with your other marketing efforts. Put your web site address on your business cards, stationery, brochure, and anything else printed having to do with your business. Whenever you talk to anyone, mention your web site address. That is why you want it simple like "stuffofheroes.com."

USING BANNERS   Banners are the color advertisements you see floating around all over the World Wide Web. You click them, and they send you to the associated web site. The key here is to spend your advertising dollar for banners only where prospective clients hang out. Amazon.com, the online bookseller, puts banners all over the Web. But each banner is specific to the topic of the web site in which it appears. Even so, much of their advertising dollar is wasted because frequenters of some web sites are probably not readers or buyers of books. If your product or service has to do with a certain industry, and you put a banner in that industry's trade association, you probably get more business.

You can get banner advertising free by putting someone else's banner on your site. One way is to find noncompetitive but compatible sites and offer a one-for-one exchange. There are also banner exchange services. If you use them, it may not be a one-for-one exchange. That is, you may need to carry two ads for every one of yours. The reason is that these companies make their money by selling those extra ad impressions to companies willing to pay for more exposure. Here are some banner exchanges services to try:

- http://www.bannerco-op.com.
- http://www.bannersxchange.com.
- http://www.linkbuddies.com.
- http://www.textlinkbrokers.com.
- http://linksmanager.com.
- http://www.linkexchanged.com.
- http://www.powerlinks.com.
- http://www.1st-work-at-home.com.
- http://www.linkvalley.com.
- http://www.powerlinks.com.
- http://www.linkadage.com.
- http://www.worldbannerexchange.com.

You can have banners created or get software to create your own banners at:

- http://www.animationonline.com.
- http://www.banner4u.net.
- http://www.coder.com/creations/banner.
- http://www.koolprint.com/home.asp.
- www.worlddesignservices.com.

CYBERLINKS   Cyberlinks are electronic links connecting one web site to another. You point, using your mouse, to a particular link and click. Presto, you're taken to that web site.

Like much of marketing on the World Wide Web, it's a case of using proven concepts in another environment. Find noncompeting consultants and offer to exchange links. Your web site contains a cyberlink describing the other businesses, products, or services and linking your site with theirs. On their site, you describe your service, and there is a similar link to your web site.

We are talking about a win-win for everyone. The other business gets additional prospects, and so do you. Moreover, the clients win too, because you can build a directory of these links, which can attract people to your web site as a source directory of products and services that are of interest to your customers or prospects but which you may not offer. Link Swapper at http://www.link-swapper.com/ offers a free link exchange plug-in and directory.

PROVIDING FREE INFORMATION TO CUSTOMERS AND PROSPECTS   The concept of giving information away seems to confirm the law that whatever you give away comes back to you many times over. That is the concept of the newsletter. If you put a newsletter on your web site and come out with a new issue every month or so, you get some people returning every month to read the newsletter. And of course, you can also promote your newsletter.

You can also put articles you have published on your web site. Of course, you can put all the information in your brochure on your web site. But, in reality, your web site is one big brochure with almost unlimited space and no printing or mailing costs.

One interesting twist for articles and the like is not to put the article or newsletter on your web site directly, but to put a link whereby your client or prospect can download this information to his or her computer. That way, you also can build a list of prospects by their e-mail address. This list is extremely valuable for Internet marketing, as we will see later.

Usenet Marketing

The Usenet consists of interactive discussion groups. They are also called news-groups. People participate by reading postings done by others and, maybe, by adding their own postings in response. Some Usenets screen postings, but on others, you can post whatever you want. Newsgroups have their own protocol and etiquette that you need to master before you market on them. A mass marketing of your services through postings would be ill-advised. That is called "spamming." It can get you banned by some ISPs, and many won't do business with you once you do it. It is important to know the culture of the newsgroup you're dealing with before you begin to market.

You can reach the newsgroup through your browser. Here are a few directories of newsgroups to begin with:

- http://www.cyberfiber.com/index.html.
- http://www.harley.com/usenet.
- http://www.ii.com/Internet/messaging/newsgroups.
- http://www.mailgate.org.
- http://www.netinformations.com/Usenet/Newsgroup_Directories.

E-Mail Marketing

E-mail is electronic mail. You type in a letter, press a button, and the message is instantly sent anywhere in the world. Now, what if you had the e-mail addresses of 1,000 or 10,000 or even 100,000 potential prospects. You hit one button, and zap—you send your message to all these potential prospects instantly, and it doesn't cost you a cent. Pretty good, right? There must be a catch. Well, there is, but it is a small one. If your message is unwelcome or hasn't been requested in some way, that's spamming just as with the newsgroups. Trust me, spam and you are going to regret it.

So it looks like a Catch-22. Here is this wonderful method of direct marketing that is instantaneous and costs nothing, but you are ill-advised to use it. So what to do? There are three solutions. They all depend on sending the advertisement only to someone who wants it. Here are three methods to do this:

1. Do your research, offer something for free, and be certain it is something the recipient is interested in.
2. Ask visitors to your web site if they would like to receive additional updates about your offering. Those that answer "yes" get on your e-mail list.

3. You can rent e-mail lists of people who have specifically requested information about the kinds of products or services you are offering. These names are collected by others and rented to you.

If you use either options two or three, you should note in your advertisement that this was information they specifically requested. That's just a little reminder to them and let them know that you are not spamming.

Unfortunately, there are a lot of unscrupulous people in this business of compiling and renting e-lists. Some claiming to offer only "opt-in" prospects (those that ask to receive e-mail advertising) actually use any e-mail address they can get hold of. Others claiming to offer large numbers of a particular category of prospects that may be interested in your offering actually contain no segmentation at all. So a reputable company is extremely important. The following three were listed in the Direct Marketing Association's (DMA) directory and are therefore DMA members. You can checkout DMA's complete list of list brokers and compliers at http://www.the-dma.org/cgi/slsearch. Not all on this list handle e-mail lists, however:

Alpha Marketing and Consulting
800 Summer Street, Ste. 315
Stamford, CT 06901-1023
Phone: (203) 359-2420
E-mail: gerry@internationallists.com
Web site: http://www.internationallists.com

Focus, United States
2 University Plaza, Ste. 500
Hakensack, NJ 07601-6222
Phone: (201) 489-2525
E-mail: info@focus-usa-1.com
Web site: http://www.focus-usa-1.com

Kahn & Associates, Inc.
857 Bryn Mawr Ave.
Penn Valley, PA 19072-1523
Phone: (610) 668-8080
E-mail: perrykahn@aol.com

Using E-Mail to Get Publicity Coverage for Your Business   You can get a lot of mileage through publicity to media, which promotes your business using e-mail. However, again you must be careful to avoid spamming or your publicity backfires. Direct Contact Publishing carries a number of articles on this subject at http://www.imediafax.com.

Publicity expert Paul Krupin says that the Golden Rule for e-mail promotion to the media is to target and personalize. He gives 10 commandments for sending e-mail to the media:

1. Think, think, think before you write. What are you trying to accomplish? Would a media professional publish it or toss it?

2. Target narrowly and carefully. Go for quality contacts, not quantity.

3. Keep it short—no more than three to four paragraphs filling one to three screens.

4. Keep the subject and content of your message relevant to your target.

5. If you are seeking publicity for a product or service, or want to get reviews for a new book or software, use a two step approach. Query with a "hook" and news angle before transmitting the entire news release or article.

6. Tailor the submittal to the media style or content.

7. Address each e-mail message separately to an individual media target.

8. Reread, reread, and reread and then rewrite, rewrite, rewrite before you click to send.

9. Be brutally honest with yourself and your media contacts—don't exaggerate or make claims you can't prove.

10. Follow up in a timely manner with precision writing and professionalism.[1]

Why Not an E-Mail Newsletter?   You can easily develop your newsletter and distribute it by e-mail. That way, you save all sorts of printing and mailing costs. Or you can use both forms for increased effectiveness.

E-Zinez.com publishes an entire free handbook on how to publish an e-mail newsletter at http://www.e-zinez.com. Some years ago, All Real Good Internet had a lot of useful information for newsletter publishers. Unfortunately, I could no longer locate them on the Internet. However, here are a few of their do's and don'ts from their former web site:

- Review your intention and content. It must provide needed information, not be a pure brag sheet.

- Make it attractive and in the simplest format for your readers. Usually simple ASCII text within the body of the newsletter is best.

- Keep it short, with a URL (Internet address) for more information.

---

[1] Paul Krupin, "Ten Tips for Using E-Mail to Get More News Coverage and Publicity," *Imediafax.* Accessed November 24, 2004 at http://www.imediafax.com/article.src?ID=16.

- Include easy unsubscribe information with each newsletter.
- Do not send your newsletter out unsolicited.
- Do not send it out too frequently. Once a month is a good starting point.[2]

Here are some additional web sites that can help if you decide to use a cyber newsletter to promote your business:

- http://123ezine.com/3/create-your-own-newsletter.html
- http://www.coollist.com
- http://www.ehow.com/how_8454_create-own-e.html

The potential for doing research and promoting your business on the Internet is incredible. Yet, not everyone takes advantage of the opportunity the Internet presents. Integrate online marketing and research with traditional methods of business and you may not find your productivity much increased, but you may get far more bang for each marketing buck you spend on promoting your business and the products or services you sell.

Sources of Additional Information

Books

Advertising on the Internet, by Robbin L. Zeff, Brad Aronson, and Bradley Aronson, published by John Wiley & Sons.

Beginning ASP.NET 1.1 E-Commerce: From Novice to Professional, by Cristian Darie and Karli Watson, published by APress.

Business to Business Internet Marketing, by Barry Silverstein, published by Maximum Press.

The Complete E-Commerce Book: Design, Build, and Maintain a Successful Web-Based Business, by Janice Reynolds, published by CMP Books.

The Complete Idiot's Guide to Starting an Online Business, by Frank Fiore, published by Que.

The Consultant's Guide to Getting Business Online, by Herman Holtz, published by John Wiley & Sons.

E-Commerce: Business, Technology, Society, 2nd ed., by Kenneth C. Laudon et al., published by Addison Wesley.

E-Commerce for Dummies, by Don Jones, Mark Scott, and Rick Villars, published by For Dummies Press.

---

[2] "Create Your Own E-mail Newsletter," *All Real Good Internet*. Accessed December 2000 at http://www.allrealgood.com/email_publishing/resources/create.shtml.

Internet Marketing for Dummies, by Frank Catalano and Bud E. Smith, published by For Dummies Press.

Internet Marketing for Less Than $500 Year: How to Attract Customers and Clients Online Without Spending a Fortune, by Marcia Yudkin, published by Maximum Press.

Low-Budget Online Marketing, by Holly Berkley, published by Self-Counsel Press.

101 Ways to Promote Your Web Site: Filled With Proven Internet Marketing Tips, Tools, Techniques, and Resources to Increase Your Web Site Traffic, by Susan Sweeney, published by Maximum Press.

Planning Your Internet Marketing Strategy: A Doctor Ebiz Guide, by Ralph F. Wilson, published by John Wiley & Sons.

Selling Online: How to Become a Successful E-Commerce Merchant, by Jim Carroll and Rick Broadhead, published by Dearborn Trade.

Starting an Online Business for Dummies, 3rd ed., by Greg Holden, published by For Dummies.

The Unofficial Guide to Starting a Business Online, by Jason R. Rich, published by John Wiley & Sons.

Internet

Note: Because Internet sites frequently go down, multiple sites are listed for similar subject matter.

About.com—Online Business. Small business e-commerce resources for business owners wanting to learn more of maximizing net profits and developing an e-commerce strategy. Accessed November 16, 2004 at http://sbinformation.about .com/od/ecommerce.

E-Commerce Guide. News, information, and products pertaining to e-commerce at http://www.ecommerce-guide.com.

E-Commerce Times—Small Business. Information on doing business on the Internet, including news and products at http://www.ecommercetimes.com/perl/section /smllbz.

Info: Small Business E-Commerce. Sources of software and services for small business at http://www.software-e-commerce.com/e-commerce.asp?cerca=small+business +e-commerce.

Monster Small Business Solutions for Online Selling. Articles, links, products, and more at http://www.monstersmallbusiness.com/ecommerce_articles.asp.

SBDCnet-E-Commerce Guide. Sources and links to information on all aspects of e-commerce business at http://sbdcnet.utsa.edu/SBIC/e-com.htm.

Web Marketing Today. Links and articles on web marketing at http://www.wilsonweb .com/articles/checklist.htm.

DOWNLOADABLE WORKSHEET 14.1
Checklist for Developing a Web Site

Actions to Take	Done	Date to Complete
Pre-Setup		
Target market identified		
Purpose of web site established		
Look at competitive web sites		
Features needed on your web site documented		
General layout of home page and others noted		
Name of site and desired universal resource locator (URL) chosen		
Frequency of site updating considered		
Duties and responsibilities of those running site fixed		
Means and costs for promoting the site documented		
Consider potential links to other sites		
Setup		
Internet service provider (ISP) selected		
URL registered		
Software program for developing the site selected		
Site developed		
Site loaded online		
Check site for appearance, graphics, speed, navigation, use with different browsers		
Correct site where needed		
Post-Setup		
Send link requests to other sites		
Begin search engine submittals and optimization		
Begin web site marketing campaign		

To customize this document, download it to your hard drive from the John Wiley & Sons web site at www.wiley.com/go/cohenentrepreneur. The document can then be opened, edited, and printed using Microsoft Word or another popular word processing application.

DOWNLOADABLE WORKSHEET 14.2
Checklist for Getting Listed in a Top Position with Search Engines

Actions to Take	Done	Date to Complete
Develop and register your domain name.		
Select and include keywords and phrases describing your product or service frequently and prominently in your web site.		
Ensure keywords and phrases are included in your *title* tag.		
Ensure *meta* tags containing a more detailed description include your keywords and phrases.		
Ensure that the first paragraph of your web page again repeats your keywords and phrases.		
Check repeats of major keywords and phrases. Unless crucial to your presentation, don't repeat more than 5 times in the title, headings or first paragraph, and more than 10 times per page.		
Start your campaign to link to other web sites—popularity demonstrated by number of links and frequency of clicks counts!		
Ensure that your site has one consistent theme. You can sell many products or services, but they should all relate to one theme used throughout your site.		
Monitor your site frequently in rankings with major search engines and keep your site up-to-date.		

To customize this document, download it to your hard drive from the John Wiley & Sons web site at www.wiley.com/go/cohenentrepreneur. The document can then be opened, edited, and printed using Microsoft Word or another popular word processing application.

DOWNLOADABLE WORKSHEET 14.3
Checklist for Promoting Your Web Site

Actions to Take	Done	Date to Complete
Think of your site as a sales document—it is! Ensure it is supporting your basic concept, theme, and what you are trying to accomplish.		
Check your site for grammatical and spelling errors. Seek perfection.		
Make certain that everything on your site works properly. Check it visually not only on your computer but also on other computers as well.		
Choose keywords and phrases to optimize your site for search engines.		
Submit your web site to the major search engines.		
Start a campaign to promote an exchange of links to other web sites.		
Consider the use of banners on other sites to link to your site.		
Write articles that appear in media read by your target audience that note your site (see Chapter 11).		
Develop a short speech of interest to individuals interested in your offering (see Chapter 11).		
Try to find a publicity hook, which might interest media in what you do, and create a publicity release (see Chapter 11).		
Think of a way of linking your web site to non-Internet advertising read by your target audience.		

To customize this document, download it to your hard drive from the John Wiley & Sons web site at www.wiley.com/go/cohenentrepreneur. The document can then be opened, edited, and printed using Microsoft Word or another popular word processing application.

CHAPTER 15

How to Develop a Marketing/Business Plan

For a small business, the marketing plan and the business plan are identical, so I will speak about your plan from now on as if it is a marketing plan, although it includes a lot more than promotional aspects. Your plan is essential for efficient and effective marketing of any product or service, and every entrepreneur or small business marketer should be able to develop a marketing plan that ultimately leads to success. Seeking project success without a marketing plan is much like trying to navigate a ship through rather perilous waters with the competition shooting at you and with neither a map nor a clear idea of your destination. Therefore, the time it takes to develop a marketing plan is worthwhile and allows you to visualize clearly both where you want your business to go and what you want it to accomplish. At the same time, a marketing plan maps out the important steps necessary to get from where you are now to where you want to be. Further, you will have thought through how long it takes to get where you want to go and what resources in money and personnel are needed and must be allocated from your company. In fact, to obtain this allocation of resources, a competent and thoroughly thought-out plan is essential. Without a marketing plan, you do not even know whether you have reached your objectives!

The Planning Mystique

Not long ago a candidate for president of the United States was presented with a campaign plan developed by his staff. That plan helped get him elected.

Two Harvard Business School students, Mike Wigley and Jerry De La Vega, got an idea about how to promote audio recordings. Their idea was to enable people to order any recording they wanted—right from their own homes. Twelve months later, using their marketing/business plan as a basis, they started their company with David Ishag another Harvard classmate. The three entrepreneurs advertised on a cable television network that aired rock 'n' roll videos 24 hours a day. They called their company Hot Rock, Inc. Hot Rock, Inc. received 50,000 inquiries in the first 17 days. Sales grew 10 to 14 percent a month. They expected sales of $6.7 million for the first year. Yet, this was no surprise—they started with a plan.

In another part of the country, Stouffers Lean Cuisine, a line of frozen food, suddenly boosted its market share by more than 30 percent in the $500 million frozen-entree food market. This caught the entire industry by surprise—but not those at Stouffers.

The Clorox Company had reached $1 billion in sales but profits were unimpressive. Shortly after that, half of the $1 billion revenue disappeared when a key division was sold. Yet, only six years later Clorox again hit $1 billion in sales. Moreover, this time profits were double—Clorox had predicted and fully expected these figures.

Gordon Bethune is now CEO of Continental Airlines, one of the largest U.S. airlines. In 1994, it was bankrupt. Then Bethune took over. Since then, it has become one of America's most admired corporations, winning numerous prestigious awards. A few of these include: Best Transatlantic Airline, Top International Airline—*National Airline Quality Rating Study*, No. 1 in Customer Satisfaction by J.D. Power and Associates, No. 1 in On Time Performance by the U.S. Department of Transportation, in *Fortune* magazine's top 100 of U.S. companies to work for, and more. Despite setbacks since 9/11, Continental has steadily moved toward profitability while it continued to win awards despite the industry-wide recession that caused the demise of competitors.

What do these vastly different organizations, from start-up to giant corporations and a presidential campaign have in common other than their success? The answer is their plans. In each case, a plan played a major role in enabling the organization to reach its goals and the success it had previously planned. This surprised everyone else, but not those who did it. They had a plan.

What Could a Marketing Plan Do for You?

A properly developed marketing plan can accomplish a lot for a relatively small amount of focused effort. A marketing plan may:

- Act as a road map to help you reach your goals.
- Assist with management control and implementation of strategy.
- Inform new participants of their roles in implementing the plan and reaching your objectives.
- Assist in obtaining financial and other resources for implementation of the plan.

- Stimulate your thinking and help make better use of limited resources.
- Assign responsibilities, tasks, and timing.
- Predict problems, opportunities, and threats.

We next look at each of these benefits in turn.

Acts as a Road Map

Perhaps, the basic purpose of the marketing plan is to act as a road map and tell you how to get from the beginning of the plan to your objectives and goals. Like a road map, the plan describes the environment you are likely to find along the way. A road map might describe the geographical terrain as well as the type and classification of the conditions along the way, such as distances and available stops for emergencies, gasoline, or lodging. In the same fashion, the marketing plan describes the environment of the marketplace including your competitors, politics, laws, regulations, economic and business conditions, state of technology, forecast demand, social and cultural factors, and demographics of the target market, as well as the company's available resources.

Assist with Management Control and Implementation of Strategy

If you're on a trip, your strategy is the route that you plan to take. Your road map shows the route along with the expected physical and geographical environment. As you proceed, various problems may occur, which could interfere with your planned strategy. You may need to detour due to unplanned circumstances, such as road maintenance or severe weather. In fact, it is certain that almost nothing goes exactly as originally planned. Yet, because your road map helps anticipate potential changes in your environment, you can continue toward your destination with ease. In the same way, the marketing plan allows you to spot and redirect your activities toward alternate paths to arrive at your objective with minimum difficulty. You see clearly the difference between what happened during implementation of your strategy and what you planned. This gives you control of the situation and allows you to take the corrective action necessary to put your project back on track and to keep it on track to reach your final objective.

Inform New Participants of Their Roles in Implementing the Plan and Reaching Your Objectives

Successful implementation of a strategy requires integration of many actions, usually by many different people both inside and outside your business. Timing is frequently critical. And it is most important that all concerned individuals understand what their responsibilities are as well as how their tasks or actions fit into the overall strategy. Having a marketing plan enables you to describe the big picture in detail. It allows everyone to see how their actions fit in with the actions of others. New people may be assigned to activities involving your plan. They can be brought immediately up-to-date regarding their responsibilities, what they must do, and how to adapt to the work of others. Thus, the marketing plan is a document that can be used to inform all participants of your objectives and how and why these objectives are done: by whom, with what, and when.

Assist in Obtaining Financial and Other Resources for Implementation of the Plan

You may find that your resources to accomplish any project are far from unlimited. This is true whether you are an individual entrepreneur attempting to obtain money from a potential investor or even if you head up a giant corporation. A marketing plan plays an important part in persuading those who have the money to lend limited resources—money, people, and other assets—to your project. And with resources scarce, you must convince these individuals that you are going to use capital, goods, and labor in the most effective and efficient manner. You must not only persuade them that your objectives are achievable, but that, despite competition and other potential threats, you can ultimately reach your goals. So your marketing plan is also a sales tool. Even more, the marketing plan helps to prove your control over the project from start to finish. It shows that you not only can see the final objective but also that you know what you must do at every point along the way. This includes actions, costs, and alternatives. When you master the project on paper, you're already halfway there. Those who have the resources you need are more likely to see the potential and give or lend you the resources you are looking for.

Stimulate Your Thinking and Help Make Better Use of Limited Resources

Because your resources are limited, you must get the maximum results from what you have. A good marketing plan helps you make the most of what you have—to make $1 do the work $10. It helps you build on your strengths and minimize your weaknesses. It also helps you obtain a differential advantage over your competition. You can always do this by economizing where it doesn't count, and concentrating superior resources where it does. This leads to success. As you do the research for your marketing plan and analyze your strategic alternatives, your thinking is stimulated. As the plan unfolds, you change and modify it as new ideas are generated. Eventually, you reach the optimum: a well-organized, well-integrated plan that makes efficient use of the resources available and assists in anticipating most opportunities that help, or obstacles that hinder, your progress.

Assign Responsibilities, Tasks, and Timing

No strategy is ever better than those who implement it. Therefore, timing and the assignment of responsibilities are crucial. A marketing plan clearly outlines these responsibilities, so there is no question where they lie. You also want to schedule all activities to maximize the impact of your strategy, while taking full advantage of the environment that is expected to exist at the time of its execution. Hard thinking during development precludes suboptimization. This occurs when one small element of the plan is optimized to the detriment of the overall project. Let us say that you are working on a marketing plan for a new personal computer. If the technical details alone are optimized, you may put the bulk of the funds on product development. This allocation may allow you to develop the best computer on the market, but insufficient funds to promote it. You may have a far superior product, but few are able to buy it because they won't know about it. Because of suboptimization, the product fails. Yet, a less grandiose technical solution might have satisfied the market and been better than your competition at a lower development cost. Funds would then be available to promote it properly.

A good marketing plan ensures that every task is assigned to someone in the correct sequence, and that all elements and strategies are coordinated synergistically to maximize their effect and ensure the completion of the project with the resources available.

Predict Problems, Opportunities, and Threats

You may intuitively recognize some of the problems, opportunities, and threats that can occur as you work toward your objectives. Your marketing plan may not only document those of which you are already aware but also help you identify others that you couldn't see until you started working on your plan. It enables you to think strategically and to consider what must be done about opportunities, problems, and threats that lie in the future. The more analysis and thinking you do, the more pitfalls you see. That is not necessarily bad. Better to note them on paper before you get started than later when it's too late. These potential problems must never be ignored. Instead, construct your marketing plan to take maximum advantage of the opportunities, think up solutions to the problems you find, and consider how to avoid the threats.

Getting in a Competitive Position before You Start

With a marketing plan, you are ahead of your competition even before you begin to execute your plan. You have systematically thought it through from start to finish. You already know where the future may lead. On paper, you have coordinated all efforts to attain a specific objective. You have developed performance standards for controlling objectives and goals and you have sharpened your strategy and tactics to a much greater extent than would otherwise have been possible. You are much better prepared than any of your competitors for sudden developments. You have anticipated those that are potential problems and know what to do when they occur. Finally, more than any competitor, you have a vivid sense of what is going to happen and how to make it happen. Your competitors are going to react, but you have already acted in anticipation of their actions.

A good marketing plan needs a great deal of information gathered from many sources. It is used to develop marketing strategy and tactics to reach a specific set of objectives and goals. The process is not necessarily difficult, but it does require organization. This is especially true if you are not developing this plan by yourself and are depending on others to assist you or to accomplish parts of the plan. Therefore, it is important to plan for planning. The time spent pays dividends later. You get back more than the time you invest up front.

To prepare for planning, you must look first at the total job you are going to do, and then organize the work so that everything is done in an efficient manner and nothing is left out. If you do this correctly, every element of your plan comes together in a timely fashion. This means that you won't be completing any task too early and then waiting for some other task to be finished before you can continue. It also means that no business partner or member of your planning team is overworked or underworked. To do this, you must consider the structure of the marketing plan and all of its elements. You must organize your major planning tasks by using a marketing plan action-development schedule. This gives an overview of the entire marketing planning process, including who is going to do what and when each task is scheduled for completion.

The Structure of the Marketing Plan

Every marketing plan should have a planned structure or outline before you start. This ensures that no important information is left out and that everything is presented in a logical manner. One outline I recommend is shown in the marketing plan outline in Figure 15.1. However, there are other ways to organize a marketing plan that are at least as good. You may be required to use a specific outline by the agency from which you are seeking a loan. Or you may be able to

Executive Summary (overview of the entire plan, including a description of the product or service, the differential advantage, the required investment, and the anticipated sales and profits).

Table of Contents

I. Introduction
What is the product or service? Describe it in detail and explain how it fits into the market.

II. Situational Analysis
- A. The Situational Environs
  1. Demand and demand trends. (What is the forecast demand for the product? Is it growing or declining? Who is the decision maker? Who is the purchase agent? How, when, where, what, and why do they buy?)
  2. Social and cultural factors.
  3. Demographics.
  4. Economic and business conditions for this product at this time and in the geographical area selected.
  5. State of technology for this class of product. Is it high-tech state-of-the-art? Are newer products succeeding older ones frequently (short life cycle)? In short, how is technology affecting this product or service?
  6. Politics. Are politics (current or otherwise) in any way affecting the situation for marketing this product?
  7. Laws and regulations. (What laws or regulations are applicable here?)
- B. The Neutral Environs
  1. Financial environment. (How does the availability or unavailability of funds affect the situation?)
  2. Government environment. (Is current legislative action in state, federal, or local government likely to affect marketing of this product or service?)
  3. Media environment. (What's happening in the media? Does current publicity favor this project?)
  4. Special interest environment. (Aside from direct competitors, are any influential groups likely to affect your plans?)
- C. The Competitor Environs
  1. Describe your main competitors, their products, plans, experience, know-how, financial, human and capital resources, suppliers, and strategy. Do they enjoy favor with their customers? If so, why? What marketing channels do the competitors use? What are their strengths and weaknesses?
- D. The Company Environs

FIGURE 15.1 Marketing Plan Outline. Note under the marketing strategy and tactics sections how your main competitors are likely to respond when you take the action planned and what you will then do to avoid the threats and take advantage of the opportunities.

III. The Target Market
Describe your target market segment in detail by using demographics, psychographics, geography, lifestyle, or whatever segmentation is appropriate. Why is this your target market? How large is it?

IV. Problems and Opportunities
State or restate each opportunity and indicate why it is, in fact, an opportunity.

State or restate every problem. Indicate what you intend to do about each of them. Clearly state the competitive differential advantage.

V. Marketing Objectives and Goals
State precisely the marketing objectives and goals in terms of sales volume, market share, return on investment, or other objectives or goals for your marketing plan and the time needed to achieve each of them.

VI. Marketing Strategy
Consider alternatives for the overall strategy; for example, for new market penetration a marketer can enter first, early, or late, penetrate vertically or horizontally, and exploit different niche strategies.

If the marketing strategy is at the grand strategy or strategic marketing management level, a market attractiveness/business capability matrix and product life-cycle analysis should also be constructed.

VII. Marketing Tactics
State how to implement the marketing strategy(s) chosen in terms of the product, price, promotion, distribution, and other tactical or environmental variables.

VIII. Implementation and Control
Calculate the break-even point and make a break-even chart for your project. Compute sales projections and cash flows on a monthly basis for a three-year period. Determine start-up costs and a monthly budget, along with the required tasks.

IX. Summary
Summarize advantages, costs, and profits and restate the differential advantage that your plan offers over the competition and why the plan will succeed.

Appendices
Include all supporting information that you consider relevant.

FIGURE 15.1 *(Continued)*

use any outline you like. What is important is that your plan be presented in a logical way with nothing omitted. So, whether you are given a specific outline to follow or are allowed to develop your own, keep these two goals in mind: leave nothing out and present your material in a logical manner.

Let us examine each section of the marketing plan structure in Figure 15.1 in more detail. Many sections are common to all marketing plans.

The Executive Summary

The first part of the marketing plan structure or outline is the executive summary. It is a synopsis or abstract of the entire plan. It includes a description of the product or service, the differential advantage of your product or service over that of your competitors, the investment needed, and the results you anticipate. These can be expressed as a return on investment, sales, profits, market share, or in other ways.

The executive summary is especially important if your marketing plan is going to be used to help you to obtain the resources for implementation. Corporate executives are busy. There may be more than just your marketing plan on which they must make funding decisions. If you submit your marketing plan to a venture capitalist, he will have many competing plans. A venture capitalist receives hundreds, sometimes thousands, of plans every year. Yet, he only funds a few. Therefore, it is hard to overestimate the importance of your executive overview.

The executive summary is a summary of the entire plan. It may be as long as a single paragraph or a few pages in length. From it, a busy executive can get a quick idea whether to spend time on the project without reading the entire plan. Therefore, no matter how good the main body of your plan, your executive summary must be well thought out and succinct. It must demonstrate that you know what you're talking about and that your proposal has potential and a reasonable likelihood of success. If not, the executive judging your plan may read no farther.

Usually, the executive summary is one of the last elements to be prepared. This is because it is impossible to summarize accurately until you complete every other part. But even though you save it for last, remember that it comes at the beginning of the plan's documentation and must persuade the reader to continue.

The Table of Contents

A table of contents sounds rather mundane and you may feel that it is unnecessary. You might be inclined to discard the idea if your marketing plan is short. But a table of contents is absolutely necessary. It makes no difference whether your marketing plan is only a few pages or a hundred pages in length. It is required, never optional, because of a psychological factor that affects those who evaluate your marketing plan for approval or disapproval.

If you are using your plan to acquire money or other resources to implement your project, the table of contents is important because many individuals from many functional disciplines are sitting on the review board. Some may be experts in the technical area, interested primarily in the technical details of your product or service. Others are financial experts; they want to examine your break-even analysis, the financial ratios you have calculated, and other financial information. In fact, every expert tends to look first at his or her own area. If you submit a table of contents, this is fairly easy to do. The reader scans the list of subjects and turn to the correct page. But if you fail in this regard, the evaluator of your plan has to search for the information. If you are lucky, he or she is able to find it anyway. Unfortunately, you won't always be lucky. When many plans must be reviewed, the evaluator may spend only a few minutes or even a few seconds in the search. That is where the psychological factor comes in. If the information can't be found easily, the evaluator may assume it's not there. This not only raises questions of what you don't know, but may also give the competitive edge to someone who submitted a table of contents making the information easier to find.

The need for a table of contents is especially critical when your plan is being submitted to venture capitalists. Venture capitalists risk large sums of money and invest in businesses that already have a track record and have a marketing plan for future growth. They want to minimize those risks.

Typically, funds are available for investment in less than 1 percent of the plans that are submitted. One venture capitalist I know said that he receives more than 1,000 marketing plans every month, each of which contains a minimum of 30 pages. Some exceed 100 pages. Under the circumstances, do you think that anyone could actually go over all of these plans in great detail? Of course not. Accordingly, this venture capitalist looks first at the executive summary, and, if it appears to be interesting, spot-checks the plan using the table of contents for items of particular interest. If he can't find the information he wants after a few seconds' search, he discards the plan. With so many plans to look at, he just doesn't have the time to do more. In this initial screening, most of the plans are dropped, leaving only a few for a more detailed reading and a final decision. So don't forget the table of contents and be certain that it is an accurate list of all the important topics in your marketing plan.

Introduction

The introduction is the explanation of the details of your project. Unlike the executive summary, it is not an overview of the project. Its purpose is to give the background of the project and to describe your product or service so that any reader understands exactly what it is you are proposing. The introduction can be a fairly large section. After reading it, the evaluator should understand what the product or service is and what you propose to do with it.

Situational Analysis The situational analysis contains a vast amount of information and, as the term indicates, is an analysis of the situation that you are facing with the proposed product or service. The situational analysis comes from taking a good hard look at your environment. Many marketing experts refer to the process as *environmental scanning*.

I like to approach the situational analysis by dividing it into four categories that I call the environs of the marketplace. The four categories are situational environs, neutral environs, competitor environs, and company environs. Let us look at each in turn.

SITUATIONAL ENVIRONS Situational environs include demand and demand trends for your product or service. Is this demand growing, is it declining, or has it leveled off? Are there certain groups in which the demand is growing and others in which demand is declining? Who are the decision makers regarding purchase of the product and who are the purchase agents? Sometimes the decision maker and purchase agent are the same, but often they are not. For example, one member of a family may be the decision maker with regard to purchasing a certain product, say a brand of beer. But the individual who actually makes the purchase may be another family member. Who influences this decision? How, when, where, what, and why do these potential customers purchase? What are the social and cultural factors? Are demographics of consumers important? Then, maybe you need to discuss educational background, income, age, and similar factors. What are the economic conditions during the period covered by the marketing plan? Is business good or is it bad? High demand can occur in both a good and bad business climate depending on the product or service offered. What is the state of technology for this class of product? Is your product high-tech state-of-the-art? Are newer products frequently succeeding older ones, thus indicating a shorter product life cycle? In sum, how is technology affecting the product or service and the marketing for this product or service? Are politics, current or otherwise, in any way affecting the marketing of this product? What potential dangers or threats do the politics in the situation portend? Or do the politics provide opportunities? What laws or regulations are relevant to the marketing of this product or service?

NEUTRAL ENVIRONS Neutral environs have to do with groups or organizations. Does government have an impact on this project? Is legislation on the state, federal, or local level likely to affect the demand or marketing of the product or service? What is happening in the media? Does current publicity favor your project or does it make any difference? Look at special interest groups. Might they have some impact? Are any influential groups (e.g., consumer organizations) likely to affect your plans for marketing this product or service?

COMPETITOR ENVIRONS Competitor environs are those businesses competing against you. They are important because they are the only elements of the environment that intentionally act against your interests. In this section of the situational analysis, describe in detail your main competitors, the products they offer, their plans, experience, know-how, financial, human and capital resources, and suppliers. Most important, discuss their current and future strategies. Note whether your competitors enjoy favor with their customers and why. Describe and analyze your competitors' strengths and weaknesses, what marketing channels they use, and anything else that you feel is relevant to the marketing situation as it exists when you implement your project.

COMPANY ENVIRONS   Company environs describe your situation in your business or company-to-be and the resources that you have available. It describes your current products, experience, know-how, financial, human and capital resources, suppliers, and other factors as you did in competitor environs. Do you enjoy favor with your customers or potential customers and why? Summarize your strengths and weaknesses as they apply to your project.

The Target Market

The target market is the next major section in your plan. Describe exactly who your customers are and what, where, when, why, how, how much, and how frequently they buy.

You may think that everyone is a candidate for your product or your service. In a sense this may be true, but some segments of the total market are far more likely candidates than others. If you attempt to serve every single potential customer segment, you cannot satisfy those who are most likely to buy as well as you should. Furthermore, you dissipate your resources by trying to reach them all. If you pick the most likely target market, or markets, you can devote the maximum amount of money to advertising your product or service in a message that your most likely customers can best understand.

Remember, the basic concept of strategy is to concentrate your scarce resources at the decisive points. Your target markets represent one application of this concept. You usually cannot be strong everywhere. You must be strong where it counts, in this case, in the markets you target.

You should also indicate why the target market you have selected is a better candidate for purchase than others. Include the size of each market.

How will you define your target markets? First, in terms of (1) demographics (i.e., such vital statistics as age, income, and education); (2) geography (i.e., their location); (3) psychographics (i.e., how they think); and (4) lifestyle (i.e., their activities, interests, and opinions). There are other ways of describing, and perhaps segmenting your market. Knowing your customers is as important as knowing yourself (the company environs), your competitors (the competitor environs), and the other environs that you have analyzed.

Problems and Opportunities

The problems and opportunities section is really a summary that emphasizes the main points you have already covered in preceding sections. As you put your plan together, developed your situational analysis, and described your target market, you probably implicitly covered many of the problems and opportunities inherent in your situation. Here you should restate them explicitly and list them one by one. Group them first by opportunities, then by problems. Indicate why each is an opportunity or a problem. Also indicate how you intend to take advantage of each opportunity and what you intend to do about each problem.

Many marketing planners do well in showing how they take advantage of the opportunities, but they do not explain adequately what they do about the problems. To get full benefit from your plan, you must not only foresee the potential problems and opportunities, but also decide what actions you must take to overcome the problems.

This foresight helps you during implementation. It also favorably impresses those who decide whether to allocate resources for your particular project. In most cases, those who evaluate your plans know when you omit a problem. That instantly makes a bad impression. An evaluator then gets one of two perceptions: Maybe you are intentionally omitting a difficult problem because you didn't know what to do about it, or maybe you didn't even recognize that you had a problem! Stating your problems and how you handle them gives you a decided edge over others who submit plans but do not take the time or trouble to consider the solutions to potential problems they might face in implementation.

Note that in both the strategy and tactics sections, there are additional potential problems to address. For example, when you initiate a particular strategy, a competent competitor isn't going to sit still and let you take his or her market. Competitor counteractions constitute a potential problem. You may discuss these counteractions in those sections. You do not have to add these new potential problems and/or opportunities to this section. This is a summary section for your initial scan of your environment.

Marketing Goals and Objectives

Marketing goals and objectives are accomplishments you intend to achieve with the help of your marketing plan. You have already prepared your reader by your earlier analysis of the target market. In this section, you must spell out in detail exactly what you intend to do.

What is the difference between a goal and an objective? An objective is an overall goal. It is more general and may not be quantified. "To establish a product in the marketplace" is an objective. So is "to become the market leader" or "to dominate the market." Goals are quantified. "To sell 10,000 units a year" is a goal. Goals are also quantified in terms of sales, profits, market share, return on investment, or other measurements. There is one major cautionary note here: Don't get trapped into setting objectives or goals that conflict. For example, your ability to capture a stated market share may require lower profits. Make sure that all your goals and objectives fit together. You can do this by adjusting and reconfirming your goals and objectives after you have completed the financial portions of your plan.

Marketing Strategy

In this section, you describe what is to be done to reach your objectives and goals. Your strategy may be one of differentiating your product from that of its competitors, of segmenting your total market, of positioning it in relation to other products, of carving out and defending a certain niche, of timing in entering the market, and so on. Marketing strategy is a what-to-do section.

One important part of the marketing strategy section that is frequently left out and that you shouldn't omit is what your main competitors are likely to do when you implement your planned strategy, and what you do to take advantage of the opportunities created, solve potential problems, or avoid serious threats. Herein is another opportunity for you to demonstrate what a terrific marketing strategist and planner you are.

Marketing Tactics

Just as strategy tells you what you must do to reach your objectives, tactics tell you how to carry out your strategy. List every action required to implement each of the strategies described in the preceding section and the timing of these actions. These tactical actions are described in terms of what is called the "marketing mix," or the "4 Ps" of marketing: product, price, promotion, and place. Sometimes the 4 Ps are known as strategic variables. However, these variables are really tactical because they are actions taken to accomplish the strategy you developed in the preceding section.

Implementation and Control

In the implementation and control section you are going to calculate the break-even point and forecast other important information to help control the project once it has been implemented. You are also going to compute sales projections and cash flow on a monthly basis for a three-year period and calculate start-up costs in a monthly budget. After implementation, you can use this information to keep the project on track. Thus, if the budget is exceeded, you know where to cut back or to reallocate resources. If sales aren't what they should be, you know where to turn your attention to realize an improvement. You should also complete a marketing plan action development schedule that indicates who or what the company is doing during implementation. Worksheet 15.1 at the end of this chapter will help you.

You may find a spreadsheet program, such as Excel, to be extremely useful for this purpose. In fact, one of the most common computer uses for business is that of the spreadsheet. A spreadsheet program can be used to do sophisticated calculations, provide data for graphs, do forecasts, view results by changing various "what if" variables, estimate costs, and the like. Basically, a spreadsheet is simply a chart with rows and columns filled with numbers. But the beauty of this type of program is that you can do the formula calculations to fill in these rows and columns with hundreds of accurate numerical results almost instantly.

There are also computer programs that can help do your planning. Some of these are found in the Sources of Additional Information, Internet section at the end of this chapter.

The Summary

In the summary, you discuss advantages, costs, and profits, and clearly state, once again, the differential advantage that your plan for this product or service offers the competition. The differential or competitive advantage is what you have that your competitors lack. Basically, it says why your plan succeeds.

Appendixes

The appendixes in your plan can contain important financial information, marketing studies, or other information bearing on your project, and biographical sketches of the planned major participants in your business, emphasizing their qualifications for the job they are going to do. The appendices complete your marketing plan outline. You now have a good idea of the information that you need for your marketing plan.

Worksheets are provided to assist in completing every section of the marketing plan that we've talked about. As you complete these forms, you automatically complete your marketing plan.

Keeping Your Material Organized

It is very important to keep your material together to guard against loss and for updating as new data is received. A loose-leaf notebook is a helpful tool. Each section can be marked: executive summary, introduction, situational analysis, target market, problems and opportunities, marketing goals and objectives, marketing strategy, marketing tactics, implementation and control, and summary. As additional information is received in its rough form, it can be added to the appropriate section.

Sources of Additional Information

Books

Basics of Successful Business Planning, by William R. Osgood, published by AMACOM.
Building Your Business Plan, by Harold J. McLaughlin, published by John Wiley & Sons.

Business Plans for Dummies, by Paul Tiffany, Steven Peterson, and John Schultze, published by For Dummies.

The Marketing Plan, 4th ed., by William A. Cohen, published by John Wiley & Sons.

The Executive Guide to Operational Planning, by George L. Morrisey, Patrick J. Below, and Betty L. Acomb, published by Jossey-Bass.

How to Prepare and Present a Business Plan, by Joseph R. Mancuso, published by Prentice-Hall.

The Art of the Strategist, by William A. Cohen, published by AMACOM.

The Definitive Business Plan, by Richard Stutely, published by Financial Times Prentice-Hall.

Model Business Plans for Product Businesses, by William A. Cohen, published by John Wiley & Sons.

Model Business Plans for Service Businesses, by William A. Cohen, published by John Wiley & Sons.

Planning /or Nonplanners, by Darryl J. Ellis and Peter P. Pekar Jr, published by AMACOM.

Internet

Note: Because Internet sites frequently go down, multiple sites are listed for similar subject matter.

Business Plans. BPlans.com provides advice on writing a business plan and sample plans at http://www.bplans.com.

Business Plan Archive, by Robert H. Smith School of Business, University of Maryland. An archive of business plans kept on file at a university at http://www.businessplanarchive.org.

Business Plans Software, Samples, and Strategy. Center for Business Planning provides business plan samples with associated information including software at http://www.businessplans.org.

Business Plan Software. Business Planware provides links to a lot of free information and products for creating business plans, including software—from Ireland at http://www.planware.org.

Free Business Planning Resources. BizPlanit provides insights into the fundamentals of writing an effective business plan including detailed descriptions of recommended sections at http://www.bizplanit.com/vplan.htm.

Marketing Plans, Programs, and Small Business Management. Marketing Plan.com has articles, outlines, links, and more at http://www.web sitemarketingplan.com.

Marketing Planning Resources. Mplans.com offers instruction, sample plans, articles, and news at http://www.mplans.com.

Marketing Survival Kit, by Joel Sussman. Marketing Strategies, marketing plans, marketing tools and templates, articles, software, ideas, and more at http://www .marketingsurvivalkit.com.

DOWNLOADABLE WORKSHEET 15.1
Marketing Plan Action Development Schedule

Weeks After Project Initiation

Task	1	2	3	4	5	6	7	8	9	10	11	12

Instructions: Write down every task that needs to be accomplished to complete the plan and indicate who will complete the task. In columns 1 through 12, indicate when the task starts and when it should be completed. You can also write in the amount of money each task is estimated to cost on a weekly basis. This allows you to compare total task costs and to schedule tasks in the most efficient manner.

To customize this document, download it to your hard drive from the John Wiley & Sons web site at www.wiley .com/go/cohenentrepreneur. The document can then be opened, edited, and printed using Microsoft Word or another popular word processing application.

DOWNLOADABLE WORKSHEET 15.2
Information You Need for Your Marketing Plan

Target Market

Geographical location _____

Special climate or topography _____

Consumer Buyers

Cultural, ethnic, religious, or racial groups _____

Social class(es) _____

Groups buyers refer to for input _____

Sex (male, female, or both) _____ Age range _____ Education range _____

Household size and description _____

Family status (single, married, divorced, with children, without children, etc.) _____

_____

Family work status with occupations: Husband _____ Wife _____

Family decision maker _____ Those in family influencing purchase decision _____

Family buyer of product or service _____

Perceptions of risk to buyer (if any) _____

Income of each family member _____

Additional descriptions, classifications, and traits of target market _____

_____

_____

_____

Target market wants and needs _____

_____

_____

General description of product _____

_____

_____

Frequency of usage _____ Traits _____

Size of target market _____ Growth trends _____

Media Habits	**Hours/Week**	**Description**
Television	_____	_____
Radio	_____	_____
Magazines	_____	_____
Newspapers	_____	_____
The Internet	_____	_____

To customize this document, download it to your hard drive from the John Wiley & Sons web site at www.wiley.com/go/cohenentrepreneur. The document can then be opened, edited, and printed using Microsoft Word or another popular word processing application.

(continued)

Organizational Buyers

Decision makers _____

_____

Primary motivation of each decision maker _____

_____

_____

Amount of money budgeted for purchase _____

Purchase history _____

Additional descriptions, classifications, and traits of target market _____

_____

_____

Target market wants and needs _____

_____

_____

General description of product _____

_____

Frequency of use _____ Traits _____

Size of target market _____ Growth trends _____

Media Habits	**Hours/Week**	**Description**
Television	_____	_____
Radio	_____	_____
Magazines	_____	_____
Newspapers	_____	_____
The Internet	_____	_____
	Number/Year	**Description**
Trade shows	_____	_____
Conferences	_____	_____

The Competition

Competitor	Products	Market Share	Strategy

Resources of the Firm

Strengths:

1. _____
2. _____
3. _____
4. _____
5. _____

Weaknesses:

1. _____
2. _____
3. _____
4. _____
5. _____

Technological Environment

_____
_____
_____

Economic Environment

_____
_____
_____

Political Environment

_____
_____
_____

Legal and Regulatory Environment

_____
_____
_____

(continued)

Social and Cultural Environment

_____

_____

_____

Other Important Environmental Aspects

_____

_____

_____

Problems/Threats

_____

_____

_____

Opportunities

_____

_____

_____

DOWNLOADABLE WORKSHEET 15.3
Goals, Objectives, and Differential Advantage

Objectives:

- _____
- _____
- _____
- _____
- _____
- _____
- _____

Goals:

- _____
- _____
- _____
- _____
- _____
- _____
- _____

Statement of Differential Advantage:

_____
_____
_____
_____
_____
_____
_____

Instructions: Objectives are general: "To establish ourselves as a major company in this industry." Goals are specific: "Achieve $200,000 in sales by the end of year one." Differential advantage is what you have that your competitors do not, and it is what will cause you to be successful.

MANAGEMENT PROBLEM SOLVING

Protecting Your Ideas

This chapter discusses ways in which the entrepreneur and small business person can protect his or her ideas. He or she may be able to get the exclusive right to some invention, product, service, or name, which can be applied to his or her business and no other. Clearly, this is of value and consequently this chapter may be one of the most important to your success.

Patents

A patent for an invention is a grant by the government to an inventor, which permits him or her certain rights. In the United States, a patent is granted by the government acting through the U.S. Patent and Trademark Office. The patent is good for 17 years from the date on which it was issued, except for patents on ornamental designs, which are granted for 14 years. The term may be extended by a special act of Congress, but this is extremely rare. Once the patent expires, the inventor has no control over his invention, and anyone has the free right to use it. This right extends only throughout the United States and its territories and possessions. A U.S. patent does not give you protection in foreign countries. For such protection, you must obtain a separate patent in each country in which protection is desired. There has been increased movement toward international cooperation in recent years. You can find more information on the web site of the World Intellectual Property Association at http://www.wipo.int.

What Can Be Patented and What Cannot

According to the patent law, any person who "invents or discovers any new and usable process, machine, manufacture or composition of matter, or any new and useful improvements therefore, may obtain a patent."

The statute specifies that the subject matter must be "useful." This means that whatever it is that you have invented must have a useful purpose and that it must be able to perform its intended purpose.

The courts have made various interpretations of this statute, and, through these interpretations, they have defined the limits of the subject matter that can be patented. The courts have ruled that methods of doing business, such as "total quality management," cannot be patented. Similarly, printed matter cannot be patented, although it can be copyrighted, and we look at that later. Also, with regard to mixtures of ingredients, a patent cannot be granted unless there is more to the mixture than the effect of the individual components. Therefore, the combination of two or more components or ingredients in a single concoction cannot be patented unless the synergistic effect of the ingredients or components causes some greater benefit.

The statute also says that the invention must be new to be patentable. The invention cannot be patented if "(a) the invention was known or used by others in this country or patented or described in a printed publication in this or a foreign country before the invention thereof by the applicant for a patent, or (b) the invention was patented or described in a printed publication in this or a foreign country or in public use or sale in this country more than one year prior to the application for a patent in the United States." This means that if the invention for which you seek a patent has been described in a printed publication anywhere in the world or if it has been in public use or on sale in this country before the date that the applicant made his invention, a patent cannot be issued. If the invention has been described in a printed publication anywhere or has been in public use or on sale in this country more than one year before the date on which an application for a patent is filed, a valid patent cannot be obtained.

Note that it's immaterial when the invention was made or whether the printed publication or public use was by the inventor himself or by someone else. Therefore, if you, the inventor, describe the invention in a printed publication such as a magazine, use the invention publicly, or place the invention on sale, you must apply for a patent before a year has gone by or your right to patent it is lost.

Your invention must also be sufficiently different from a similar invention that has gone before. Even if what you seek to patent involves a few differences, a patent may be refused if the differences are obvious and not novel. According to the Patent and Trademark Office, the subject matter that you seek to patent must be sufficiently different from what was described before or used before so that it may be said to amount to invention over the prior art. Small advances that would be obvious to a person having ordinary skill in the art are not considered inventions capable of being patented by this interpretation. For example, simply substituting one material for another material would not enable you to patent an idea as an invention.

Who Can Apply for a Patent?

According to the law, only the inventor may apply for a patent on an object, with certain exceptions. If the inventor is dead, a legal representative may make the application. If the inventor is insane or is otherwise under legal guardianship, his or her guardian may represent him or her. If an inventor is missing or refuses to apply for a patent, a joint inventor or a person having a proprietary interest in the invention may apply on behalf of the missing inventor. If a person who is not the inventor applies for a patent and is granted one, this patent would be void. Also, if an individual states that he or she is the inventor of an item and in fact he or she is not, the individual is subject to legal prosecution. If two or more persons make an invention jointly then they can apply as joint inventors.

Even through it is possible for an inventor to prepare the application for his or her own patent, this may not be a good idea. The procedures are very complex, and even if a patent is granted, it is unlikely that an untrained individual will secure all the rights he or she could to protect his or her invention through the patent. If you do decide to patent your invention by yourself, I recommend reading books available on this subject. A few are listed at the end of this chapter.

Most inventors employ the services of persons known as patent attorneys or patent agents. Only certain patent attorneys and patent agents are authorized to practice before the Patent and Trademark Office, and this office maintains a registry of these attorneys and agents. Those listed meet certain qualifications and demonstrate them by passing an examination. There are currently more than 20,000 attorneys and 6,000 agents authorized in the United States.

The difference between patent attorneys and patent agents is that patent attorneys are also attorneys at law. While patent agents are not attorneys, both are fully qualified for preparing an application for a patent and conducting the prosecution in the Patent and Trademark Office. However, patent agents cannot conduct patent litigation in the courts or perform various other services, which the local jurisdiction considers to be practicing law.

You can get a complete list of those attorneys and agents registered to practice before the U.S. Patent and Trademark Office from the Superintendent of Documents, P.O. Box 371954, Pittsburgh, PA 15250-7954, or through any district office of the U.S. Department of Commerce. You can also find a patent attorney through the Yellow Pages or you can also search for an attorney or agent near you at http://www.uspto.gov/web/offices/dcom/olia/oed/roster/index.html. If you don't have Web access, USPTO Contact Center provides a list of names of attorneys and agents for a particular city or zip code. Call (800) 786-9199 or (703) 308-4357.

Once you employ a patent attorney or an agent, you execute a power of attorney or authorization of agent. This must be filed in the Patent and Trademark

Office, and is usually part of the application papers. Once an attorney has been appointed, the Patent and Trademark Office won't communicate with you directly, but conducts all correspondence with your attorney, although, of course, you are free to contact the office concerning the status of your application. You can remove the attorney or agent from your patent case by revoking the power of attorney.

Protecting Your Idea Prior to Patenting

How do you protect your idea prior to its patenting? One recommended method of protecting your invention is to get a close friend or someone who understands your invention to sign his or her name on a dated diagram or written description of the invention. In fact, you can do this during the process of your inventing. Every couple of days, as your work progresses, you can have someone sign as a witness to your notes. This provides evidence of the time you came up with your idea or invention in case of a dispute with others as to who developed the invention first.

Another way of protecting your invention prior to patenting is through a program established by the U.S. Patent and Trademark Office. This is known as the Disclosure Document Program. You file a disclosure document with the patent office, which remains on file. This protects you for a two-year period. The current fee for this service is only $10. If you are interested in this program, complete information is available at the government's web site at http://www.uspto.gov/web/offices/pac/disdo.html.

Patent Procedures

One of the first steps in patenting, before you begin to prepare the application, is to ensure that you have established "novelty." According to the patent office, this is one of the most crucial and difficult determinations to make, and it involves two things. First, you must analyze your device according to standards specified by the patent office for patentability, and second, you must see whether anyone else has patented the device first.

"Novelty" sounds simple. If you are doing this yourself, go to the Patent Office's web site at http://www.uspto.gov/ and search under "novelty." The only sure way of accomplishing the second requirement is to make a search of the patent office files.

Searching Existing Patents and Technical Literature   It used to be that someone had to go to the search room at the Scientific Library of the Patent and Trademark Office and do a search manually. You could search and examine U.S.

patents granted since 1836 arranged according to the Patent and Trademark Office classification system, which included over 300 subject classes and 64,000 subclasses. Or you could go to one of the Patent Depository Libraries, which has a numerically arranged set of patents. A complete list of these libraries, found in every state is at http://www.uspto.gov/go/og/1998/week31/patlibs.htm. You can still do these hands-on searches; however, an easier quicker search can be done online by going to http://www.uspto.gov/patft/index.html.

The Application for a Patent

The application for a patent is made to the commissioner of patents and trademarks. It includes the following: (1) a written document, which comprises a specification of description and claims and an oath or declaration; (2) a drawing in those cases in which a drawing is possible; and (3) the filing fee.

There are some general requirements with regard to the form in which the application is submitted; however, much can be done online. You can even do electronic filing for some types of patents. Although current basic fees are several hundred dollars, with search fees, attorney fees, and more, you can expect to spend several thousand dollars to obtain a U.S. patent. For the latest information, go to http://www.uspto.gov/ebc/efs/index.html.

Use of "Patent Pending" Marking

If you make or sell patented articles, you are required to mark the articles with the word "patented" and the number of the patent. The penalty for failure to do this is that you may not recover damages from a patent infringer unless the infringer was notified of the infringement and continued to infringe after the notice. However, the marking of an article as patented when it is not patented is against the law. Some inventors mark articles with the terms "patent applied for" or "patent pending." These phrases have no legal effect, but they warn everyone that an application for a patent has been filed in the U.S. Patent and Trademark Office. Thus, a potential infringer knows that if he or she tools up to manufacture the item that has such a marking, when and if a patent is granted, he or she infringes on your patent and could be subject to a lawsuit. However, the protection afforded by a patent does not start until the actual grant of the patent. The law imposes a fine on those who use these terms falsely.

Limitations and Disadvantages of Protection with Patents

There are disadvantages and limitations to the use of patents. Here are some that you should consider before you apply for a patent.

First, your patent can be designed around. If your patent shows how to accomplish a certain task, you're only being given a patent for that particular method of accomplishing that task. Someone else can then see what you are doing, think of a different way to do the same task, which does not infringe on your patent, and patent a new invention himself.

Infringement of a patent consists in the unauthorized making, using, or selling of your patented invention within the territory of the United States during the term of the patent. However, if the patent is infringed, the government itself does not sue. That is your job. You may sue for relief in the appropriate federal court and you may ask the court for an injunction to prevent the continuation of the infringement, and award of damages because of the infringement. However in such a suit, the defendant may raise the question of the validity of your patent. This is an important point. The court can invalidate your patent, even after it has already been granted to you. One survey reported that 70 percent of patents taken to court for infringement are actually invalidated. These inventors received nothing for their effort or for their expense in obtaining their patents, not even the court costs.

Another disadvantage of a patent is the cost. As stated, it amounts to several thousand dollars at a minimum: And this only gets you a patent in the United States. Remember that a U.S. patent does not protect you in foreign countries, and each country has its own patent laws. While you can certainly obtain patents in foreign countries through your patent attorney, this costs more money. Therefore, the cost of a patent must be weighed against its value prior to applying for it. Many inventors have the idea that it is possible to make a fortune simply by having a patent granted. This is not true. It gives you certain protection only. Production, marketing, and everything else need to be accomplished to make any money.

Another disadvantage is the specifics on the invention required by the patent office. It is for this reason that many chemical processes, even though they can be patented, are not. It has been reported that the inventor of the correction paper, which corrects typewriting mistakes, made a gross error in patenting because the chemical works over a large range of percentages of the impregnation of the paper, whereas the patent office required a specific percentage to the nearest tenth. From the information in the patent itself, many others were able to copy the idea simply by impregnating the paper with other amounts of the chemical. This did not infringe on the patent awarded, even though it certainly was an infringement in reality. To prevent this sort of infringement, the formula for Coca-Cola has never been patented and still remains a secret.

Copyrights

A copyright is a form of protection given to the authors of original works of authorship, be they literary, dramatic, musical, artistic, or even certain other types of intellectual works. Section 106 of the U.S. Copyright Act generally gives the owner of the copyright the exclusive rights to do and to authorize the following:

- To reproduce the work in copies or phonorecords.
- To prepare derivative works based on the work.
- To distribute copies or phonorecords of the work to the public by sale or other transfer of ownership, or by rental, lease, or lending.
- To perform the work publicly, in the case of literary, musical, dramatic, and choreographic works, pantomimes, and motion pictures and other audiovisual works.
- To display the copyrighted work publicly, in the case of literary, musical, dramatic, and choreographic works, pantomimes, and pictorial, graphic, or sculptural works, including the individual images of a motion picture or other audiovisual work.
- In the case of sound recordings, to perform the work publicly by means of a digital audio transmission.

It is illegal for anyone to violate any of the rights provided to the owner by the copyright. However, these rights are not unlimited in their scope, and Sections 107 through 118 of the Copyright Act provide for limitations.

Typical of items that can be copyrighted are the following: literary works; musical works including any accompanying words; dramatic works including any accompanying music; pantomimes and choreographic works; pictorial, graphic, and sculptural works; motion pictures and other audiovisual works; and sound recordings. This list is, however, not all-inclusive. For example, a computer program or software is registerable as a literary work. Maps are also registerable as pictorial, graphic, or sculptural works, and so forth. Computer programs and most "compilations" may be registered as literary works. All of these can be copyrighted.

Some Material Cannot Be Copyrighted

There are several categories of material that are not eligible for copyright protection. These include: (1) works that have not been fixed in a tangible form of expression, for example, works that have not been written down, recorded, or photographed; (2) titles, names, short phrases and slogans, mere symbols or designs, mere variations of typographic ornamentation, lettering, or coloring, mere listings of ingredients or contents; (3) ideas, procedures, methods, systems, processes, concepts, principles, discoveries, or devices, as distinguished from a description, explanation, or illustration; and (4) works consisting entirely of information that is common property and containing no original authorship. Examples here would include standard calendars, height and weight charts, tape measures and rules, schedules of sporting events, and lists of tables taken from public documents or other common sources.

Who Can Copyright?

As with a patent, only the author or someone deriving rights through the author can rightfully claim copyright. It is important to realize that, unlike a patent, a copyright is done automatically and does not require an attorney even for registration. The procedures for copyright registration are very simple. Copyright protection exists from the time the work is created in any fixed form.

The copyright in the work of authorship immediately becomes the property of the author who created it. There is an exception to this if you are working for someone else. In this case, it is the employer, not the employee, who is considered the author, because it comes under a copyright statute defining "work for hire," which is work prepared by an employee within the scope of his or her employment, or a work specially ordered or commissioned for use as a contribution to a collective work. If there are two or more authors of a joint work, all are co-owners of the copyright unless there are agreements to the contrary.

How to Apply for a Copyright

A copyright is secured automatically upon creation. The way in which copyright protection is secured under a new law in the United States is sometimes confused with the way it worked under the old law. Under the old copyright law, copyright was secured by publication with the copyright notice or registration in the copyright office. However, under the new law, no publication or registration or other action in the copyright office is required to secure copyright. You should also recognize that this differs from a patent, which must actually be granted by the U.S. Patent and Trademark Office.

Prior to 1978, when the new copyright law came into effect, copyright was secured by act of publication with the notice of copyright, publication meaning the distribution of copies of a work to the public by sale or other transfer of ownership, or by rental, lease, or lending. Even though publication is no longer required for copyright, the concept of publication is important in the copyright law because when a work is published, several important consequences follow:

- Works that are published with a notice of copyright in the United States are subject to mandatory deposit with the Library of Congress.
- Publication of a work can affect the limitations on the exclusive rights of the copyright owner that are set forth in the law.

- The year of publication is used in determining the length of the copyright protection for anonymous and pseudonymous works, when the author's identity is not in the records of the copyright office, and for works made for hire.
- Deposit requirements of published works differ from those of registration of unpublished works.

If you are publishing your work, let's talk first about the notice of copyright. The copyright notice should have three elements:

1. The symbol ©, or the word "copyright" or the abbreviation "copr." (I would recommend the © plus the word "copyright," because in some countries this gives additional international protection.)
2. The first year of publication.
3. The name of the owner of the copyright.

Thus, a typical copyright would read as follows: Copyright © by William A. Cohen, 2006.

If you are copyrighting phonograph records or similar items, instead of ©, use the symbol ® in the same fashion, put down the year of first publication and the name of the owner of the copyright.

How to Register Your Copyright

Remember, you receive your copyright automatically. However, there are several advantages to registering your copyright with the U.S. Copyright Office. Here are a few from the U.S. Copyright Office's web site:

- Registration establishes a public record of the copyright claim.
- Before an infringement suit may be filed in court, registration is necessary for works of U.S. origin.
- If made before or within five years of publication, registration establishes *prima facie* evidence in court of the validity of the copyright and of the facts stated in the certificate.
- If registration is made within three months after publication of the work or prior to an infringement of the work, statutory damages and attorney's fees are available to the copyright owner in court actions. Otherwise, only an award of actual damages and profits is available to the copyright owner.
- Registration allows the owner of the copyright to record the registration with the U.S. Customs Service for protection against the importation of infringing copies. For additional information, request Publication No. 563 "How to Protect Your Intellectual Property Right," from U.S. Customs

Service, P.O. Box 7404, Washington, DC 20044. Also see the U.S. Customs Service web site at www.customs.gov for online publications.

Registration may be made at any time within the life of the copyright. It is highly recommended. Moreover, unlike patenting, copyrighting can be done without professional help. It is also very inexpensive to do, costing at the present time no more than $30 per copyrighted work. Basically, you need to submit only three things: (1) a completed application form, (2) the fee per application, and (3) a deposit of the work being registered. The copy requirements may vary in different situations. For links to all the necessary forms go to http://www.copyright.gov/circs/circ1.html#wci.

How Long Is a Copyright Valid?

The law has changed several times over the past 25 years or so, but under the present laws, you can expect protection for 70 years after the author's death, or 70 years after the last author's death if there is more than one author. That should be enough protection for anyone!

International Copyright Protection

As with patents, there is no such thing as an international copyright that automatically protects an author's writings throughout the entire world. However, most countries do offer protection to foreign works under certain conditions, and these conditions have been greatly simplified by international copyright treaties and conventions. The United States is a member of the Universal Copyright Convention (UCC), which came into force in 1955. Under this convention, a work by a national or domiciliary of a country that is a member of the Universal Copyright Convention or a work first published in a Universal Copyright Convention country may claim protection under the Universal Copyright Convention, as long as the work bears the notice of the copyright in the foreign position specified by the Universal Copyright Convention. It is for this reason that I advise you to use the word "copyright" as well as the symbol ©. However, any author who wants protection for his or her work in a particular country should find out about that specific country. Also see the government's Circular 38a online at http://www.copyright.gov/circs/circ38a.pdf.

The Trademark

A trademark includes any word, name, symbol, device, or any combination thereof adopted and used by a manufacturer or merchant to identify his goods and distinguish them from those manufactured or sold by others. The primary function of the trademark is to indicate origin. Among other functions, trademarks also guarantee the quality of the goods bearing the mark and through advertising help to create and maintain a demand for your product. You may also come across the term "service mark." It is essentially the same thing as a trademark but for a service rather than a product.

Rights in a trademark are acquired only by use, and the use must ordinarily continue if the rights so acquired are to be preserved. This means that although you may register a trademark in the Patent and Trademark Office, this by itself does not create or establish any exclusive right. Such registration is only recognition by the U.S. government of the right of the owner to use the mark in commerce to distinguish the mark from those of others.

Benefits of Registration

While federal registration is not necessary for trademark protection, registration on the Principal Register does provide certain advantages:

- An explicit notice of your claim of ownership.
- A legal presumption of your ownership of the mark and exclusive right to use the mark nationwide in connection with the goods and/or services listed in the registration.
- The ability to sue regarding the trademark in federal court.
- The use of the U.S registration as a basis to obtain registration in foreign countries.
- The ability to file the registration with the U.S. Customs Service to prevent importation of foreign goods that infringe on your trademark.

How to Register for a Trademark

The registration application for a trademark must be filed in the name of the owner of the mark. The owner may file and prosecute his own application for registration, or he or she may be represented by an attorney or other person authorized to practice in trademark cases.

There are four parts to the application for a trademark:

1. A written application.
2. A drawing of the mark.
3. Five specimens or facsimiles.
4. The required filing fee.

Filing is easy and can be done online at http://www.uspto.gov/teas/index.html. If you don't have Internet access, you have two options. First, you can access Trademark Electronic Application System (TEAS) at any Patent and Trademark Depository Library throughout the United States. You may either mail or hand deliver a paper application to the USPTO. You can call the USPTO's automated telephone line at (800) 786-9199 to obtain a printed form. The mailing address to file a new application is: Commissioner for Trademarks, P.O. Box 1451, Alexandria, VA 22313-1451. The current fee is $335.

Trademark Notice

Once a federal registration is issued, you can give notice of registration by using the ® symbol. Although it is not required, prior to registration many trademark owners use a TM or SM (if the mark identifies a service) symbol to indicate a claim of ownership, even if no federal trademark application is pending. However, you are not allowed to use the ® symbol until after your registration has been approved.

Renewal of Trademarks

Trademarks must be renewed between the ninth and tenth anniversary of registration, and can be renewed indefinitely so long as you maintain use. Renewal fees are currently $100.

Trademark Search Library

A record of all active registrations and pending applications is maintained by the USPTO to help determine whether a previously registered mark exists, which could prevent the registration of an applicant's mark. You may conduct a search free of charge on the USPTO web site using the Trademark Electronic Search System (TESS) at http://tess2.uspto.gov/bin/gate.exe?f=login&p_lang=English&p_d=trmk. You can also conduct a trademark search by visiting the Trademark Public Search Library, between 8:00 A.M. and 5:00 P.M. at their Public Search Facility—Madison East, 1st Floor, 600 Dulany St., Alexandria, VA 22313. Similar to patents, you can also conduct a free search at a Patent and Trademark Depository Library near you. See the section on patents for an online list.

Sources of Additional Information

Books

The Concise Guide to Patents, Trademarks, and Copyrights, edited by Solomon J. Schepps, published by Bell Publishing Co., a division of Crown Publishers.

Copyright Law of the United States of America, published by the U.S. Copyright Office.

Digital Copyright: Protecting Intellectual Property on the Internet, by Jessica Litman, published by Prometheus Books.

From Patent to Profit, by Bob Dematteis, published by Perigee Books.

General Information Concerning Patents, published by the U.S. Superintendent of Documents.

General Information Concerning Trademarks, published by the U.S. Superintendent of Documents.

The Copyright Handbook, by Stephen Fishman, published by Nolo.com.

The Inventors Patent Handbook, by Stacy V. Jones, published by Dial Press.

Patent It, by Hrand M. Munchergan, published by Tab Books.

Patent It Yourself, by David Pressman, published by Nolo Press.

Patent Pending in 24 Hours, by Richard Stim and David Pressman, published by Nolo Press.

Patents and How to Get One, by the U.S. Department of Commerce, published by Dover Publications.

Patents, Copyrights, and Trademarks for Dummies, by Henri Charmasson, published by For Dummies Press.

The Entrepreneur's Guide to Patents, Copyrights, Trademarks, Trade Secrets and Licensing, by Jill Gilbert, published by Berkley Publishing Co.

Internet

Note: Because Internet sites frequently go down, multiple sites are listed for similar subject matter.

Copyright Law of the United States. Complete version of the U.S. Copyright Law in PDF format at http://www.copyright.gov/title17.

Copyright web site. Complete copyright registration and information resource at http://www.benedict.com.

Michael J. Colitz Jr. Patent Attorney. A complete overview of the patenting process at http://colitz.com/site/flow.htm.

Intellectual Property Web Server. Patents.com provides links to frequently asked questions on all aspects of patents, copyrights, trademarks, and more. Furnished by the law firm of Oppedahl & Larson at http://www.patents.com.

Trademarks. Official U.S. government site. Basic facts about trademarks, Depository Libraries, and more at http://www.uspto.gov/main/trademarks.htm.

U.S. Copyright Office. Official site for the government office featuring recent publications, forms, law resources, and registration information at http://www.copyright.gov.

U.S. Patent and Trademark Office. Official government web site with links to everything you need to know at http://www.uspto.gov.

DOWNLOADABLE WORKSHEET 16.1
Checklist for Obtaining a Patent

Task	In Process	Done
Maintain invention records and periodic review and signature by two witnesses, if process not yet started.		
Obtain services of a U.S. patent attorney, if desired. (See list through web links in this chapter.)		
Research material at U.S. Patent and Trademark Office web site to decide on type of patent required.		
Submit patent disclosure through U.S. Patent Office's disclosure program. (See web link in this chapter.)		
Search for prior patents at Patent Office, Depository Libraries, or web link provided in this chapter.		
Prepare patent application and submit.		
Include "patent applied for" on the copies of the invention you produce.		
Consider patenting in foreign countries and, if so, obtain services of a foreign attorney.		
Revise application and resubmit if required.		
Include the U.S. patent number on the copies of the invention once the patent has been awarded.		

To customize this document, download it to your hard drive from the John Wiley & Sons web site at www.wiley .com/go/cohenentrepreneur. The document can then be opened, edited, and printed using Microsoft Word or another popular word processing application.

DOWNLOADABLE WORKSHEET 16.2
Checklist for Obtaining a Copyright

Task	In Process	Done
Research material at U.S. Copyright Office web site to decide on type of copyright needed.		
Decide on type of copyright indicia to be included with your publication.		
Put the copyright indicia on the publications you produce (remember, that unlike patents, a copyright is automatic as soon as you create the publication—you're just registering it).		
Obtain copyright registration forms from the U.S. Copyright Office or through web links provided in this chapter.		
Submit completed form with fee and copy of your published material.		

To customize this document, download it to your hard drive from the John Wiley & Sons web site at www.wiley.com/go/cohenentrepreneur. The document can then be opened, edited, and printed using Microsoft Word or another popular word processing application.

DOWNLOADABLE WORKSHEET 16.3
Checklist for Obtaining a Trademark

Task	In Process	Done
Research your desired trademark to ensure it hasn't been previously adopted.		
Put "TM" or "SM" on your material.		
Obtain the necessary forms from the U.S. Patent and Trademark Office and/or through the links provided in this chapter to register your trademark.		
Once registration is complete, put the ® on your material instead of "TM" or "SM."		

To customize this document, download it to your hard drive from the John Wiley & Sons web site at www.wiley.com/go/cohenentrepreneur. The document can then be opened, edited, and printed using Microsoft Word or another popular word processing application.

CHAPTER 17

How to Recruit and Hire New Employees

Since recruiting can have a major impact on the future effectiveness and efficiency of your business, this activity is one of the most important you can do. The process can be divided into four basic steps:

1. Establishing requirements for staffing.
2. Establishing job specifications for each position.
3. Recruiting.
4. Hiring.

Establishing Requirements for Staffing

The first step in the hiring process is to plan ahead for your company's needs. To do this, it is best to set a time period of several months to a year and decide what your organization's objectives are and what the attainment of these objectives involves. For example, if you are expanding, do you require more salespeople or production people over the coming months or years? Are you going to develop a new product and need more technical people? Whatever future activities you plan, you must ensure that you have the necessary personnel on board. Now is the time to start laying out your future personnel requirements.

The way to establish these personnel requirements is first to establish what your company is going to do and then to break down the overall objective into smaller steps or tasks. You can then describe the kind of individual you need to perform the task and estimate how many labor hours are needed from that person for each month over the selected period. This also tells you whether you need more than one individual to perform this function. If you already have individuals in your company who can do the job, you merely indicate this. But if you do have needs in the personnel area, Worksheet 17.1 in this chapter, Forecasting Manpower Requirements, helps.

In some cases, your needs are immediately evident, because of a termination, someone leaving, or unexpected new business. When this happens, you must readjust your forecasts and complete a new worksheet to help you determine the personnel requirements of the job. With an updated forecast, you always know your requirements in detail.

Establishing Job Specifications

Once you complete Worksheet 17.1, you have a list of individuals you need for the coming year as well as the month that they should be hired.

Your task now is to write a detailed description of the job you want these individuals to perform along with other factors that you consider important. For this purpose, use Worksheet 17.2, Job Specification Form, which details the job title, to whom the individual reports, the background on why you need the individual, the task that the individual performs, desired prior experience, desired education, special problems, factors that would definitely exclude a candidate from consideration regardless of other qualifications or accomplishments, travel requirements, salary range, other compensation, and some ideas about why someone should take the job.

Note that your requirements are not cast in iron. You may change the job title at any time, and tasks can be added or reduced in number or in scope. Prior experience and education also should be flexible because it is what you want the individual to do and not what he or she has done already that is important. Past experience and education are important only as indicators of the potential to perform work. For this reason, requirements such as a certain number of years of experience should always be flexible. The salary that you intend to pay should be a range rather than as a specific value, but even the range is a guideline, and as you interview and talk to various candidates, you can begin to narrow to an appropriate salary range. Detailing information about the advantages of taking the job is also very important because it allows you to put yourself in the candidate's shoes and see things from his or her perspective. Why would the type of individual that you have specified want to work for you? If there are few perceived advantages, you are not going to get the kind of individual you want. If you want good people, then there should be sufficient reasons motivating them to work for your company rather than going somewhere else or staying at their present place of employment. This section is very useful for you in your recruiting, whether you do it yourself or go through someone else, such as a personnel agency, counselor, or headhunter.

Recruiting

The following are all sources of personnel that you should consider:

- Personnel currently in your own company.
- Personnel from other companies.
- Newly graduated individuals or students about to graduate from colleges or universities.
- Currently unemployed individuals.
- Temporary employment agencies.

Personnel Currently in Your Own Company

Staffing from within your own company is a good idea in many instances, and certainly when personnel for tasks required are currently available. This not only saves money in recruiting but can also motivate all of your employees. This is especially true if the new job is a promotion and the individual in your company can handle the job. There are additional advantages. An individual recruited internally is already familiar with the practices, procedures, personnel, policy, special characteristics, and other employees of your company. Therefore, in general, there is less time required to bring the individual up to speed for the job that you want him to perform.

However, when recruiting from your own company, you must be concerned with who takes over the job that the individual is doing. You must also be sure that the change of job creates no problems. Does the individual really want the job? Do not automatically assume this to be the case, even if it means a promotion. Do other employees present problems that this individual must deal with in his or her new role? These are all things you must consider.

Personnel from Other Companies

In many instances, the necessary personnel do not exist within your own company and you must go outside the organization to recruit them. Going outside the organization has advantages. If you have sufficient time, you can hire an individual who has been successful in an identical or similar job with another company. This can increase his or her chances of success in the job that you have planned. In addition, bringing new people into your company also brings in new ideas from other companies. Of course, there are disadvantages to recruiting outside of your company. These include the additional expense, the fact that the new personnel are unfamiliar with your company's way of operating, and possible dissatisfaction on the part of current employees.

It is generally accepted that an individual can move from one company to another if the new company can offer a better job opportunity, and that any individual is free to go from one company to another for personal betterment. However, in considering individuals from other companies, you should attempt to ascertain his or her current state of mind, because it affects the candidate's readiness to come to your company and it also influences how you handle the employment interview. This is true even if an executive recruiter is successful in going into a firm and pulling out an individual for a specific job for your firm. This does not necessarily mean that the individual is unhappy in his or her former job. Quite the opposite may have been true. The individual may have been perfectly happy in his or her old job, and executive recruiters often argue that these individuals make the best new employees; if they were happy in their former employment they should be happy in your employ as well. With a job candidate who is currently happily employed, you need to present the job situation in its best light. This is where your reasons why someone should take this job are very important.

Newly Graduated Individuals or Students about to Graduate from Colleges or Universities

Many recently graduated students go to larger companies, since larger companies offer training programs that initiate them into the industry and functional area they have chosen and can usually offer higher salaries. Also, because large companies send recruiters all over the country in search of newly graduated talent, it may be difficult for you as a small company to compete for this source of candidates. However, you can offer certain advantages to a college graduate that a larger company cannot offer. These include the possibility of rapid advancement, better visibility to top management, and more responsibility, earlier. In fact, many consider small companies more fun to work for and even seek them out. Further, if there are colleges or universities close by, you do not even have to bear a heavy travel expense to do this type of recruiting. All you need to do is to call the placement offices of colleges and universities in your geographical area. By emphasizing what you have to offer, you can successfully (and inexpensively) compete with larger companies for many top-quality college graduates.

Currently Unemployed Individuals

A potential employee for your company may be currently unemployed because he or she was fired, quit, or was laid off from a previous job. None of these reasons need reflect unfavorably on your candidate. However, it should be routine to find out as much as you can about the former employment and why the individual left the former job. Many companies do not like to hire unemployed individuals, preferring individuals who are currently holding a job. However, this is a prejudice that has little validity. Many unemployed individuals are outstanding candidates, even for high-level jobs in your company.

Temporary Employment Agencies

Temporary employment agencies are known by various names, some less than flattering, but they are a source of skilled temporary help, although, even in many large companies this temporary help may be used for as long as a year or more. What these temporary employment organizations offer you is an individual who is rented out to you on an as-needed basis. The agency hires the employee and pays all fringe benefits concerned as well as salary. The advantage to the temporary employee is that he or she is paid at a higher rate than if he or she were working for one company and is guaranteed continued employment with less chance of a layoff from work than might otherwise be the case. To you, the advantage is that you have needed personnel for short-term projects but you do not need to retain them when there is no more work. Also, you may find that the employee is so good that you want to offer him or her a full-time position even though the project ends. Of course, there is a disadvantage as well: It is difficult to make a temporary employee an integral part of your company. He or she is unlikely to be as committed to your goals as your permanent employees since the term of employment is limited.

Selection of the Right Recruiting Method

The recruiting methods that you use depend on many factors including your company, industry, the type of employee you seek, the job market at the time that you're doing your recruiting, and how long you are willing to look.

The methods discussed in the following paragraphs each have advantages and disadvantages. Some methods are very time consuming: Advertising in magazines read by the type of individual for which you're looking, for example. The lead time for the ad to appear may be several months. Other methods may be very expensive: executive recruiting firms, for instance. You may be expected to pay as much as 30 percent of the annual compensation of the candidate in return for the firm finding you a suitable candidate. Even employment agencies require a fee of 10 to 15 percent of annual compensation for their services. Some methods, such as word of mouth, which costs nothing are fine if you are not in a hurry, but may not be desirable at all if you need someone at once.

Word-of-Mouth Recruiting Word-of-mouth recruiting is perhaps the easiest and the least expensive method. You or someone in your employ simply calls around to likely sources, such as friends and professional associates, and asks them if they would be interested in the available position, or if they know someone who meets the qualifications that you seek. This method has several advantages. As indicated before, it doesn't cost anything. It is also easy; there is no special procedure involved, and anyone can do it. And either you know the individual yourself or your friends or associates know the individual. However, there are also disadvantages with this type of recruiting campaign. First, you do not reach as many potential candidates as you might otherwise. Also, if you are receiving recommendations from people who are friends of the candidate, the qualifications of the candidate may be somewhat colored by this relationship. If for one reason or another you want your hiring to be done without the knowledge of others, potential competitors or potential customers, you are not able to use word of mouth. Finally, this process may not work quickly.

Advertising for Candidates Advertising for new candidates is expensive, but if your advertisement is reasonably well put together it brings in qualified applicants. If you are in a hurry, then you should run display or classified advertisements in the business section of your local paper or the *Wall Street Journal*. Alternatively, if you have time, it may be wise to consider advertising in professional magazines that are read by individuals in the desired field. Such magazines may require a month to six weeks or more of lead time before the advertisement appears.

It is possible when you advertise to keep secret the fact that you are searching for new employees to fill certain designated positions. You can run a "blind ad," which gives a box number instead of the name of your company. The box number is provided by the newspaper or magazine that you have chosen. For a slight additional fee, they collect all the responses to your ad and forward them to you. When considering a blind advertisement versus an open advertisement, however, you must also recognize that a blind advertisement pulls fewer responses than an open advertisement because some potential candidates are concerned about the identity of the advertiser. They don't want their present company to know that they have responded as a potential candidate for a new job.

If you are going to advertise, you should know the competition for the employees you seek to hire. This competition can be readily assessed by viewing the "Help Wanted" section of your local newspaper. Check the classified ads under the appropriate job description and also the display ads in the business section. By studying competitive ads, you get a general idea of what jobs are being offered in your geographical area and how to structure your ad.

One major advantage of advertising is that you are able to locate candidates fairly rapidly for the position. Also, the method is reasonably certain. Unless the competition is overwhelming, your ad is really poorly constructed and written, or the terms that you advertise are just not competitive, you are going to get enough responses to enable you to fill the position.

The biggest disadvantage of advertising as a method of securing candidates is the cost. Even a single display ad can run a thousand dollars or more. Another disadvantage is the fact that you only reach candidates who are seeking a position. This would appear to be an advantage—isn't that what you want, after all, individuals who are looking for work? However, for some positions, you may want to recruit individuals who are perfectly happy and content and performing well for other companies. This may be especially true for high-level jobs. You do not reach such individuals through advertising because they are not looking in the employment section of newspapers. Also, even if by chance such an individual reads your ad, rarely is the information a sufficient enticement to encourage this candidate to send a resume to you. Finally, if you are seeking a job specialty, which is in great demand at the time of your search, you may not be able to find sufficient potential candidates or qualified candidates through advertising.

Government Employment Agencies   Government employment agencies, local and state, may be of assistance in finding suitable employees for your company. The quality of candidates that they provide varies widely from place to place and time to time. Candidates from government employment agencies generally appear to be somewhat less well qualified for professional positions than candidates from other sources. The reason for this is that many professionals do not register with government employment agencies except as a last resort. However, it is always worthwhile checking with government employment agencies. It costs you nothing and you may find just the right candidate.

Employment Agencies and Executive Recruiters   Although employment agencies and executive recruiters are collectively known as "headhunters" and in both cases you pay money for their services, the two differ in a number of ways.

Executive recruiters or executive search firms generally go after higher-level candidates than do employment agencies. In theory, executive recruiters or search firms actually go into other companies by telephone and find and recruit exactly the right candidate for you. For these services, you may pay 30 percent of the new employee's annual compensation or more. Many times these firms operate only on retainer, and you must pay them a basic fee for a candidate who is sent to you even if you ultimately do not hire the person. For this reason, this type of recruiter should be reserved for very top candidates and used only at a time when you can afford this special service.

Employment agencies may recruit from other companies as well, but they tend to rely primarily on applicants who register with them, and while some may require a retainer in the same way as search firms, most operate on contingency only. This means that you only pay the employment agency if you hire a candidate that the employment agency sends to you for an interview. Obviously, this has major advantages for the small firm, which cannot afford to finance a search that is not successful. Each individual agency has its own fee schedule; they generally start at 10 percent and may go as high as 30 percent.

There are also agencies that collect fees from the individual job applicant. You must be much more careful with the candidates that you interview coming from this source because the agency is far more likely to try to sell you a candidate than to send you the best person available for the job.

If you are dealing with a professional recruiter, whether he or she is in a search firm or an agency, this source of candidates can offer a number of advantages to you. For one thing, you can be very precise in the requirements that you set for potential candidates. This can save you a great deal of time screening numerous resumes and interviewing applicants who are not qualified for the job. Also, if you yourself recruit from a competing firm, you can run into legal difficulties. However, if a search firm or employment agency does this for you, you are probably off the hook legally. Finally, there is usually some type of guarantee if you hire the candidate and he or she quits after a short period of time or for some reason proves to be unsatisfactory. This is something you most definitely should investigate prior to giving the okay to any type of headhunter. Guarantees may run up to as long as a year, with the firm required to return your money or to recruit a new candidate for you.

You should expect any personnel agency, employment agency, or search firm that you deal with to screen the candidates for you. How much screening you get really depends on the agency involved. On the low end, if you are paying something like 10 percent, probably all you're going to get is basic screening of resumes. On the high end, with an executive search firm on a retainer, you can expect many candidates to be approached, some candidates to be screened face-to-face, references to be checked, and three to five candidates, all of whom meet your qualifications, to be submitted to you for your consideration. Other firms' services fall somewhere in the middle. Perhaps references are checked, candidates are talked to and screened, but the screening is not done in as thorough a manner as would be the case if you were paying on a retainer basis.

If you're going to use a headhunter, it is a good idea to talk to other small businesspeople who have also used headhunters since the quality varies so much.

One final word on the use of headhunters: Get some idea as to how fast the recruiter is going to work and when you can expect to interview the first candidate.

Another type of employment agency that you should consider contacting is a national organization known as "Forty Plus." This is a self-help agency composed of individuals who have reached the age of 40 or older and who are currently unemployed. These individuals pay a small fee and may donate their time to helping an organization. The result is that you see qualified candidates, and even if you hire them, you pay nothing.

Recruiting through the Schools   School recruiting is an excellent way for a small businessperson to acquire outstanding candidates for professional positions. For one thing, such candidates are frequently well trained, having received their bachelor's degree or an advanced degree and are eager to start work. They can be easily motivated to do a good job for you, and yet their salaries are much lower than you would have to pay for a more experienced but perhaps less well-qualified employee.

As pointed out earlier, you do not need to run around the country recruiting, as does a major company. In fact, you need not do any face-to-face recruiting at all. If you are fortunate enough to live near a large city where there are many colleges and universities, place a telephone call to the career development office or to the department that teaches a subject likely to produce candidates for the job that you have open. This can produce very good results. Over the phone, you should indicate that you have a position open, what the qualifications are, some advantages for coming to work for you, and where you can be reached to set up an interview.

Depending on how lucrative the position is and the job market in your area for these new graduates, you may get a number of candidates for your job. This is a very easy way to recruit, and a very inexpensive one. You should not overlook it when seeking potential employees.

Internet Recruiting   The Internet has become a major vehicle for locating job candidates. You can post your own offering and search through literally millions of job candidates at relatively low cost. Here are just a few employment sites that you may find useful:

- http://www.monster.com.
- http://hotjobs.yahoo.com.
- http://www.ajb.org.
- http://www.careerbuilder.com.
- http://www.jobs.net.

Yahoo! offers a free guide to online recruiting that you can request from their jobs web site at: http://www.hotjobs.com.

Professional Associations   Many professional associations allow you to place recruiting advertisements in their newsletters or act as a clearinghouse for job openings as a service to the members of the association. In many cases, this costs you nothing—a major advantage for using this method. The disadvantage, as with many other low-cost methods, is that there are no assurances that you get large numbers of candidates. In fact, you may not receive any applicants at all for the job. But you should consider professional associations as a supplemental source of job candidates.

Some Additional Recruiting Tips

- Make sure you know exactly what you are looking for and the skills required, and develop a complete job specification as shown on Worksheet 17.2 of this chapter, every time it's necessary for you to do recruiting.

- Make certain that whoever answers the phone at your company has full information about the position so that he or she can answer inquiries about it if you are unavailable.

- If your recruiting is going to bring in large numbers of resumes of candidates, then set minimum standards for these candidates and establish a list of these minimum standards so that someone else can screen these resumes for you.

- Let your other employees know about the position and give them a brief description from your job specification so that they can do free recruiting for you.

- Select your recruiting methods based on your particular situation, but be certain to use all appropriate means of bringing in job candidates, especially those that are free.

- If an advertisement under one heading fails to bring in an adequate number of qualified candidates, then try a different job heading or a slightly different job title.

- If you decide to use a recruiter or an employment agency, visit the firm so that you can know better the headhunter who is working for you. Also, ask if they can supply you with three names of clients not in your business, who have been happy with their operation, whom you may contact.

- If you do a great deal of hiring, conduct an audit from time to time to see what your hiring costs are and which recruiting methods work best.

- When you receive job applicants from organizations or associations that do not get paid, be certain to thank them for their time and effort in referring candidates or applicants to you.

Hiring

The hiring process consists of three steps: screening, interviewing, and making the offer. Let us look at each in turn.

Applicant Screening

If you used an employment agency or a search firm, the applicants have already been screened prior to the interview. In this case, you are presented with a number of candidates and the amount of work you have to do along these lines is greatly reduced. Alternatively, if you've used any of the other methods, then you have received resumes—sometimes quite a few. For example, a really good job at the professional level may bring in 500 to 800 resumes if you are located in a large urban area. Going through this number of resumes is a time-consuming and exacting task. However, if you establish basic requirements and communicate them to someone else, it may be easier and less expensive for a secretary or some other employee to go through these resumes for you and reduce them to a reasonable amount. If the initial screening fails to weed out very many, then you can tighten up on the requirements and continue screening until you have a workable number. Remember that interviewing a candidate for a job also takes time. Therefore, the initial screening should pare the number of candidates down so that you see no more than 6 to 10. Some companies have the human resources manager do the initial screening, selecting 10 candidates from the resumes, and then the human resources manager sees these 10 him- or herself, and selects five candidates who are interviewed by the executive doing the hiring. Use your own judgment in this, but don't spend all of your time interviewing, especially if it is not for a top-level job.

Opinions differ as to whether you should talk to references of the applicants prior to the interview. My feeling is not to do so until mutual interest has been established. If you only call three references for each candidate, and you are considering five candidates, that's 15 telephone calls. Also, many candidates or applicants do not give you references until mutual interest is established as a result of the interview. The reason for this is that they do not want their references bothered by every single company with whom they interview. However, regardless of when you do a reference check, make certain that it is done prior to hiring. In fact, if you delay the reference check until after the offer, the offer should be contingent upon favorable references. Perhaps the best method is to interview the candidates and get permission to check references of the one or two candidates you are seriously interested in. Assuming the references check out, you can extend the offer. Regardless of when the reference check is made, the following items should be checked:

- How long the reference has known the candidate.
- Under what circumstances he or she has known the candidate.
- The candidate's personal qualities—honesty, reliability, dependability, and so forth.
- The candidate's general background.
- Specific items that you feel are relevant to this particular position, including years on the job, managerial experience if applicable, and what exactly the individual accomplished while working on the job.

Don't be surprised if occasionally a reference does not check out, even though the candidate appears outstanding for the job. Sometimes a reference that the candidate feels is a good one turns out to be a negative one because of jealousy or some other reason. When that happens, look at the overall situation. If two out of three references are positive and only one is bad, you might want to ask for additional references. Alternatively, if the general pattern of references is bad, you may wish to drop the candidate.

Another thing you must not overlook when checking references is questioning an individual who has supervised the candidate in the past. A candidate would have to be very foolish to give you the name of someone he or she knows may not give a good reference. However, he or she doesn't always have the same control when dealing with former employers.

Interviewing the Candidate

To get the maximum out of the interview, you must prepare for and plan the interview ahead of time. One of the most important steps and one that is frequently overlooked is to be sure that you are not continually interrupted during the interview. If you are, your train of thought is broken, and the candidate may be unimpressed with your lack of consideration for him or her. It may cause the candidate to turn down the offer even though he or she is ideal for the job.

If you have time prior to the interview, mail out a job applicant's form about a week before the interview and ask the candidate to complete the form and return it to you. The job applicant's form is more valuable than a resume in that it forces the candidate to list more complete information in some sort of chronological order. A clever applicant for a job can structure his or her resume around your requirements and keep information that may negatively affect his or her chances at the job out of your reach. But it is to your advantage to get all the information that you can. In a job application form, you can ask for employment and educational information, including supervisors in the former and have this information structured chronologically. You may NOT ask for information regarding age, marital status, race, religion, or ethnic group.

Before the actual interview, you should review the application form, resume, and other information you have about the candidate. Write down information you feel is missing or that you want to get from the candidate. Also, review the candidate's background against your job specification form very carefully and develop a list of questions you want to ask. Write down a syllabus for the candidate's interview. Also, put down things that you wish to take place. Doing this planning ahead of time makes the interview more fruitful for you and for the candidate. It shows your interest in seeing that he or she is happy in the position, and he or she learns something about the company and has an easier time making his or her decision to come to work for you.

If possible, arrange for the candidate to be interviewed by at least two individuals in your company beside yourself. Select these individuals carefully; they should be individuals who have a good understanding of what the job requires and what the company is looking for. Such multiple interviewing has many advantages. For one thing, it brings in someone else's opinion. Also, sometimes other interviewers pick up things that you did not. Finally, it allows the candidate to meet other members of your company and gives the candidate a better idea of what your company is like and what's going to be required of him or her as a part of the job.

Do not put the candidate under pressure during the interview unless being under pressure is part of the job. First, ask very general and open questions to put the candidate at ease. Also, note those aspects of the candidate that you would like to know more about and write these down. Then, ask the more specific and detailed questions you wrote down during your planning. Allow the candidate to do most of the talking. At some point, you should try to find out what you can about the candidate's current or former compensation and what salary figure he or she has in mind for the position. Finally, even if you do not have a company tour, let the candidate know that you are interested by telling him or her more about the job and its importance to the company, fringe benefits, and so forth. Promise to get back to the candidate as soon as a decision is made, but do not make an offer at this time, no matter how good the candidate seems. Always wait to think it over and if possible to compare notes with other interviewers.

If the candidate is a skilled interviewee, he has done his homework and learned everything possible about your company and the job. The interviewee may even have made up a list of questions to ask you. The purpose of these questions is to exhibit his alertness and interest. The candidate may also wish to learn exactly what you want so that he can best answer your questions when you ask them. Do not allow yourself to be drawn into answering questions in detail until you have your own questions answered.

Here are some tips you should consider in any interview that you conduct to recruit new employees for your company:

- Allow the applicant to feel comfortable and attempt to establish a friendly, personal relationship.
- Make certain that you ask the questions that you have listed prior to the interview before the applicant asks questions of you.
- Ensure that the applicant has the necessary qualifications for the job.
- Determine whether the applicant has the personal characteristics required for the job.
- Try to discover what the applicant's attitude toward the position in your company is. Remember, you are looking for someone for a long-term relationship and do not want the person you hire to quit after a few weeks or a few months.
- Always let the applicant do more talking than you do. In fact, a good way to start is to ask the candidate to tell you something about him- or herself.
- Take notes on any information that you think is important or that you may wish to talk or ask about later.
- Probe to get some idea of what the applicant is seeking in the way of compensation. This may affect your own tactics when making the offer later on.
- Ensure that all of your questions conform to equal employment opportunity practices as required by the law.

You should know and be able to explain everything about the job, including the basic duties, the salary range, the fringe benefits, any overtime hours expected, possibility of travel, and so forth.

Background Checks over the Internet There are many company that can do background checks for you over the Internet, some for quite reasonable amounts. Considering the investments you must make in all new employees, and the payoff for good ones, this is usually a good investment. Here are a few companies that do background checks:

Background PI.com
Web site: http://www.backgroundpi.info

Consumer Intelligence Agency
Phone: (310) 630-3700
Web site: http://www.ciadata.info

Informus Corporation
Phone: (800) 364-8380
Web site: http://www.informus.com

Instant People Check
Web site: http://www.instantpeoplecheck.com/default.asp

You can also find a number of companies listed at:

Best Background Checks
Web site: http://www.bestbackgroundchecks.com/personal.html

Equal Employment Opportunity Laws   Equal employment opportunity laws state that you may not discriminate against an applicant on the basis of the applicant's race, religion, sex, national origin, or age. You can find out important information and questions and answers about these important laws at the U.S. government's web site at http://www.eeoc.gov/facts/qanda.html.

Making the Offer

Once you have settled on the best candidate, state your offer either by telephone or in person. Generally, assuming the salary amount is fair; you should open at from 10 to 15 percent lower than what you think the person may accept. Some candidates state a minimum figure, which is really the maximum amount they feel they can get, and they may be perfectly willing to accept 10 to 15 percent less if this is a fair amount and not lower than the approximate going rate for the work. If the person is inflexible regarding the amount that he or she wants and you really wish to hire the candidate, you can always allow yourself to be negotiated up to a higher figure in your predetermined range.

If the candidate asks for an unreasonably high figure, which is well out of your range, you can explain to the candidate that while you want to hire him or her, the salary is too high and is not reasonable considering the going rate. Offer what you think the job is worth and emphasize other positive aspects of the job such as promotion opportunities, fringe benefits, and so forth.

Always keep in mind that your objective during negotiations is not to hire at the lowest figure possible, as even if you succeed in doing this it probably makes for an unhappy employee, and that you definitely don't want. Rather, your objective is to hire at the lowest fair price.

What to Do about Candidates You Do Not Hire

You should always let unsuccessful candidates or applicants down gently. After all, they've gone to considerable trouble for you, submitting resumes, being interviewed, and allowing their references to be checked. Every candidate who has seen you in a face-to-face interview should be contacted after you have made your decision. You should explain to each that while he or she was an outstanding finalist for the job, you have made the decision to hire someone else. Thank him or her for considering your company. If true, tell the unsuccessful candidate that you would like to consider him or her for future positions with the company. In this way, you keep on good terms with everyone that you contact and can even use some of the unsuccessful candidates as potential candidates for future jobs. This could be extremely important if something goes wrong with the deal you've already struck. If for any reason the candidate you hire cancels out prior to beginning work, you don't want to start from the beginning all over again if you have another candidate who was almost as good. In the final analysis, all hiring decisions are subjective. It may turn out that your second or third choice was really the best person for the job.

Sources of Additional Information

Books

Finding and Hiring the Right Employee, Small Marketers Aids No. 106, by Rudolph Raphelson, published by the Small Business Administration.

High Impact Hiring, by Del J. Still, published by Management Development Systems.

Hire with Your Head, by Lou Adler, published by John Wiley & Sons.

Hiring and Keeping the Best People, (no author listed), published by Harvard Business School Press.

Hiring Great People, by Kevin Klinvex et al., published by McGraw-Hill.

Hiring Smart, by Dr. Mornell Pierre et al., published by Ten Speed Press.

Hiring the Best, by Martin Yate, published by Adams Media Corporation.

Hiring the Right Man, Small Marketers Aids No. 106 (no author listed), published by the Small Business Administration.

Management's Talent Search, by Paul W. Maloney, published by AMACOM.

Ninety-Six Great Interview Questions to Ask before You Hire, by Paul Falcone, published by AMACOM.

Recruiting and Selecting Employees (no author listed), published by the Small Business Administration.

The Selection Process, by M. M. Mandell, published by AMACOM.

Internet

Note: Because Internet sites frequently go down, multiple sites are listed for similar subject matter.

Ask the Headhunter. Inside information about the hiring process at http://www .asktheheadhunter.com.

Business.com. Links to hundreds of recruiting, hiring, and retentions material at http://www.business.com/directory/human_resources/hiring_and_retention.

Fast Company. Interesting articles about various aspects of hiring at http://www .fastcompany.com/guides/hire.html.

Free Advice. Answers a number of legal questions regarding hiring at http://employment -law.freeadvice.com/hiring.

U.S. Department of Labor. Links to important employment issues in the areas of affirmative action, the hiring of veterans and foreign workers, the employment of workers under the age of 18, and how to implement drug-free workplace programs at http://www.dol.gov/dol/topic/hiring.

DOWNLOADABLE WORKSHEET 17.1
Forecasting Labor Requirements

Project/ Task	Type of Individual Required	Hours of Work Estimated by Month											
		Jan	Feb	Mar	Apr	May	Jun	Jul	Aug	Sep	Oct	Nov	Dec
Monthly Labor Requirements by Title (1)													
Current Labor Resources on Hand (2)													
Additional Labor Required (1) – (2)													

To customize this document, download it to your hard drive from the John Wiley & Sons web site at www.wiley.com/go/cohenentrepreneur. The document can then be opened, edited, and printed using Microsoft Word or another popular word processing application.

DOWNLOADABLE WORKSHEET 17.2
Job Specification Form

1. Job title: _____   2. Required by (date): _____

3. Reporting to: _____

4. Background: _____
   _____
   _____
   _____

5. Required tasks/duties: _____
   _____
   _____
   _____

6. Desired prior experience: _____
   _____
   _____
   _____

7. Desired education: _____
   _____
   _____
   _____

8. Special issues: _____
   _____
   _____
   _____

9. Factors that would exclude a candidate from consideration: _____
   _____
   _____
   _____

10. Travel requirements: _____
    _____
    _____
    _____

---

11. Salary range: _____

    _____

    _____

    _____

12. Other compensation: _____

    _____

    _____

    _____

13. Why should someone take this job? _____

    _____

    _____

    _____

CHAPTER 18

How to Manage Your Most Valuable Resource: People

Human resource management is the management of people, and people are the most important resource in your business. Chapter 17 covered how to find and hire new personnel. This chapter discusses developing job descriptions, wage scales and compensation plans, doing performance appraisals and counseling your employees, dealing with disciplinary problems, motivating employees, terminating employees, and using temporary help services.

Performing a Job Analysis and Developing Job Descriptions

Good job descriptions assist you in hiring, in establishing wage scales and compensation, in constructing a valid means of performance appraisal, and in hiring temporary help services. Good job descriptions are the basis of most actions that you must take in human resource management. The job description itself is based on a job analysis—a methodology for discovering the most important factors concerning any job in your company. The analysis answers the four major questions for the job description and job specification:

1. What physical and/or mental tasks does the worker perform? These may include cleaning, fabricating, judging, managing, word processing, planning and numerous other functions.

2. How does the worker do the job—what methods are used and what equipment or machinery, if any, is involved? For example, does the job require use of a lathe, a cash register, a computer, and for what purpose are these or other equipment used?

3. Why is the job done? In this part of the analysis, you should develop a short explanation of the objective of the job and how it relates to other jobs that are done in your company. Here you may indicate, for example, that your copywriter writes copy that is used in advertising and promotional materials.

4. What qualifications are needed to perform this job? List knowledge, skills, training, personal characteristics, and so forth required of the worker. For example, a sales engineer may need a bachelor's degree in engineering, ability to get along with people, a pleasing personality, persuasiveness, and energy.

In summary, the job analysis provides a complete picture of the job, including what the worker does, how he does it, his job's relationship to other jobs that must be performed, and the knowledge, skills, training, and education that the worker must have to do the job.

Conducting a job analysis is not difficult. The easiest way is simply to sit down and think through the various aspects of the job as mentioned previously. If you already have an employee in the job and you wish to redefine it, you may speak with her and her supervisor. Or you could talk with people in other companies who have similar jobs. You could also ask the employee or supervisor to list the duties and responsibilities and qualifications he or she feels are important in performing the job. You can then modify this information as appropriate. To assist you in doing this, use Worksheet 18.1, Job Analysis, at the end of the chapter.

Once you have completed the job analysis, you have the material necessary to develop a job description and job specifications. There is a distinction between job descriptions and job specifications. A job description is part of the job analysis that describes the responsibilities of the job, how the job is done, and how it ties in with other jobs in your business. The job specification, which is used directly in your recruiting efforts, describes those qualifications required of someone to do the job properly. Therefore, to prepare a job description, simply summarize the important facts about the job that you have analyzed. Write down in a clear, concise way the essential facts including a job title that is descriptive of the position; a brief summary of the work to be performed; responsibilities of the job including knowledge of equipment that may be necessary, decision making, and scheduling; major job duties that are performed only occasionally; and the relationship of the job to other positions in your firm, including whom the employee would supervise and to whom the employee would report. To assist you with this, use Worksheet 18.2, Writing a Job Description, at the end of this chapter.

Wage Scales and Compensation

How much you pay your employee for a particular job is very important. Unfortunately, the question has no simple answer. If you pay too little, many of your better employees leave to do the same work elsewhere or to work on their own, and in general only the poorer, less motivated, and less able employees remain to work for you for the lower pay. Alternatively, overpaying has a drawback. It can affect the price you charge for the product or service that you are offering, or leave less financial resources for other areas, or cut unnecessarily into your profits.

Also, an important consideration is the fact that compensation is measured in more than mere dollars, and many compensation programs fail because the business does not recognize this fact. Back in the 1880s, Congress, in a serious cost reduction effort, failed to appropriate money for the salaries of army officers. Thus, army officers received no compensation whatsoever for services rendered. Many faced dangers and great hardships on the frontiers protecting pioneers and settlers. They were able to support their families at subsistence level only because they were granted government quarters and were able to eat at no cost at government mess facilities. Yet, despite this draconian measure at cost reduction, there were no mass resignations. Clearly, the compensation received was other than monetary, for these officers continued to work without pay for almost two years.

Compensation obviously does consist of elements other than salary. These include working environment, terms of employment, status, and fringe benefits. We come back to salary, but, because of their importance, let's look at these other elements first.

Working Environment

Working environment is an extremely important element of compensation. It encompasses a wide range of factors. These include working conditions, the facilities in which your workers work, and the esprit de corps that you as the head of a company are able to develop in the group of employees that work for you.

Terms of Employment

The terms of employment include many different aspects of the job, not all tangible. Aside from compensation these can include the security that your company offers, work hour flexibility, the number of holidays and vacation days, sick days, and other benefits.

Status

Status may come from your company and its relative position in the industry as well as from the title that you give the job that the employee holds. If yours is a small company, it may at first appear unlikely that you have anything to offer in the way of status. However, even suitable titles for the various jobs that people do for you as employees can create status. In fact, it can be a major portion of the compensation that you pay. I once encountered a multilevel marketing firm that awarded each of its independent contractors the title of chief executive officer (CEO). Technically, they were correct, and as far as I know you are at liberty to assign titles in any way you wish, so long as they are not fraudulent.

Fringe Benefits

There are basically two types of fringe benefits. There are those that everyone who works for you receives and those that are reserved for key personnel. Certain fringe benefits have become very common with many companies, even small ones. These include life insurance policies, retirement plans, medical and hospital insurance, and the like. In many cases, such supplements to salary are expected. For example, if you are trying to recruit someone who already has one or more of these benefits at his or her current place of employment, it may be difficult to hire this person if you cannot duplicate the benefits offered. Fringe benefits for key personnel include stock options, use of a car, club memberships, and so on. These fringe benefits for key personnel can be even larger than the salary element of compensation.

Bonuses

Bonuses are an addition to the normal salary. For maximum benefit to you, they should be tied in some way to the performance of the individual as well as to the performance of your company. You must be very careful with bonuses. Used correctly, a bonus element of compensation can help motivate maximum performance. Used incorrectly, it can cause frustration and hurt your personnel policies and the performance of your employees.

The Salary Component of Compensation

In determining the salary component, consider the following principles:

- Higher pay should be given for work requiring more knowledge, skill, or physical exertion.

- Pay should be competitive with that given for similar work in other companies.
- Total earnings should reflect the employee's contribution to the performance of your company.
- So far as possible, all employees should know pay scales.
- Secrecy usually leads to erroneous speculation and hard feelings. If compensation is fairly awarded, it is rarely resented.
- Overqualified employees should not be paid exorbitant amounts more than fully qualified employees for the same position and same work.

You should strive to be as fair as possible in the application of these basic principles of salary compensation, as well as in compensation in general for your employees.

Developing a Compensation Package

The first step in developing a total compensation package for a position is to document all the nonsalary elements including insurance, unique things about your company, the title you have given the job, and others. You should also try to find out what compensation other firms are paying for similar work. You can obtain such data from professional organizations and associations, industrial organizations, your local chamber of commerce, the U.S. Bureau of Labor Statistics, independent management consultants, and executive recruiters. An Internet search can also be very helpful; try the following sites:

- http://www.wageweb.com.
- http://www.realrates.com.

There are additional sites listed under Sources of Additional Information at the end of the chapter.

Once you have gotten these data, you can list them on Worksheet 18.3, Compensation Comparisons. Try to quantify in dollars those factors that are measurable financially. Naturally, some intangibles cannot be quantified, such as stability of employment, the reputation of your company in the industry, or a job title. The final result of this work is a range of quantitative compensation figures along with a list of important intangible variables that you are offering.

Develop the compensation package for every position in your organization. Do not finalize any until all have been analyzed. In this way, you ensure that the system that you're putting together for your firm is cohesive, makes sense, and is fair to all.

How to Administer Your Compensation System

If you administer your compensation system in a fair and effective way, you obtain and keep good employees. To do this, base salary increases on the following:

- Merit increases to recognize performance and contribution.
- Tenure increases for time spent working at your company.
- Increases for market and economic conditions.
- Supply and demand for certain types of employees.
- Promotion increases for employees assigned to higher-level jobs.

To allow for these increases, a planned and scheduled review should be accomplished for all your employees, generally on a yearly basis, either all at one time or on anniversary of hire. This annual review should consider all of the factors regarding a pay and salary increase. However, salary increases should not be automatic or tied to a cost-of-living benefit. Further, merit increases should not be made unless performance actually warrants it. To do otherwise, does not motivate your employees for high performance.

Performance Appraisal and Counseling

Performance appraisal and counseling are essential for your business, and a well-designed performance appraisal system enables you to do the following:

- Select individuals for promotion fairly and wisely.
- Determine merit increases fairly.
- Identify individual needs for special training.
- Provide an opportunity for a complete discussion of performance, career goals, progress, organizational policies, and other areas of interest to you and your employees.
- Obtain feedback from your employees.

Performance appraisal systems can be rather informal, especially for the small company. However, they should always be documented, both for reference in the future and to enable you to compare different employees and their performance.

There are seven basic methods for performance appraisal. These are:

1. Graphic rating scale.
2. Forced distribution.

3. Forced choice.

4. Critical incidents.

5. Ranking.

6. Essay appraisals.

7. Management by objectives.

The Graphic Rating Scale

The graphic rating scale is a scale that can be either numerical or descriptive in which an individual is rated on a variety of attributes, which you feel are important for the particular job. Because it can be numerical, the method allows for a total score and therefore easy comparison if you have large numbers of personnel. Because each factor has a score, it is easy to identify those areas in which an individual may be doing well or may need to improve. See Worksheet 18.4 at the end of this chapter.

Forced Distribution

In the forced distribution method, whoever is doing the performance appraisal must rate a certain number of individuals and place each number into a different percentage category—for example, upper 25 percent, middle 50 percent, lower 25 percent—according to some criteria. The forced distribution scale is also used when there are large numbers of people to be rated. One advantage of the forced distribution system over the graphic rating scale alone is that it eliminates the danger that the rater is either too severe or too lenient because he or she is forced to place everyone in one category or another. However, forced distribution also has a major disadvantage in that it assumes that all groups within any organization have identical percentages of poor, fair, or outstanding performance, which is, of course, highly unlikely.

Forced Choice

The forced choice method of rating forces the appraiser to choose a most and least descriptive statement about the individual being rated out of several statements that are listed together in the same group. A number of these groups make up a rating form. See Worksheet 18.5 at the end of this chapter.

In using this method, some of the raters' choices are disregarded by whoever is analyzing the results. These include those descriptions that are not highly relevant to the job that the individual is performing. The main advantage in forced choice rating is that it also minimizes the rate of bias. Research has also shown some evidence that forced-choice rating correlates better with productivity than many other types of ratings. However, forced choice does have serious drawbacks. It is expensive, and the forms must be specially prepared and carefully administered.

Critical Incidents

With the critical incidents method, the appraiser begins by making up a list of requirements that are considered critical to the performance of the job. This can be done with the assistance of the job description and job specifications that you prepared earlier. Once the list of critical requirements is prepared, the rater notes incidents during the rating period, both positive and negative, which pertain to each of the critical requirements listed. The main advantage of this system is that it provides specific examples of performance rather than generalities to discuss during the counseling period of performance appraisal. The difficulty is trying to compare the ratings of one individual and another based solely on qualitative data. However, the critical incident method adapts very well to the purposes of a small company.

Ranking

The ranking method is very easy, especially if you have a small number of employees. You simply rank the individuals reporting to you, starting with your best individual and proceeding down the list to your worst. Clearly, ranking is very valuable in determining promotions, raises, layoffs, and the like. However, it is of very little use during an interview or during the annual salary review, and the question of fairness is raised when comparing individuals performing totally different jobs and having totally different functions.

Essay Appraisals

With the essay appraisal, the rater simply writes a descriptive essay on the individual performance during the period of rating. Essays may make use of critical incidents, and they are very useful because of this for the evaluation interview and for documenting recommendations for promotion and other personnel actions. Again, the problem is one of making comparisons among different performances; also, these essays may be time consuming.

Management by Objectives

Management by objectives (MBO) is both a performance rating method and a management tool. It provides for specific quantifiable performance goals that are decided upon by you and the individual rated at the beginning of the performance-rating period. At the end of the performance-rating period, usually a year, you sit down with the employee and review these agreed-on goals. In doing this, you are also critiquing actual performance.

There are clearly advantages to using MBO. These include a closer relationship between you and your employees, the fact that your subordinates have the opportunity to discuss problems with you that otherwise they might not bring up for discussion, and the focus on future performance rather than the past. However, there are also serious problems in using MBO. These include the fact that the goal may be set too low, that MBO stresses those things that are quantifiable when many goals that you wish the employee to reach during the oncoming year may not be quantifiable, and that MBO does not encourage flexibility. Therefore, if company goals are changed during the period of rating, MBO goals must be changed as well. If you don't do this, then the MBO goals may bear no relationship to the direction that you want to see your company take.

Any of these methods of performance appraisal can work for your company. However, you should be sure that the method of performance appraisal adopted is spelled out clearly to all your employees and also that you use a standard appraisal form with all your employees and managers who may be doing appraisals. A typical form, regardless of which performance appraisal method is used, should include job performance factors such as dependability, initiative, job knowledge, volume of work accomplished, the quality of performance, results achieved, ability to work with others in your firm, and effectiveness in dealing with others outside of your company, including customers, suppliers, and so forth.

While the annual, semiannual, or biannual performance appraisal is an excellent time to sit down with your employees and discuss past performance, counseling should never be reserved for such occasions. You should see your employees if you are dissatisfied with the job they are doing, and counsel them one-on-one as to what you expect and why they are not performing up to your expectations. In fact, to keep communications open and your organization running smoothly, you may want to have periodic talks with key employees whether or not you have something specific to say. That is, a one-on-one meeting is useful just to review problems, how they feel about their jobs and the way they are doing them, and what you can do in order for them to be able to do their job better.

Although the performance appraisal is an excellent tool and your employees should be counseled whenever you use it, do not make this the only counseling you ever have with your employees.

Dealing with Disciplinary Problems

You may not like confrontations with employees over disciplinary problems. Few do. But, in a way, it is a cost of doing business. You can minimize disciplinary problems by creating an atmosphere of mutual trust, understanding, and common purpose in which all of your employees know your company rules, as well as the reasons for them, and therefore do everything possible to support them.

Some rules may be similar at all firms, including those pertaining to absenteeism, tardiness, drunkenness, drug use, theft, and so forth. However, above and beyond this, here are a few guidelines for establishing company rules that help foster the positive climate of discipline that you are seeking:

- The rules and standards that you establish must be reasonable and perceived to be reasonable by your employees.

- Whatever rules you establish should be communicated, so they are known and understood by all employees. This means not only that the words are understood but also the reasoning behind them and why they are essential.

- There should be no favoritism. What is expected of one employee should be expected of all employees.

- Even though you have established rules, which all employees are expected to adhere to, if some extenuating circumstances exist that make a rule either extraordinarily harsh or unreasonable, it can be waived for that specific instance.

- Your employees should be aware that they can and should tell you if they are dissatisfied with rules they consider unfair or unreasonable, and that you may consider modification or elimination of these rules if it is as they perceive it to be.

- The punishment for breaking certain important rules should be spelled out and understood by your employees.

- When you are developing these rules, you should consult your employees before adopting them; get their thoughts, and, if you get some good ideas, adopt them. However, you've got to make it clear at the beginning that even though they may have good ideas, you may not be able to adopt them due to other factors.

- There should always be an appeals procedure available so that an employee who feels that you have made an unfair decision in applying the rule can be heard.

How to Motivate Your Employees

Motivation is extremely important. Unmotivated employees can have an extremely negative impact on your business. These include friction on the job, substandard output in quality, a high turnover of employees, absenteeism, tardiness, and other problems that you want to avoid. Motivated employees produce to their maximum abilities for your company.

Over the years, researchers have developed different theories regarding motivation. Frederick Taylor, for example, felt that motivation should be primarily through economic means, and Frederick Hertzberg, discovered a number of job satisfiers and dissatisfiers and developed the theory that motivation could be achieved primarily through something called "job enrichment." Other theories would have employees participate more in the management of the company and in general decision making, or would have motivation depend primarily on management style. Following are 15 actions you can take or avoid taking to promote motivation among employees in your company:

1. Care about the people who work for you. The people who work for you don't have to become friends, but they are individuals and you should recognize them as such. You should be concerned with their problems and their opportunities both on the job and off.

2. Take responsibility for your actions. This means that when you make a mistake, you should acknowledge it freely and don't try to blame it on an employee or someone else.

3. Be tactful with your employees. They are not pieces of machinery. They have feelings, thoughts, and ambitions. Therefore, they deserve respect and to be treated with tact.

4. Give praise when a job is well done. If your employee does something good, show that you appreciate it by your public recognition.

5. So far as possible, foster independence in your employees. Let them have as much authority and responsibility as they can handle in doing their jobs. The military used to give this advice: Tell people what to do, not how to do it.

6. Be willing to learn from your employees. You are not an expert on everything. Acknowledge the expertise of those who work for you.

7. Always exhibit enthusiasm and confidence. Enthusiasm and confidence are catching, and if you are enthusiastic and confident, your employees are also.

8. Keep open lines of communication to your employees so they can express their opinions, even if they disagree with you or you them.

9. If your employee has a problem doing his or her job, don't just give orders. Give as much help as you can to allow your employee to do the job as best he or she can.

10. Set standards for yourself and your company. Communicate these standards to your employees.

11. Always let your employees know where they stand—when you are happy with them and when you are unhappy. Never leave them in doubt about your feelings.

12. Keep your employees informed about what's going on in the way of future plans in your company. If your employees can understand the big picture, they can help you better by orienting their jobs to your overall objectives.

13. Encourage initiative, innovation, and ingenuity in your employees. Do not turn off ideas submitted by someone who works for you simply because he or she is not supposed to come up with an idea. Good ideas are hard to come by, and you want all you can get.

14. Be aware of your own prejudices and biases toward certain people. You may not be able to rid yourself of your personal prejudices and biases. However, never allow these prejudices or biases to interfere with the way you treat your employees or your evaluation of their performance.

15. Always be flexible. The fact that you have done something one way since you started your business does not mean that it has been done right. Or maybe it was right at one time, but not now. Always be ready to change for something better.

If you follow these 15 pieces of advice, you have gone a long way toward motivating your employees toward high performance.

Termination

Sometimes it is necessary to terminate employees. This should never be taken lightly. Remember that in hiring an individual you have invested considerable time and effort. You have invested further effort in training your employee to do the job. If possible, prior to dismissal, a warning and a second chance should be given. However, sometimes dismissal is absolutely required. To keep some employees, either because of violation of rules or their low level of performance pulls down the performance of other employees and causes problems with morale and motivation.

In terminating an employee, you should have an exit interview in which you inform them forthrightly but tactfully why they are being released. Do not be angry or unpleasant. Remember that this employee, even though he or she may not work for you again, probably has to work for someone else in the future. Further, regardless of his or her performance for you, this person may work for someone else quite satisfactorily.

Here is some further guidance on termination:

- Warn and counsel an employee whose dismissal is contemplated prior to the dismissal decision.
- Once it is definitely decided to dismiss an employee, do not delay.
- Hold a termination interview with the employee, explaining tactfully but straightforwardly the reasons for termination.
- Be sure that you have the employee's correct forwarding address and telephone number.
- Pay all wages that are due to the employee.
- If severance pay is part of the contract, be sure that it is paid.
- Maintain a file on terminated employees that includes the reasons for termination.
- Respond to any requests for information from the Workers' Compensation Disability Insurance or Unemployment Insurance Board if your terminated employee applies for any of these benefits.
- Because the employee did not work out for you does not mean that the employee cannot do just fine somewhere else. You need to know this, as does the employee you are terminating.
- In rare cases of dispute or legal complications, an attorney may need to be present. I don't much like this, and I mention it reluctantly. However, we have become a very litigious society. If there is any possibility that the dismissal could result in a future lawsuit, consult an attorney.

Using Temporary Help Services

Sometimes it is better for your company to use temporary labor rather than permanent labor. Such services may be necessary when a rush order comes in or the workload suddenly increases but you know that it will drop back to a normal level after the rush order is completed. Temporary help may be necessary if many of your employees are sick at the same time or when a key employee is ill, or a special project or a seasonal demand must be fulfilled. Under these circumstances, bringing in temporary help is far better than hiring and then having to fire, lay off, or pay for services that are not being fully utilized.

Temporary Help Services versus Hiring Your Own

Before considering temporary help of any kind, you should consider paying overtime for additional work from your present employees. However, sometimes this isn't possible, either because they are already working overtime or for some other reason. Once you decide on temporary help, you have two choices. One choice is to hire your own temporary help. The problem is the experienxe of finding this help and hiring this help. If you go to a temporary help service, you avoid these difficulties. A temporary help service has already hired these individuals as employees. Therefore, they are fully covered by insurance and generally understand the specific types of jobs that you may have for them. In essence, you are relieved of any problems with recruiting, interviewing, screening, testing, and training. Another advantage is that if the employee works out, most temporary help firms have procedures that allow you to hire the employee on a permanent basis. What this means is that you can also use temporary employees as a sort of "try before you buy." If you like the person, you can offer him a permanent position. If not, the temporary services are for a fixed period. When they are over, the temporary worker simply disappears without the necessity of a formal termination.

Of course, there are some disadvantages. These include the fact that although the individual may be competent for the type of work being done, he or she does not know your particular company and some orientation may be necessary before the job is done exactly as you want. Also, the temporary worker may not be as motivated or devoted to your company mission as your regular employees.

There are about a thousand firms in the temporary help industry in the United States. They are usually located near large population centers. You can generally find these firms in the Yellow Pages, or you can easily do an Internet search for your city. Look under "employment—temporary," or "employment—contractors, temporary help." The cost varies depending on the firm, the location, and other relevant factors. It is higher than the basic salary or wage you would pay for a similar permanent employee. This is because for this one price, you are paying not only for the hours worked but for other things such as payroll taxes, Social Security, workers' compensation, and, of course, the expenses and profits of the temporary help firm.

Sources of Additional Information

Books

Affirmative Action and Equal Employment: A Guide Book, published by the U.S. Government Printing Office.

American Salaries and Wages Survey, by Helen S. Fisher, published by the Gale Group.

Compensation, by Robert E. Sibson, published by AMACOM.

Effective Psychology for Managers, by Mortimer R. Feinberg, published by Prentice-Hall.

Grievance Handling: 101 Guides for Supervisors, by Walter E. Baer, published by AMACOM.

Handbook of Modern Personnel Administration, edited by Joseph J. Famularo, published by McGraw-Hill.

Handbook of Wage and Salary Administration, by Milton L. Rock, published by McGraw-Hill.

Outlook Handbook, published by the U.S. Department of Labor.

The American Almanac of Jobs and Salaries, by John Wright, published by Avon.

The OSHA Compliance Manual, by Donald C. Petersen, published by McGraw-Hill.

Personnel Management, by Michael J. Jucius, published by Richard Irwin.

Internet

Note: Because Internet sites frequently go down, multiple sites are listed for similar subject matter.

Career Babe. Provides links to other sites with salary information at http://www.careerbabe .com/salarysites.html.

CareerInfonet. List salaries and trends for many different industries at http://www .acinet.org.

Economic Research Institute. Lists various services and links regarding executive compensation both in the United States and abroad at http://www.erieri.com.

Job Star. Contains links to over 300 salary surveys at http://www.jobstar.org/tools /salary/index.cfm.

U.S. Department of Labor. An unbelievable number of links to salary information and statistics at http://stats.bls.gov.

Job title: _____   Employee reports to: _____

Tasks to be performed by employee: _____

_____

_____

_____

Why is this job necessary? _____

_____

_____

_____

What special equipment, if any, will the employee need to do the job? _____

_____

_____

_____

How is the job performed procedurally? _____

_____

_____

_____

What qualifications are needed to do the work? _____

_____

_____

_____

With whom will the employee interact within and outside of the organization? _____

_____

_____

_____

What special issues need to be addressed? _____

_____

_____

_____

_____

To customize this document, download it to your hard drive from the John Wiley & Sons web site at www.wiley .com/go/cohenentrepreneur. The document can then be opened, edited, and printed using Microsoft Word or another popular word processing application.

DOWNLOADABLE WORKSHEET 18.2
Writing a Job Description

Job title: _____   Supervisor: _____

Duties: _____

_____

_____

_____

_____

_____

_____

Degree, licensure, or other requirements: _____

_____

_____

_____

_____

_____

Experience requirements: _____

_____

_____

_____

_____

_____

Personal characteristic requirements: _____

_____

_____

_____

_____

_____

_____

To customize this document, download it to your hard drive from the John Wiley & Sons web site at www.wiley .com/go/cohenentrepreneur. The document can then be opened, edited, and printed using Microsoft Word or another popular word processing application.

DOWNLOADABLE WORKSHEET 18.3
Compensation Comparisons

Company	Salary	Bonus	Life Insurance	Health Insurance	Retirement Plan	Other Quantitative Benefits	Total Quantitative Benefits	Non-Quantitative Benefits

To customize this document, download it to your hard drive from the John Wiley & Sons web site at www.wiley.com/go/cohenentrepreneur. The document can then be opened, edited, and printed using Microsoft Word or another popular word processing application.

DOWNLOADABLE WORKSHEET 18.4
Graphic Scale Performance Rating

Performance Rating Factors	Not Observed or Not Applicable	Far Below Acceptable Performance	Below Acceptable Performance	Acceptable Performance	Exceeds Acceptable Performance	Greatly Exceeds Acceptable Performance
Work quality						
Productivity						
Job knowledge						
Planning and organizing						
Management of available resources						
Leadership						
Flexibility						
Oral communications						
Written communications						
Professionalism						
Ability to work with others						
Other						

To customize this document, download it to your hard drive from the John Wiley & Sons web site at www.wiley.com/go/cohenentrepreneur. The document can then be opened, edited, and printed using Microsoft Word or another popular word processing application.

DOWNLOADABLE WORKSHEET 18.5
Forced Choice Employee Rating Sheet

Instructions: For each group of statements, choose a most and least descriptive statement for the individual being rated. The objective is to obtain an accurate performance picture of the individual's performance over the rating period.

Group 1

Statement	Most	Least
Shows a high degree of job knowledge		
Highly productive		
Is a good planner and organizer		
An efficient manager of resources		

Group 2

Statement	Most	Least
An outstanding leader		
Is flexible when things go wrong		
Communicates well orally		
Shows a high degree of job knowledge		

Group 3

Statement	Most	Least
Communicates well in writing		
Demonstrates a high degree of professionalism		
Works well with others		
Highly productive		

Group 4

Statement	Most	Least
Produces high-quality work		
Highly productive		
Is flexible when things go wrong		
Communicates well orally		

To customize this document, download it to your hard drive from the John Wiley & Sons web site at www.wiley.com/go/cohenentrepreneur. The document can then be opened, edited, and printed using Microsoft Word or another popular word processing application.

(continued)

Group 5

Statement	Most	Least
Demonstrates a high degree of professionalism		
Shows a high degree of job knowledge		
Communicates well orally		
Communicates well in writing		

CHAPTER 19

How to Avoid Getting Ripped Off

Unfortunately, crime is rising in the United States. In fact, in just five years losses due to crime in small business have risen more than 100 percent, and this percentage is based on official figures that involve only reported crimes. Probably, in actuality, the number of crimes is even higher. The subject of crime is very important to a small business. In fact, the Small Business Administration says that crime contributes to 30 to 40 percent of business failures. Furthermore, a small business is 35 times as likely to be a victim of crime as a large business. In this chapter, we cover the methods of preventing major crimes for small business owners. These crimes include:

- Burglary.
- Robbery.
- Shoplifting.
- Internal theft.
- Bad checks.
- Credit card fraud.

Burglary

Burglary is any unlawful entry to commit a felony or a theft, whether or not force was used to gain entrance. Statistics show that burglaries have doubled in the past several years, and so it is a major crime with which small business must contend.

Prevention of Burglary

There are methods that can prevent burglary in your small business. These include: locks, alarm systems, key control, lighting, burglar-resistant windows, window screens, safes, guards or patrols, watchdogs, and frequent cash deposits. Let us look at each in turn.

Locks   Locks are important because even if they fail to keep a burglar out, the burglar must force his or her way into your premises. This is important because in many standard burglary insurance policies, you must have evidence of a forced entry to collect.

Many experts on locks consider the pin-tumbler cylinder lock, with a variable number of pins, to provide the best security at a reasonable cost. You should consider a lock with at least five pins because burglars can easily pick a lock with fewer pins. It is also wise to utilize dead-bolt locks. A dead-bolt lock is one having a lock bolt that must be moved positively by turning the knob or key without action of a spring. Sliding a piece of flexible material or tool between the door edge and doorjamb cannot open it. If you use a double cylinder dead-bolt lock, the door cannot be opened without a key on either side. This is important, especially in the case of glass doors, because if the burglar breaks the glass and attempts to open the door by reaching through, he or she is not able to do so. A double cylinder dead-bolt lock also provides protection where a thief remains concealed during the day and then attempts to break out with his loot (your goods) after closing time. It is advisable to be particularly careful about the rear door because burglars favor back doors. You may consider barring this door in addition to locking it. A competent locksmith should install all locks; even the best lock available is not effective in preventing burglaries if it is not installed properly.

Alarm Systems   A silent central station burglar alarm generally is better protection than a local alarm such as a siren or a bell. This is because a silent alarm alerts only the specialist who knows how to handle the burglary and does not notify the burglar of his detection, as does a loud local alarm system. Alternatively, if your intention is to frighten the burglar off prior to his entrance, it is the better type of protection.

Regardless of whether you want a silent alarm or a local alarm, there is a wide choice of sensory devices available for the system that you adopt. These include: ultrasonic detectors, photo beams, radar motion detectors, vibration detectors, and auxiliary equipment such as an automatic phone dialer that notifies the police when the alarm system has been triggered.

Each type of alarm has advantages and disadvantages, depending on your situation. Therefore, I recommend that you get professional guidance to determine which alarm is best for you. For example, local alarms may be useless in areas that are not frequently patrolled or are in secluded neighborhoods.

Key Control   Key control is as important as the lock the key opens. You should avoid key duplication by having the key stamped "Do not duplicate." You should caution employees who have access to keys not to leave store keys with parking lot attendants or anywhere else where someone may gain access to them. You should keep a record of each of your keys and who has custody of it at any given time. When employees leave your employ or if a key is lost, you should install new locks and issue new keys. Do not use the same key for outside doors as for the door to your office. Remember that if you use a master key, it weakens your security system because one key opens all the locks. Do not have your keys plainly marked as to specific store or specific lock. Use a code with key numbers. Do everything possible to make it tougher for a potential burglar.

Lighting   Burglars prefer the darkness because of the protection that it offers. Therefore, illuminating exterior and interior parts of your premise at night discourages burglars. In addition, indoor lighting allows police or patrol cars to see silhouettes in your store and helps them spot something amiss.

It is possible to control lighting with a photoelectric eye system, which turns on your lights automatically at dusk and turns them off at dawn. This saves you a trip on weekends, and means one less thing for you to remember to do. Motion-sensing lights are another means of letting someone know you have a problem and of warning intruders off.

Burglar-Resistant Windows   Windows, especially storefront windows that offer a burglar access to the store's interior, are very vulnerable to hit-and-run attacks by burglars who break the glass, enter the store, steal something, and leave immediately. Using tempered glass, laminated glass, or impact-resistant plastic windows can reduce the likelihood of such an attack occurring.

Window Screens   Steel mesh screens or bars are available to give added protection to windows, transom skylights, ventilator shafts, air vents, and manholes. Such protection is particularly important in screening areas that are not in view, as they are an excellent entry and exit route for burglars. Heavy window screens or gratings are also available to protect show windows. After closing time, these screens are shut and locked into place and allow no room for entry of an object that could break your window.

Safes   Many safes are available that provide excellent protection for your money and other valuables. Along these lines, you should recognize that a fire-resistant safe is not necessarily burglar resistant. In fact, being made of fire-retardant materials may make it easy to break open if it is not also burglar resistant. Note that the operant word is "resistant." Any safe can be broken open if the burglar has enough time. Because of this, many burglars attempt to carry a small safe off rather than try to open it on your premises.

While many types of burglar-resistant safes are available, the "E" safe is considered adequate under most situations. "E" safes are more expensive; however, many insurance companies give a reduction in premiums for use of this type of safe.

Four precautions regarding your safe help to reduce burglaries:

1. Bolt the safe to the building structure. Surprisingly, even very heavy safes have been carted off by enterprising thieves.
2. Put the safe where it can be seen from the street, if possible. Also, make sure that the safe is well lighted at night.
3. Never leave the combination to your safe on store premises.
4. When an employee who knows your safe combination leaves your employ, always change the combination to your safe.

Guards on Patrols Special and private guards and private police patrols can be hired to stay on your premises during certain hours or check your office at regular intervals. Such private help may also assist you in training your employees and auditing your building or buildings for areas that may give easy access to potential burglaries.

Although the cost of private guards and police patrols is not low and may be prohibitive for a small operation, you may be able to get around this by joining with several other businesses in your vicinity, all of you contributing to a common fund for this purpose. Private guards and police patrols can be located in the Yellow Pages or through the Internet.

Watchdogs Watchdogs can be very valuable in preventing burglaries because they have the ability to render an alarm and to confront the potential burglar with an immediate physical threat. Also, word of your watchdog soon gets around and may even deter an attempt to break in. You do not need to own your own watchdog. You can also rent one at a monthly rate. Frequently, a noisy dog that barks and gives the alarm is just as valuable, or maybe more so, than a dog that provides a physical threat. However, be aware that what you think you know about watchdogs may be wrong. For example, American pit bull terriers are infamous for being a vicious breed, with fantastic strength and fanatical courage. You might have assumed that this breed makes a good watchdog. Pit bull terriers have the strength and courage, but contrary to what you may have heard, pit bulls are not vicious and are far too friendly to make good watchdogs.

Frequent Cash Deposits   One sure way to minimize losses is to make frequent bank deposits. In fact, having little cash on hand provides less motivation for a burglar to take the risk of attempting to burglarize your business.

Robbery

Technically, robbery is stealing or taking anything of value by force, violence, or the use of fear. Robbery is the fastest growing crime in the United States. Also, the greatest increase has been found in retail stores where holdups alone have increased 75 percent in recent times. Robbery is a violent crime and in the majority of cases the robber uses a weapon. As a result, robbery victims are frequently hurt. So it is naturally in your interest to do everything possible to prevent robbery.

Prevention of Robbery

Some of the means to prevent burglaries also prevent robberies. For example, frequent cash deposits remove some of the motivation, but you must be very careful here. The sight of the money may trigger a robbery. Therefore, it is wise to vary your hours and routes to the bank if possible, and not carry your deposits in obvious money containers. An armored car service may be of value here. Such services offer a safe alternative with pickup items scheduled to meet your needs with guaranteed delivery. Special safes may also be available in conjunction with an armored car service. These special safes, known as dual control safes, can only be unlocked jointly by the armored car guard and the business owner.

One safe that is helpful in preventing robberies has an inner compartment, with a special drop slot for cash deposits. Such a safe works on the same principle as a dual control safe—the advantage being that only the manager or owner of the store as opposed to the cashier has access to the second compartment once the cash has been deposited.

The Importance of Opening and Closing Routines

Special routines for opening and closing your place of business may be of great assistance in preventing robberies. You may make this a two-person operation. Your assistant observes your actions as you open, enter, and check the burglar alarm. If you do not reappear at a prearranged time, this should be the signal for your partner to call the police. If everything is all right, you reappear and signal to your assistant. The closing routine at night is similar, with your assistant again waiting outside and observing.

A trained guard dog can be of value in preventing robbery. A guard dog would be in your presence at all times and would be trained to attack anyone who threatens you. These guard dogs can't be rented because of the personal nature of the defense—they usually must be owned by the business owner.

Physical Deterrents

Certain devices assist you in minimizing the effect of robberies once they take place. One is a surveillance camera that, if robbers know it exists, may also act as a deterrent. Other types of silent alarms, including footrail switches, cash door contacts, and holdup buttons, can also be of great assistance in catching robbers once the act has taken place.

A handgun may also be of use during a robbery, if it is legal and if you are trained in its use. A handgun is like any other tool: safe if the operator knows what he is doing, extremely dangerous if he or she does not.

Cautions on Night Calls

You should be particularly cautious if you are called at night to return to your business for some purpose. If the reason given is a malfunction of your burglar alarm system, you should phone the police department and ask that someone meet you at your place of business. If the problem is some sort of repair that must be done, make sure to phone the repair company and ask that the service truck meet you. Call before you leave your home, not from your office. If you arrive at your office and do not see the police car or the repair truck, don't park near your store or enter it. Verify all phone calls you receive after store hours.

Shoplifting

Shoplifting is the most commonplace of all small business crimes, and shoplifters are stealing more than $10 billion (yes, that's billion with a "b") worth of merchandise annually. Everything that you can do to spot, deter, apprehend, prosecute, and prevent shoplifting is much to the advantage of your business and other businesses across the country.

Types of Shoplifters

Shoplifting expert Terrence Shulman divides shoplifters into six categories:[1]

1. Addictive-compulsive shoplifters, the largest majority who frequently steal items that are often inexpensive, and then give them to others as gifts. This group consists of 85 percent of the total.
2. Professionals who steal expensive items. These constitute only 2 percent of the total. They may carry tools and utensils on them to assist with the theft. Most likely, this group resists arrest if confronted and attempts to flee the store.
3. Impoverished who steal out of economic need. This group is about 5 percent of the total. They tend to steal necessities, such as food, diapers, toiletries, or children's clothing.
4. Thrill seekers who steal for excitement are about 5 percent. Teenagers tend to fall into this group. Unlike the other categories, they may operate in a group.
5. Drug addicts who steal to support their habits. They are about 2 percent and steal high-end items like the professionals.
6. Kleptomaniacs. This small group of about 1 percent doesn't know why they steal. They tend to be impulsive and are often careless.

Tactics of Shoplifters

Basic shoplifter tactics include putting on clothes and simply walking out wearing them. Another common tactic is for two or more shoplifters to work as a team: while one uses some tactic to distract the store owner or salesperson, the other commit the theft. Another tactic is simply to switch price tags and in this way to pay lower prices for more expensive items. Many shoplifters use a palming tactic whereby the merchandise to be taken is placed under a handkerchief, between the folds of a newspaper, or with some similar item used to cover the item, which is shoplifted. If close to an exit, some shoplifters simply grab what they want and run. Common items such as pocketbooks, umbrellas, baby strollers, and briefcases are also used as depositories for items that are shoplifted, or the shoplifter may slip the item into a jacket pocket or within a dress. Professionals are a little more sophisticated, using items known as booster boxes, which are empty cartons disguised in gift wrappings. These booster boxes have hidden openings, which allow shoplifters to pick up the

[1] Terrence Shulman, "Different Types of Shoplifters," *CASA*. Accessed January 5, 2005, at http://www.shopliftersanonymous.com/types.htm.

item quickly without being observed. Professionals may also use hooker belts, which are worn around the waist. These belts support hooks on which stolen items can be attached. You should be aware of all of these tactics used by shoplifters.

Deterring Shoplifters

To deter shoplifters, take four basic actions:

1. Educate your employees on what to expect or what to do.
2. Plan the layout of your business considering shoplifters.
3. Use protective equipment.
4. Use protective personnel.

Educating Your Employees You should brief your employees regarding shoplifter tactics as well as the various types of shoplifters. You should also instruct them to watch for suspicious-looking shoppers and shoppers carrying possible concealing devices such as those described. If you operate a clothing store, your salespeople should keep careful count of the number of items carried into and out of dressing rooms. Employees should be especially aware of groups of shoppers who enter the store together and who may be trying diversionary tactics. The salespeople should also be watchful of individuals who handle a great deal of merchandise, but take an especially long time to make their decision. Watch for loitering customers in any one area and customers who only shop during certain hours when sales personnel on duty are few. Individual employees who accept payment for goods such as cashiers should be careful of switched price labels and purchased items, which can be containers for stolen goods, such as garbage cans or toolboxes.

Frequently, local police conduct training seminars for store personnel. Such courses can be very helpful in showing you and your personnel how to spot shoplifters, and teaching you the latest methods of prevention. To find out if such training is available, contact your local police.

Planning Store Layout Not to consider store layout would be a terrible mistake that costs you dearly in lost merchandise. Plan your store with deterrents in mind, such as maintaining adequate lighting in all areas of the store, maintaining merchandise in standard groups of three or four items per display so that your salespeople notice when something is missing, keeping small items of high value behind a counter or in a locked case with sales personnel on duty, keeping your displays orderly, and positioning your cash register so that it provides complete and unobstructed views of aisles of goods. Finally, if fire regulations permit, you should lock all exits, which are not to be used by your customers. Those exits that are not locked should have alarm systems attached to them, which make a noise when someone enters or leaves. Close and block off unused check-out aisles.

Using Protective Equipment   Using protective devices can greatly decrease the amount of shoplifting to which your store is subjected. Protective equipment includes two-way mirrors, one-way viewing mirrors, peepholes, closed circuit television, and convex wall mirrors. The use of special electronic tags prevents much shoplifting. If someone attempts to leave when electronic tags are not removed or rendered inoperative, an alarm goes off. Other tags are almost tamper-proof because they are either attached to hard-to-break plastic or constructed in such a fashion that they cannot easily be removed or switched. Price labels marked by rubber stamps or pricing machines are also very useful in preventing removal and switching and are better than handwritten price tags because they cannot be switched or altered. You can also institute a system to alert your employees when a package has been paid for. For example, you can instruct your cashiers or salespeople to staple receipts to the outside of all packages that have been paid for. A simple system but it works.

Protective Personnel   Another method of preventing or deterring shoplifting is using protective personnel. These include detectives disguised as customers who can better observe what is going on in your store than your salespeople can, and uniformed guards who stand as visual deterrents to shoplifting.

Apprehending Shoplifters

Apprehension of shoplifters must be done with some finesse because you certainly don't want to disturb your regular customers or accuse an innocent person. Not only do you lose future sales, but you could also be sued. Therefore, apprehension should be carefully thought out and policies established beforehand. In general, to make shoplifting charges stick, do the following:

- See the shoplifter take or conceal store merchandise.
- Positively identify the merchandise as belonging to you.
- Testify that it was taken by the shoplifter with the intent to steal.
- Prove that the merchandise was not paid for.

Failure to meet these basic criteria leaves you open to counter-charges of false arrest. False arrest does not necessarily mean arrest by police but may simply mean that you have prevented a customer from conducting normal activities.

Therefore, you should be extremely careful and check laws pertaining to shoplifting in your state with your lawyer or your local police or both. Be especially careful that the shoplifter is not able to dump the merchandise after you have decided to arrest him. In fact, a good rule is: If you lose sight of the shoplifter for even an instant, forget it. If the shoplifter succeeded in getting rid of the merchandise, you could be in for a lot of trouble.

Internal Theft

The Department of Commerce estimates that dishonest employees are responsible for 75 to 80 percent of all retail shortages. This costs U.S. business over $50 billion annually. Some estimates show that 75 percent of all employees steal from their employers at least once throughout their careers and at least half of these steal multiple times from their employer.[2] The most common type of internal theft is embezzlement in which cash is received and your employee merely pockets it without making a record of the sale. A slightly more complicated type of internal theft or embezzlement is called "lapping." With this type of theft, the embezzler withholds receipts, such as payments on accounts receivable, temporarily, perhaps with the intent to repay. The amount withheld is eventually paid by "borrowing" from yet another account, which is intended to be a payment on accounts receivable. In this way, borrowing may increase and the amounts grow larger and larger; in fact, sometimes this type of fraud may run on for years, and when it is finally detected the amount is in the tens, or even hundreds, of thousands of dollars.

Internal theft is frequently concealed, and therefore you must look for clues to the fact that it is going on. Here are six different occurrences, which should lead to an investigation to see if an embezzler is ripping you off:

1. Decline or an unusually small increase in cash or credit sales. This could mean that some sales are not being recorded.
2. Increase in overall sales returns. This might mean a concealment of accounts receivable payments.
3. Inventory shortages. This could be caused by fictitious purchases, unrecorded sales, or some other means of theft.
4. Profit declines and expense increases. This could be a sign that cash is being taken from your accounts in some way.

---

[2] Justin A. Walsh, "Employee Theft," *IFPO*. Accessed January 12, 2005, at http://www.ifpo.org /articlebank/employee_theft.htm.

5. Slow collection. This could be a device concealing lapping (mentioned previously).

6. Unusual bad-debt write-offs. This could cover some sort of internal theft scheme.

In general, there are two major ways to cut down on internal theft. First, screen your employees well—follow the good hiring practices discussed in Chapter 17. Then, control your business operations and remove or reduce theft hazards. For example, price items by machine or rubber stamp, not by handwriting. Permit only authorized employees to set prices and mark merchandise. Make unannounced spot checks to be sure that actual prices agree with authorized prices and price charge records.

With refunds, insist on a merchandise inspection by someone other than the person who made the sale. Match items to the return vouchers and then return the merchandise back into stock as quickly as possible. Keep a tight control on all credit documents. Spot check customers by mail or telephone to make sure they got their refunds.

Be careful of your cashiers. Keep a sharp eye open for signals—nods, winks, and so on—between cashiers and customers. Pay special attention to cashiers when they are surrounded by clusters of people. Be alert to the use of over-ring slips to cover up shortages. Watch for items bypassed when ringing up sales. Check personal checks to make sure they are not being used to cover up shortages. Use a professional shopper to check for violations of cash register and related procedures.

Control all shipments. Have a secondary check by a worker or a salesperson on all incoming shipments. Insist on flattening all trash cartons and make spot checks of trash after hours. Prohibit employees not essential to this part of your operation from parking near receiving door or dock. Keep receiving door locked when not in use. Make sure the locked door cannot be raised a few inches. A receiving door should be opened only by a supervisor who remains in the area until it's relocked. The alarm on the door should ring until turned off with the key held by the store manager. Distribute door keys carefully and change lock cylinders periodically.

Summary for Preventing Embezzlement

Here are some important actions to take to prevent embezzlement:

- Only hire honest people.
- Verify important information on employment applications.

- Talk to references and former employers.
- Use credit checks to discover if an applicant has financial problems.
- Use pre-employment tests that reveal dishonesty.
- Check for criminal convictions.
- Deal fairly with your employees.
- Maintain internal controls.
- Use a separate employee responsible for paychecks preparation and another responsible for payroll distribution.
- Separate the functions of company records maintenance and handling cash receipts.
- Personally approve all checks over a certain amount.
- Pay only from an original invoice.
- Personally reconcile all bank statements, and do so promptly.
- Spot check invoices, receipts, and other forms.
- Hire an expert in computer-related embezzlement part-time.
- Randomly spot check anything having to do with money.
- Supervise and verify everything of financial importance.[3]

Bad Checks

The Department of Commerce estimates that more than $2 billion worth of losses a year can be attributed solely to bad checks. Another source says $23 billion![4] In the United States, it is estimated that more than 450 million bad checks are written every year. It's worth your effort to prevent a portion of this huge amount from coming out of your pocket. You are a lot less likely to accept bad checks by the simple act of requiring identification and consider certain other key points before you hand over the cash.

Require Identification

You should always require identification to make sure that the person presenting you with a check is the same person whose name is printed on the check. It is

---

[3] Lynn Westergard, "Preventing Embezzlement," *The Bottomline Online.* Accessed January 12, 2005, at http://www.nelsonlambson.com/nlco-articles/embezzlement.htm.
[4] No author listed, "Experience the Benefits of Electronic Check Services," *Regions.* Accessed January 12, 2005, at http://www.regions.com/business/merchant_ecs.html.

better to require at least two pieces of identification. Usually, these should be a driver's license and a major credit card. Recording information such as the serial number from the driver's license and the number from the credit card helps deter the person from passing the bad check, and it also helps locate the individual if the check turns out to be bad.

Of course, identification is not foolproof. Any identification can be forged. However, some pieces of identification are more difficult to forge than others. The following types of identification are more difficult and are therefore better for check cashing purposes: automobile operator's license, automobile registration card, credit cards, government identifications, and identification cards issued by companies that carry a photograph, description, and signature.

The following are not good identification because they are so easily forged: Social Security cards, business cards, club organization cards, bank books, work permits, insurance cards, learner's permits, letters, birth certificates, library cards, and voter registration cards.

Check Key Points

The following key points should be considered when the check and identification materials are presented:

- Compare signature from the check with signature on the identification.
- If the check is not written for a local bank, make sure the customer's out-of-town as well as his local address and telephone number are written on the back of the check.
- Check the date, including day, month, and year. Do not accept checks that are not dated or postdated, or checks on which the date is more than 30 days past.
- Be sure that the numerical amount agrees with the amount described in writing.
- Be sure that the check is legibly written, signed in ink, and does not have any erasures or written-over amounts.
- Be sure that you are the payee, or your firm is. If a check is a two-party check; that is, a check that is written to the individual presenting you with the check and is to be endorsed over to you, be sure that you get full information and take special care.
- It is safer to take personal checks only for the exact amount of purchase. Of course, whether you do this is your decision.
- Set a limit on the amount for which you cash a check. Post the amount for your customers to see and accept none beyond that amount except for amount of purchase.

- Statistically, checks with low serial numbers are returned more often than checks with higher numbers. Therefore, be especially cautious about low numbers.
- Statistically, bad checks tend to be in the $25 to $35 range, according to the Small Business Administration. Be particularly careful of checks around this amount or under $50.
- Look for lack of concern about the price of the merchandise purchased. Lack of concern may indicate that the check is no good.
- Make sure the name and address is printed on the check. If the phone number is printed, check to make certain it is a working phone.
- Ensure that you have a street address, no P.O. boxes.

Bad Check Protection Services and Equipment

Certain devices and services assist you in minimizing bad checks. You can photograph the individual who cashes the check with a Polaroid camera. This procedure is definitely a deterrent because bad check passers do not want to be photographed. There is a check verification service available in many states for a small monthly fee. A central computer contains only negative information about check passers. You can get this information as a participating businessperson by calling a central number and giving the customer's driver's license number. Another mechanical deterrent is a fingerprint register. This fingerprint register works without the traditional black, messy ink. It involves only one thumbprint on the back of the check, which is registered by the machine. Obviously, bad check passers do not wish to be fingerprinted.

You can find out more about check protection equipment by checking in the Yellow Pages, through the Internet, and also by talking with other merchants who are using similar devices.

You Are Under No Obligation to Take a Check

Never forget that you are not obligated to take anyone's check, even if the individual presents identification and all of the key points described previously are positive. Naturally, you may wish to do so to make a sale and for goodwill. But you are well advised not to accept a check if the person acts suspiciously. However, be aware that if you tell a customer that you cannot accept his check because he is a college student, lives in a bad neighborhood, or give a similar response in such a way as to discriminate, you may be in violation of a state or federal law on discrimination.

Reference Check Services on the Internet

Nowadays, computer checking and the Internet can permit background checks for everything from criminal convictions to other reference information to confirm checks. Chapter 17 listed some of these under the "Hiring" section. Here are a few dealing specifically with check verification:

Cash Flow Specialists, Inc.
Phone: (800) 669-2700
Web site: http://www.cashflowspecialistsinc.com/services/verification

PayQuickly
Phone: (888) 872-2285
Web site: http://www.payquickly.com/check_guarantee.htm

Vantage Card Services, Inc.
Phone: (800) 397-2380
Web site: http://www.vantagecard.com/solutions/check-guarantee.html

Credit Card Fraud

The Los Angeles area has one of the largest credit card usages in the world. Here is what the Los Angeles Police Department recommends to prevent credit card fraud from *Credit Card and Computer Fraud*, published by the Department of the Treasury, U.S. Secret Service:[5]

- Train employees to follow each credit card company's authorization procedures.
- Be skeptical of a customer with only one credit card and one piece of identification.
- Be aware of the customer who makes several small purchases by check or credit card that are under the amount for manager approval.
- Is the item being purchased one that could be easily fenced for cash? (Examples include televisions, stereos, cameras, and other portable items.)
- If you are suspicious of the purchaser, make a note of appearance, companions, any vehicle used, and identification presented. Call your local police department.

---

[5] No author listed, "Small Business Crime Prevention," *LAPD Online*. Accessed January 12, 2005, at http://www.lapdonline.org/bldg_safer_comms/prevention/sm_bus.htm.

- Look for "ghost" numbers or letters. Many times criminals change the numbers and/or name on a stolen card. To do this they either file or melt the original name and numbers off. Both of these processes can leave faint imprints of the original characters.
- Examine the signature strip on the credit card. A criminal may cover the real card owner's signature with White-Out and sign it on the new strip.
- Compare the signature on the card with the signature on the sales slip.

Sources of Additional Information

Books

Avoiding Cyber Fraud in Small Business, by G. Jack Bologna and Paul Shaw, published by John Wiley & Sons.

Employee Theft: How to Spot It, How to Stop It! by Ron Jennings, published by Business Owners Press.

Loss Prevention and the Small Business, by J. Robert Wyman, published by Butterworth-Heinemann.

Mind Your Own Business, by Norman Jaspen, published by Prentice-Hall.

Protect Your Business against Crime—A Guide for the Small Businessman, published by Drake Publishers.

Security and Loss Prevention, by Philip P. Purpura, published by Butterworth-Heinemann.

Sticky Fingers, by William W. McCullough, published by AMACOM.

Shop Lifting and Shrinkage Protection for Stores, by Loren E. Edwards, published by Charles C. Thomas.

Stopping Employee Theft, by Richard W. Decker, published by Diverse Assets Creations.

Internet

Note: Because Internet sites frequently go down, multiple sites are listed for similar subject matter.

Common Sense Methods Preventing Employee Theft. An article published by the U.S. Small Business Administration with a summary approach as to what needs to be done at http://www.sba.gov/gopher/Business-Development/Success-Series/Vol6/theft.txt.

Crime Prevention by Rutgers University. Provides links to get information on preventing employee theft using situational crime prevention, and ideas on how not to hire thieves in the first place at http://crimeprevention.rutgers.edu/crimes.htm.

Fraud Protection Services from Verisign. Learn how to protect your online business from the risks of fraud, including fraud prevention. Information and free guide called

"What Every Merchant Should Know About Internet Fraud" at http://www
.verisign.com/products-services/payment-processing/online-payment/fraud/index
.html?sl=t50080175426021000.

Global Polygraph Network. This company sets up polygraph testing anywhere in the world
at http://www.polytest.org.

National Crime Prevention Council. Numerous links to crime and business crime prevention topics at http://www.ncpc.org/ncpc/ncpc/?pa=resCenter&sa=searchResults
&topicId=175.

DOWNLOADABLE WORKSHEET 19.1
Burglary Prevention

Task	Complete	In-Progress	Needs to Be Started
All outside entrances and inside security doors have deadbolt locks.			
Padlocks are made of steel with serial numbers from locks removed to prevent unauthorized keys from being made.			
All outside or security doors metal lined and secured with metal security crossbars; all exposed hinges pinned to prevent removal.			
Windows have secure locks and burglar-resistant glass.			
You can see easily into your business after closing.			
The inside and outside of business is illuminated, especially around doors, windows, skylights, or other entry points.			
Covers installed over exterior lights and power sources to deter tampering.			
Parking lot has good lighting and unobstructed views.			
Cash register is in plain view from the outside of business.			
Safe is fireproof and securely anchored.			
Alarm system installed.			

To customize this document, download it to your hard drive from the John Wiley & Sons web site at www.wiley .com/go/cohenentrepreneur. The document can then be opened, edited, and printed using Microsoft Word or another popular word processing application.

DOWNLOADABLE WORKSHEET 19.2
Robbery Prevention

Task	Complete	In-Progress	Needs to Be Started
Check the layout of store, eliminating any blind spots that may hide a robbery in progress.			
Ensure windows are clear of displays or signs.			
Make sure business is well lighted.			
Tell employees to write down and report any suspicious activity or person immediately.			
Put cash registers in front of store where they are easily seen.			
Use a drop safe into which large bills and excess cash are dropped by employees and cannot be retrieved by them.			
Post signs alerting would-be robbers that employees do not have large amounts of cash.			
Ask local law enforcement regarding procedures in case you are robbed.			
Display street number outside prominently.			

To customize this document, download it to your hard drive from the John Wiley & Sons web site at www.wiley .com/go/cohenentrepreneur. The document can then be opened, edited, and printed using Microsoft Word or another popular word processing application.

DOWNLOADABLE WORKSHEET 19.3
Shoplifting Prevention

Task	Complete	In-Progress	Needs to Be Started
Train employees how to reduce opportunities for shoplifting and how to apprehend shoplifters.			
Use mirrors to eliminate blind spots in corners that could conceal shoplifters.			
Keep merchandise away from store exits.			
Keep expensive merchandise in locked display cases.			
Keep store and merchandise display orderly.			
Limit the numbers of expensive merchandise items shown to customers at any one time.			
Use an electronic surveillance system at exits.			
Design exits so that merchandise must pass in front of or be examined by security personnel.			
Ensure that the cash register is inaccessible to customers.			
Keep dressing rooms locked and under surveillance.			

To customize this document, download it to your hard drive from the John Wiley & Sons web site at www.wiley .com/go/cohenentrepreneur. The document can then be opened, edited, and printed using Microsoft Word or another popular word processing application.

CHAPTER 20

How to Use the Computer and Advanced Technologies to Stay Ahead of the Competition

In previous chapters, I've talked about the use of computers for financial management, tax preparation and planning, record keeping, and marketing. I now tell you that this is only scratching the surface. A computer does more to raise your productivity than any other single tool. If you have never used a computer before, or have done so only for recreation, you are going to be amazed. Chances are, however, that you are already computer literate and well versed with much of a computer's capabilities. Either way, I think this chapter provides valuable insight for using a computer in your business, even if you are already using one.

How the Computer Can More than Double Your Productivity

Word processing by itself allowed me to double the work I turned out in a given amount of time and the quality of work was better, too. But I soon discovered other things that I could do with my computer that saved me time, money, and made all of my business operations more efficient. Here are a few that I briefly covered in previous chapters.

Desktop Publishing

In the old days, I used to pay a graphic artist and designer to do my layout and typesetting for brochures, flyers, and booklets. This usually cost a minimum of $100 per job and took at least a week before I could even proofread the designer's first efforts. Now, using a software program, which came already loaded on my computer, I can do everything myself in short order. I have dozens of choices of different fonts and sizes. Moreover, I get the work done immediately and never need to wait to see what the final product is going to look like. I don't mean that I never use a graphic artist now, but most of the routine work I can do myself.

The same is true of overhead transparencies that I use for my seminars. It used to take at least a week, and there were always typos, some of which I caught too late to have corrected before my presentation. With a desktop publishing program, all that is past. I do all my own stuff, with the advantages I mentioned above. Now, using Microsoft's PowerPoint, I rarely make transparencies except for backup. Through the use of this program, a laptop computer, and a projector, I have full-color overhead projections for my seminars at no additional cost. Moreover, the program allows me to integrate my own notes with each view and to print handouts with smaller versions of each projection (up to nine miniature projections per page) to enable my audiences to take notes and retain a permanent copy of each projection.

There are all sorts of programs, many of them free, which can help you set up your own web site. I noted some of them in Chapter 14. Some programs that may cost you a little are well worth the money. With them, you can turn out web sites, CD ROMs with your entire catalogue on them, and more. In Chapter 14, I also mentioned the FrontPage program, which I used for this purpose. Although this can be purchased separately, it was already loaded on my computer when I got it.

I am able to save all of my material so that if I ever want it again, or want it with minor changes, it's a piece of cake to make the changes and print out the new material.

Mailing Advertisements Using Merge

There are all sorts of programs that let you merge your customer list with a sales letter. This means that every letter is personalized to that individual customer. What once had to be done by someone else can now be done by you in your own office. Your program addresses both letters and envelopes. This is especially valuable for relatively small mailings, as it isn't cost effective to have them done by a letter shop that handles very large mailings more economically.

Your word processing program may already have this feature built in. But if you want to look at some separate more powerful programs, visit these web sites:

e-campaign
http://www.mailsoft.biz

e-mail Marketing Director and Campaign Enterprise
http://www.arialsoftware.com

Gammadyne Mailer

http://www.gammadyne.com/mmail.htm

Let the Computer Fix Your Writing

I mentioned earlier that programs exist to correct your spelling. But there are also programs available to correct your grammar, programs to give you choices of the words you may want to use (a thesaurus program), programs that help you to write so that your writing is more readable, and so on. Many are integrated into your word processing program. But these too are only a small part of what is available.

A computer software program can't turn you into an instant professional writer, but it can turn you into a more competent one. If you want help with copywriting for your ads, there are programs for this also. They can create headlines, theme lines, slogans, and jingles. Other programs help pick the perfect name for your product or service or design your letterhead and business cards. When you consider that there are companies that charge several thousand dollars for this you can appreciate just what an advantage it is to be able to do this for yourself.

Here are a few web sites that you may find useful:

- SmartAuthor.com publishes a number of writing programs for generating publicity releases, articles, essays, and more. See their web site at http://www.instantwritersoftware.com.

- For help with general writing, take a look at *Writer's Workbench*. It is described fully at http://www.emo.com.

- According to the description, *Wizards 4 Word* "automatically formats and fixes your manuscript, generates correct headers, footers, footnotes, page layouts, plus more, and helps speed up the writing and editing process, saving you time, money, and big headaches." See a full description at http://www.wizards4word.com.

- If you want help with advertising headlines, see the web site for Headline Creator Professional at http://www.easy-headlines.com.

Analyzing Potential or Present Employees

Big companies pay big fees to consultants to obtain complete psychological evaluations on potential or current key employees. Even this has been computerized and you can obtain programs in which you input data by merely answering questions posed by the program based on a short personal interview with the candidate.

The output tells you how the individual is likely to behave under different situations, as well as how best to influence his or her or others' opinion regarding the employee's behavior. If you want to use handwriting analysis as an assist in evaluation, these kinds of programs are available as well. Here are a few examples:

- Dipolar publishes *Professional Quest* software to enable so-called 360 degree evaluations. That is, feedback from multiple sources about an employee including, managers, suppliers, customers, peers, and so on. You can see what they have to offer at http://www.dipolar.com.au/default.asp.

- MBA Ware.com offers many programs for evaluating current employees and for hiring. *Smart Hire* guides you through the interview process. *Survey Solutions* helps you with employee surveys. Full descriptions are at http://www.mbaware.com.

- Sheila Lowe produces the *Handwriting Analyzer* software. Full information is available at http://www.sheilalowe.com/software.html.

- *Succession Wizard* at http://www.successionwizard.com/ helps you do succession planning. I can think of a number of companies, some giant corporations, that could use this software package.

Marketing Research

There are probably hundreds of marketing research programs available. They help you, not only to design your research tool, but also to analyze your data and interpret the results as well. Best of all, the following examples are FREE!

CCOUNT is a free software package for market research/marketing research data cleaning, data weighting, manipulation, cross tabulation, and data analysis. You find it at http://pan-data.dyndns.org/ccount.

Survey Crafter Professional survey software helps in writing, administering, and analyzing web, paper, and telephone-based surveys that combine ease of use and flexibility. You can print your questionnaire on paper for a paper survey, publish it on your own Linux, Unix, or Windows-based web server for a web survey, or use the built-in Interviewer for a telephone survey. You can locate it at http://www.surveycrafter.com/interim2.

For the trained marketing researcher, Decision Analyst provides their free statistical analysis software called STATS. This marketing research software performs several commonly needed statistical functions for marketing research including:

- Generating random numbers.
- Calculating sample sizes needed for surveys.
- Computing the mean, standard deviation, standard error, and range for keyboard-entered data.

- Determining the standard error of a proportion.
- Performing significance testing between two percentages from independent samples.
- Calculating statistical significance between two percentages from dependent samples.
- Performing significance testing between two averages from independent samples.
- Contingency table analysis (i.e., Chi-Square).

You can locate this program at http://www.decisionanalyst.com/download.asp.

Business Simulation

If you want to fine-tune your business decision-making tools, there are programs around that place you in a number of business situations requiring you to make tactical and strategic business decisions. The programs analyze your decisions and teach you about factors that you may not have considered. Thus, you can learn some things by experience without the hard knocks and loss of time and money in the real world.

Decision Pro helps you to improve your business decisions by applying proven management techniques including decision tree analysis, Monte Carlo Simulation, linear programming, and advanced forecasting methods. You can get full details at http://www.vanguardsw.com/decisionpro/jgeneral.htm.

Witness Simulation by the Lanner Group enables dynamic simulation modeling of business activities and allows integration of various tools to deliver the optimum choice to a plethora of potential solutions. It is fully described at http://www.witness-for-simulation.com.

For over 100 (currently 167) business simulation product links, go to http://dmoz.org/Science/Software/Simulation.

The Internet

We have already looked at the Internet in previous chapters. I don't see how any business can operate without an Internet connection today. Through the Internet you are able to access data banks of information all over the country and do research on things, people, competitors, and potential vendors and business partners from any business location, even if it's your home. You have a mailbox that allows customers to communicate with you and you to communicate with customers in the blink of an eye. Moreover, you can build your own mailing list with instantaneous connections to customers so that you can send special offers, catalogues, and newsletters (see Chapter 14) without costing you a penny.

There are many ways of hooking up to the Internet. The right method for you depends on speed, cost, convenience, and availability. Three of the most popular are standard modem, cable, and digital subscriber line (DSL).

Standard Modem

A modem is a device that attaches to your computer and connects you to the Internet via your telephone line. That means that you either need a phone line dedicated to Internet usage or, while you are online, you can't use that telephone line for either outgoing or incoming calls. There is also a frustrating delay until the dial up is completed, which doesn't exist with other methods.

One advantage of the standard modem is that it is inexpensive, usually costing less than $100 for the equipment and less than $30 a month for usage. Another advantage is that it is easily and widely available. Most computers come with modems. However, the standard connection is slow—the top being 56K bps, and, as noted previously, modems tie up a phone line. (By the way, bps refers to bytes per second. At this speed, some of the information you want, especially graphics, can take a long time to download.) For a business, I don't really recommend 56K bps.

Integrated Services Digital Network (ISDN) is one step up. Like a 56K dial up, an ISDN establishes a connection to your service provider when you access the Internet. However, ISDN circuits are faster and fully digital, so the dial-up connection is established almost instantaneously. Moreover, the speed is faster at 64Kbps to 128Kbps. The equipment costs considerably more, and you may be billed $20 to $40 per month plus per minute charges. However, the speed and the fact that you don't tie up a phone line more than make up for the difference. However, the ISDN is obsolescent and is probably on its way out as a system.

Cable

Cable connects you to the Internet through a coaxial cable, usually the same line that carries your cable TV service. If you can't get DSL or don't have the budget to get another system, it may be your only viable high-speed option. Cable connections offer very high connection speeds, 500k bps to 2 Mbps, at low costs. The modem runs you up to about $200 and it costs you about $50 a month for the service. I use cable myself, and I have found very few if any negatives in doing so.

Digital Subscriber Line

Digital subscriber line (DSL) is fast and works over a shared phone line. You get to choose a variety of high speeds and pay accordingly. These are from a low of 128Kbps to a high of 1.54Mbps and the costs are from about $50 a month on up. Modem costs may be a little less than for cable. The biggest problem is that DSL isn't available everywhere.

There are also systems for very high-speed connections, but they cost you an arm and a leg, and for most businesses, 2Mbps is plenty.

I hope I've said enough to show you what a computer might be able to do for you. Of course, there are many other things that a computer can do including maintaining lists of customers, finding new customers, and doing media research. Your local business software store or some of the Internet URLs I give you can show a lot more. If you live in a town that doesn't have a store that sells software, go to your newsstand and get a copy of one of the many computer magazines that are now being published. You see many programs advertised and described right in the magazine, and you can obtain catalogues from companies that publish hundreds of other programs that can help you run and build your business.

What You Need to Know about Computers

First, let me say that you really don't need to know much. But if you are unfamiliar with computers, it all seems confusing. I'm going to clear up that confusion right now. When you buy a desktop computer, you need a keyboard, the computer proper, which includes one or more disk drives, a visual indictor (called a monitor), and a printer. I am going to suggest that it's very handy to have a CD ROM drive. The current state of the art is 16X or better. The 16X is 16 times larger than the first models of just a few years ago. You may also want a rewritable capability to enable you to write on blank CDs and save information or graphics. You can also make the masters for your catalogues on CD if you have this capability or make copies of your CD ROMs. Finally, I recommend a color scanner with which you can scan images into your computer and save them on your hard drive.

The keyboard attaches to the computer and is very similar to the one found on typewriters in the old days. It has a few more keys, but the instructions with any program tells you what keys to press to get the computer to do what you want. If you're writing (the term used is "word processing"), each time you push a key, you're telling the computer to make that mark on the screen of your monitor.

A mouse is a pointing device, which also gives commands to your computer, and at a much faster rate than you could give commands using your keyboard.

You point to a symbol on the screen, click a button on your mouse, and the computer reacts to a command.

The disk drives work like a record player. You play your computer programs on them. The programs themselves can be bought on the disks or CD ROMS, or the programs may already be loaded up when you buy your computer. The programs are known as "software."

Now, back to the hard disk I noted earlier. In addition to containing software programs that you may want to run, disks are also used for storing data: your advertising brochure, customer lists, sales letters, and so forth. Each small disk allows you to store 1,440,000 bits or 1.44 megabytes of information. Now I know that this sounds like a lot, but you may soon discover that it's not. The beauty of a hard disk is that it stores not only megabytes of data but also gigabytes of data, depending on what you buy. What this means is that programs and data you want stored can all go on a hard disk. The speed and convenience of accessing this data is amazing. Now one way or another, you're going to need at least two disk drives in addition to your hard disk. You need the one regular disk drive to input new programs that you buy. Nowadays, this is usually a CD drive. The other will be a 1.44 MB drive. How many megabytes or gigabytes for your hard disk? Once again, my general advice is more than you think. Once you start using a computer—and you see more potential for it in your business—your needs grow exponentially and fast, and the most advanced programs today require more storage memory on hard disks and in RAM.

RAM stands for "random access memory." This is the temporary memory you need on your computer to operate one or more programs, and, yes, you can operate programs simultaneously today. It is called multitasking. Having too little RAM denies access to many business software programs that you may want to use.

You also want to pay attention to the speed of the processor in your computer: the faster, the better.

You can tell the requirements for any given program by looking on the package or in the instructions supplied with it. For most business programs today, I would recommend a computer with a Pentium 133 megahertz (MHz) or higher processor, 128 MB of RAM or better, and hard disk storage of at least 20 to 30 gigabytes (GB). You also want to make certain you have sound and graphics cards, and a display with Super VGA (800 × 600) or higher resolution monitor with 256 colors. Remember, these are minimums. The more you get, the faster and better your computer's performance.

Apple/Macintosh or IBM Compatible?

The two biggest personal computer types on the market today are IBM/IBM compatible and Apple's Macintosh. The biggest advantage of the IBM types is the amount of software available. Everybody and his brother develop software for the IBMs. There are plenty of programs available for the Macintosh as well, and its major advantage is advanced technology and ease of use. Most professionals who deal with graphics prefer the Apple/MacIntosh system; the IBM system is probably the most popular for other purposes.

What Kind of Printer to Buy

Printer prices have really come down and you can get a high speed laser printer for a few hundred dollars on up. I would also recommend a color printer. Color laser printers are still relatively high in price. A good ink jet or similar printer is perfectly adequate for most purposes, but a little slower.

Other Useful Computer Equipment

Computer technologies and software are still developing and what is cutting edge one month is obsolescent only a few moths later. So, I have tried to give you more web sites under Additional Sources of Information later for comparison of the latest basic and ancillary equipment. But I want you to know about the following, which while not essential, exist today if you want to buy them.

Laptop, Palmtops, and so On

It is easy now to have just about full computing capability in a computer that slips into your briefcase and may weigh five pounds or less. I travel all over the world with my palmtop and it weighs about two pounds. It does anything my laptop computer does. In fact, for some laptop models you can get a cradle so that you use it as a desktop computer and then simply release it from its cradle and slip it into a case to be completely portable.

Miniature Drives

Memory drive sticks are extremely useful and handy. I have several. One is less than two inches long and a half-inch wide and weighs only a few ounces. Yet, it is essentially a hard drive with a capacity of 1 gigabit (GB).

In the old days, I had to carry an entire portfolio of disks. If I had to carry around 1 GB worth, they would fill a suitcase. Now, one end of this small, but important, accessory plugs into a universal serial bus (USB) receptacle found on most new computers. I can slip this into my pocket and access my files wherever I find a computer.

As I did the research for this chapter, I found one miniature drive that is part of one of those mini-Swiss Army knives. For about $75, you get a 128MB drive along with a nail file, scissors, and small knife all rolled into one. However, my 1 GB drive also cost less than $80. By the time you read this, there may be 2 GB drives out and the most inexpensive probably won't cost a lot more.

Voice Recognition Software

If you are a fan of the original 1960s Star Trek series on television, you may recall a man from the future who came back and prepared his written reports by simply talking to his typewriter. Well, its really here, only of course, you talk to your computer, and you may no longer need to dictate your letters or reports to a secretary. You may pay several thousand dollars, however, there are products costing a lot less. ComputerSearch.com compares a number of programs and gives you pricing and where to buy it. The top rated program is only $150! For additional information, go to http://productopia.consumersearch.com/computers /voice_recognition_software/.

Sources of Additional Information

Books

Absolute Beginners Guide to Basics, by Michael Miller, published by Que.

Alternative Computer Access: A Guide to Selection, by Dennis Anson, published by F. A. Davis Company.

Don't Make Me Think: A Common Sense Approach to Web Usability, by Steve Krug, published by New Riders Press.

How Computers Work, by Ron White and Timothy Downs, published by Que.

Illustrator CS for Windows and Macintosh: Visual QuickStart Guide (Visual

QuickStart Guides), by Elaine Weinmann and Peter Lourekas, published by Peachpit Press.

PCs for Dummies, by Dan Gookin, published by For Dummies Press.

Teach Yourself Desktop Publishing, by Christopher Lumgair, published by McGraw-Hill.

10-Minute Guide to Buying a Computer, by Shelly O'Hara, published by Alpha Books.

The Internet for Dummies, by John R. Levine et al., published by For Dummies Press.

Webster's New World Dictionary of Computer Terms, by Bryan Pfaffenberger, published by Hungry Minds.

Internet

Note: Because Internet sites frequently go down, multiple sites are listed for similar subject matter.

About Buying a Computer. Life Advice provides good general information about buying a computer and a glossary of computer terms prepared by MedLife Consumer in conjunction with the Federal Consumer Information Center at http://www.pueblo .gsa.gov/cic_text/misc/buy-computer/buycomp.htm.

CNET.com. All sorts of computer product reviews and related stories about computer equipment at http://www.cnet.com.

PC World. This magazine available online has a review section, where the best computers and ancillary equipment selected by *PC World* are reviewed at http://www.pcworld .com/reviews/index.asp.

Internet Connections. Techsoup.org provides free newsletters, weekly news, how-to, and more having to do with the Internet. Intended for nonprofits, but very helpful for business at http://www.techsoup.org/howto/articles.cfm?topicid=4&topic=Internet+Connections.

Productopia. This is a terrific site. All kinds of products, especially those having to do with computers, are compared and rated. ConsumerSearch.com reviews hundreds of product reviews, analyzes them, distills the information shoppers need and recommends the best products and tells where to find them at http://productopia .consumersearch.com.

DOWNLOADABLE WORKSHEET 20.1
Computer/Equipment Comparison Checklist

Equipment	Computer 1	Computer 2	Computer 3
Processor/motherboard			
RAM			
Hard drive			
Video card			
Sound card			
Speakers			
Modem			
CD/DVD drive			
Monitor			
Operating system			
Floppy drive			
Mouse			
Keyboard			
CD-Writer/re-writer			
Scanner			
Printer			
Surge protector or uninterrupted power supply (UPS)			
Software included			
Price			

To customize this document, download it to your hard drive from the John Wiley & Sons web site at www.wiley .com/go/cohenentrepreneur. The document can then be opened, edited, and printed using Microsoft Word or another popular word processing application.

Useful Internet Sites for Entrepreneurs and Small Businesses

Advertising and Publicity

Advertising—Basic, by Businesstown.com. Links to numerous articles on advertsing and promotion. http://www.businesstown.com/advertising/basic.asp.

Advertising for your Small Business, by Ian White. Links to numerous articles and free guides at http://www.access2000.com.au/Guides/Advertising/advertising.htm.

Advertising Media, by Hairong Li. A good general article on advertising media with statistics on various advertising methods at http://www.admedia.org.

Publicity.com, by Bill Stoller. Free sample issue of free publicity newsletter with many good ideas. http://www.publicityinsider.com.

Small Business Advertising, no author listed. Numerous links to articles and advertising web sites at http://www.boiseadvertiser.com/smadv.htm.

"Word of Mouth Advertising," *Market Navigation, Inc.* A collection of articles through links with a number of articles regarding what some consider one of the most effective methods of promotion at http://www.mnav.com.

Your First Job Is to Get Them to See Your Advertising, by Noel Peeples. A lot of good information and link to free mini-course on advertising at http://www.marketleadersltd .com/Advertising_Of_Small_Business.htm.

Borrowing and Loans

ABC's of Borrowing. A complete booklet by the SBA at http://www.sbaonline.sba.gov /library/pubs/fm-1.doc.

A Venture Capital Primer for Small Business. Explains how to deal with venture capitalists to borrow money at http://www.sbaonline.sba.gov/library/pubs/fm-5.doc.

Bank Rate.com. Enables comparison of borrowing rates for small business no matter what State you live in at http://www.bankrate.com/brm/biz_home.asp.

Borrowing for Your Small Business. This site sponsored by Eastern Bank has links to all sorts of loan categories at http://www.moneyfitness.com/mc3/topic.php?b =24550218&c=491.

Entrepreneur Capital Finance. Sponsored by BPPubs.com, the site has links to a variety of articles on borrowing at http://www.bppubs.com/SOHO_and_Small_Business /Financing.

"Applying for a Loan," *SBA*. Good advice on what you must do at http://www.sbaonline .sba.gov/financing/basics/applyloan.html.

SBA CAPLines Loan Program. The umbrella program under which the SBA helps small businesses meet their short-term and cyclical working-capital needs at http://www .sbaonline.sba.gov/financing/loanprog/caplines.html.

SBA Credit Factors. Explains factors that help or detract from your ability to get a loan at http://www.sbaonline.sba.gov/financing/preparation/qualify.html.

SBA Disaster Relief Loans. Complete information including questions and answers at http://www.sbaonline.sba.gov/disaster_recov/loaninfo/property.html.

SBA Disaster Area Loans. If where you are doing business is declared a disaster area, go to http://www.sbaonline.sba.gov/disaster_recov/loaninfo/ecoinjury.html.

SBA Export Working Capital Program (EWCP). This program was designed to provide short-term working capital to exporters. Information online is available at http://www.sbaonline.sba.gov/financing/loanprog/ewcp.html.

SBA International Trade Loans. This program is for businesses preparing to engage in or already engaged in international trade, or adversely affected by competition from imports at http://www.sbaonline.sba.gov/financing/loanprog/tradeloans.html.

SBA Defense Loan and Technical Assistance Program (DELTA). The DELTA program provides financial and technical assistance to defense-dependent small businesses that have been adversely affected by defense reductions. Eligibility and other rules are available at http://www.sbaonline.sba.gov/financing/loanprog /military.html.

SBA Loan Package Checklist. SBA's complete Loan Package Checklist is at http://www .sbaonline.sba.gov/starting_business/financing/loanpackagechecklist.html.

SBA Military Reservist Disaster Relief Program. If you are a military reservist you may get special consideration. Check this out at http://www.sbaonline.sba.gov /disaster_recov/loaninfo/militaryreservist.html.

SBA Pollution Control Loan Program. The program is designed to provide financing to eligible small businesses for the planning, design, or installation of a pollution control facility at http://www.sbaonline.sba.gov/financing/loanprog/pollution.html.

SBA Preparing a Loan Proposal. Good advice for preparing a loan proposal at http://www.sbaonline.sba.gov/starting_business/financing/loanproposal.htm.

SBA Qualified Employee Trust Loan Program. The objective of this program is to provide financial assistance to Employee Stock Ownership Plans at http://www.sbaonline .sba.gov/financing/loanprog/trusts.html.

SBA U.S. Community Adjustment and Investment Program (CAIP). CAIP is intended to assist U.S. companies that are doing business in areas of the country that have been negatively affected by the North America Free Trade Agreement (NAFTA) at http://www.sbaonline.sba.gov/financing/loanprog/caip.html.

Small Business Investment Companies (SBICs). A complete list of SBICs at http://www .sbaonline.sba.gov/INV.

Small Business Loans. A quick review by SmallBusinessNotes.com at http://www
.smallbusinessnotes.com/financing/loans.html.

The ABC's of Borrowing. Another slant on borrowing by the Agora Business Center at
http://www.agora-business-center.com/borrowing.htm.

Business Insurance

Business Insurance. Business search engine and directory including company and industry profiles, news, financials, statistics, competitive analysis, and more at:
http://www.businessinsurance.com.

Business.Com. Information, resources, data, and publications for insurance providers, actuaries, agents, and so on at http://www.business.com/directory/financial_services
/insurance/index.asp.

Business Insurance Oracle. A practical guide to understanding and buying business insurance at http://www.insuranceoracle.com.

Free Advice on Legal Questions and Problems—Business Insurance. Free Advice's business insurance law information helps businesses to understand their legal rights
through questions and answers at http://www.freeadvice.com/insurance_law
/business_insurance.

Insurance for USA.com. Business insurance quotes. Fill out one form here and receive quotes from 3 agents in your area at http://www.insurance4usa.com
/business-insurance.cfm?affiliateid=433.

Most Choice Business Insurance. Information about business insurance choices and how to
get best values at http://www.mostchoice.com/business_insurance_overview.html.

My Own Business—Business Insurance. Provides free information about insurance for
entrepreneurs at http://www.myownbusiness.org/s5.

Computer and Ancillary Equipment

"About Buying a Computer," *Life Advice™.* Good general information about buying a
computer and a glossary of computer terms prepared by MedLife Consumer in
conjunction with the Federal Consumer Information Center at http://www
.pueblo.gsa.gov/cic_text/misc/buy-computer/buycomp.htm.

CNET.com. All sorts of computer product reviews and related stories about computer
equipment at http://www.cnet.com.

PC World. This online magazine has a review section where the best computers and ancillary equipment selected by *PC World* are reviewed at http://www.pcworld.com
/reviews/index.asp.

"Productopia," *ComputerSearch.com.* This is a terrific site. All kinds of products, especial
those having to do with computers are compared and rated. ConsumerSearch.com
reviews hundreds of product reviews, analyzes them, distills the information shoppers need and recommends which products are the best and tells where to find them
at http://productopia.consumersearch.com.

"Internet Connections," *Techsoup.org*. Free Newsletters, weekly news, how-to, and more having to do with the Internet. Intended for nonprofits, but very helpful for business at http://www.techsoup.org/howto/articles.cfm?topicid=4&topic=Internet+Connections.

Credit (Extending)

ACA International. Association of Credit and Collection Professionals at http://www.collector.com.

Credit and Credit Collection. Links to important sites and resources at http://www.worldwidewebfind.com/sites/Business/FinancialServices/CreditandCollection.

Credit and Credit World. This is an online credit resource for professionals including daily news at http://www.collectionsworld.com.

Credit Guru.com. A newsletter about credit at http://www.creditguru.com.

Creditworthy. Offers information about credit and collection management, bankruptcy, credit reporting agencies and their reports, and other financial matters at http://www.creditworthy.com.

Lawdog Center. Covers all legal aspects, including laws, state by state at http://www.lawdog.com.

E-Commerce

About.com—Online Business. Small business e-commerce resources for business owners wanting to learn more of maximizing net profits and developing an e-commerce strategy at http://sbinformation.about.com/od/ecommerce.

Banner Creation

http://www.animationonline.com.

http://www.banner4u.net.

http://www.coder.com/creations/banner.

http://www.koolprint.com/home.asp.

http://www.worlddesignservices.com.

Banner Exchanges

http://www.bannerco-op.com.

http://www.bannersxchange.com.

http://www.linkbuddies.com.

http://www.textlinkbrokers.com.

http://linksmanager.com.

http://www.linkexchanged.com.

http://www.powerlinks.com.

http://www.1st-work-at-home.com.

http://www.linkvalley.com.

http://www.powerlinks.com.

http://www.linkadage.com.

http://www.worldbannerexchange.com.

E-commerceGuide.com. News, information, and products pertaining to e-commerce at http://www.ecommerce-guide.com.

E-Commerce Times—Small Business. Information on doing business on the Internet, including news and products at http://www.ecommercetimes.com/perl/section/smllbz.

Info: Small Business E-Commerce. Sources of software and services for small business at http://www.software-e-commerce.com/e-commerce.asp?cerca=small+business +e-commerce.

Link Swapper. Offers a free link exchange plug-in and directory at http://www .link-swapper.com.

List brokers and Compliers. This list is maintained by the Direct Marketing association at http://www.the-dma.org/cgi/slsearch.

MonsterSmallBusiness Solutions for Online Selling. Articles, links, products, and more at http://www.monstersmallbusiness.com/ecommerce_articles.asp.

Newsgroup Directories

http://www.cyberfiber.com/index.html.

http://www.harley.com/usenet.

http://www.ii.com/internet/messaging/newsgroups.

http://www.mailgate.org.

http://www.netinformations.com/Usenet/Newsgroup_Directories.

Newsletter (Cyber) Advice

http://123ezine.com/3/create-your-own-newsletter.html.

http://www.coollist.com.

http://www.ehow.com/how_8454_create-own-e.html.

Programs for Building a Web Site

http://www.buildyoursite.com.

http://www.coolpage.com/cpg.html.

http://www.easywebeditor.com/?vov_web_page_software.

http://www.homestead.com.

http://sitebuilder.serveryard.com.

http://www.virtualmechanics.com/index.html.

http://www.webbuild.net/?Source=Overture.

http://www.webpage-maker.com.

SBDCnet-E-Commerce Guide. Sources and links to information on all aspects of e-commerce business at http://sbdcnet.utsa.edu/SBIC/e-com.htm.

Search Engine Information

http://www.addpro.com.

http://www.highrankings.com.

http://searchenginewatch.com.

http://selfpromotion.com.

http://www.seoinc.com.

Web Marketing Today. Links and articles on web marketing. http://www.wilsonweb .com/articles/checklist.htm.

Financial Management

Basic Guide to Financial Management in Small For-Profit Businesses, by Carter McNamara. A complete guide on the basics at http://www.mapnp.org/library/finance /fp_fnce/fp_fnce.htm.

Financing for the Small Business, U.S. Small Business Administration. Overview of financing for small business at http://www.sbaonline.sba.gov/library/pubs/fm-14/.doc.

Business Finance Magazine. This is an online magazine with links to all sorts of information regarding business financing at http://www.businessfinancemag.com.

Financing Basics. A complete discussion with links provided by the U.S. Small Business Administration at http://www.sbaonline.sba.gov/financing/basics/basics.html.

Links to Hundreds of Business and Finance Journals. Look Smart Find Articles list more magazines than you can read on the subject matter at http://www.findarticles .com/p/articles/tn_bus.

Understanding and Controlling Cash Flow. An SBA sponsored booklet on the Internet at http://www.sbaonline.sba.gov/library/pubs/fm-4.txt.

Small Business Finance (Business.com). Numerous links broken down into categories at http://www.business.com/directory/financial_services/small_business_finance.

Finding/Developing New Products and Services

About Inventors—Trade Shows and Conventions. a listing of the major inventor shows worldwide at http://inventors.about.com/od/eventsconventions/index_a.htm.

NASA TechFinder. This site lists U.S. government inventions available for licensing at http://technology.nasa.gov.

NASA TechBrief. This site describes engineering and manufacturing solutions and more at http://www.nasatech.com.

"New Product Development," *Wikipedia*. Free article of new product development at http://en.wikipedia.org/wiki/New_product_development.

"New Product Introduction (NPI)," *Better Product Design*. Complete discussion with links pertaining to management of the new product development process at http://www.betterproductdesign.net/npi.

"Product Development Forum," by DRM Associates and PD-Trak Solutions. New Product Development, concurrent engineering, IPD, QFD, target costing, and DFM information, best practices, resources, and links at http://www.npd-solutions.com /pdforum.html.

"The PDMA Glossary for New Product Development," *Product Development and Management Association*. Web site of organization devoted to the study and practice of new product development at http://www.pdma.org/library/glossary.html.

"Product and Service Management," by Carter McNamara. Discussion and many links pertaining to activities necessary in the development of new products at http://www.mapnp.org/library/prod_mng/prod_mng.htm#anchor1332959.

The Official Gazette of the U.S. Patent Office. This bulletin is published weekly and lists all the patents granted by the patent office at http://www.uspto.gov/web /patents/patog.

The Thomas Register of Manufacturers. This publication consists of several volumes listing manufacturers of all types of items in the United States at http://www .thomasregister.com.

U.S. Government Patent and Trademark Office. This site is the official U.S. government site and has lots of useful information about potential new products at http://www.uspto.gov.

Legal Aspects

Circular E, Publications 15, *Employer's Tax Guide*, and 15-A, *Employer's Supplemental Tax Guide*. IRS Circular E describes employer tax responsibilities: withholding, depositing, reporting, and paying taxes at http://www.irs.ustreas.gov/pub/irs-pdf/p15.pdf.

Checklist for Going into Business. An online checklist published by the U.S. Small Business Administration at http://www.sba.gov/library/pubs/mp-12.doc.

Government Regulations and Your Business. This SBA web site has links to all sorts of regulatory material required by the government. It is at http://www.sbaonline .sba.gov/starting_business/startup/guide4.html.

IRS Tax Credit Information. The latest information on tax credits at http://www.irs .gov/publications/p334/ch04.html.

Legal Advice about Going into Business. Free Advice.com provides legal advice on starting a business written by lawyers and attorneys in a Q&A format at http://freeadvice .com/law/517us.htm.

Selecting the Legal Structure of Your Business. Booklet developed by the U.S. Small Business Administration at http://www.sba.gov/library/pubs/mp-25.doc.

Online Classroom. This complete online class on taxation is available through the U.S. Internal Revenue Service at http://www.irs.ustreas.gov/businesses/small/article/0,id =97726,00.html.

Managing People

Career Babe. Provides links to other sites with salary information at http://www.careerbabe .com/salarysites.html.

CareerInfonet. List salaries and trends for many different industries at http://www .acinet.org.

Economic Research Institute. Lists various services and links regarding executive compensation both in the United States and abroad at http://www.erieri.com.

Job Star. Contains links to over 300 salary surveys at http://www.jobstar.org/tools/salary /index.cfm.

RealRates.com This is a specialized salary comparison site for the comuter industry at http://www.realrates.com.

U.S. Department of Labor. An unbelievable boatload of links to salary information and statistics at http://stats.bls.gov.

WageWeb.com. This site has information regarding salary surveys so you can make comparisons at http://www.wageweb.com.

Marketing and Business Planning

"Business Plans," by *BPlans.com.* Advice on writing marketing and business plans and sample plans at http://www.bplans.com.

"Business Plan Archive," by Robert H. Smith School of Business, University of Maryland. An archive of business plans kept on file at a university at http://www .businessplanarchive.org.

"Business Plans Software, Samples, and Strategy," by *Center for Business Planning.* Business plan samples with associated information including software at http://www.businessplans.org.

"Business Plan Software," by *Business Planware.* Links to a lot of free information and products for creating business plans, including software—from Ireland at http://www.planware.org.

"Free Business Planning Resources," by *BizPlanit.* Insights into the fundamentals of writing an effective business plan including detailed descriptions of recommended sections at http://www.bizplanit.com/vplan.htm.

"Marketing Plans, Programs, and Small Business Management," by *Marketing Plan.com.* Articles, outlines, links and more. Emphasizes the Internet at http:// www.websitemarketingplan.com.

"Marketing Planning Resources," by *Mplans.com*. Offers instruction, sample plans, articles, and news at http://www.mplans.com.

"Marketing Survival Kit," by Joel Sussman. Offers marketing strategies, marketing plans, marketing tools and templates, articles, software, ideas, and more at http://www.marketingsurvivalkit.com.

Marketing Research

Free Marketing Research Sources. ResearchInfo.com provides numerous links to marketing research resources at http://www.researchinfo.com.

PJ Marketing Research. Provides links to worldwide marketing research experience, including how to write a market research report at http://www.pj-marketing.com.

Market Research and Internet Marketing Research. KnowThis.com provides links to articles at http://www.knowthis.com/research.

Marketing Research Home Page. This is an online supplement that accompanies Donald R. Lehmann, Sunil Gupta, and Joel H. Steckel's *Marketing Research*, a textbook. This site provides you with access to a multitude of marketing research information sources and links, arranged by topic at http://www.prenhall.com/lehmanngupta.

Quirk's Marketing Research Review. Quirk has a great deal of information, articles, and so on at http://www.quirks.com.

Protection (of Ideas)

Copyright Registration Complete information on how to do this at http://www.copyright.gov/circs/circ1.html#wci. Also registering with U.S. Customs Service to block imports at www.customs.gov.

Copyright Law of the United States. Complete version of the U.S. Copyright Law in PDF format at http://www.copyright.gov/title17.

Copyright Web Site. Complete copyright registration and information resource at http://www.benedict.com.

Finding an agent or patent attorney near you. Go to U.S. government web site at http://www.uspto.gov/web/offices/dcom/olia/oed/roster/index.html.

Libraries with Patent Files. From the U.S. Government at http://www.uspto.gov/go/og/1998/week31/patlibs.htm.

Michael J. Colitz, Jr. Patent Attorney. A complete overview of the patenting process at http://colitz.com/site/flow.htm.

Patents.com Intellectual Property Web Server. Links to frequently asked questions on all aspects of patents, copyrights, trademarks, and more furnished by the law firm of Oppedahl & Larson at http://www.patents.com.

Patent Application. This is up-to-date information for applying for a U.S. patent at http://www.uspto.gov/ebc/efs/index.html.

Patent Search Online at http://www.uspto.gov/patft/index.html.

Protect Your Idea without a Patent. This U.S. Government web site shows you how to get temporary protection at http://www.uspto.gov/web/offices/pac/disdo.html.

Trademark Registration Online. At http://www.uspto.gov/teas/index.html.

Trademarks. Official U.S. government site. Basic facts about trademarks, Depository Libraries, and more. Accessed December 8, 2004, at http://www.uspto.gov/main/trademarks.htm.

Universal Copyright Protection. See http://www.copyright.gov/circs/circ38a.pdf.

U.S. Copyright Office. Official site for the government office featuring recent publications, forms, law resources, and registration information at http://www.copyright.gov.

U.S. Patent and Trademark Office. Official government web site. Links to everything you need to know at http://www.uspto.gov.

World Intellectual Property Association. Information about patents and protecting your intellectual property worldwide at http://www.wipo.int.

Protecting Your Business from Fraud, Bad Checks, Robbery, and so On

Cash Flow Specialists, Inc. This company can verify checks. It currently has access to 145 million accounts that reside within this network. Participating financial institutions include, but are not limited to, Bank of America, Wells Fargo, Chase, and Citibank at http://www.cashflowspecialistsinc.com/services/verification.

Common Sense Methods Preventing Employee Theft. An article published by the U.S. Small Business Administration with a summary approach as to what needs to be done at http://www.sba.gov/gopher/Business-Development/Success-Series/Vol6/theft.txt.

Crime Prevention, by Rutgers University. Provides links to get information on preventing employee theft using situational crime prevention, and ideas on how not to hire thieves in the first place at http://crimeprevention.rutgers.edu/crimes.htm.

Fraud Protection Services from Verisign. Learn how to protect your online business from the risks of fraud, including fraud prevention. Information and free guide "What Every Merchant Should Know About Internet Fraud" at http://www.verisign.com/products-services/payment-processing/online-payment/fraud/index.html?sl=t50080175426021000.

Global Polygraph Network. Sets up polygraph testing anywhere in the world at http://www.polytest.org.

National Crime Prevention Council. Numerous links to crime and business crime prevention topics at http://www.ncpc.org/ncpc.

PayQuickly. Payquickly automatically gives the full amount of any check it approves, when the merchant follows simple procedures and requirements at http://www.payquickly.com/check_guarantee.htm.

Vantage Card Services, Inc. Guarantees checks using a check reader. Full information is at http://www.vantagecard.com/solutions/check-guarantee.html.

Pricing

"Pricing Introduction," *tudor2u*. Definitions and theories with links to notes and key pricing terms at http://www.tutor2u.net/business/marketing/pricing_introduction.asp.

"Pricing New Products," by Michael V. Marn, Eric V. Roegner, and Craig C. Zawada. *Inc.com* reprint from *The McKinsey Quarterly*. Article originally published by famed consulting firm for clients at http://www.inc.com/articles/2003/07/pricing.html.

"Small Business Pricing Strategies," by Sharon Senter, *WebMarketing Articles.com*. Article on some interesting pricing tactics at http://www.webmarketingarticles.com/Pricing_Strategies.htm.

"Strategies for Pricing a Product or Service Optimally," *Ideas for Marketing*. Article discusses pricing strategies and link to manual on pricing at http://www.ideasformarketing.com/pricing.html.

"The Pricing Strategy," by Ken Evoy, *East Home Business*. Article discusses pricing strategies and tactics and has a link to a free 5-day pricing course at http://www.easy-home-business.com/better-business-price.html.

Record Keeping

Businesstown.com—Basic Accounting. Basic accounting steps you need to run your small business and keep track of your finances using the standard accounting tools at http://www.businesstown.com/accounting/basic.asp.

BuyerZone.com. FREE Accounting and Bookkeeping Services Quotes from Multiple Suppliers at http://www.buyerzone.com/professional_services/accounting/qz_questions_694.jhtml?_requestid=15628.

Powerhomebiz.com. Basic Business: Good Record Keeping, by "Wild Bill" Montgomery. An article on the basics at http://www.powerhomebiz.com/vol11/recordkeeping.htm.

Setting Up a Record Keeping System, by Cheryle Jones Syracuse. Part of a Ohio State University small business series at http://ohioline.osu.edu/cd-fact/1152.html.

The Small Business Advisor: Accounting and Record Keeping. Covers the basics with links to resources and additional information at http://www.smallbusinessadvice.com/acct.html.

Starting a Business and Keeping Records, by the Internal Revenue Service. U.S. Government record keeping requirements at http://www.irs.ustreas.gov/pub/irs-pdf/p583.pdf.

Recruiting and Hiring

Ask the Headhunter. Inside information about the hiring process at http://www.asktheheadhunter.com.

Business.com. Links to hundreds of recruiting, hiring, and retention materials at http://www.business.com/directory/human_resources/hiring_and_retention.

Fast Company. Interesting articles about various aspects of hiring at http://www.fastcompany.com/guides/hire.html.

Free Advice. Answers legal questions regarding hiring at http://employment-law
.freeadvice.com/hiring.

U.S. Department of Labor. Links to important employment issues in the areas of affirmative action, the hiring of veterans and foreign workers, the employment of workers under the age of 18, and how to implement drug-free workplace programs at
http://www.dol.gov/dol/topic/hiring.

Selling

Ambassador of Selling. This site contains many articles on selling at http://www
.sellingselling.com/articles.html#Anchor-Article-59579.

Market News Magazine. This is a free online course on salesmanship published for the
Canadian electronic industry. At http://www.marketnews.ca/training_sales.cgi.

Positive Results. Numerous articles on selling plus a newsletter at http://www.positiveresults
.com/sen/archives/index.asp.

Sales Dog.com. Offers a free weekly newsletter with lots of articles and advice at
http://www.salesdog.com.

Sales Vault. Many articles on salesmanship and selling at http://www.salesvault.com.

Starting a Business

Starting a Business Test. Sales Creators, Inc. developed this test at http://www
.salescreators.com/SCI/Sales_Consultants_for_New/New_Business/Starting_A
_Business_TEST/starting_a_business_test.html.

The Entrepreneur Test. The Small Business Know-How Resource on the Internet developed this test at http://www.liraz.com/webquiz.htm.

The Self-Employment Test. The New York State Department of Labor developed this self-
employment test at URL http://www.labor.state.ny.us/business_ny/entrepre/test.htm.

Self-Employed Attitude Test. Here's an attitude test developed by the Small Business
Information Resource at the Business Bureau-UK in England at http://www
.businessbureau-uk.co.uk/new_business/attitude_test.htm.

SBA's Entrepreneurial Test. This test was developed by the U.S. Small Business Administration and its Online Women's Business Center at http://www.onlinewbc.gov
/docs/starting/test.htm.

SBA Small Business Success Quiz. Here's another SBA self test at http://www.sbaonline
.sba.gov/gopher/Business-Development/Success-Series/Vol1/Quiz/quizall.txt.

Trade Shows

BizWiz. Publishes an online Resource Guide Convention/Trade Show at http://www
.bizwiz.com/resource/ConventionTradeShow.htm.

Family Shows. Publishes a listing of trade shows and conventions at http://www
.familyshowpromotions.com/trade_shows/convention-trade-show.html.

Federation of International Trade Associations. Directories, member associations, and how to join, newsletter and more at http://www.fita.org.

How Trade Shows Work. An article provided by howstuffworks.com with plenty of meaty information at http://money.howstuffworks.com/trade-show.htm.

Successful Meetings Magazine. Publishes conference and trade show information at http://www.successmtgs.com/successmtgs/index.jsp.

Trade Shows and Missions. Information on international trade shows and how to get involved with them at http://www.fas.usda.gov/agexport/shows/tsopage.html#why%20participate.

Trade Show Quotes. Provides competitive quotes for putting various aspects of shows together for small to midsized companies. http://www.trade-shows.org.

Trade Show Week. Contains lists of shows, industry reports, and more at http://www.tsnn.com.

Trade Show Week. Publishes an online directory at http://directory.tradeshowweek.com/directory/index.asp.